P9-AGX-693

AMERICAN INDIAN MEDICINE WAYS

EDITED BY
CLIFFORD E. TRAFZER

AMERICAN INDIAN
MEDICINE WAYS

Spiritual Power, Prophets, and Healing

THE UNIVERSITY OF
ARIZONA PRESS
TUCSON

The University of Arizona Press
www.uapress.arizona.edu

© 2017 by The Arizona Board of Regents
All rights reserved. Published 2017

Printed in the United States of America

22 21 20 19 18 17   6 5 4 3 2 1

ISBN-13: 978-0-8165-3716-7 (cloth)
ISBN-13: 978-0-8165-3717-4 (paper)

Cover design by Miriam Warren
Cover art: *Gaan Dancer* © War Soldier Artworks, courtesy of Sherman Indian Museum,
Riverside, California.

Research for this publication was made possible in part from funds provided by the University
of California, Riverside, Rupert Costo Endowment in American Indian Affairs.

Library of Congress Cataloging-in-Publication Data
Names: Trafzer, Clifford E., editor.
Title: American Indian medicine ways : spiritual power, prophets, and healing / edited
    by Clifford E. Trafzer.
Description: Tucson : The University of Arizona Press, 2017. | Includes bibliographical references
    and index.
Identifiers: LCCN 2017012671| ISBN 9780816537167 (cloth : alk. paper) | ISBN 9780816537174
    (pbk. : alk. paper)
Subjects: LCSH: Indians of North America—Religion. | Indians of North America—Medicine.
Classification: LCC E98.R3 A44 2017 | DDC 299.7/14—dc23 LC record available at https://lccn
    .loc.gov/2017012671

∞ This paper meets the requirements of ANSI/NISO Z39.48-1992 (Permanence of Paper).

In memory of Troy Johnson and Al Logan Slagle

*In honor of the following contemporary healers who have
shared their knowledge:
Eleonore Sioui (Wendat-Huron)
Kenneth Coosewoon (Comanche)
Rita Coosewoon (Comanche)
Larry Eddy (Chemehuevi)
Matthew Hanks Leivas (Chemehuevi)
Andrew George (Snake River–Palouse)
Vivienne Jake (Southern Paiute)
Mary Jim (Snake River–Palouse)
Paul Ortega (Mescalero Apache)
Jim Henson (Cherokee)
Beverly Sourjohn Patchell (Cherokee)
Crosslin Smith (Cherokee)*

CONTENTS

PREFACE

IN THE SPRING OF 2008, a former colleague and university professor visited me in my office in the Department of History at the University of California, Riverside. I had not seen her in years. Remarkably, as she walked into my office and closed the door behind her, she burst into tears, crying uncontrollably. I tried to comfort her and asked what was wrong. Through her tears and deep emotion, she told me she had been diagnosed with stage 4 cancer. I asked what I might do to help her. She responded by saying she knew that I researched Native American medicine ways and that I knew several medicine people among the tribes of North America. She asked if I would consult a healer on her behalf and see if someone might be able to help her.

The next day, I flew to Oklahoma City to meet Beverly Sourjohn Patchell, a Cherokee–Muskogee Creek woman then directing the American Indian Nursing Program at the University of Oklahoma's Health Sciences Center in Oklahoma City. In addition to her academic work, Beverly had been trained by several American Indian healers and had in-depth knowledge of medicine ways of indigenous people. She took me to her homeland east of Tulsa, and we visited healers living near Tahlequah, Oklahoma. Two of them offered their help to assist my friend with cancer. Jim Henson stood up immediately, saying, "We better pray for her right now." For fifteen minutes, Jim prayed in the Cherokee language for my friend, and then he began singing a common power song among the Cherokee. He gave me his telephone number and asked me to pass it along to the woman.

The next day, Beverly and I drove to Oklahoma City, where the American Medical Association's Commission to End Health Care Disparities met at the University of

Oklahoma Health Sciences Center. I was the first speaker at the conference in Oklahoma City. More importantly, at this gathering I met Kenneth and Rita Coosewoon, both medicine people who opened the meeting with songs, prayers, and good words for all in attendance. That afternoon, I interviewed Kenneth and Rita for three hours. When we finished the oral interview, I told them about my friend with cancer. Kenneth closed his eyes and began praying for a few minutes before blurting out, "We are going to get that cancer. We're going to kill it. We are going to be able to destroy it. You tell that woman I will do the ceremony for her and I have been told she is going to be OK!" Kenneth reported he had been told the woman would be healed.

I returned to California and told my friend what Kenneth had said but told her that Kenneth and Rita stressed the point that she had to believe that healing was possible. I sent a photograph of the woman to Kenneth who took it into the sweat lodge during the ceremony. Three weeks after my return, my friend visited me again and told me that during her preop appointment, the surgeons imaged her body and then biopsied her. They could no longer find the cancer; the biopsy showed not one cancer cell. She was cancer free and has been since then. When I called Kenneth and Rita to report the outcome of my friend's examination, Kenneth laughed and said, "Good, good." When I told Beverly about the outcome of this patient, she responded, saying, "What did you expect? This is how our medicine works." Several Native Americans would agree with Beverly, especially indigenous people familiar with the healing and medicine ways of their people. People with wisdom and knowledge of traditional ways of medicine and healing continue to practice some form of Native medicine in many parts of contemporary Indian Country.

Healing and medicine are tied to religion and spiritual beliefs of specific tribes. Some pan-Indian ways of knowing exist today, but most tribes and individual healers have their own ways of dealing with physical, mental, and spiritual ailments. They seek to bring people back into balance by using a host of techniques too numerous to mention here. Healers, spiritual leaders, and men and women of wisdom are not new to the Native Universe. Most people believe that the power to heal and care for others developed on earth at the time of origin when the Creator or Creators brought power to the earth and assigned certain people the gift of helping and healing others. Over the course of centuries, American Indian men and women of wisdom kept alive beliefs in medicine ways and knowledge of how to concentrate power to help individuals and groups of people. Such individuals have had enormous influence over the course of history. Only a few of these people are well-known, but many once lived among the Indian tribes of North America.

This volume offers a collection of ten essays about people with power, wisdom, and knowledge. Some of the studies found here deal with spiritual healing for individuals, tribes, and intertribal groups of people. Some offer broad strokes about the medicine ways of particular tribes, providing ways of knowing among select tribes, religious movements, and healings. The project began in 1977 when I moved from the Navajo Reservation to teach at Washington State University. When I arrived in the Palouse Country, I decided to research the history of the Palouse Indians of the Great Columbia Plateau, which I accomplished with the able assistance of Richard D. Scheuerman. Together, we explored many topics, including the influence of the Wanapum Prophet, Smohalla, and the Washani religion (Seven Drums) on the history of the Palouse Indians. Since the 1970s, we have learned a great deal about Smohalla, Puck Hyah Toot, and the Longhouse religion of the inland Pacific Northwest. As a result of this work, I contacted various historians then researching American Indian holy people, healers, prophets, and wisdom people.

While working on the Palouse book, I presented my research on the Palouse, Wanapum, and Smohalla at professional meetings. I knew R. David Edmunds had researched Tecumseh and Tenskwatawa, and he introduced me to the work of Joseph Herring, who was then working on Kenekuk. Through my associates at Oklahoma State University, I contacted L. G. Moses, who had researched James Mooney and Wovoka. At the same time, I learned that Al Logan Slagle, an attorney teaching at the University of California, Berkeley, had researched the Indian Shaker Church of the Tolowa in California. I asked these scholars and a few others to join me in creating a special edition of the *American Indian Quarterly* on "American Indian Prophets and Revitalization Movements." The journal published this special issue in the summer of 1985, and a year later, Sierra Oaks, a small press in Newcastle, California, received permission to reprint the special issue in a book, *American Indian Prophets: Religious Leaders and Revitalization Movements.*

Over the years, other scholars published exciting new literature on American Indian prophets, religious movements, power, and medicine. Like all scholars, the authors and I are indebted to many researchers that came before us. All of the authors presented in this work thank particular researchers that have worked in their specific field of study. I particularly thank Vine Deloria Jr., Anthony F. C. Wallace, Donald Fixico, Alfred Cave, Gregory Evans Dowd, Peter Nabokov, Donald Bahr, Christopher Miller, Calvin Martin, Gregory Smoak, William Lyon, Paul Robert Walker, John Grim, James Mooney, Lewis Mehl-Madrona, Sam Gill, and Wolfgang G. Jilek, whose works over many years have influenced my work. The present study is a collection that will introduce readers to a select number of subjects associated with spiritual knowledge, power, healing, and indigenous wisdom. All of these broad topics influenced the course of American history and Native American history, and all of them have influenced contemporary society—especially Indian Country. The authors thank the University of Arizona for interest in this work, which the authors hope will encourage young people to engage in new research in spiritual healing and prophetic movements past and present. Native American people and communities, rural and urban, contain a great deal of knowledge about various indigenous medicine ways. This knowledge has yet to be explored to the fullest, which will provide new details and ways of knowing.

I wish to thank the authors of the present work for their research and willingness to share their work with a broader audience. Since the beginning of this new work, two authors have passed on, including Troy Johnson and Al Logan Slagle. I thank the families of both men for giving permission to use their work. In doing so, their contributions continue to inform people today. Many libraries, archives, historical societies, and special collections at several institutions helped the authors and me collect data and photographs for this book. In particular, I thank Tillie George Sharlo, Philip Klasky, the Pauline Murillo family, Carrie Jim Schuster, John Clement, Richard Scheuerman, and the following institutions for providing photographs and permissions: Sherman Indian Museum, Colville Confederated Tribes, Dorothy Ramon Learning Center, Yakima Valley Libraries, State Indian Museum of the California State Parks, Nevada Historical Society, and Kansas State Historical Society. American Indian scholars actively helped in the production of some of these essays, and we thank them for sharing their knowledge. I also wish to thank Lorene Sisquoc, curator of the Sherman Indian Museum, and the War Soldier family, for permission to use the painting of an Apache *gaan* by Billy War Soldier Soza for the cover of this volume.

Several universities and institutions provided research funding for the production of this work, including the Rupert Costo Endowment; University Senate; and College of Humanities, Arts, and Social Sciences at the University of California, Riverside. I wish to thank the following people for assisting me with my research: Kim Wilcox, Cindy Larive, Milagros Peña, Kiril Tomoff, Randolph Head, Thomas Cogswell, Allison Hedge Coke, Wesley Leonard, Gerald Clark, James Brennan, Thomas Patterson, Wendy Ashmore, Sterling Stuckey, Ray Kea, James Sandoval, Joshua Gonzales, Rebecca Kugel, Benjamin Jenkins, Henry Vasquez, Ronald Cooper, James Fenelon, Robert Przeklasa, Beverly Sourjohn Patchell, Kenneth and Rita Coosewoon, Matthew Hanks Leivas, and the entire Native American Studies faculty at the University of California, Riverside.

I owe a great debt of gratitude to the outstanding professional staff at the University of Arizona Press. Kristen Buckles has graciously supported this project from its inception, and Director Kathryn Conrad approved the project. Amy Maddox, Stacey Wujcik, Leigh McDonald, Amanda Krause, Julia Balestracci, Allyson Carter, Scott De Herrera, Abby Mogollon, Nora Evans-Reitz, Rosemary Brandt, and Miriam Warren all have improved the project from its original presentation and furthered the production of the book into a handsome presentation. I also thank the three outside reviewers for the time they spent reading and commenting on the manuscript.

Their comments contributed to the final version of the manuscript, which benefitted greatly from their constructive criticisms.

Finally, I thank my family for giving me time to research and write. Louise, Tess, Hayley, and Tara encouraged my work every step of the way, and Lee Ann contributed greatly as a historian and scholar. Lee Ann gave up time from her own research and teaching to read drafts, edit, and comment on the work. Without Lee Ann, I could not have completed this collection. I greatly appreciate my family for their continued support and encouragement of my research.

Clifford E. Trafzer
Palm Desert, California

AMERICAN INDIAN MEDICINE WAYS

INTRODUCTION

꽃

O N DECEMBER 4, 2012, Kim Marcus, a Cahuilla-Serrano tribal elder, stood before a large audience on the lawn of the new interdisciplinary building at the University of California, Riverside. With microphone in hand, he explained the indigenous tradition of blessing people, lodges, and open spaces with the use of tobacco, "blowing smoke ceremonially," and offering song and prayer. He carefully took a rolled cigarette from a medicine bundle, lit the cigarette, and began singing a prayer. With his daughter, Mallory; son, Raymond; and a group of young Cahuilla-Serrano Indian men behind and beside him, he blew smoke in the four directions, praying in his language and asking the spiritual world for the safety and well-being of every person that would ever enter the building. He prayed for the students that would learn and gain knowledge within the building. He prayed for the professors, so they would be clear in their teachings so students might gain knowledge. And he prayed for safety, peace, and harmony throughout the building and within the people using the structure.[1]

Once Marcus had blown smoke in the four directions and sung his prayers, he led the singers in a series of Bird Songs, an ancient song complex that emerged among Cahuilla people at the time of creation when men, women, and children scattered like birds on great journeys to visit different landscapes. Through song, the singers reported on the geography, flora, fauna, and natural resources of a vast region of the world before settling in the desert, mountains, and passes of Southern California. The elder completed the blessing by dancing with a group of young Cahuilla-Serrano men near the skeletal head of a bighorn sheep, one of the most sacred and celebrated animals of the region. Many Cahuilla, Serrano, Luiseño, Chemehuevi, Cupeño, Kumeyaay,

FIGURE I.1. Chemehuevi Salt Song singer Matthew Hanks Leivas at the Oasis of Mara. He spoke at the edge of the oasis pond about the power and significance of water in Native American cultures, offering support for the water protectors of the Standing Rock Indian Reservation of South Dakota. Editor's photograph.

and others say that bighorn sheep can be shamans, returned to earth to watch over the people from lofty heights and impart power and wisdom to those earnestly seeking help and supplication.[2]

Kim Marcus is one of thousands of contemporary Native Americans carrying forward the old songs, rituals, ceremonies, and traditions of ancient cultures born of the Native Universe of the Western Hemisphere. He is also one of many indigenous people that believe spirits live within the universe and influence the course of human history. Many indigenous people in America and around the world believe that creators placed power on earth at the time of origins, power to use in positive or negative ways. Many American Indians—past and present—had and have the ability to use power to access wisdom, knowledge, spiritual understanding, and help in human activities. In return, spiritual powers may act independently of mankind and elect to help those in need and those seeking help. Spiritual powers may also do harm to people. Humans may decide to use their spiritual gifts in many ways, most often working for the benefit of their people and themselves. But humans also have the capacity to misuse power, sometimes directing it in evil, harmful, or deadly ways that can cause illness, misfortune, or even death. But ancient creation stories generally dwell on heroes who sought to find power to kill monsters, feed their people, learn new laws, or heal the lame and sick. Ancient concepts exist today among many Native Americans, as these beliefs are part of living traditions.[3]

Beliefs about spiritual power are not new in Indian Country. Indigenous people of wisdom have offered prayers of power, protection, and healing since the dawn of time. They conducted ceremony, prayers, and rituals, calling on the spiritual world to help humans and their relationships with each other and the natural world.[4] Native Americans have long believed in powerful spirits living within the environment that significantly influenced the course of American Indian cultures, languages, social structures, laws, and histories long before the arrival of newcomers. When traveling on land or water, indigenous people often left rock cairns, prayer feathers, arrows, and other offerings to ask for safe journeys. Spirit power has had an impact on all indigenous communities, creating common bonds between the spiritual world and individuals, clans, bands, and families.[5] Still today, many American Indians believe creators placed spirit power throughout the earth and universe, concentrating special power in certain areas on earth and giving particular people the ability to access and harness power to do good or evil.[6]

Many indigenous people still believe the intensity of spiritual power varies in variety and influence in specific ways, depending on its assigned duty to cure, protect, give knowledge, or offer heroic leadership. Native Americans often view power as a network endowed with intelligence and agency, working independently to act with will. In fact, indigenous power can operate like a spider web with current that may be continual or intermittent. This power often operates on various levels of being with humans and the environment. All levels of power may function on an invisible level, which makes it unseen to most human eyes. Power may operate above, below, or around human beings. Still, all levels of power can influence humans, plants, animals, rivers, and a host of other elements of life on earth. This power source may also influence the weather, cosmos, volcanic action, and other natural events on earth. These are shared beliefs of many indigenous people of the United States and globally.[7]

The present work addresses specific examples of people and power, past and present, among a select number of Native American people and tribes. The authors provide only a few examples, but the authors address the way spiritual power played an important role in tribal cultural and political history and the lives of particular Native American people over time, including in contemporary society. The book opens with an introduction to spiritual power, using examples throughout American history. The discussion begins with examples of creation stories and songs that Native Americans know through oral traditions, which people have shared from generation to generation. Today, many of these stories and songs appear in the scholarly literature, written in English, French, Spanish, and indigenous languages.

Contemporary Indian people remember many of these stories, and they continue to teach their communities, especially children, to encourage Native identities and beliefs. For centuries before the arrival of settler-colonists, Native American men and women of wisdom and spirit lived within their villages, bands, communities, and tribes. The people honored and feared these men and women of power, as they could use their spiritual gifts to help or harm others. Many of them received their power from the spiritual world. All of them gained wisdom over time through life's experiences and a cultural relationship with the spiritual world that the people featured in this work truly believed existed on another plane of being on earth. In the past, each group of Native Americans knew multiple spirits by name and knew their residences within the environment. Elements of sacred knowledge exist today within tribal groups. Spirits manifested themselves in many ways to human beings. Some spirits offered negative, even deadly, power, but others gave positive power to people to heal, sing, hunt, plant, fish, fight, farm, prophesize, and conduct many other activities. Most of the emphasis of this volume centers on people of wisdom or ways specific people know the spiritual world. The work offers case studies to illustrate elements of complex spiritual beliefs, ceremonies, and cultural ways that remain extant in Indian Country today.[8]

No utopia ever existed in indigenous America. Most people tried to conduct their lives in positive ways in accordance with "staying medicine." According to Piman shaman Juan Gregorio of the Tohono O'odham, known through the research of anthropologist Donald Bahr of Arizona State University, the causation of spiritual illnesses among tribal people originates from the violation of tribal "laws" or commandments.

Diverse rules of living exist for each particular tribe or group of people. Creative forces that put the world together at the beginning of time for a particular people provided specific laws or commandments by which people should live. Creators gave these laws to American Indian people at the beginning of time, and contemporary people know these laws through song and stories handed down through oral traditions. Commandments might differ from tribe to tribe and include such things as marriage laws, rules to prepare for hunts, how to handle fishing nets, the proper way to dress a deer, or the correct steps taken to weave a basket. Each tribe had and has its own laws, and violation of a law could cause physical, mental, or spiritual sickness. Gregorio described disease and inflictions caused by the transgression of cultural norms such as breaking marriage laws, ill treatment of animals, trespassing into sacred sites, or incorrectly handling certain objects such as pipes, feathers, weapons, bundles, or stones. Spiritual causes of disease remained specific to a group and did not travel like infectious diseases. Thus, Gregorio claimed that the cultural laws or communal commandments remained within the group and did not travel, thus staying within the particular group. Cures for such diseases were unique to that tribe. Neither the disease causation nor the remedy traveled. Both remained unique and within the group, thus the term "staying medicine."[9]

Healers focused on caring for specific parts of the body or the body as a whole. Native American doctors often specialized in pre- and postnatal care, internal medicine, pharmaceuticals, orthopedics, dentistry, psychology, wounds, poisons, bites, and more. Among diverse tribes, medicine people became doctors that focused on mending bones, calming intestinal disorders, and curing eye and ear infections and skin eruptions. Wounds could arise from accidents, war, and supernatural causes, including witchcraft and violations of cultural norms. American Indian doctors used many techniques to bring patients into balance—including conversations, prayers, rituals, songs, stories, ceremonies, and medicinal actions that might include eating certain herbs or foods, drinking teas and water from specific sources, or washing with liquids infused with power from prayers, plant materials, animal parts, or minerals from the earth—but it is spiritual power and knowledge that provided these doctors with the underlying power to heal.[10] After a lengthy discussion of plant medicines used in healing by Wendat-Hurons of Wendake, Quebec, tribal healer Eleonore Sioui once explained, "You keep worrying about the plants. The power is not in the plants. The Spirit places the healing agents into the plants, infusing them with holy power to heal. That's how it happens."[11] Medicine men and women know how to use their power to bring the spiritual and healing properties into the plants. Thus the key to healing is the healing power within the agent, making that agent (such as plant leaves, roots, or fruit) more powerful and able to do the healing.[12]

Spiritual power also enabled warriors to have special abilities in war. Warriors often received their gift of fighting through a spiritual process, especially through dreams. Among all communities in the world, external and internal conflict emerged from time to time. The ability to fight and resist enemies had a spiritual component as certain people, most often men but sometimes women, tapped into spiritual power to become great warriors. These individuals had to give their lives to fighting on behalf of their people and protecting indigenous families.[13] Mohave and Quechan (pronounced Kwitsan) Indian warriors of California and Arizona received their power to be warriors through dreams, which brought the future warrior into contact with powerful entities that emerged in their dreams. Spiritual agents giving power to warriors could be one of the Yuman gods or familiars such as plants, animals, wind, rain, bones, clouds, or other natural elements that visited the person in a dream or vision. In one dream, a person engaged a large Yuman warrior dressed in a buckskin skirt with his body painted black and red. The character in the dream carried a lance and shield. He appeared in the dream in the foothills of Pilot Knob (a small mountain that straddles Baja and Alta California, near the western banks of the Colorado River). The painted Yuman warrior walked up to and stood in the shade of a brush arbor, where he watched travelers passing by on a walking trail leading to the sacred mountain. The dream captured one element of spiritual power that may come to Native Americans and guide their ways of being and thinking.[14]

At times, men, women, and children attempted to capture the power of spirits and use them to help themselves and others; Native American prophets, holy people, healers, storytellers, singers, ceremonial officials, and prayer leaders function as spiritual interpreters that usually acted as heroes to benefit others. People of power and spirit, found within sacred narratives as well as historically, have the capacity to act benevolently or misuse power, selfishly causing accidents, mishaps, illness, and death. Songs and stories taught people tribal wisdom, and this process remains alive today.

Characters of creation songs and stories included Coyote, Cougar, Cloud, Salmon, Huckleberry, Raven, Rabbit, Spiders, Wolf, Water Babies, Bugs, and Bear.[15] According to indigenous people, these and other characters, often described as "people" of the first creation, put the universe into motion and made mountains, oceans, rivers, lakes, and special places. Through their actions they taught Native Americans holy commandments for their particular people. Creators made humans and taught them how to be members of certain groups of people. Each tribe has their own sacred narratives, and people learned their identity and history through narratives, songs, and places within their environments. Thus the laws of Iroquoian people differed from those of Mohave, Hupa, Comanche, or others. Non-Native settlers did not understand the diversity of people and their laws. The marriage laws of the Southern Paiute, for example, created chaos within that community and the settler community when in 1909 a Chemehuevi named Willie Boy formed a forbidden relationship with Carlota Mike, one of his second cousins. In doing so, Willie violated the incest laws of the Southern Paiute people. Tribal elders past and present say that many deaths followed as a result of this violation, including the death of headman William Mike; his daughter, Carlota; and Willie's

FIGURE I.2. Pedro Chino was a *pa'vu'ul*, a high-ranking shaman of the Agua Caliente band of Cahuilla Indians with extraordinary powers. Chino lived at the hot springs in Palm Springs, which he used as part of his healing. He is a legendary *puul*. Courtesy Agua Caliente Cultural Museum, Palm Springs, California. All Rights Reserved.

grandmother, Mrs. Ticup. Willie lived out his days near Las Vegas, Nevada, where he lived with other Southern Paiute people. There he found refuge and healing, but only after shamans urged the people to help Willie Boy regain some semblance of balance. Ultimately, Willie Boy died of tuberculosis, perhaps a result of his past actions.[16]

Among the Wendat-Huron people of Wendake, Quebec, Eleonore Sioui and her children, particularly her son Georges, use the wisdom of the spirit world to guide them as they work to keep their indigenous beliefs alive and pass on their culture to others.[17] Eleonore always considered herself a daughter of Ataentsic, better known as the Woman Who Fell from the Sky. Like other Iroquoian-speaking people, Eleonore and her family believe this world began when Ataentsic fell from the sky world onto earth, which was composed only of water. Big Turtle gave his back so Ataentsic would land on a solid surface and use medicine to begin creating Turtle Island (the Western Hemisphere). In his work as a renowned historian teaching at the University of Ottawa, Georges continues his mother's work of cultural preservation through formal education. The Sioui family is one of many indigenous families in the modern world that continue working in contemporary society from the spirit of the past.[18]

Since the time of origins, Native Americans have personified foods and places. Haudenosaunee or Longhouse people (Iroquoian Nations) consider corn, squash, and beans personified as three sisters. People consider these foods to be spirit personalities who physically, mentally, and spiritually nourish human bodies and minds, offering a sacred connection between humans on earth and the spiritual world. In like fashion, the Chemehuevi and other Southern Paiute of California, Arizona, and Nevada personify yucca. They say yucca and agave have been a part of their culture since the time of creation on the Spring Mountains of Southern Nevada. Yucca provides edible flowers, stalks, and dates, and the Chemehuevi people personified the plants, calling characters of the origin stories by the name Yucca Date Sisters. Similarly, in the Pacific Northwest, Indians personified Salmon, Deer, and the Huckleberry Sisters. These characters within the stories and songs acted out tribal laws, teaching humans by example how to be indigenous. In the Northwest, one narrative explains that Coyote acted as a hero against five monsters.[19]

According to the story from the Northwest Plateau, five monster sisters, known collectively as the Tah Tah Kleah, built a fish dam on the Columbia River. Blocking the natural flow of the river and the migration of salmon upstream compromised the lives of the fish and the people living there. The dam violated the law established by holy actions at the beginning of time. Coyote agreed to break the fish dam by disguising himself as a baby and using five sturdy sticks to dig out the dam. With his digging sticks, Coyote worked diligently for five days to break the dam. On the fifth day, one of the monsters broke her digging stick. This was a sign to the sisters that something was wrong, so they hurried home to find Coyote breaking their dam. They immediately took up clubs to beat Coyote to death, clubbing his head. To protect himself, Coyote placed bighorn sheep antlers on his head as helmets. Coyote kept digging, breaking the dam and allowing the Columbia River to run into the Pacific Ocean in accordance with the first law of creation. The salmon could then swim up the Columbia to spawn, so Coyote led them there, determining which tributaries would receive fisheries.

As he traveled inland, Coyote met a series of problems he could not solve. When this occurred he called on the five Huckleberry Sisters, which he kept in his stomach, for advice. On one occasion Coyote needed nourishment and attempted to capture a salmon by hand, but the fish was too slippery. The Huckleberry Sisters told him to stand on a sandbar and call to the salmon so that the fish rolled in the sand, providing Coyote with a grip on the slippery fish. After they provided advice to Coyote, the wily one always commented, "Yes, I knew that all along." With the help of the sisters, Coyote opened the river in accordance with natural laws and led the salmon inland to spawn.[20]

Native American stories sometimes portray Coyote as a trickster and buffoon, but like human beings, Coyote can also be a hero. Coyote is just one of many personified characters found in traditional Native American stories and songs. Coyote's actions and that of other ancient characters—Rabbit, Crow, Bear, Cougar, Rattlesnake, Huckleberries, Yucca—emerged from power placed on earth at the time of creation and from the influence of unseen creative spirits that many Native Americans say remain in rivers, rocks, ravines, mountain tops, caves, and other selective sites on earth. Many indigenous people consider these places sacred today, and American Indian leaders, prophets, medicine people, warriors, and holy people knew where to go to call on spirits for assistance, healing power, and communal protection. Among the Chemehuevi and their Southern Paiute relatives, *puhagaants* (literally meaning "where power sits"), or medicine people, made pilgrimages to special places—including Charleston Peak, Nevada; Old Woman Mountains, California; and Hawaiyo on the west side of the Colorado River—where *puha*, or power, might be gifted to them for the benefit of the people.[21]

Knowledgeable humans, when properly instructed, may still seek and obtain spiritual healing power today. With the help of spirits, people believe they can heal the sick, protect communities from natural disasters, and mediate power of many kinds between the spiritual and temporal worlds. People with wisdom and the knowledge of spirits and places of power remain an integral part of tribal cultures today. They are often the connective cloth between the ancient past and the present. The influence of such men and women remains significant to future generations of Native Americans.

Many tribal people view the development of knowledge, wisdom, and power in two stages. The first phase occurred when spiritual forces made the cosmos and the natural world on earth. The first creation brought forth life and the physical world as the first beings prepared the earth for humans. The second phase of creation included the emergence of mankind, sometimes in the current form and sometimes in other forms that evolved into humans. Often, stories related how mist, moisture, water, breath, movement, and action created the first life. In addition, songs of creation include dualities. Positive and negative elements charged life from the outset. Male and female, good and evil, physical and spiritual, and courage and cowardice all have existed since the time of creation, and tribal people know of these dualities through origin songs and stories. They also know the cultural heroes of their people. Origin accounts contain a blend of the sacred and profane. The first wisdom spirits often appear to have lived in physical form on earth before becoming invisible, retreating into rock formations, mountains, lakes, rivers, canyons, clouds, plants, and other special sites.[22]

A Quechan elder related how a great transformation occurred in the Whipple Mountains along the west bank of the Colorado River north of present-day Parker, Arizona. During the time of creation and on this site, a creator named Marxokuvek transformed spirits into animals and plants. This creator also sent his favorite spirits to inhabit specific mountain ranges where they reside today, waiting for human interaction. These spirits have the ability to gift power to Quechan people, but humans must approach these places with respect and humility, asking spirits for particular power to deal with issues significant to human welfare and health. When asked if these spirits remain within the environment today, a contemporary tribal elder replied, "Of course, they are still waiting for us to ask for their help."[23]

Yavapai-Prescott elder Ted Vaughn once explained that the *kakaka* (mountain spirits known as "Little People") remain in the mountains east of the Colorado River in Arizona in spite of the fact that in 1873, the United States Army forcefully removed the Tulkapaiya (Western Yavapai) at gunpoint from their homelands in the mountains and deserts to Camp Verde and to the San Carlos Indian Reservation. They were later allowed to leave, and some of them congregated in Prescott and others at Camp Verde. In 1942, General George Patton took over a huge portion of the former Yavapai and Quechan homeland in Southwestern Arizona. Today, the United States Army Command controls this vast landscape as the Yuma Proving Grounds, and they do not permit indigenous people to return to their homelands without special permits. As a result, the people have lost contact with the *kakaka* and their places of power. Nevertheless, indigenous power through the *kakaka* remains on the base, waiting for human interaction. Matthew Hanks Leivas once explained, "Sacred sites and spirits of power did not go away but remain close by so we can call on them to come when we need them."[24]

Contemporary people of wisdom and knowledge, including Vaughn and Leivas, still interact with nature and places of power. Indigenous power, placed there at the time of creation, still sits in places within the natural environment today.[25] On one occasion, Leivas visited a dried-up spring at Hawaiyo in the Mojave Desert. He sang, prayed, and inserted a small stick into the ground, which brought forth water from the underground spring. People of spiritual power knew how to appeal to the sacred and ask for such blessings as water. They also enjoined the spiritual world to address pertinent issues of health within Native communities. In the historical literature and within contemporary society, non-Indians have denigrated indigenous belief systems, sometimes labeling healers, prophets, and intellects as fakes, frauds, charlatans, and witch doctors. Christian missionaries, agents, soldiers, and settlers often denied the efficacy of American Indian people of power, but other observers offered written testimony about miraculous and inexplicable events, including healings.[26]

Tribal leaders with special abilities used spiritual power to accomplish needed tasks. Larry Eddy, a contemporary Chemehuevi leader on the Colorado River Indian Reservation, explained that when his grandfather wished to heal someone, he called his familiar—which came to him in the form of a bat—summoning it with songs.[27]

The bat carried *puha* from the mountains and caves where it lived, places where *puha* concentrated. Although the duties of some Indian healers and leaders have changed over time, people still expect them to act in the best interest of the people—not their own self-interest. Long before the arrival of Leif Erickson, Christopher Columbus, or Chinese junks, individuals with spiritual power enjoyed an elevated place within American Indian societies. Some Native American healers still maintain power to access the spiritual plane, but others are more grounded in mundane affairs.

This volume presents only a small sample of events and people associated with the spiritual world historically and their relationship to religious, social, and military movements among various communities. Although most of the essays are grounded in American history and archival research, many of them have implications within contemporary indigenous societies. According to indigenous interpretations, the subjects and events analyzed here received their power from the spiritual world and enjoyed a close relationship with unseen forces that influenced the course of American Indian history. The people and events also influence contemporary American Indian societies.[28]

This collection pulls together specific examples of wisdom, spiritual power, and forces within tribal communities that influenced the past and may influence the future. Many of the spiritual leaders and their beliefs presented here intended to serve the best interest of the American Indian people as defined by the actors. Some of the people supported violent confrontations with settler-colonial societies, but others sought peaceful means of coexisting with non-Indian newcomers. Still others provided healing ways for their people using songs, prayers, and spiritual medicine. Authors presented here draw on written and oral sources, but much of the cultural information presented stems from a strong oral tradition that lives today among many Native Americans. Authors also employed Native accounts of creation narratives, oral histories, and songs that speak of healers, spirits, and power. Within tribal creation stories, special characters or spirits taught members of the group proper behavior and methods by which to access and use power wisely. Creators taught tribal laws and commandments for proper behavior. According to the Quechan of the lower Colorado River region, Kukumat (or Kumat) created indigenous plants and animals. Kukumat, his son, Kumastamho, and his helper, Marxokuvec, put the world into motion.[29]

Kukumat created the first human beings, molding them from clay and animating them with light, breath, and movement. For the Quechan, Kukumat served as the first teacher, training the people in the Dark House, which contemporary Quechan people consider the first cultural schoolhouse. He also traveled the Native Universe, giving names and power to people, places, plants, and animals. For example, he endowed Rattlesnake with poison but instructed him not to harm the people. Rattlesnake became a great healer and grew large and arrogant, full of himself and his power. For no reason, one day he murdered Rabbit, biting him with his fangs, abusing his power and breaking

Kukumat's law by using his poison. Rattlesnake grew so large and became so full of himself that he grew two heads (some tribal scholars say he had four heads). Rattlesnake made his home on a great mountain called Castle Dome, located in the Arizona desert northeast of present-day Yuma. Because Rattlesnake had broken the Creator's law, Kukumat sent his son to kill Rattlesnake. Kumastamho, the culture hero of the Quechan, set a trap for Rattlesnake, surprising him, wresting him to the ground, and cutting off his heads before tossing his body to the west. Rattlesnake left a lengthy, permanent imprint in the ground near the eastern banks of the Colorado River, known today as Yuma Wash, and forming the Pacific coastal ranges from South America to Alaska.[30]

Kukumat, Kumastamho, and other creators found in ancient oral narratives of Quechan people served as the first "people" of power. They taught by example through their actions, and they established relationships and laws between plants, animals, places, and people. Out of the tradition of the "first people" came human beings who interacted with their particular communities and local environments. They used spiritual power to define their ways of life and execute their innate sovereignty, given to them by creators and known through song and story. People of power and wisdom within diverse Native communities left a legacy followed by traditional leaders and teachers. Tribal people have used traditional knowledge to help guide their group in order to keep their worlds together and in balance in spite of many changes.

Every American Indian community within North America had their own people of wisdom and spiritual power. They were sometimes revered, sometimes feared. At the beginning of time, animals often filled the role of educators, acting out human activities and teaching by example, teaching through positive or negative experiences. Coyote, Raven, Rabbit, and many other characters taught lessons shared through song and story. Each indigenous community could write its own history about these individuals, but we have chosen to write about a select number of leaders and communities to illustrate the roles of spiritual leaders, medicine people, and prophets that influenced the course of Native American and American history.

For example, Popé (*Po'png*, or Pumpkin Mountain) played a significant role within many Pueblo Indian communities of New Mexico during the late seventeenth century. The Tewa Indian man said that he had a revelation when he visited Shibapu, a lake in northern New Mexico, where he met masked dancers called *katsinas* (or kachinas) who promised to help the Pueblos rid themselves of Spanish colonial settlers, especially soldiers and missionaries. From an underground kiva, or ceremonial chamber, Popé proclaimed his mission and offered a ceremony to initiate a revolt against the Spanish and their Christian religion.[31] Many leaders became involved in the Pueblo Revolt, which they successfully launch in 1680, driving the Spanish from the Río Grande Valley until 1699, when the ruthless Diego de Vargas returned to reclaim New Mexico. Even before his return, however, the Pueblos unseated Popé and his attempted central government, preferring the old way of village rule that has prevailed into the twenty-first century. During the seventeenth century, many Pueblos scattered to live with Apache, Navajo, Ute, and other Indians with whom they shared Pueblo culture.[32]

The arrival of white people encouraged people with spiritual power to speak about against the invasion. They opposed the theft of Native American lands and resources. Passaconaway, a Penacook *powah*, or medicine man, among the Indians of New Hampshire and Western Massachusetts, worked with Abnaki and Massachusetts Indians to form an effective confederacy that repelled the great Mohawk Nation and its well-known warriors. Passaconaway served his people as a warrior, diplomat, and healer, preferring to negotiate and deal with Puritans rather than fight them. He gained his power from spiritual entities and was open to learning about the Christian path. When John Eliot, the famous Puritan minister, asked to Christianize the Indians of the Penacook Confederacy, Passaconaway agreed. Yet as an elder of one hundred years, he had a prophetic experience that revealed to him that white people would bring destruction to Indian people. Indians, he proclaimed, would be "rooted off the earth" by non-Indians. Still, Passaconaway advised against war and urged his son, Wannalancet, the grand sachem of the Penacook, not to fight the English but to live in peace with them, a path the tribe followed even during King Philip's War, 1675–1676.[33]

Several people of wisdom urged their tribes to live in peace with white settlers while still maintaining elements of their traditional cultures.[34] Neolin, the Delaware Prophet, lived in east central Ohio along the Muskingum River and its tributaries. He had seen the devastation resulting from the French and Indian War, and like many Indian people living in the Old Northwest, he favored the French over the English and their American allies. In 1762, as the French power waned, Neolin preached among the Indian villages, calling for a union of the Indian tribes and a rejection of European and American manufactured good, including guns, ammunition, metal tomahawks, pots, pans, knives, and manufactured cloth. He urged Native Americans to return to their traditional cultures and material items that did not depend on Euro-American traders, goods, and military largess. To seek greater spiritual power and understanding, Neolin set out to meet the Master of Life. After several days' journey, Neolin found three illuminated paths, which he took, one by one, until he reached the narrow path.[35]

According to Neolin, during his vision he met a beautiful woman in a white deerskin dress who told Neolin the Master of Life (Creator) lived on top of a steep mountain. She instructed him to disrobe, bathe, and follow a unique path to the top. The Master of Life met Neolin, took him by the hand, and instructed him in sacred ways. He told Neolin that the people must live in harmony and balance together, take only one wife, and end their dependency on manufactured goods. Before leaving the mountain, the Master of Life gave Neolin a prayer stick with carved symbols and a prayer to be repeated by Native Americans. Neolin received messages and teachings from the Master of Life, which led him to teach among the Indian people of Ohio, Pennsylvania, Michigan, Indiana, and Canada. His words influenced Pontiac, the great Ottawa war chief, who used Neolin's concepts and ideas to rally many indigenous people against the English and Americans. On April 27, 1763, Pontiac addressed several hundred Indians south of Detroit on the banks of the Ecorse River, saying, "Drive from your lands those dogs in red clothing."[36]

Neolin's teachings led many Native Americans to call him a prophet. He taught the people that non-Indians blocked the path between earth and the spiritual world of the Master of Life. Pontiac used Neolin's words and philosophies to inspire tribal nations, and his teachings influenced Native Americans to stand against the British in the Great Lakes region.[37] In 1763, at the end of the French and Indian War, Pontiac led many tribes with their leaders in a war against the British and Americans. At first the war went well for Pontiac, but in the end, the British prevailed. But Neolin and Pontiac, both people of wisdom and spirit, inspired other Native American leaders in their dealings with newcomers. During the American Revolution, many Native Americans of the Northeast, Old Northwest, and South sided with the British against the Americans who had expanded onto Indian lands and threatened to take more Indian territory and resources.[38]

The American Revolution proved disastrous for thousands of Native American men, women, and children from a host of Indian tribes. At first the British supplied Native American warriors with arms and ammunition. British traders provided food, intelligence, arms, and assistance to indigenous fighters, but as the war wore on after the Battles of Oriskany and Cherry Valley, fortunes turned against Indian people. The Peace of Paris of 1783 ended the American Revolution. Tribes that had allied with the United States and those that had fought for the new nation found that the states and their citizens harbored a great deal of racism against the first nations. Tensions arose between national and state governments over Indian policies, and many American Indians sought to understand their new position within newly constituted states and the new nation. Among some Indian tribes, cultural disarray ensued, including spousal and child abuse, alcoholism, and witchcraft.

Under pressure from settlers, state representatives, federal agents, and military officials, some tribal people (leaders and nonleaders) agreed to treaties, including the Treaty of Big Tree among the Seneca, who were members of the Haudenosaunee, or the Iroquois League. Like so many Native nations, the Seneca secured for themselves only a minute portion of their former lands, and white settlers, including many Christians, moved onto these lands near Indian villages. Haudenosaunee chief Cornplanter of the Seneca served as a prominent political and military leader during and after the American Revolution. He had secured lands in Pennsylvania along the Allegheny

River for the Seneca. Handsome Lake, Cornplanter's brother, served as a chief as well. Like Cornplanter, he was a man of power, drawing on holy energy to heal others through spiritual and plant medicine. He lived with Cornplanter but started drinking, dancing, and singing sacred songs while drunk. This was a grave violation of Iroquoian law. Many Indians, including Cornplanter, felt that Handsome Lake had traveled down a destructive path that violated the laws of the Iroquoian people. After one of his drunken parties, Handsome Lake became ill and died.[39]

Some Native Americans believed he was dead for two hours before he awakened to announce that he had seen three spirits dressed like human Indian men, wearing ceremonial clothing, and carrying huckleberry branches in one hand and bows and arrows in the other. With their faces painted red, the spirits reported that the Master of Life had sent them. Handsome Lake experienced his first revelation in a vision on June 15, 1799, and he had subsequent visions, the most important of which took place on August 7, 1799, while his friend Quaker Henry Simmons visited Handsome Lake.[40] Simmons documented this spiritual experience. According to Native American accounts, Handsome Lake traveled into the Milky Way with the Creator to learn lessons and new laws to ensure the survival of all Iroquoian people. When Handsome Lake awoke from his visions, he began preaching and teaching the Gaiwiio, the Good Word of Handsome Lake, which taught the Iroquois to unify themselves around the Longhouse religion or Handsome Lake Church. The new law included an end to witchcraft, whiskey, gambling, and child and wife abuse. Handsome Lake emphasized many aspects of the old religion to renew his people through spiritual wisdom.

Many Iroquois followed the Gaiwiio but others, like Chief Red Jacket, rejected the Seneca prophet. Red Jacket served his people throughout his life as a religious and political leader, taking a Seneca delegation to visit President Thomas Jefferson, who acknowledged the leadership of Handsome Lake and sent farming equipment to aid in agriculture. Jefferson stated that Seneca people would never forget Handsome Lake, saying "Your children's children, from generation to generation, will repeat your name with love and gratitude for ever." Each year at the Strawberry Festival, members of the Longhouse speak at great length about the Gaiwiio.[41]

During the War of 1812, Handsome Lake counseled the Iroquois not to become involved with the teachings of the prophets of war, including Tenskwatawa (the Shawnee Prophet), and Hildis Hadjo (or Josiah Francis, the Muscogee-Creek Prophet). Today, historians and students of Native American history know a great deal about Tenskwatawa and his older brother, Tecumseh, through the cutting-edge scholarship of Cherokee historian R. David Edmunds. In his books *The Shawnee Prophet* and *Tecumseh*, he argues that Tenskwatawa began the unification of eastern tribes against the United States during the first decade of the nineteenth century through a spiritual movement. Further, the famous Tecumseh, often referred to as "the prophet's brother," used the religious movement to enlarge the effort to stand against the United States through a political and military means, which made far greater sense to settlers than a spiritual movement. Native Americans believed Tenskwatawa and Tecumseh both had spiritual power, and they used their abilities to wisely form a confederacy of Native Americans to halt the advance of white settlers and preserve traditional cultures of the Indian tribes east of the Mississippi River. Shawnees once lived in present-day Virginia, Kentucky, and Pennsylvania, but settlers and soldiers pushed them out of their homeland, and they moved north of the Ohio River.[42]

Tecumseh and Tenskwatawa's father was Shawnee, a great warrior and chief, and their mother was Muscogee Creek. Tecumseh was born in 1768 and Tenskwatawa was born in 1775, both at the village Piqua on Mad River near present-day Springfield, Ohio. Soldiers killed their father in battle, and their mother moved south to the Muscogee Creek, leaving the boys in the care of an older daughter. As a child, his family called Tenskwatawa by the name Lalawethika, which meant the "Noise Maker" or "Rattle."[43] He had a troubled childhood and lost an eye running with an arrow. While Lalawethika was known as a clumsy boy, his brother, Tecumseh, excelled as a hunter, warrior, and leader. Tecumseh often helped feed his brother's family. Lalawethika also drank to excess at times and contributed little to his family and people. In 1805, while sitting by the fire, Lalawethika fell over and stopped breathing. His wife wailed and prepared him for burial, but before they placed his body into the ground, Lalawethika awoke and proclaimed he had been to paradise, where he communicated with the Master of Life. As a result of this experience, Lalawethika changed his name to Tenskwatawa, "the Open Door," and became an influential spiritual leader known as the Shawnee Prophet. Tenskwatawa taught that the Master of Life wanted all Native Americans to unite against the encroaching settlers and remain on the land.

The new doctrine called for the end of whiskey and witchcraft. The prophet asked the people to share property and food, stop familial and tribal conflicts, and end marriages with white people. Like Neolin and Handsome Lake before him, Tenskwatawa told the people to end their dependency on manufactured goods offered by white traders. Indigenous people had become dependent on goods provided by newcomers, and the prophet sought to end this dependency. He asked the people to return to their bows, arrows, leather clothing, and old material culture. He claimed he could heal the sick, outmaneuver enemies, and overcome death. Although writers and historians have portrayed Tenskwatawa as a fake and a fraud, Native Americans considered him a receiver of spiritual power with the ability to communicate with the Master of Life. He may have been influenced by the teachings of Neolin, Handsome Lake, and a Shawnee medicine man, Penagashea, as well as by white Shakers, but his teachings made sense to American Indian people of the time and soon garnered a huge following. In the early nineteenth century, Indians considered Tenskwatawa a prophet, healer, and holy man determined to use the wisdom and spiritual guidance attained in his vision to help the people under assault from settlers, soldiers, and speculators. His message was an answer to their prayers.[44]

Tenskwatawa preached, sang, and experienced trancelike states, informing the people of the knowledge he gained through divine visions. He also encouraged people to root out witches and to torture and burn them to death. When the Delaware killed some witches, Ohio governor William Henry Harrison responded by writing a letter to the Delaware, saying if Tenskwatawa "is really a prophet, ask him to cause the sun to stand still." The governor punctuated his challenge, writing, "If he does these things, you may believe that he has been sent from God."[45] Tenskwatawa took the challenge, appointing the day that he would blot out the sun, which he did on June 16, 1806, during a full eclipse of the sun. The Shawnee Prophet shouted to his followers, "Did I not speak the truth? See, the sun is dark." The crowd was in awe of his great medicine power.[46] Perhaps he had learned of the eclipse from a *Farmer's Almanac*, or maybe not. No one knows. Regardless, the reputation of Tenskwatawa rose mightily among a large indigenous population after he blotted out the sun.

At first wary of his brother's newfound fame, Tecumseh soon used Tenskwatawa's spiritual revelations to launch a political and military movement among the tribes to resist westward expansion. When Governor Harrison announced the need for more Indian land, Tecumseh responded, "These lands are ours. No one has the right to remove us, because we were the first owners. The Great Spirit above has appointed this place for us, on which to light our fires, and here we will remain."[47] The teachings of Tenskwatawa and speeches of Tecumseh stirred the hearts, minds, and souls of listeners, and so many people came to their village to hear the messages. So many people visited the village to hear the prophet preach that the leadership moved their village to present-day Indiana at a place called Kehtipaquononk, "the Great Clearing," which whites called Tippecanoe. There they built Prophetstown, and for three years it was a hub of spiritual, political, and military activity.[48]

In 1809, Harrison met with progovernment chiefs who signed a new treaty ceding three million acres to the United States for $5,000 worth of goods and annuities. The Senate and the president signed the Treaty of Fort Wayne, making it the supreme law of the land. Land speculators and surveyors hurried to open former Indian lands to settlers, selling Indian lands for a profit. Tecumseh prepared for battle. In 1813, he traveled to the South to seek military alliances with the Cherokee, Choctaw, Chickasaw, Seminole, and Muscogee Creek. All of the southern tribes rejected his plea, even great warriors and war chiefs like Choctaw chief Pushmataha. But that group of Muscogee Creek known as the Red Sticks joined Tecumseh's confederacy. Hildis Hadjo, or Josiah

Francis, dedicated himself to stopping the advance of settlers and soldiers onto Indian lands, primarily leading the militant Muscogee as a prophet. Although his father was white, Hadjo dedicated himself to protecting Native American sovereignty.[49]

Hadjo and Tecumseh both knew and respected Seekabo, the Muskogee Creek elder and healer. Seekabo took Tecumseh to see Hadjo, who had earned a reputation as a charismatic, intelligent, and learned man with special powers to fly and live underwater for weeks. Hadjo said he possessed a strong spirit helper that guided his actions. He had convulsions, jerking and trembling when the spirit came upon him or when he met a person opposed to fighting the Americans or joining Tecumseh's confederacy. Hadjo, William Weatherford, Peter McQueen, and others joined the Red Sticks in support of the Indian confederacy in the South against the United States. Other Muscogee Creek leaders, especially Big Warrior, opposed the confederacy that he felt would ultimately fail, bringing more harm to the Creek Nation. Big Warrior rejected Tecumseh, so the Shawnee promised to stamp his foot when he returned to Ohio. Not long after leaving the South, the large Muscogee town of Tookaubatchee experienced a deadly earthquake that it.[50]

In 1813, the federal government built a national road from Georgia into Alabama, the heart of Muscogee Creek Country, and Indian Agent Ben Hawkins pushed for assimilation, urging indigenous people to turn their backs on their traditional cultures, ceremonies, economies, laws, and languages. Hawkins, like Harrison, wanted indigenous people to seek "civilized" lives and become Christians. Some Muscogee Creek became successful plantation farmers, while others rejected the new ways. Threatened by westward expansion, the Red Sticks launched their own campaign against soldiers, settlers, and slaves, killing many at Fort Mims. Hadjo did not participate in the battle and ruthless killings but retreated to Ecunchatee, or Holy Ground, to establish two villages as safe havens for his followers. In retaliation for Fort Mims, General Ferdinand Claiborne, supported by Chief Pushmataha and Choctaw warriors, attacked Holy Ground, where Hadjo had magically created a death barrier that no soldiers could compromise. The barrier did not work, and Hadjo and his followers fled to Spanish Florida, where they readjusted to their new home. Meanwhile, the Red Sticks took up quarters at Horseshoe Bend, where they suffered a stunning defeat by the forces of Andrew Jackson and his Choctaw allies under the leadership of Pushmataha.[51]

In 1814, Hadjo was on board a ship with British admiral Alexander Cochrane when the Redcoats engaged Andrew Jackson's forces at the Battle of New Orleans. Learning of the decisive American victory, Hadjo traveled to London, where British officials made him a brigadier general, giving him a bright red uniform fitting the position and 325 pound sterling for his service to the crown. Some Red Sticks continued the fight the Americans, but Hadjo remained in Florida, where he paid for his son to learn to read and write Spanish and English. While living in Florida, Hadjo and Himollemico, another Muscogee leader, saw a ship approaching flying the Union Jack. Thinking a British friend had sailed into port, Hadjo and Himollemico paddled out in a canoe to greet their friend. Once on board, they realized the ship belonged to the Americans. The navy made prisoners of the two Muscogee chiefs and hanged them on April 18, 1818.

Hadjo supported the Red Stick cause as a loyal supporter of Tecumseh. While Hadjo used his spiritual power to bring the Red Sticks together during the early part of the War of 1812, Tecumseh returned home to find his confederacy in shambles. In his absence, Tenskwatawa had sent his warriors into battle, saying he would cast a spell on Harrison's troops, killing half of them and driving the other half insane. While Tenskwatawa sang and prayed, warriors attacked Harrison at four in the morning. In terms of numbers killed and wounded, the battle proved a draw, but Harrison's troops drove the warriors from the battle and burned Prophetstown. Tecumseh and others blamed the Shawnee Prophet for the defeat, which harmed the Indian confederacy. Tecumseh threatened to kill his brother if he attempted to lead warriors in the future, and both he and Tenskwatawa moved to Canada with many followers to continue the cause. On October 5, 1813, Harrison and Tecumseh fought at the Battle of the Thames. Tecumseh died a warrior's death as a patriot. Tenskwatawa, no longer a prophet, remained in Canada until the United States hired him as a government chief to convince the Shawnee to sign a removal treaty and move to Indian Territory. In May 1828, Tenskwatawa took many Shawnee to the site of present-day Kansas City, Kansas, where they settled on a new reservation. There, Tenskwatawa reunited with old friends, including Sac, Fox, and Kickapoo. He lived out his last days in Kansas, dying in November 1836 near Kansas City.[52]

Many eastern tribes living in Indian Territory suffered severely during the 1850s when the United States began to unravel over the question of slavery and the extension of slavery into the western territories. During and after the American Civil War, Native American leaders called on their experience, wisdom, and spiritual power to deal with Union and Confederate forces operating in Indian territories west of the Mississippi River. Some tribes held peace councils and tried to avoid fighting, while others joined Confederate or Union armies. The Civil War proved devastating to many tribes in Indian Territory and elsewhere. The United States used the Civil War and Reconstruction eras to force tribes to accept the peace policies of reservations, relocations, and consolidations. Some tribes fought back, including Navajo (Diné) people. Kit Carson's campaign ended military resistance of the Navajo, and General James Carleton condemned the people to a reservation on the Pecos River, where they declined in numbers.[53]

In 1868, Navajos learned that a peace commission led by William Tecumseh Sherman would decide their fate. Navajo people of power called on their gods to determine their fate. In 1868, before Sherman's arrival, Navajos conducted a Coyote Way Ceremony. Scholars today know of the ceremony through the oral histories of contemporary Navajo people and through military records. Significantly, a Navajo Naat'anni conducted the Coyote Way Ceremony, asking spiritual forces known as Holy People to guide him and the people to know their future. One day, every able-bodied person gathered on an open plain outside Fort Sumner. They formed a huge circle, clacking rocks and sticks together while walking toward the center of the circle. They moved slowly and purposefully with good thoughts and prayers, making the circle smaller and smaller until they trapped a coyote within the circle. They did not kill the animal. The coyote rolled over and played dead, lying on its side in a meek manner. In ritual fashion, with songs and prayers, Chief Barboncito, a holy man, opened the coyote's mouth and placed a white shell bead (abalone shell) inside so the animal swallowed the divining medicine. Once this was completed, Barboncito and the people backed away from the coyote, which trotted off in a westerly direction, indicating that General Sherman would send them home.[54]

Like American Indians throughout the Native Universe, Barboncito and the Navajos held prisoner prayed their gods would return them to Dinetah, the sacred land of the Navajo people. Their tie to their holy homeland began at the time of creation, when the people emerged from the Third World into the Fourth World, the earth as we know it today. At that time, Diné people settled in the vast territory inside their four sacred mountains. Spirits inhabited the land at the time. Navajo people call these beings Diyin Diné'e, or Holy People. They once lived on earth and put the world into motion, charging the earth with power and designating the lands that would always be for Diné. Their enchanted lands are literally filled with spirits. They gave Diné people all things on earth and made the world ready for Earth Surface People, or humans.[55] A time existed when Earth Surface People existed at the same time as Holy People, and they were directly related to each other. After living together for a spell, the Holy People decided to become invisible and live in the rocks, valleys, mountains, water, clouds, and all places within the environment of the earth. They taught Diné people how to use song and ceremony to call on them for help, which Earth Surface People have done ever since. During the ceremony, Diné medicine men call on Holy People to enter ceremonial hogans and travel through sand paintings into the bodies of patients, through the central nervous system to heal the afflicted person. The connection between modern Diné people and Holy People continues today, just as Barboncito and his people had a direct relationship to the Spirit People that lived within their landscape.

When Sherman arrived at Fort Sumner to negotiate the Navajo Treaty of 1868, he met with Barboncito in a grand council. Barboncito represented the people and their attachment to their sacred homeland. Because he and others had performed a Coyote Way Ceremony, Barboncito dealt with General Sherman with wisdom and calm, saying the reservation at the Bosque Redondo in eastern New Mexico "has caused a great decrease of our numbers, many of us have died, also a great number of our animals."[56] He explained that at the time of creation, Holy People had taught "that we were never to move east of the Rio Grande or west of the San Juan rivers." When Sherman pressed the point about moving the Navajo to Kansas, Barboncito responded, "I am speaking to you now as if I was speaking to a spirit." Later, the chief said, "I hope to God you will not ask me to go to any other country except my own." Barboncito, a man of power and wisdom, prayed to the Holy People to convince Sherman to return Navajo people to their beloved Dinetah. On May 29, 1868, Sherman informed the Navajo that the United States would send them to their former homeland. With joy, Barboncito told his people they would return to Dinetah, a gift of the spirit world.[57]

Chief Barboncito is one of many powerful patriots that protected his people from abuses by invading forces. In 1876–1877, Toohoolhoolzote, a Nez Perce *towat* (medicine or holy man, sometimes called *twati*), argued vehemently with General Oliver O. Howard when the United States demanded the removal of nonreservation Nez Perce, Palouse, and Cayuse onto the Nez Perce Reservation. Toohoolhoolzote reminded Howard that the Nez Perce had signed the first Nez Perce Treaty in 1855 at the Walla Walla Council. However, he pointed out that a few Nez Perce, with only one chief, had signed the "Thief Treaty" of 1863 that reduced the reservation by 6,932,270 acres for eight cents per acre. The amount of money never mattered. The theft of land violated Nez Perce law and sovereignty. Neither Toohoolhoolzote nor any of the other leaders had agreed to the Thief Treaty, and from 1863 to 1877, they refused to leave their homelands.[58]

At the Lapwai Council of 1877, Howard asserted his authority and executed his orders. He disliked the Washani religion, calling the followers "Dreamers," which he meant as a derogatory term. Howard also referred to the Indians as heathens, followers of a "new-fangled religious delusion" led by Toohoolhoolzote, a "wizard" and "magician." Young Chief Joseph represented the feelings of many when he explained, "The Creative Power, when he made the earth, made no marks, no lines of division or separation on it." The earth was the mother of all people. Toohoolhoolzote explained Indian law (*tamanwit* or *tamanwal*) came from the creation, not man. In frustration, Howard jailed Toohoolhoolzote and forced the nontreaty chiefs to remove to the reservation. These actions contributed to igniting the Nez Perce War of 1877. Joseph later stated that Howard was the grizzly bear and the Indians were deer.[59]

The Nez Perce, Palouse, and Cayuse fought in the Nez Perce War, and General William Tecumseh Sherman ordered the exile of Nez Perce, Palouse, and Cayuse prisoners of war to Fort Leavenworth, Kansas, the Quapaw Agency, and the Ponca Agency in Indian Territory. During their exile in Eekish Pah (Hot Country), the people sang and prayed in their longhouses, asking the Creator to send them home. In 1885, all the

survivors returned to Idaho or Washington, where they live today. The people contin-
ued the Longhouse faith through the Seven Drums religion, which is extant today.
The loud beat of *kookoolots*, or hand drums, mixed with strong voices still rings out
during ceremonies at the longhouses on many reservations of the Columbia Plateau.
Many Indians followed the old religion, revitalized in the mid-nineteenth century by
Smohalla and his nephew, Puck Hyah Toot.[60]

Puck Hyah Toot taught the children of Palouse elder Mary Jim, including Carrie
and Tom. For many years, Palouse and Nez Perce holy man Andrew George followed
the teachings of the old ones, singing and praying for the benefit of others. Andrew
George, a *twati* (medicine man) believed strongly in spiritual power and called on
spirits for healing. He also doctored people suffering from negative spirit medicine,
including Josiah Pinkham and his sister. Using songs, prayers, and water, Andrew
drove the negative energy from their bodies. He included the blowing of water on their
bodies and slapping of their bodies as a means of ridding them of ill health. At public
functions on and near the reservations, people pray and sing, asking spirits to assist
them in all matters large and small.[61] In the twentieth century, many Native American
spiritual leaders continued this tradition, including the Wendat-Huron religious leader
and professor Eleonore Sioui, of Wendake, Quebec. Sioui became a noted medicine
woman after the 1950s through her Tecumseh Center, where she treated patients for
numerous illnesses. She advocated for her tribe and all Indian people, calling on spiritual power to protect sacred lands, traditional environments, flora and fauna, and leaders fighting on behalf of First Nations people. In like fashion, Cherokee healer Beverly Patchell serves Indian people as a traditional healer, prayer leader, and professor.
Patchell explained that she asks Grandfather for power and wisdom so she can help
others through prayers, herbal medicine, message, oils, and the sweat lodge. Whenever Comanche medicine man Kenneth Coosewoon needs her, she assists him so
that the presence of male and female energy will bring better healing into the sweat
lodge.[62]

Some California Indians also practice the sweat lodge ceremony. Many variations
exist, but all the leaders call on the spiritual world to help cure people or assist them in
dealing with life's trials. In Northern California, Winnemem Wintu healer Flora Jones
received her power on an eighty-mile trek near indigenous sacred places on the slopes
of Mount Shasta.[63] After completing her education at an Indian boarding school and
Lowell High School in San Francisco, Jones returned to the McCloud River in the
shadow of Mount Shasta to continue her healing ways. She often took patients to Panther Meadows on the slopes of the great mountain, where many Indian people believe
the Creator placed a great woven basket in the lofty mountain cone. According to
Native Americans in the region, the mountain basket gives out blessings and goodness to the world. The people maintain the power emanating from the basket by sing-

ing, praying, and conducting ceremony using songs, prayers, and stories. In 2003, Jones died, but her grandniece, Caleen Fisk, carries forward her medicine, spirit, and political advocacy to regain federal tribal recognition and protect the tribe's sacred places that are threatened by farmers and bureaucrats eager to raise Shasta Dam and destroy holy places of the people. In 1980, the Bureau of Indian Affairs took federal recognition away from this band of Wintu, making it easier for federal, state, and private agencies and developers to destroy the cultural traditions and places of the people. Sisk is one of many women that calls on spiritual power to assist her in the tribe's preservation efforts, praying ceremonially for the protection of Winnemem Wintu people and their grand environment in the shadow of Mount Shasta.[64]

In Southern California and surrounding states, Martha Manuel Chacon, Vivienne Jake, Pauline Murillo, Dorothy Ramon, Jane Dumas, Sarah Martin, Lorene Sisquoc, Barbara Drake, June Leivas, Lorena Dixon, Jane Penn, Carmen Lucas, Barbara Levy, Daphne Poolaw, Rose Ann Hamilton, and Katherine Siva Saubel spent their lives in the service of their people. All of these women have power, sharing their wisdom and experiences with others in order to preserve and protect their cultural heritage. Chacon, Murillo, and Martin—all women, not men—kept their ceremonial Big Houses (ceremonial lodges) alive and functioning on the San Manuel and Morongo Reservations and guarded the sacred bundles for many years after the last shamans died. The people considered their Big Houses to be alive and highly sacred places. On these two reservations, the Big House functioned as a tribal meeting place, a site of ceremony for the dead, and a place of annual celebrations connecting the living with spirits of the dead. All of the women kept traditions alive within the cultures of the Cahuilla, Serrano, Kumeyaay, Kwaaymii, Mohave, Quechan, and Luiseño Indians, and all of them serve or served their people as spiritual leaders who call on the Creator and spirits living within the indigenous environment to assist the Indian people with blessings of family, food, friendship, love, and historic preservation of traditional songs, stories, ceremonies, and language.

Henry Rodriquez, Mark Macarro, Matthew Hanks Leivas, Claudia White, James Ramos, Lorey Cachora, Gary Dubois, Sean Milanovich, Anthony Madrigal (Sr. and Jr.), Richard Arnold, Pauline Murillo, Barbara Levi, Katherine Saubel, Michael Tsosie, Ernest Siva, and Manfred Scott are only a few of the many indigenous contemporary leaders, singers, storytellers, and historians of California, Arizona, and Nevada. They access the sacred to gain power to help their people continue the old cultural fires and teach young people indigenous traditions. Many cultural and spiritual leaders exist in California and in the vast Native Universe of the Western Hemisphere, far too many to mention here. But people with indigenous wisdom—people of the past and present—significantly influenced the course of American history, and these kinds of special Native Americans continue to influence the modern indigenous world.

Cherokee people also continue the healing traditions of the past, and healers continue to help others today in the communities near Tahlequah, Oklahoma. Cherokee elders Watt Cheeters, Jim Henson, Crosslin Smith, and Beverly Patchell are four of many Cherokee medicine people in Oklahoma, and they use their knowledge and commitment to serve others through a healing community. Jim Henson received his healing gift from his grandfather, who passed it on to him after the elder's death. According to Henson, his grandfather appeared to him in his home one night and in the Cherokee language said, "It is time!" When he questioned his grandfather's ghost about the meaning of his statement, his grandfather told him to think about it! The vision disappeared but reappeared another night, asking him, "Have you thought about it?" Henson responded that he had and believed his grandfather wanted him to end his hedonism and follow the Good Red Road.[65]

Henson had grown up assisting his grandfather in the medicine, helping people whenever they asked. His grandfather passed along the power of healing to him, instructing him to retrieve the old man's medicine bundle carefully buried at the old place. When Henson dug up the medicine bundle and opened it, a forceful wind came out of the bundle and struck him in the chest. In this way, Henson explained, the healing spirit entered his mind and body, infusing him with his grandfather's healing power. People started asking him for help, and he healed them with the new power, benefiting the people and bringing his own life into balance.[66]

Historically, many people of wisdom and power served their communities as prophets, healers, and teachers. Other indigenous leaders organized their people militarily to fight the United States. Some of these individuals appear in the introduction and in the body of this book. War leaders sought power to protect their people, often through preemptive strikes against the United States Army and volunteer solders, believing they could defeat their enemies through spiritual power and violence supported by creative forces. Other leaders called on spiritual power to protect their people from enemies, attempting to live by acculturating—not assimilating—into the non-Indian world but maintaining their identities as Native Americans. In most regions of North America, American Indians held on to the most fundamental element of their Native identities—their cultural and spiritual beliefs, which include various and diverse means of communications with the spiritual world.

Throughout Indian Country today, people continue to conduct prayers, rituals, songs, and ceremonies with the intention of connecting with spiritual worlds and powers. Not all Native Americans participate in such activities, especially those that have converted to other faiths intolerant of Native ways, but other American Indians participate in indigenous ceremonies, rituals, healings, and beliefs and in Christianity. In some cases they blend together. Reverend Sheldon Swick, a Christian minister and Mohave man living on the Colorado River Indian Reservation, explained that Mastamaho, one of three Mohave creators, lives in spirit today on the mountain Avikwamé, located west of the Colorado River above Needles, California. Swick explained that Mastamaho is the same as the Jewish and Christian god of the Holy Bible, only Mohave call the Creator by another name. The Almighty, Swick said, manifested in different ways to different people, but he believes there is only one god, known by many names, including Mastamaho.[67]

In the twenty-first century, many Native American communities continue to use traditional medicines and believe in spiritual healing, not just through herbal medicines but also through spiritual medicine ways, ceremonies, songs, and rituals tied to people and places. It is impossible to analyze the depth and breadth of historical figures with wisdom, power, and significance. The essays found in this volume offer brief studies of a select number of communities and people associated with spirit and power. All of the Native people and indigenous cultural traditions presented here are directly related to the spiritual world of Native America. The subjects share a common bond through human attempts to receive and use power for knowledge, healing, war, peace, protection, diplomacy, politics, economic stability, cultural preservation, and other uses. The works found herein feature some well-known figures and subjects of American history and others not so well-known and are written by some of the foremost historians of Native Americans in the late twentieth and early twenty-first centuries.

American Indian medicine ways and spiritual power remain extant within indigenous worlds of the Western Hemisphere today. A direct link exists between past indigenous medicine beliefs in power and the present. Although the various forms of medicine may have changed over the years, the core beliefs within tribal communities still continue today, and people draw on them to preserve, protect, and heal their people. Most members of tribal groups use some form of Western medicine, but they have not forsaken their ancient beliefs and methods. Indigenous and Western medicine ways intersected over time, and American Indian communities, clinics, and hospitals today often encourage the use of both medicine ways to help tribal members heal and live healthier lives. At hospitals and clinics, patients and their families may conduct ceremonies, sing, and offer prayers. Indigenous medicine people may use pipes, bundles, songs, feathers, and other material items to help patients. Medicine people and family members sometimes place bundles or prayer feathers above the patient's head or in the corners of hospital rooms. The intersection of Western and indigenous medicine ways has enhanced healing for American Indian people today.

In 2016, Dr. Juliet McMullan established a positive relationship between the School of Medicine at the University of California, Riverside (UCR), and Riverside-San Bernardino Indian Health. Through a program known as the Gathering of Good Minds: Engaging Native Americans and Wellness, California Indians, urban Indians, and professors from UCR seek to bring together indigenous and Western medicine ways. Each gathering begins with prayer and a talking circle, where everyone in attendance has an opportunity to share their lives and any trouble then plaguing them. The group of Western medical doctors, community nurses, medicine people, and tribal members meet to discuss ways of healing and moving forward together to benefit the health of American Indian people. Trust is at the heart of each fellowship meeting, as diverse people and medical methodologies exchange with each other in mutually beneficial ways that have brought about healing and will bring people together in a positive manner. A long-term relationship will develop out of the Gathering of Good Minds.[68]

This introduction offers a general overview, with specific examples of Native Americans using spiritual means to engage power and wisdom in the best interest of their people. Some Indians and non-Indians opposed the Native American leaders highlighted in the essays, and some people dismiss the spiritual beliefs and power of individuals or movements found in this volume. Such is the human condition, but the chapters offer one way of understanding indigenous communities and Native Americans of power, leadership, and healing during tumultuous times in American history. The volume offers a means by which students may learn about selective elements of American Indian medicine ways.

CHAPTER DESCRIPTIONS

The authors of the forthcoming essays deal with human interaction with the spiritual world through a discussion of omens, prophecies, war, peace, ceremonies, rituals, and material culture such as masks, prayer sticks, sweat lodge, peyote, and other items. Clifford E. Trafzer and Benjamin Jenkins present chapter 1, "Spirits, Landscape, and Power: Ways of Quechan, Navajo, and Apache." The essay introduces the subject of spiritual power by examining three diverse tribes and focusing on creation stories, spiritual power, Athabascan masking, and ceremonies, and the continuance of these concepts today.[69] The tribes share a strong relationship with spirits, which have influenced the course of history since the time of creation and continue this relationship today. Diné (Navajo) hand tremblers, crystal gazers, and stargazers seek the help of supernatural powers to learn the cause of sicknesses and advise patients which ceremony they need. Navajo medicine men had and still have a sophisticated ceremonial system that calls on the power of many Holy People who once inhabited the earth before disappearing into the landscape where they reside.

Through ritual, ceremony, sacred art, song, and dance, Navajo and Apache medicine men ask the Holy People to come to the ceremonial site to enter the patient's body and expulse disease-causing agents. Navajo people consider the entire ceremonial system an integral part of their culture and life, a component that ties Earth Surface People with the supernatural world. Navajo people are direct descendants of Holy People, who put the earth into motion, and both have an obligation to interact with each other to keep the world in balance and heal those suffering from illnesses. Quechan, Navajo, and Apache each had a warring tradition that drew on spiritual power to defeat enemies and protect their people. The chapter introduces elements of the warring tradition, but chapter 2 begins a discussion of the spiritual side of war.

Native Americans often connected war with the spiritual realm, seeking support for their causes through spiritual means. R. David Edmunds demonstrated this thesis in his works on Tenskwatawa and Tecumseh, and he furthers the theme in chapter 2, "Main Poc: Potawatomi Wabeno." A contemporary, ally, and friend of Tecumseh and Tenskwatawa, Main Poc (Cripple Hand) grew up in the thick deciduous woods of the Kankakee River in Illinois. He had no fingers or thumb on his left hand, but he grew into a large, strong warrior with great medicine associated with fire. Main Poc handled fire and ate hot coals, placing them on his body and in his nose with no ill effects. Potawatomi, Kickapoo, Ottawa, and others said he exhaled fire, blowing it in various directions and creating fireballs to toss at his enemies. Main Poc received power by communicating with spirits, casting positive spells to protect himself and his warriors, and casting negative spells to harm his enemies. This huge, muscular chief fought the United States during the War of 1812, contributing to the early successes of the Indian confederacy. He fought with Tecumseh many times but took his people into northern Michigan rather than fight Harrison at the Battle of the Thames. He died in 1816, but his people lived on in the northern woods and in Indian Territory, where the army relocated so many Indian tribes after the War of 1812.[70]

Joseph B. Herring contributed chapter 3, "Kenekuk, the Kickapoo Prophet." Rather than call on the spirit world to fight the United States, Kenekuk prayed for the survival of his people. He maintained his focus on continuing an Indian identity by acculturating some elements of American society and Christianity without assimilating. Like Main Poc, Kenekuk lived in Illinois. Kenekuk was a member of the Vermillion Kickapoo of Illinois, where he was a wild young man. He drank a lot and murdered his uncle, but a Catholic priest counseled the young Kickapoo, which began a life-changing transformation. Kenekuk used his Kickapoo culture as the foundation of a new movement among his people to lead a good life, rejecting evil and embracing temperance and peace. Kenekuk rejected Calvinism but blended Indian culture with a belief in God, Jesus, the Virgin Mary, heaven, and hell. He taught that living a good life and caring for others led Indians on the path to heaven. He encouraged his followers to speak Kickapoo, not English, and to sing, dance, and celebrate through ceremonies in the old ways of the people. He asked his congregation of four hundred people to be tolerant of other faiths but to remain loyal to the Kickapoo way and preserve their land and resources on the Kickapoo Reservation in Kansas.[71]

Troy Johnson, now deceased, offers chapter 4, "Masking and Effigy in the Northeastern Woodlands." Although this chapter focuses heavily on the Haudenosaunee (or Iroquois; People of the Longhouse), other data provided in this chapter pertains to the belief systems and cultures of other Native Americans living east of the Mississippi River, including the Algonquin-speaking people. Masking and the making of wood and stone effigies emerges as a common theme among Native Americans of the Northeastern Woodlands, and most often the material culture is tied to the sacred and spiritual elements of Native cultures. The False Face society of the five or six Iroquoian nations is sacred and well-known today, although the carved faces of spirits from a live tree are highly charged holy objects used ceremonially. During the time of creation, a spirit challenged the Creator to a duel of power, so they agreed to sit facing the east and see which of them could cause the Appalachian Mountains to move from the west to the east. The spirit man tried first but could not move the mountain, and so the Creator instructed the spirit not to look back while he moved the mountain.[72]

The spirit disobeyed, turning his head and finding the full force of the mountain smashing into his face. This broke his nose and taught him that the Creator had far more power than the spirit. The Creator charged Broken Nose to form the False Face society to help and heal the people, and so he did. Johnson introduces some of the masks and their functions, including the longnose, straight-lipped, whistling, and pig-head masks and the Husk Faces, or Bushy Heads. These are elements of the spirit, full of wisdom and healing for the people who still benefit greatly when the False Faces appear in their homes, longhouses, and in ceremony.

"Spiritual Traditions of the Great Plains" is the title of chapter 5. Written by Troy Johnson, the chapter provides specific analysis of selective spiritual traditions among the northern and southern Plains tribes. Johnson introduces the Sun Dance and sacred pipes, two central elements of the holy among many Plains Indians. Johnson offers a broader understanding of the Sun Dance, spiritual visions, *yuwipi* ceremony, and the sacred pipe through the lives of Frank Fools Crow, Daniel and Grady Dull Knife, and Stone Forehead. Keeper of the Sacred Arrows, Cheyenne holy man Stone Forehead, smoked the sacred pipe with Colonel George Armstrong Custer, who promised peace with the tribes. Stone Forehead emptied his spent tobacco from the sacred pipe on Custer's boots, telling him that if he did not live up to his solemn promise, the colonel and his men would lose their lives. This prophecy came true when warriors defeated Custer and the Seventh Cavalry at the Battle of the Little Bighorn.[73]

Johnson also discusses Hidatsa shaman Wolf Chief, who had a profound relationship with the spiritual world and used his medicine items, such as a buffalo skull, to find buffalo, protect warriors, and seek power to heal others. Tavivo, a Paiute prophet of the 1870s, originated the first Ghost Dance religion, which called on spiritual forces to end the world and bring back the dead, animals, and cultural ways of Native Americans. His son, Wovoka, is best known for the Ghost Dance, and details of his life are provided in chapter 8 by L. G. Moses. Johnson ties Tavivo and Wovoka to the spread of the Ghost Dance to the Lakota, which led to the Seventh Cavalry slaughtering Lakota men, women, and children along Wounded Knee Creek in South Dakota.[74]

Johnson foreshadows the chapter written by Moses by providing material not addressed by Moses. Johnson provides a brief analysis of Comanche chief Quanah Parker and Delaware leader John Wilson, who started the Native American Church in Indian Territory, using peyote as a sacrament and means of communicating with the divine. They were the first road men, traveling about Indian Country offering peyote services to Native Americans, and they helped spread the Native American Church to Apaches, Navajos, Utes, and others. In chapter 5, Johnson also deals briefly with the power of Geronimo, a medicine man and warrior known to have prevented the sun from rising until he and his warriors could find sanctuary in the mountains away from pursuing troops.

Chapter 6 offers "Smohalla, Washani, and Seven Drums: Religious Traditions on the Northwest Plateau" by Clifford E. Trafzer and Richard D. Scheuerman. The chapter opens with an explanation of spiritual power on the Columbia Plateau, where the Nez Perce, Yakama, Palouse, Cayuse, Umatilla, and others believe in *tamanwit*, or the laws of creation, which bound the tribes together into a cultural unit that has survived many generations and which remains an integral part of the tribes today. The death and rebirth of Smohalla, a Wanapum Indian holy man, helped revitalize the old Washani religion, often referred to as the Dreamer religion. Smohalla awoke during his own funeral service to tell the people that he had visited the Creator (Naamii Piap, or Elder Brother) and returned with a message that the Indian people should return to their old ways, ceremonies, and customs. He opposed reservations and allotments, which emerged as a major topic at the Walla Walla Council in 1855 and during discussions among the Nez Perce, Cayuse, and Palouse at the Lapwai Councils of 1863 and 1877 when the federal government pushed the Nez Perce and their allies into a destructive war. From the start, Chiefs Joseph, Stickus, Owhi, and many others opposed reservations because it broke *tamanwit*. Many other Indian leaders believed that federal Indian policies contradicted the precepts of Native American creation, which required humans to respect plants, animals, and places so they could remain connected with the Creator, the giver of life. This chapter also provides a reference to John and Mary Slocum, who originated the Indian Shaker Church. The brief mention of the Shake provides foreshadowing for the next chapter, which deals with Shakers in California.[75]

Al Logan Slagle, now deceased, was a Cherokee scholar and member of the Indian Shaker Church. He provided chapter 7, "Tolowa Indian Shakers: The Role of Prophecy at Smith River, California." Slagle provides background information on the origins of the Shake and the Tolowa Indian community in Northern California. John Slocum, a Nisqually Indian, had death and rebirth experiences in 1882 at Mud Bay, Washington. During Slocum's afterlife experiences, he learned what Jesus Christ required of Indian people, and Slocum's teachings, with the important assistance of his wife, Mary, formed the corpus of the Shaker doctrine. Slocum told the people that God is good and generous, a loving god, and he wanted Indian people to act better toward each other and all humans on earth. Slocum taught, and the people of Smith River practice, a religion asking the Holy Spirit to heal people of physical, mental, and spiritual conditions.

When people meet in the Shaker Church, they ask God to heal them through the Holy Spirit, and they pray that evil stays away from their communities. The people of Smith River believe the Holy Spirit first came among them during the first Ghost Dance of 1870, but then it became latent, reemerging with Wovoka, the Feather religion, and Native World Renewal Ceremonies. The people call on the spirits through dreams, dance, songs, prayers, and the ringing of brass school bells, asking the spiritual world to intervene among humans to bring health, happiness, and prosperity to members, as well as to keep negative forces from the congregation. The Shaker brought about a new spiritual community, the foundation of which is distinctly Native and Tolowa.[76]

L. G. Moses offers chapter 8, "'The Father Tells Me So!': Wovoka, the Ghost Dance Prophet." He continues the theme of spiritual power, teachings, and wisdom first addressed in brief by Troy Johnson, who introduced the Ghost Dance of the 1870s. Wovoka's father, Tavivo, communicated with the spirit, bringing the Ghost Dance into being, but it failed to stir the tribes in the same manner as the second Ghost Dance. During the 1870s and 1880s, many Indian people say the Ghost Dance did not die but became latent, rising again through Wovoka when the Great Spirit determined the time appropriate for the movement to rise again. Moses centers his essay on the Ghost Dance of Wovoka, who experienced death and rebirth on New Year's Day, 1889, a day punctuated by a total eclipse. On that day, Wovoka died, traveled to heaven, met the Grandfather, and returned to life in order to share the things he had learned directly from the Creator. Like Kenekuk, Smohalla, and other prophets of the nineteenth century, Wovoka provided a peaceful message, not one of war, conflict, and destruction.[77]

In accordance with lessons learned from the Grandfather, Wovoka told the people to end quarrels, work hard, and do others no harm, including abstention from whiskey, theft, or familial abuse. He wanted Indians to live in peace with whites. Native Americans, Wovoka preached, should unite so they could enter the heavenly world together, where no suffering, sickness, sadness, or starvation existed. To hasten the great event when the Indian world would live forever in peace and harmony with the Great Spirit, they had to perform a special dance for five consecutive nights, which made them tired and ghostlike. Indians from many regions of the American West traveled to hear Wovoka and return to their people with his message.

In the late nineteenth century, Native Americans struggled to survive in the face of wars, diseases, confinement, theft, and domination by the army and the Bureau of Indian Affairs. Wovoka provided hope for Native America, and the Lakota delegation brought the Ghost Dance from California to the Great Plains, where it spread quickly but with a militant twist. Military and civilian officials feared the Lakota and began rounding up Ghost Dancers. When Big Foot and his Ghost Dancers fled the agency to Wounded Knee Creek, Custer's old unit, the Seventh Cavalry, followed, setting up Hotchkiss guns on the hills overlooking the Indian camp. On December 29, 1890, the hostile parties started shooting at each other, creating a great American tragedy, the Wounded Knee Massacre.[78]

Some scholars argue the Ghost Dance died after Wounded Knee, but Native Americans know the religion continued and lives today in parts of the American West, including California, where men and women use the Ghost Dance to revitalize old religions, including the Earth Lodge religion and World Renewal Ceremonies of California's First Nations, and dances performed by Chemehuevi and other Southern Paiute people. Michelle Lorimer and Clifford Trafzer present an original essay for chapter 9, "California Indian Women, Wisdom, and Preservation." The chapter begins with a discussion of the Bole Maru and the works of Essie Parrish, Annie Jarvis, and Mable McKay in Northern California.[79] They also address the spiritual work of Wintu healer Flora Jones, who lived along the McCloud River and practiced her medicine on the slopes of Mount Shasta. They also address the spiritual works of women from Southern California, including Katherine Siva Saubel, Pauline Murillo, Carmen Lucas, and Jane Dumas. Like the women of Northern California, these unique and powerful women drew on the spiritual world for their power and their work in cultural preservation.

Many California Indian women have fought for the preservation of their cultures, which includes preservation of plants, animals, and places. They have led the cause to protect American Indian sacred sites and human remains in Southern California, where the federal government through the Bureau of Land Management, with the support of President Barack Obama and Governor Jerry Brown, opened thousands of acres of pristine desert lands for the "Great Barbeque" of energy companies that have destroyed human remains, cremations, cultural resources, and sites to hastily build wind and solar energy projects funded by public gifts and loans without proper federal or state oversight.

FIGURE I.3. Chemehuevi and Southern Paiute *puha'gaants* wore feathered headdresses during ceremonies. Dutch Eddy wore such a headdress during wakes. The Twenty-Nine Palms band of Mission Indians cares for this headdress, sharing it with other Southern Paiute tribes. Editor's photograph.

Carmen Lucas, Katherine Saubel, Lolita Schofield, Linda Otero, Daphne Poolaw, Barbara Levy, Linda Cachora, Willa Scott, and many other Native American women in Southern California protested some projects based on the harm those projects brought to indigenous sites, features, environmental sources, and sacred places. The government and energy companies ignored the pleas of American Indian men and women, and rushed to complete their renewable energy projects and collect huge dividends for their efforts. Throughout the efforts to make energy companies and federal officials more responsive to Native American protests, California Indian women prayed to the spiritual world for strength and wisdom. Their spiritual efforts formed the foundation of their preservation work.

Native American spiritual leaders hold an elevated place within Native American communities. For hundreds of years they have influenced the course of Native American history, and many people among tribes today have received special powers from the spiritual world to heal, sing, conduct ceremony, and perform other functions within communities. The late Kiowa elder and former leader of the Native American Church in Oklahoma, Harding Big Bow, healed people with much success through the peyote religion. During funerals and one-year memorials, Chemehuevi singers Matthew Hank Leivas, Vivienne Jake, and Larry Eddy use Salt Songs to heal Southern Paiute people during times of stress and grief. These and other traditional healers help people in alternative ways, calling on spiritual healing and medicine to assist patients. This is the case of Kenneth Coosewoon and his wife, Rita, who use the power of the healing spirit today to heal others through the sweat lodge ceremony. In chapter 10, "Coosewoon: Visions, Medicine, and Sweat Lodge," Clifford Trafzer analyzes the life and spiritual experiences of Comanche healer Kenneth Coosewoon. According to Coosewoon, during a sweat lodge ceremony in eastern Oklahoma, a powerful spirit came to him to tell him to lead the sweat lodge and heal people. The essay explores Coosewoon's journey into the world of spiritual healing, providing an example of a modern healer that has received and used spirit wisdom and power for forty years to help Indians and non-Indians in need. The work offers an example of one man that has *puha* or spiritual wisdom, power, and understanding from spiritual sources and has used these gifts to heal others.[80]

Coosewoon is one example of a contemporary Native American medicine man drawing on wisdom spirits for power to help others, not enhance his own lifestyle or position within the world. He is an effective and generous medicine man, a healer that has devoted his life to assist others with mental, physical, and spiritual illness. He is part of a long tradition within the Native American world of people and communities that believe in spiritual power that influences human beings. In 2015, Kenneth Coosewoon suffered his own health setback and now lives in the Veterans Center in Lawton, Oklahoma. But his medicine remains strong, and he continues to use his wisdom and power of healing by helping other veterans and their families as a prayer leader.

This volume offers several examples of the ways in which Native American beliefs in spirits have been and remain a fundamental aspect of American Indian history and culture. Historically, spiritual power influenced the cultural heritage of Native American tribes through their prophets, war leaders, medicine people, civilian leaders, and holy people, including those featured in this work. And spiritual power remains a powerful and permanent element in the lives of those Native Americans following in the cultural traditions of their ancestors. Students interested in American Indian history and culture might embrace a better understanding of these influences among tribes, tribal people, and cultural landscapes. Many sites have power, wisdom, and knowledge. Recently, Cahuilla-Serrano elder Kim Marcus explained, "From generation to generation, our elders have taught us to approach our ancestors and the spirits with good intentions and to call on them when we need help, blessings, and the right path."[81]

FIGURE I.4. Eleonore Sioui was a medicine woman and indigenous scholar of the Wendat-Huron people of Wendake, Quebec. Born into a family of chiefs, Sioui dedicated her life to spiritual and herbal healings. Editor's photograph.

American Indian prophets, holy leaders, and medicine people functioned in many ways within the Native communities of North America. They acted as psychologists, pharmacists, and spirit doctors, advising patients and sometimes calling on the spirit world to help them diagnose problems of the mind and body. People of wisdom used many methods to help others. Among many Algonquin Indians, people of wisdom called on spirit people through a shaking tent, which they constructed from logs and tightly wrapped skins or cloth, thereby creating a medicine lodge. Medicine people entered the lodges to sing and pray, calling on healing spirits to help them help others. When the spirits arrived to instruct the shamans or provide healing, the tent shook violently, swaying to and fro. Sometimes observers from outside the shaking tent heard voices, songs, and noises that let them know the shaman had connected with spirits of wisdom.

For traditional people, medicine people and prayer leaders are the connective tissue between the temporal and divine, the sacred and profane. Creative forces brought the breath of life to specific tribes and established their earth, cosmos, and all that exists. Life came from their creative power and forces, and throughout history, through positive and negative actions, wisdom spirits have taught people how to be or how not to be. From the beginning of time, they taught others the world was filled with life and death, joy and sorrow, day and night, light and dark, water and drought, plenty and want, health and illness, and many other dualities. Humans with spiritual power and wisdom provided some predictability and supplication for their people. They asked the spiritual world for help in bringing about good weather, water, hunting, healing, loving, farming, fishing, gathering, and other elements of life on earth. They prayed for world renewal and helped bring balance, maintain health, and general protection of the people. These men and women were and are part of an ancient but continuing tradition of indigenous people who harness spiritual power and use it to serve their people. American Indian medicine ways remain alive today in Indian Country, manifesting themselves in many forms and making medicine available to people of good hearts and those seeking to benefit others.

NOTES

1. In spring 2012, Stephen Cullenberg, then dean of the College of Humanities, Arts, and Social Sciences at the University of California, Riverside, planned the opening of a new interdisciplinary building by inviting tribal elder Kim Marcus to offer a Cahuilla and Serrano Indian Blessing Ceremony. Marcus and singers blessed the building and the people using the structure with songs, prayers, and ceremony.

2. Ibid.

3. For an overview of different forms of negative medicine or witchcraft among Native Americans, see William S. Lyon, *Encyclopedia of Native American Shamanism* (Santa Barbara, Calif.: ABC-CLIO, 1998), 130–33, 140–41, 150–54, 193, 209, 236–37, 242, 260–61, 305–6, 358.

4. Ake Hultkrantz, *The Religions of the American Indians* (Berkeley: University of California Press, 1979), 9–65, 84–102; Jeffrey Ostler, *The Lakotas and the Black Hills* (New York: Penguin Books, 2010), 3–27.

5. Richard D. Scheuerman and Clifford E. Trafzer, *River Song: Naxiyamtáma (Snake River-Palouse) Oral Traditions from Mary Jim, Andrew George, Gordon Fisher, and Emily Peone* (Pullman: Washington State University Press, 2015), 1–43, 47–50, 74–76, 155–62; Clifford E. Trafzer and Richard D. Scheuerman, *The Snake River-Palouse and the Invasion of the Inland Northwest* (Pullman: Washington State University Press, 2016), ix–xviii, xxii–xxiv, 1–20, 172–91; Ostler, *Lakotas and the Black Hills*, 3–22; Vine Deloria Jr., *The World We Used to Live In: Remembering the Powers of the Medicine Men* (Golden, Colo.: Fulcrum Publishing, 2006), 125–48.

6. Kathleen Van Vlack, Richard Stoffle, Evelyn Pickering, Katherine Brooks, Jennie Delfs, *Unav-Nuquaint: Little Springs Lava Flow Ethnographic Investigations*, Bureau of Applied Research in Anthropology (BARA) (Tucson: University of Arizona, 2013), 23–25, 140–42. Richard Stoffle, Richard Arnold, Kathleen Van Vlack, Larry Eddy, and Betty Cornelius, "Nuvagantu, 'Where Snow Sits': Origin Mountains of Southern Paiute," in *Landscapes of Origin in the Americas: Creation Narratives Linking Ancient Places and Present Communities*, ed. Jessica Christie (Tuscaloosa: University of Alabama Press, 2009), 32–44.

7. Lowell John Bean, ed., *California Indian Shamanism* (Menlo Park, Calif.: Ballena, 1992), 22–23; Gregory Evans Dowd, *A Spirited Resistance: The North American Indian Struggle for Unity, 1745–1815* (Baltimore: Johns Hopkins University Press, 1992), 1–9; Christopher L. Miller, *Prophetic Worlds: Indians and Whites on the Columbia Plateau* (New Brunswick, N. J.: Rutgers University Press, 1985), 2–5, 14–21, 42–45; Calvin Martin, *Keepers of the Game: Indian-Animal Relationships in the Fur Trade* (Berkeley: University of California Press, 1978); and Martin, *The American Indian and the Problem of History* (New York: Oxford University Press, 1987).

8. Clifford E. Trafzer, introduction to *American Indian Prophets: Religious Leaders and Revitalization Movements*, ed. Trafzer (Newcastle, Calif.: Sierra Oaks Publishing Company, 1986), ix–xiv.

9. Donald M. Bahr, "Pima and Papago Medicine and Philosophy," in *Handbook of North American Indians*, vol. 10, *Southwest*, ed. Alfonso Ortiz (Washington, D.C.: Smithsonian Institution Press, 1983), 195–96.

10. For general works, see William S. Lyon, *Encyclopedia of Native American Healing* (New York: W.W. Norton, 1996); Robert A. Trennert, *White Man's Medicine: Government*

Doctors and the Navajo, 1863–1955 (Albuquerque: University of New Mexico Press, 1998); Lewis Mehl-Madrona, *Coyote Medicine* (New York: Scribner, 1997).

11. For this concept, see Georges E. Sioui, *Huron-Wendat: The Heritage of the Circle* (East Lansing: Michigan State University Press, 1999), 16–41.

12. Eleonore Sioui, oral interview by Clifford E. Trafzer, May 24–28, 2001, Wendake, Quebec.

13. Two sources focused on Mohave and Quechan warriors include Kenneth M. Stewart, "Scalps and Scalpers in Mohave Indian Culture," *El Palacio* 76 (Summer 1969), 25–30; and Jack D. Forbes, *Warriors of the Colorado: The Yumas of the Quechan Nation and Their Neighbors* (Norman: University of Oklahoma Press, 1965).

14. During the course of the editor's research with the Quechan Indian Cultural Committee, a person related this dream. The dream took place in 2011 at Fort Yuma Indian Reservation. For the report on the research, see Clifford E. Trafzer, *Quechan Indian Historic Properties of Traditional Lands on the Yuma Proving Ground* (Riverside: California Center for Native Nations, 2012). For an understanding of the spiritual and temporal power of dreams, see C. Daryll Forde, *Ethnography of the Yuma Indians* (Berkeley: University of California Publications in American Archaeology and Ethnology, University of California Press, 1930–1931), 158–60, 201–4.

15. Numerous books and articles have been published with traditional oral narratives of Native Americans. For examples provided by two Native American women in their tribal languages and in English, see Dorothy Ramon and Eric Elliott, *Wayta' Yawá* (Banning, Calif.: Malki Museum Press, 2000), 6, 47, 75, 97, 177, 294; Katherine Siva Saubel, *'Isill Héqwas Wáxish: A Dried Coyote Tail*, vol. 1 (Banning, Calif.: Malki Museum Press, 2004), 129, 181, 266, 272, 305, 308, 310, 312, 529.

16. Clifford E. Trafzer, *A Chemehuevi Song: The Resilience of a Southern Paiute Tribe* (Seattle: University of Washington Press, 2015), 176–209.

17. G. Sioui, *Huron-Wendat*, 14–125.

18. Ibid.

19. Clifford E. Trafzer, ed., *Grandmother, Grandfather, and Old Wolf: Tamánwit Ku Súkat and Traditional Native American Narratives from the Columbia Plateau* (East Lansing: Michigan State University Press, 1998), 97–109.

20. Ibid., 107–9.

21. Clifford E. Trafzer, "Where Puha Sits: Salt Songs, Power, and the Oasis of Mara" (paper presented at the Indigenous Environments Conference, University of East Anglia, UK, July 8, 2016).

22. Trafzer, *Grandmother, Grandfather, and Old Wolf*, 97–109.

23. Lorey Cachora, interviews by Clifford Trafzer, June 23, 2012, and July 26, 2012, Fort Yuma Indian Reservation. During an interview with Yavapai-Prescott elder Ted Vaughn on September 10–11, 2009, at the Yavapai-Prescott Indian Reservation, the tribal scholar provided the comment regarding the continuation of mountain spirits.

24. Vaughn, interview; Matthew Hanks Leivas, oral interview by Clifford E. Trafzer, November 27, 2013; Trafzer, *Yavapai-Prescott Cultural Ethnography of Lands* (Riverside: University of California, California Center for Native Nations, 2009), 67.

25. C. F. Black, *The Land is the Source of the Law* (London: Routledge, 2011), 23–61. Black provides us with a profound indigenous interpretation of the power of the earth and its significance in providing the fundamental laws of all Native people.

26. In the last book of his life, Vine Deloria Jr. provided numerous written examples of the efficacy of Native American medicine and medicine people. See this exceptional piece of Native American history, *World We Used to Live In*.

27. Larry Eddy, oral interview by Clifford E. Trafzer, October 18, 2007, Colorado River Indian Reservation. Trafzer conducted the interviews for the National Library of Medicine, National Institutes of Health, and they can be accessed through the National Library of Medicine in Bethesda, Md.

28. For a broad representation of Native American spiritual beliefs with specific examples, see Peggy V. Beck, Anna Lee Walters, and Nia Francisco, *The Sacred: Ways of Knowledge, Sources of Life* (Tsaile, Ariz.: Navajo Community College Press, 1995), 3–32.

29. Trafzer, *Quechan Indian Historic Properties*, 36–46; John P. Harrington, "A Yuma Account of Origins," *Journal of American Folklore* 21 (1908): 234–48; Cachora, interviews.

30. Trafzer, *Quechan Indian Historic Properties*, 101–2.

31. For a Native American perspective of Pueblo people, see Joe S. Sando, *The Pueblo Indians* (San Francisco: American Indian Historian Press, 1976), 53–66; Paul Robert Walker, *Spiritual Leaders* (New York: Facts on File, 1994), 6–19.

32. Clifford E. Trafzer, *As Long as the Grass Shall Grow and Rivers Flow: A History of Native Americans* (Fort Worth, Tex.: Harcourt, 2000), 30; for a Pueblo Indian scholar's view of Pópe and his significance to Pueblo history and culture, see Sando, *Pueblo Indians*, and Sando, "The Pueblo Revolt," in *Handbook of North American Indians*, vol. 9, *Southwest*, ed. Alfonso Ortiz (Washington, D.C.: Smithsonian Institution Press, 1979). Sando and Ortiz were important Pueblo Indian scholars who wrote on Popé, thus providing a Pueblo version of the great leader of the seventeenth century.

33. Passaconaway (Papisse Coneaway, or Child of the Bear) was a spiritual leader who fought for the rights of people in New Hampshire and surrounding New England. See Leo Bonfanti, *Biographies and Legends of the New England Indians*, vol. 1 (Wakefield, Mass.: Pride Publications, 1970), 47–53, 61; Charles Edward Jr., *Passaconaway in the White Mountains* (Boston: Richard G. Badger, 1916); and Walker, *Spiritual Leaders*, 1–5.

34. Dowd, *Spirited Resistance*, 20, 33–40.

35. Dowd, *Spirited Resistance*, 23–46; Trafzer, *As Long as the Grass Shall Grow*, 92–93.

36. Alfred Cave, *Prophets of the Great Spirit: Native American Revitalization Movements in Eastern North America* (Lincoln: University of Nebraska Press, 2006), 22–39. Cave provides one of the most important books published on American Indian prophets,

providing insightful interpretations and analyses of several Native American prophets in the eastern part of the United States. For short biographies of Neolin and Pontiac, see Carole Barrett, Harvey Markowitz, and R. Kent Rasmussen, eds. *American Indian Biographies* (Pasadena, Calif.: Salem, 2005). For an outstanding scholarly work on Pontiac, see Gregory Evans Dowd, *War Under Heaven: Pontiac, the Indian Nations, and the British Empire* (Baltimore: Johns Hopkins University Press, 2002).

37. Walker, *Spiritual Leaders*, 14–19.

38. Cave, *Prophets of the Great Spirit*, 17, 39–44; Dowd, *Spirited Resistance*, 33–36, 42–45.

39. Anthony F. C. Wallace, *The Death and Rebirth of the Seneca* (New York: Random House, 1969), 239–54

40. Ibid.; Cave, *Prophets of the Great Spirit*, 183–224. Significantly, Wallace, a superior scholar, served as an advisor for Professor Cave on *Prophets of the Great Spirit*.

41. Thomas Jefferson to Handsome Lake, November 3, 1802, in *The Papers of Thomas Jefferson* (Princeton: Princeton University Press, 2011), 38:628–21; Wallace, *Death and Rebirth of the Seneca*, 239–54; Cave, *Prophets of the Great Spirit*, 183–224.

42. R. David Edmunds, *The Shawnee Prophet* (Lincoln: University of Nebraska Press, 1983), 28–41; for a broader survey centered on Tecumseh, see R. David Edmunds, *Tecumseh and the Quest for Indian Leadership* (Boston: Little, Brown, 1984). Also see Cave, *Prophets of the Great Spirit*, 45–90; and Dowd, *Spirited Resistance*, 124–29.

43. For a new interpretation and analysis of Tenskwatawa, see Adam Jortner, *The Gods of Prophetstown: The Battle of Tippecanoe and the Holy War for the American Frontier* (New York: Oxford University Press, 2012).

44. Edmunds, *Shawnee Prophet*, 28–41; Cave, *Prophets of the Great Spirit*, 97–114.

45. Edmunds, *Shawnee Prophet*, 47.

46. Ibid., 49.

47. See Tecumseh's message to President James Madison in Duane Champagne, *Chronology of the Native North American History* (Detroit: Gale Publishers, 1994), 504.

48. Ibid., 28–41; Dowd, *Spirited Resistance*, 142–47; Cave, *Prophets of the Great Spirit*, 114–39.

49. For recent interpretations on the Creek War and the role of various indigenous leaders, see Kathryn E. Braund, ed., *Tohopeka: Rethinking the Creek War and the War of 1812* (Tuscaloosa: University of Alabama Press, 2012); Kathryn E. Braund, *Deerskins and Duffels: The Creek Indian Trade with Anglo-America, 1685–1815* (Lincoln: University of Nebraska Press, 2006).

50. Frank L. Owsley Jr., "Prophet of War: Josiah Francis and the Creek War," in Trafzer, *American Indian Prophets*, 35–55; Cave, *Prophets of the Great Spirit*, 165–68, 178–79.

51. Owsley, "Prophet of War," in Trafzer, *American Indian Prophets*, 44–45.

52. Ibid., 51–52.

53. Trafzer, *As Long as the Grass Shall Grow*, 202–7, 220–28.

54. In 1977, while teaching at Navajo Community College (Diné College), the editor first learned of the Coyote Way Ceremony. According to Navajo professors in the Department of Navajo History and Culture, Navajo people held the ceremony at Fort Sumner, New Mexico, toward the end of their incarceration. Navajo scholar Ruth Roessel also reported on the ceremony in her book *Navajo Stories of the Long Walk Period* (Tsaile, Ariz.: Navajo Community College Press, 1973), 212, 238–39, 244. The editor also found evidence of the ceremony reported by the army. See Gerald Thompson, *The Army and the Navajo* (Tucson: University of Arizona Press, 1976), 151–58; and Clifford E. Trafzer, *The Kit Carson Campaign: The Last Great Navajo War* (Norman: University of Oklahoma Press, 1982), 240–41.

55. Gladys A. Reichard, *Navaho Religion: A Study of Symbolism* (New York: Pantheon Books, 1950), 50–51, 55, 57, 59, 62, 65–68, 156, 225, 330.

56. Martin A. Link, *Treaty Between the United States of America and the Navajo Tribe of Indians, with a Record of Discussions that Led to Its Signing* (Las Vegas, 1968), 1–2.

57. Ibid.; Trafzer, *Kit Carson Campaign*, 242–43.

58. Trafzer, *As Long as the Grass Shall Grow*, 259–61; Clifford E. Trafzer and Richard D. Scheuerman, *Renegade Tribe: The Palouse Indians and the Invasion of the Inland Pacific Northwest* (Pullman: Washington State University Press, 1986), 104–5.

59. Trafzer and Scheuerman, *Renegade Tribe*, 105–8.

60. For the most in-depth scholarly book on the Nez Perce, Palouse, and Cayuse in Indian Territory, see Diane Pearson, *The Nez Perce in Exile* (Norman: University of Oklahoma Press, 2008), 1–54; Clifford E. Trafzer, "The Palouse in Eekish Pah," *American Indian Quarterly* 9 (1985): 169–82.

61. Josiah Pinkham, a member of the Nez Perce Tribe of Idaho, shared this healing story with the editor in Oklahoma City, Oklahoma, at the National Cowboy Museum during a consultation. Andrew George, interview with Richard D. Sheuerman, Lee Ann Smith, and the editor, November 15, 1980, Yakama Indian Reservation.

62. Clifford E. Trafzer, Beverly Sourjohn Patchell, and Ronald Ray Cooper, *Comanche Medicine Man: Kenneth Coosewoon's Great Vision, Blue Medicine, and Sweatlodge Healings* (Camano Island: Coyote Hill Press, 2015), 163–68.

63. Peter M. Knudtson, *The Wintun Indians of California and Their Neighbors* (Happy Camp, Calif.: Naturegraph Publishers, 1977), 15–17, 59–68.

64. Beck, Walters, and Francisco, *Sacred*, 134–37.

65. For a published example of a Cherokee healer, see Robert Conley, *Cherokee Medicine Man: The Life and Work of a Modern-Day Healer* (Norman: University of Oklahoma Press, 2005).

66. Jim Henson, oral interview with Clifford E. Trafzer, April 12, 2008, Keys, Okla.

67. Clifford E. Trafzer, *Mojave of the Colorado River* (Riverside: University of California, California Center for Native Nations, 2011), 39–42. Swick, interview with Trafzer, Oc-

tober 18, 2007. The interview was conducted for the National Library of Medicine of the National Institutes of Health and may be accessed at the National Library of Medicine, Bethesda, Md.

68. In 2016, the Patient Centered Outcomes Research Institute of Washington, D.C., authorized by Congress in 2010, funded a highly significant project with the University of California, Riverside, Gathering of Good Minds: Engaging Native Americans in Wellness, which has focused on creating healthy relationships between the School of Medicine and the Riverside-San Bernardino American Indian Health Consortium. Dr. Juliet McMullan is the principal investigator. A group of people engaged in Indian health and medicine, including the editor, have participated in this two-year program, which encourages the use of traditional indigenous medicine ways of Native Americans.

69. Harrington, "Yuma Account of Origins," 324–28; Reichard, *Navaho Religion*, 11, 16, 24, 29; Keith H. Basso, *Wisdom Sits in Places: Landscape and Language Among the Western Apache* (Albuquerque: University of New Mexico Press, 1996), 105–49; John Farella, *The Main Stalk: A Synthesis of Navajo Philosophy* (Tucson: University of Arizona Press, 1985), 69–83; Ethelou Yazzie, *Navajo History*, vol. 1 (Tsaile: Navajo Community College Press, 1971), 42; Philip G. Greenfield, "Apache Masks," in *Gods Among Us*, ed. Ross Coates, (San Diego: San Diego State University Press, 1989), 86–98; Troy R. Johnson, *Native American Spiritual Practitioners and Healers* (Westport, Conn.: Oryx Press, 2002), 145.

70. Edmunds, *Shawnee Prophet*, 67–93, 117–42; Ralph Linton, "Nativistic Movements," *American Anthropologist* 45 (April 1943): 230–40; Anthony F. C. Wallace, "Revitalization Movements," *American Anthropologist* 58 (May 1956), 264–81; Ruth Landes, *The Prairie Potawatomi: Tradition and Ritual* (Madison: University of Wisconsin Press, 1970), 27–29, 46–48, 51–60, 89; R. David Edmunds, *The Potawatomis: Keepers of the Fire* (Norman: University of Oklahoma Press, 1970), 96–115, 186–88; Johnson, *Native American Spiritual Practitioners*, 220–23.

71. Joseph B. Herring, *The Kickapoo Prophet* (Lawrence: University Press of Kansas, 1988), 1–18; Cave, *Prophets of the Great Spirit*, 225–43; George Schultz, "Kennekuk: The Kickapoo Prophet," *Kansas History* 3 (1980): 38–39; Johnson, *Native American Spiritual Practitioners*, 115–18.

72. William N. Fenton, *The False Face of the Iroquois* (Norman: University of Oklahoma Press), 35, 48, 60, 95–106, 121–23, 137, 140–42, 383, 424–25; Daniel K. Richter and James H. Merrell, *Beyond the Covenant Chain: The Iroquois and Their Neighbors in Indian North America, 1600–1800* (New York: Syracuse University Press, 1987), 15–17; Johnson, *Native American Spiritual Practitioners*, 1–3, 65–67, 96–99.

73. John Epse Brown, *The Sacred Pipe: Black Elk's Account of the Seven Rites of the Oglala Sioux* (Norman: University of Oklahoma Press, 1989), 3–9, 31–44; Ruth Fulton Benedict, "A Vision in Plains Culture," *American Anthropologist* 24 (1922): 17; John Neihardt, *Black Elk Speaks: Being the Life Story of a Holy Mon of the Oglala* (Lincoln: University

of Nebraska Press, 1961), 3–6; James Mooney, *The Ghost Dance Religion and the Sioux Outbreak of 1890* (Chicago: University of Chicago Press, 1965), 62–63, 114–20, 127; Johnson, *Native American Spiritual Practitioners*, 21–24, 34–36, 38–41, 44–46, 57–60, 75–78, 120–22, 127–30, 142–45, 161–64, 194–97, 212–17, 244–49, 251–59.

74. Mooney, *Ghost Dance Religion*, 114–27.

75. Click Relander, *Drummers and Dreamers* (Caldwell, Idaho: Caxton Printers, 1956), 50–68; Virginia Beavert, *The Way It Was* (Olympia, Wash.: Consortium of Johnson O'Malley Committees, Region IV, 1974), x–xiv; Robert H. Ruby and John A. Brown, *John Slocum and the Indian Shaker Church* (Norman: University of Oklahoma Press, 1996), 310; Leslie Spier, *The Prophet Dance of the Northwest and Its Derivatives: The Source of the Ghost Dance*, General Series in Anthropology 1 (Menasha, Wisc.: George Banta Publishing, 1935), 43–44; Johnson, *Native American Spiritual Practitioners*, 60–63, 107–9, 197–208, 225–28, 241–44.

76. Homer G. Barnett, *Indian Shakers: A Messianic Cult of the Pacific Northwest* (Carbondale: Illinois State University Press, 1972), 35–38; Ruby and Brown, *John Slocum and the Indian Shaker Church*, 79, 138, 151, 207, 216; Relander, *Drummers and Dreamers*, 50, 149–52, 162–67; Johnson, *Native American Spiritual Practitioners*, 197–203.

77. Gregory E. Smoak, *Ghost Dances and Identities: Prophetic Religions and American Indian Ethnogenesis in the Nineteenth Century* (Berkeley: University of California Press, 2006), 165–75; for a detailed work on Wovoka, the Ghost Dance Prophet, see Michael Hittman, *Wovoka and the Ghost Dance*, exp. ed. (Lincoln: University of Nebraska Press, 1998), 63–105, 297–98; Johnson, *Native American Spiritual Practitioners*, 251–59.

78. The entire works of Michael Hittman offer original interpretations of Wovoka and the Ghost dance; see Hittman, "Ghost Dance, Disillusionment, and Opiate Addiction: An Ethnohistory of Smith and Mason Valley Paiutes" (PhD diss., University of New Mexico, 1973); and Hittman, *Wovoka and the Ghost Dance* (Lincoln: University of Nebraska Press, 1990); see also Paul Bailey, *Wovoka the Indian Messiah* (Los Angeles: Westernlore Press, 1957), 35, 50, 67, 207; Nat P. Phister, "The Indian Messiah," *American Anthropologist* 4 (April 1891): 105–8; Henry F. Dobyns and Robert C. Euler, *The Ghost Dance of 1889 Among the Pai Indians of Northwestern Arizona* (Prescott, Ariz.: Prescott College Press, 1967), 14–35.

79. Greg Sarris, *Keeping Slug Woman Alive: A Holistic Approach to American Indian Texts* (Berkeley: University of California Press, 1993), 8–11, 65–67, 127, 176–77, 185, 197–98; Frank LaPena, "Tradition Is Evidence for the Truth of Life," in *Surviving in Two Worlds: Contemporary Native American Voices*, ed. Lois Crozier-Hogle and Darryl Wilson (Austin: University of Texas Press, 1997), 53–60; Knudtson, *Wintun Indians of California*, 15–17; Cora DuBois, *The 1870 Ghost Dance* (Lincoln: University of Nebraska Press, 2007), 1–4; Frank LaPena, "Wintu," in *Handbook of North American Indians*, vol. 8, *California*, ed. Robert Heizer (Washington, D.C.: Smithsonian Institution Press, 1978), 324–40;

Johnson, *Native American Spiritual Practitioners*, 134–38, 164–67. For an excellent study of Wintu people that includes segments on religious movements, see Cora DuBois, *Wintu Ethnography* (Berkeley: University of California Press, 1935).

80. Stoffle et al., "Nuvagantu," 32–44. Also, see Anthony Madrigal Sr., *Sovereignty, Land, and Water* (Riverside: University of California, Riverside, California Center for Native Nations, 2008), 50–71.

81. Marcus made these statements on December 4, 2012, when he conducted the Blessing Ceremony for the interdisciplinary building on the campus of the University of California, Riverside.

1

SPIRITS, LANDSCAPE, AND POWER

꩜

Ways of Quechan, Navajo, and Apache

CLIFFORD E. TRAFZER AND BENJAMIN JENKINS

ALL AMERICAN INDIANS in the American Southwest have rich oral histories of creation that tie their peoples to the sacred, especially to spirits that still exist today. Divine creators acted in concert to originate all Native Americans in the region, including the Quechan (pronounced Kwit-san), Navajo, and Apache people. These three major tribes of the American Southwest share beliefs in powerful spirits of wisdom, knowledge, and healing that live in the environment and that have always affected the course of their tribal culture and history.

American Indians have ancient beliefs in unseen, controlling spirits that live in the environment, taking many forms and influencing humans in many ways. Anthropologists, philosophers, and scholars working in various fields of religious studies have long understood the significance of wisdom spirits. But too many historians have avoided addressing spirits as factors that influence the course of Native American history. The issues of spirits and power seem unhistorical to a number of scholars. This chapter provides a few ways of thinking about spirits within these three cultures that studious readers may apply to other tribes in Native America. Not every contemporary Native American tribe maintains beliefs in wisdom spirits, but American Indians raised deeply in their cultures believe in these living deities, often in tandem with their Christian beliefs. For many, however, spirits have always been and continue to be important cultural elements that influence events, lives, tribes, and Native interactions with newcomers.[1]

Although spirits manifest themselves differently within each group, each tribe's religion centers on creative gods that appear visibly and invisibly in ceremonies. Thus the Quechan, Navajo, and Apache enjoy a common theme of living spirits that influence human beings to bring balance, power, protection, and healing to the world. Both positive and negative spirits exist, but this treatment focuses on those that enhance lives, rather than "witches" that destroy lives.

Quechan, Navajo, and Apache Indians believe in spiritual "people" or characters that created life, including the Earth Surface People, and continue to play an active role in their daily lives. Quechan, Navajo, and Apache cultures contain layers of meaning, and their separate landscapes of cultural and spiritual meaning communicate different ideas to contemporary people. All three of these groups believe in mountain spirits and a host of other entities, some of whom manifest in ceremony through human actors, particularly those who wear masks. The Quechan and other Yuman people celebrate and reconnect with their dead through memorials called *Keruk*, participating in intimate interaction with the spirit world and their known and unknown dead. Spirits live in the environment but help the people when summoned.[2] In the same fashion, Navajo and Apache spirits participate in protection, healing, puberty, and hunting ceremonies. They live in the environment but manifest as masked dancers, traveling from the spiritual world to inhabit impersonators or dancers, reminding people of their kin relationship with the gods and their responsibilities and obligations to the holy ones.

Quechan creators put the world into motion but began life using a miraculous fluid. They did not employ water but a thick ocean where two creators stirred, emerging from the ocean.[3] In the traditions of the Quechan, Apache, and Navajo, spirits filled the earth. They became creators and holy people on the earth, establishing a bridge between humans and the spiritual world. Spirits taught Apache and Navajo to re-create the face of their gods in masks worn by humans to represent and become the spirits.[4]

Past Quechan reported, and some contemporary elders state, that their landscape has always been alive with spirits.[5] Creators charged the landscape with power and spirit, which they make available to people of wisdom. The Quechan landscape is located in present-day California and Arizona along the length of the Colorado River from Hoover Dam to the Gulf of California.[6] Since the time of creation, Quechan lived in three major groupings: the North Dwellers, living north of present-day Yuma, Arizona; the South Dwellers, who occupied land south of Yuma extending into Mexico; and the Sunflower Eaters, who lived east of present-day Yuma along the Gila River and east of the Colorado River.[7] In 1908, Quechan medicine man Tsuyukwerau, or Tsushratz (known primarily by his English name, Joe Homer), provided a short version of Quechan creation to anthropologist John Harrington.[8] Contemporary Quechan elders say creation began inside an ocean of thick, life-giving fluid or primordial soup. Two beings came out of the ocean, including Kukukmat (also known as Kukomat, Kwikumat, and Kokomut). His name means He Lies Above, Cloud Above, or Cloud Body. The other being, the brother of Kukumat, "had no name" but became

FIGURE 1.1. Sunflower Eaters of the Quechan Nation lived along the Gila River east of present-day Yuma, Arizona. They conducted cremation ceremonies in accordance with the laws given them by their creator, Kukumat. Painting by Carl Schott, from William H. Emory, *Report of the United States and Mexican Boundary Survey* (Washington, D.C.: A. O. P. Nicholson Printers, 1857), facing 110.

known as Kweraak Kutar (Old Man Who Shares, or, commonly, Blind Old Man).[9] Eventually, Kukumat (often shortened to Kumat) and Blind Old Man came to the surface, and Kukumat stood on the ocean. Through his movement in the four directions, song, and gesticulation of his finger, Kukumat envisioned and brought about dry land, the center of which became Avikwamé, a sacred mountain located at the southern tip of Nevada along the Colorado River on its California bank. In addition, Kukumat made the sun, moon, and stars. After establishing the cosmos, the creators began work on making humans, plants, and animals.[10]

From the mud left by the receding thick ocean, Kweraak Kutar lived at Avikwamé and made clay doll figures, which he envisioned as the first humans. When Kweraak Kutar made his version of human beings, Kukumat scolded him and taught him how to make them correctly. Kweraak Kutar's clay creations with webbed feet "became ducks, geese, pelicans, beavers, [and] muskrats."[11] In anger, Kweraak Kutar returned to the thick sea, creating a whirlpool and wind emitting "all kinds of sickness."[12] Kukumat continued his work on the clay dolls that would become the first human beings, making Marxokuvek, Quechan First Man, who was himself another creator. Kukumat gripped Marxokuvek under the armpits, swinging him north, west, south, and east in a counterclockwise direction.[13] Kukumat animated all Yuman people, including the Quechan, Mohave, Kumeyaay, Kwaaymii, Cocopa, Yavapai, Hualapai, Havasupai, Maricopa, and Paipai. He commanded them four times to speak, and they spoke the first language on earth, the Yuman language.[14] Kukumat and future creators taught the first people in the creation lodge called the Dark House, instructing them on laws, realities, and ways of life. Kukumat taught that no utopia would exist on earth. Life was never as perfect as the existence of the gods, and people experienced tensions, contradictions, anger, jealousy, betrayal, disappointments, and other elements of Quechan life.

Kukumat made the Quechan and Kumeyaay and Kwaaymii (pronounced Ku-me-eye and Kwhy-me, respectively) friends, and he encouraged them to marry. He directed the Cocopa to marry Maricopa, and so on among all the Yuman people. Kukumat used his own shadow, rather than human sexual reproduction, to create his son, Kumastamho, who worked with his father and Marxokuvek to help "fix up the world."[15] Thus three creators—Kukumat, Kumastamho, and Marxokuvek—created the world, plants, places, and animals. They taught the first people, and once they became spirits living in the environment, they continued to help living Quechan in all matters, including war. Kukumat never directed the Quechan and Cocopa to become enemies, but during the time of creation, conflicts sometimes arose between the two groups, resulting in pitched battles up until the 1850s.[16] Kukumat created social, political, economic, and religious laws by which people would live, establishing the Quechan Way, followed by a number of contemporary Quechan. Creators taught the Quechan how

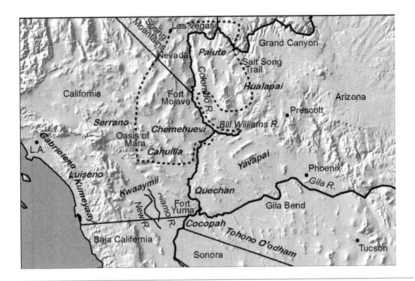

FIGURE 1.2. Map of the Southwest and selected tribes. Notice the dotted line depicting the Salt Song Trail. Salt Song singers carefully guard knowledge of the exact trail in order to protect it and prevent the looting of sacred sites of power. Editor's collection.

to live on earth, instructing through positive and negative actions and words. When the first people questioned Kukumat's laws, the Creator brought rain to the region for four days and rescued the drowning people swimming in the ocean. He turned the various people into different animals. As Joe Homer related to John Harrington, "He made from the Cocopa the mockingbird (*sukwilyla*); from the Diegueño [Kumeyaay and Kwaaymii] the deer; from the Maricopa the buzzard (*ase*)."[17] Kukumat explained that he would continue creation and proceeded singing four songs, and as he sang, floodwaters receded, revealing more of the earth. Kukumat had created the first people from mud, but then he gave them detailed instructions on how to copulate, telling them to populate the earth. Originally Kukumat created eight humans, but then he made twenty-four more.[18]

At Avikwamé, Kukumat proclaimed the site the center of the world, saying, "Here, I shall build my Dark House." The creators used the Dark House as a place of instruction, akin to a schoolhouse. Yuman people re-created the style of the Dark House as Quechan homes, replicating the architecture of logs, sticks, and adobe plastered on the structure as Kukumat, Kumastamho, Marxokuvek, and Xavasumkulaplap (Kukumat's daughter, her name meaning Blue Green Bottom of Her Foot and commonly called Xanye, or Frog) traveled the earth naming places, especially mountains.[19] Quechan homes provided a visual reminder of the Dark House, the site of creation. Creators traveled over the entire world but designated the Colorado River Basin as the center of the universe, including that area around present-day Yuma, Arizona, where some of creation occurred. Under instructions from Kukumat, Marxokuvek led the people down from the mountain. Indeed, the word *Kwitsan* (originally rendered in the Latin alphabet as Kwitsen, but today spelled Quechan), meaning "coming down," became this group's tribal name.[20] Marxokuvek led the people downriver, traveling first to Sokapai (Mount San Jacinto), back to Avikwamé, south along the Colorado River to the Whipple Mountains, and south to Pilot Knob, magically crossing the water to Cottonwood Mountain (Black Hill in Yuma), up the Gila River, and northeast to Castle Dome Mountain. From the heights of Castle Dome, Marxokuvek announced, "This is my homeland," saying he wished to be cremated in the Muggins Mountains north of the Gila River and east of Yuma. In this way, he designated a vast region for the Quechan, a landscape they still claim, and the mountains of which still contain Quechan spirits.[21] Kukumat taught the people to communicate through language and prayer, as well as rock art, intaglios, shrines, trails, and other natural features. Kukumat's power remains within the Quechan landscape today. According to contemporary Quechan elder George Bryant, the area surrounding present-day Yuma is a "storied land" that contains power and legends.[22]

The Quechan believe that the landscape features, hydrological systems, flora, and fauna of Southern California, Northern Baja California and Sonora, and the American Southwest as a whole owe their origin to Kukumat, Kumastamho, and Marxokuvek and Xanye. Quechan elders report that Kumastamho used his spittle to make the sky and stars, rubbing the stars with his fingers until they became bright with light. He made the sun move across the sky, rising in the east over the Paloma, Muggins, Castle Dome, and Kofa Mountains, and traveling west across the firmament, sinking over the mountains of western Arizona and eastern California. Marxokuvek, the First Quechan Man, is associated with the Yuma region and the sacred mountains, including Muggins, Picacho, Pilot Knob, Eagle Mountain, Castle Dome, Gila, Kofa, and others. In this area, Kumastamho stamped his foot, creating cracks on the earth's surface where numerous varieties of plants developed. His stamping also created earthquake faults that exist today, a reminder of Kumastamho's power.[23]

Kumastamho next brought the sky closer to earth, and he painted a grand face on the sky, rubbing it until "it shone brightly."[24] In this magical way, Kumastamho made Inya, the sun, which lives and dies each day. Marxokuvek made day (*inyamek*) and night (*tinyam*). Kukumat and Kumastamho created animals, many that live today in the mountains and deserts, some moving in daylight and others at night. The change of seasons also influences the lives of the Quechan. Kumastamho made rain, saying, "I have the power to cover up the face of the sun with a rain-cloud and send a rain-wind every day." He also knew that people, plants, and animals needed water. In appropriate

FIGURE 1.3. Barbara Levi of the Quechan Nation of the Fort Yuma Indian Reservation dances to a *Pipa* song accompanied by a gourd rattle. Levi is a tribal elder with great knowledge of traditional medicine. She is a well-known scholar of her tribe's history, culture, language, and religion. Editor's photograph.

amounts, rains fed humans, plants and animals, but too much rain caused floods on the Gila and Colorado Rivers. Kukumat created the first massive sandstorm, blinding and covering all living things.[25]

Kukumat created Ave (or Rattlesnake) from a muddy stick and gave him great healing power and the ability to harm others. At first Rattlesnake healed effectively, but he became egotistical and power hungry. Quechan people feared being bitten by the great snake, and one day, Giant Rattlesnake Doctor (or Rattlesnake for short) bit Marxoku-vek, who died as a result. However, with whirlwind power, Kukumat raised him from the dead so he could fulfill his purpose on earth, taking the people to the Yuma area.[26] Not long after, Rattlesnake bit and murdered another innocent, Rabbit. Kumastamho determined to rid the earth of the Giant Rattlesnake Doctor, coaxing him down from his home on Castle Dome toward the Colorado River. Kumastamho killed Rattlesnake with a flint knife, cutting off his heads and tossing his body along the Pacific coast, his body becoming the Pacific coastal range from Chile to Alaska.[27]

Although Quechan creators had great power and established power within the environment, they were not omnipotent. Kukukmat could not cure all illnesses, including bad medicine put on him. Kukumat lived in the Dark House with his daughter, Xavasumkulaplap. Like her father and Blind Old Man, she originated in the primordial ocean but usually chose to live on solid ground with her father. One day, Kukumat rested on the north side of the Dark House. Frog lay naked at the front door facing east. When Kukumat walked outside to defecate, he reached out and touched her vagina, violating incest laws.[28] After touching Frog, Kukumat went to a hill to defecate, not knowing that Frog was underneath him, where she caught his excrement and used it to poison her father. He became violently ill and traveled about, searching for a doctor to save his life, but to no avail. He told people:

I am sick, I am sick.
What made me sick?
Did rain-cloud make me sick?
Did foul-wind make me sick?
My head is sick, my belly is sick,
My limbs are sick, my heart is sick.[29]

Kukumat grew more ill, turning his head in the four directions, hoping for relief and healing. He sweated a white substance, creating a pale pigment found near Yuma.[30] People that loved Kukumat gathered around him in the Dark House and watched his life-force vanish. Feeling guilty for her part in his sickness, Frog burrowed into the earth and resurfaced three times, including once on the Colorado River, where her formation remains on a large rock today.[31] The people conducted a sweat lodge ceremony for Kukumat, but he soon died.[32] When Kukumat died, Wren (Xanavtcip) proclaimed that the Creator "is dead. He is a shadow. He is a wind. You will never know him more." She instructed the people about the cremation ceremony, explaining exactly how to ritually prepare and handle Kukumat's body and how to build the cremation pyre. Kukumat's cremation set an example for Quechan to follow. The Quechan and other Yuma people often follow this tradition today.[33] Wren sent Coyote to the east to get fire for the funeral pyre. Following these instructions, Coyote traveled toward the dawn to get white fire, but Wren had sent him away, fearing he would desecrate Kukumat's body. When Coyote saw smoke from the funeral pyre, he raced back, jumped into the middle of the cremation fire, and stole Kukumat's heart. He raced east toward present-day Phoenix to Greasy Mountain (the modern Estrella Mountains) to eat the heart and put the power of Kukumat into his body.[34]

Kumastamho sang for his father, which made the people cry once more in memory of Kukumat. Four times Kumastamho sang:

> The wind is wandering, is wandering
> The wind is wandering, is wandering
> The wind is wandering, is wandering
> The wind is wandering, is wandering.[35]

In the aftermath of his father's death, Kumastamho created the Colorado River with a digging stick. "Where he held the spear-blade flat, the river is broad. When he held it sidewise, the river-channel is narrow, and most of the water flows to one side." Kumastamho split the mountain today known as Fort Yuma Hill and Prison Hill, cutting "the mountains asunder to let the river through." Kumastamho sang a song about the river and how much he loved the water. He proclaimed that the water should flow forever: "It shall flow forever. It shall flow forever. When the weather grows hot, it shall rise and overflow its banks. It shall flow forever."[36]

Not long after, Marxokuvek took the Quechan to the Yuma area. His illness grew worse when he reached Yuma, where he asked the people to cremate him on Muggins Mountain. When the Quechan burned Marxokuvek, the entire region of Mokwintaorv, near the Muggins, Gila, and Laguna mountains, appeared on fire. Today, the Quechan identify this area also as Aaux'rakyamp, meaning Fire All Around. The Quechan believe Marxokuvek's spirit still resides in the Muggins Mountains, where contemporary Quechan may access his assistance through song and prayer.

After Marxokuvek's death, only Kumastamho lived on earth. But when he believed that his work on earth was finished, he began to sing, transforming himself from a physical entity into a spiritual one.[37] Kumastamho sang:

Into the earth I go down, go down
Nothing but earth will be seeing, will I be seeing.
I sink down into the old riverbed,
Down into the interior.[38]

As Kumastamho sang, his body sank deeper and deeper into the earth. He spun into the earth four times. The fourth time he sang and vanished into the earth, where he remained for four days. After re-emerging, Kumastamho announced that he would ascend to Avikwamé. He sang a new song, announcing his transformation into Eagle, becoming Black Eagle in the west, High Eagle in the east, White Eagle in the north, and Fish Eagle in the south.[39] Since that time, Kumastamho's spirit has lived on Avikwamé, where the Quechan seeking the power to heal visit him in dreams. The people lost their three creators, Kukumat, Kumastamho, and Marxokuvek, in physical form. Today, however, Quechan people say all three live in spirit and occupy sacred sites on the landscape where people may call on them for help.[40]

The Apache and Navajo people of the American Southwest similarly share a belief in spirits living in their landscapes. They also share a close relationship with each other and with their environments. Like the Quechan, their creation stories place a host of spirits into their environments in Arizona, New Mexico, Utah, Colorado, and northern Mexico. At special times, humans imitate some spirits, who appear in ceremonies as masks worn by humans. The people believe that the person wearing the mask becomes the spirit they impersonate. Navajos have an array of gods impersonated by humans in various ceremonies. Navajo, or Diné, as they call themselves, live in a vast geographical area they refer to as the Dinetah, the Land of the People. According to the Navajo creation story, the first people traveled through three previous worlds before arriving in the present Fourth or Glittering World where First Man built a creation hogan, a sacred lodge in which First Man made the masks.[41] Inside the creation hogan (a term that refers to a Navajo home, lodge, or place of ceremony, especially female), First Man spread a robe made of the eastern dawn, blue sky to the south, evening twilight in the west, and night darkness to the north. On the robes, First Man laid down, respectively, white shell, turquoise, abalone shell, and black jet stone. In the center of the lodge, he placed a red stone before laying a sheet of the dawn over all the robes and sacred stones. First Man spread several layers of sacred buckskin (the unwounded skin of a deer, killed by hunters who smothered the deer to death) and sky blue, evening twilight, and night darkness. He used waters, colors, clouds, and air as medicine, ultimately removing the eight layers of robes before blowing life-giving air on them.[42]

First Man replaced the robes again and did this four times, since four is the sacred number of Navajos. As First Man removed the robes four times, and seven *hashehe*, or gods, appeared, including Talking God, Calling God, Male God, Female God, and Shooting God. Contemporary Navajo elders explain that First Man made the Diyin Diné'e, or Holy People, that once lived on earth in physical form. Although the spirits could move their eyes and heads, they could not speak but only make their special sounds. First Man gave them powers, particularly the ability to heal. First Man endowed the gods with articles of power with which to do their work, including straight lightning, zigzag lightning, flash lightning, feathers, pollen, sunlight, sunray, rain rays, rainbow, stubby rainbow, and reflected sun red color. He also gave them white, blue, yellow, dark, and pink winds. The various colored winds constitute the souls of the gods, providing them the ability to stand, walk, move, and breathe. Corn Beetle blew rock crystal into their eyes, and they could see and make high-pitched sounds.[43]

Navajos believe the various gods lived on earth until the Holy People retreated to special places and homes, living as spirits in the mountains, rocky buttes, canyons, water, and other places in a huge geographic area of Arizona, New Mexico, Utah, and Colorado. But like the Quechan, Navajos can still call on them for help and healing. Some spirits retreated into the red walls behind White House ruin in the southern branch of the Canyon de Chelly and numerous other sites. Before moving into the spiritual world, they left their *nikehe*, or face prints, on white shell, turquoise, abalone shell, and jet, so Navajos could re-create their images during ceremony by wearing sacred buckskin masks.[44] Navajos call masks *jish*, meaning "pouch" or "sack," but they are commonly known as *yei* masks, a derivative of the Yeibichai (pronounced Yay-be-chay), or Talking God, the maternal grandfather of the holy people.[45]

Masked gods appear during Navajo ceremonies, including the Fire or Corral Dance, Windway, Shootingway, Beautyway, Coyote Way, Upward Reaching, Big Godway, and Downway.[46] They also visit communities, asking for goods and money to support a ceremony. *Yeis* play prominent roles in the Nightway when fourteen to twenty-four masks participate in ritual and ceremony. Nightway originated when two stricken twins sought healing from the gods, traveling from White House ruin to many sites and back again, where the *yeis* agreed to conduct the ceremony farther up the canyon. Masked gods dance publically outside the ceremonial hogan during the last night of the Nightway.[47]

Dawn Man and Dawn Woman parented Talking God, the deity of the east. Navajos use sacred buckskin to make his mask and most others, killing the deer by capture and suffocation in a highly spiritual, ritual, and religious sacrifice.[48] Mask makers use this sacred buckskin for face masks and sacred doeskin for the backside. They use sinew of both the buck and doe to sew the two pieces together and rock crystal to mark spots where an awl punches holes for the eyes and mouth. They use native almogen (*dlésh*, or plants blended to create yellow) to color Talking God's face white and black ochre to color the eyes, mouth, and corn plant placed on the god's face.

FIGURE 1.4. During many Navajo ceremonies, mask gods participate through ritual acts and dancing. This sketch of a female *yei*, or Navajo god, is one of many diverse masks worn during ceremony. Female gods danced outside the female hogan during healing ceremonies where medicine men created holy sand paintings and led healing ceremonies. Sketch by Sarah Moore. Editor's collection and photograph.

The corn plant consists of five leaves and two ears with tassels on the forehead of the mask.[49]

The marks and colors found on *yei* masks represent rain, dawn, twilight, and other elements of the environment significant to contemporary people. Many *yeis* contain freshly cut spruce around the collar, and some wear feathers from eagles, turkeys, bluebirds, and owls. Navajos use horsehair of different colors to create hair on the masks, a practice that developed when Spanish conquistadores introduced horses during their conquest of the Americas.[50] Mask makers use white shell beads, turquoise, and other "jewels" on *yei* masks. Ceremony performers who wear masks must be healthy,

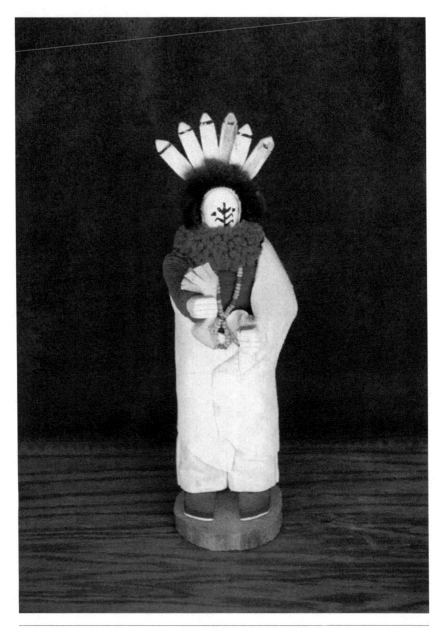

FIGURE 1.5. Talking God, or Yeibichai, is the grandfather of the *yeis* of Navajo people. He is the lead god, depicted here in the form of a carved cottonwood figure. Navajo medicine men often sing and speak of Talking God. He leads the Yeibichai dances during many ceremonies today. Editor's collection and photograph.

free of disease and open sores, and without negative attitude. Women in the midst of menstruation are not allowed to participate in the ceremony. Performers' participation must focus on the well-being of patients and the people, not their own egos or elevated places in society.[51] Dancers become the particular gods they represent, and they must act in accordance with the tradition of the gods in order to bring the power of the Holy People from their homes in the environment to ceremonial sites. For the health of the community and every Navajo person, masked dancers must be wise in their thoughts and actions on behalf of all people. Dancers impersonating Talking God, Calling God, and House God have a special role to play in the ceremonies, particularly Nightway.[52]

Talking God carries a fawn bag of sacred corn pollen or cornmeal in his left hand and a gourd rattle in his right hand, making his characteristic wu-hu-hu-hu sound. Navajos call Talking God Yeibichai or Hastseyalti, but he is only one of many gods important to the Diné and tied to their beautiful and spiritual landscape.[53] Calling God is similar to Talking God. Navajos paint his face blue, not white, and no corn plant appears on his face. During the ceremonies, particularly Nightway, Calling God accompanies Talking God, although they do not appear together in every ceremony.[54] Both of these deities are associated with the House God, or Hastsehogan, and some Navajos say that he is an equal to Talking God and Calling God. House God is the god of the west and sunset, and thus the opposite of Talking God, who is associated with the east and dawn. House God commands the homes, caves, cliff dwellings, and other sacred dwellings found in the Navajo environment. He oversees sacred places, agriculture, and game animals. Navajos paint House God with a blue face to symbolize the sky, and paint triangular eyes and a square mouth on the mask, offering many colorful symbols representing rain.

Only men wear the mask of Talking God, but women may wear other important masks, especially the *yebad*, or female mask, painted blue with triangular black eyes and a yellow ladder situated above her square mouth vertically running to her forehead.[55] The male god wears a head mask Navajos paint with a blue face and black triangular eyes, using a tubular end of a gourd or a leather tube to represent the mouth. Six male gods appear alongside the six female gods in the public dances during the last night of Nightway, and four of them portray First Dancers in that portion of the public ceremony held on the last evening of Nightway, known as Atsalei.[56]

Fringed Mouth (Dsahadoldzam) appears in ceremony in two forms, both ornate.[57] Navajo mask makers paint Tse'nitsi Dsahadoldza, or Fringed Mouth of Land, red on the right and blue on the left, while they make Tha'tladze Dsahadolza, Fringed Mouth of Water, yellow on the right and blue on the left. Navajos believe Fringed Mouth is connected to land, water, and the most powerful of elements, lightning. This deity carries lightning in his hands, using ropes of zigzag lightning. Navajos paint zigzag lightning on the dancer's chest, back, arms, legs, and shoulder blades to visually emphasize the dancer as the incarnation of Fringed Mouth.[58]

Diné call Humpback or Hunchback God Ganaskidi, who received his name by walking with his back bent over and from the black bag he carries on his back. Symbolically, the black bag represents rain clouds and planting. It contains fruits, vegetables, and other foods associated with harvests.[59] Mask makers present Humpback God's eyes with triangles and fringe his ears so he may hear from Wind. Navajos paint the face of Red God, or Hastseltsi, with red ochre and a black panel outlined in white. This area of the mask contains the eyes and mouth, both covered with white shell. Red God lives in the red walls behind White House Ruin in Canyon de Chelly. The god of racing, he appears in public during the Nightway Ceremony, challenging others to a footrace. He never dances, and he never helps the patient in the ceremonial hogan. If someone accepts his challenge to race and loses, Red God whips the person with the yucca switches. Nothing happens if Red God loses.[60]

Black, Gray, and Destroyer Gods are three important masked spirits of the Diné. Black God, or Hastsezini, an important deity, is the god of fire and celestial constellations. He invented the fire drill and introduced fire to humans. Navajos paint his face black with sacred charcoal and use white paint to present the seven sisters, or Pleiades, on his left temple or cheek. A white line runs from his nose to forehead, a half-moon appearing on the forehead of his mask. Navajos call Gray God or Water Sprinkler To'nenili. He is the Navajo rain god, the lord of heavenly waters and producer of rain clouds. He is an integral part of healing ceremonies, providing patients holy water. In the public dances, he is the clown.[61] Navajos call Destroyer or Whipping God Hadacisi. He carries yucca whips, lightly striking the afflicted part of a patient's body, driving out the ailment. Navajos paint the body of Destroyer with white circles.[62]

Except for the *yebad*, few female gods exist. The Shooting God, or Hastseoltoi, is an exception, but a male impersonates this female god of hunting, chase, and mystery. Navajos consider hunting the "feminine" form of war, and thus the female god. Shooting God is the female counter to Monster Slayer, the god of war. During Nightway, Shooting God appears with Monster Slayer and Child Born of Water in acts of exorcism. Mask makers paint Shooting God's face blue with triangular eyes. She wears a bow on her back and carries in her hand a quiver of arrows and bow case made of wildcat. She wears an old-fashioned velveteen cloth, a collar of fox fur, and Navajo jewels.[63]

Monster Slayer (also referred to as Nayenezgani or Nezyani) and Child Born of Water (or To'Baziscini) play prominent roles in the Navajo origin story. They are the offspring of Changing Woman and Sun, and they found power to fight against monsters preying on the people, including disease. Navajos consider Monster Slayer one of the most powerful of Holy People, a tremendous hero and slayer of alien gods.[64]

First Man and Sun endowed Monster Slayer with curing powers. Monster Slayer can destroy witchcraft power. He wears a dark kilt trimmed with a scarlet cloth belt and black moccasins. He dons turquoise, coral, and shell necklaces, as well as several earrings and bracelets. Navajos paint his hands white, and they paint the rest of his body in black sacred charcoal, made by burning sacred weed, gramma grass, white sage, and an herb (wood charcoal is used to make the deity in dry sand paintings but is not used to paint the body or mask of Monster Slayer).[65] Monster Slayer carries a black flint knife to fight enemies. Navajos believe Monster Slayer is endowed with power to use his bow and lightning to strike evil, which can manifest itself in disease. For this reason, Navajos paint bow symbols on the impersonator's body. Beginning with the outside part of the left leg below the knee and ending with the left side of the back, Navajos paint a total of eight bows on the body of the wearer of Monster Slayer's mask. They paint the last bow unstrung or incomplete, indicating that his job remains unfinished and will forever remain so, because the Diné will always need Monster Slayer to fight for them. This cultural hero "stands clothed in bows" living in the environment but answering the call of Navajo people in need.[66]

Monster Slayer's brother or cousin, the Child Born of Water, participates in ceremony with Monster Slayer. The Child Born of Water represents medicine and the spiritual side of war, offering prayers and power to help vanquish alien enemies. Instead of the bows worn by Monster Slayer, Child Born of Water wears symbols of a Navajo hair bundle, or queue, representing scalps taken from alien enemies by Monster Slayer. Child Born of Water oversees enemy scalps, which are highly charged and dangerous. Only spiritual leaders can handle enemy scalps since they contain the spirits of the enemy. Child Born of Water wears red moccasins and a yellow kilt and carries a black pinion rattle and cedar rattle, both of which symbolize thunder.[67]

During the Nightway Ceremony, Navajos make a patient's mask, used on the second night of the ceremony and known as Rites of Evergreen Dress. They make a *nikehe* for a female patient or a *thadilkai* for a male patient. Most often, contemporary Navajos use the female patient mask made of braided yucca or spruce. Mask makers cut out black triangular pieces for the eyes and square pieces for the mouth. Horizontal lines of black and yellow are beneath the mouth, and the makers use yucca fiber to tie the bottom of the mask to the dancer's neck. Navajos paint four sets of vertical lines under the yellow to indicate rain. A fringe of spruce is placed around the mask to represent hair. Male and female patients wear the mask and an outfit made from spruce.[68] Navajos believe the mask absorbs the patient's sickness and carries it out of the body. Monster Slayer removes the disease from the patient, sends the illness into the mask, then cuts the mask from the patient's fact, thus destroying the disease.[69]

Navajo and Apache masks are dangerous, especially after they have been used in ceremony. Navajos conduct a ceremony to discharge danger from the masks and to inform the Holy People that humans have handled the masks respectfully. On the fourth night of Nightway, Navajos hold an honoring ceremony called the Vigil of the Masked Gods. Navajos spread layers of blankets, calico, muslin, and buckskin northwest of the fire in the hogan. They place the *yei* masks and other items used in ceremony on the floor of the hogan and instruct the patient to sprinkle a pollen line down the center of each mask from top to bottom and then from right to left.[70]

The medicine man, his assistants, and the spectators follow suit, spreading sacred pollen on each mask. Outside the lodge, someone cries out loudly, announcing the next stage of the vigil.[71] A number of women carrying bowls of ceremonial foods enter the hogan, moving sunwise around the fire until the lead woman stands near the doorway at the east side of the lodge. A virgin boy and girl enter with the women, but they remain on one side of the circle. The woman sets down the sacred foods, followed by other women who enter with foods. For approximately one hour, the women and men sit smoking and singing, some shaking rattles, until the medicine man prepares sacred water for the boy and girl to christen the masks. The boy blesses the masks with two black feathers, and the girl uses two blue feathers, dipping them in water and sprinkling the masks four times before sprinkling the participants. The patient, medicine man, and assistants follow suit and fulfill other ritual rules.[72] Early the next morning, the medicine man and his assistants collect the masks, offer a long song prayer, and lay the masks out again, one on top of the other. During the course of the Vigil of the Masked Gods, the medicine man shakes and rocks each mask, handling and blowing smoke at them, thus purifying them. They conclude the vigil with songs, prayers, and pollen, ending with the Song of the Beautiful Dawn.[73]

The masked gods of the Navajos perform an integral part of many other ceremonies. Indeed, there can be no Nightway without the masked gods. Navajo and Apache people respect their tribal ceremonial traditions and believe the masks represent spirits that remain active in their worlds. Quechan have no complex masking tradition, and Quechan ceremony focuses on the dead, which is never the case with Apache and Navajo. However, despite these differences, the tribes share similar views of spiritual power, believing that spirit people live in mountains, canyons, caves, bodies of water, and other important sites in the landscape. Humans may call on these spirits for many kinds of assistance, including curing, hunting, human fertility, plant fertility, protection, rain, and abundance of food. Medicine people among all three groups call on spirits for curing power, but the Apache and Navajo, not the Quechan, use masking in their ceremonies to impersonate the gods. The people do not worship masks, but they use masking traditions to enhance their relationships with the Holy People. All three tribes believe in community-based ritual and ceremony, which benefits individuals and communities.[74]

Western Apache people on the San Carlos and White Mountain Reservations, as well as other Apache tribes, enjoy a rich masking tradition of the *gaan bitch'aa*, or "gaan his hat."[75] Like Navajo *yeis*, *gaans* live in mountains, caves, water, and the general environment of Apache people. Apaches believe *gaans* live in the mountainous areas of eastern Arizona and western and northern New Mexico (and for the Kiowa-Apaches, in special places on the southern plains). Apaches, like Navajos and Quechans, believe spirits have great supernatural power, affecting the health, curing, and overall well-being of people. They also have power over rain, lightning, thunder, deer, coyote, bear, and other animals. *Gaans* are centers of power that flow in many directions, often radiating out of their mountain homes. Thus the spaces between mountains have power, spreading out like the spokes of a wheel. Apache believe *gaans* influence success in hunting, farming, protection, and curing. *Gaans* are not animal spirits, but they have influence over animals, especially those that appear regularly in creation stories. Like Navajo masked dancers, Apache masked dancers become the *gaan* they impersonate, making the sounds of the gods, which often bear resemblance to those of animals.[76]

Dancing gods remain connected to good medicine and Apache individual and community health. Thus a ceremony focused on one person, like a young girl in the puberty ceremony, enhances the health of everyone attending the event, the community as a whole, and Apache people in general.[77] Today *gaans* appear in public gatherings and blessings, dancing to the delight of non-Apache people. For many years, Apache students from the San Carlos Indian Reservation attending Sherman Institute and Sherman Indian High School in Riverside, California, danced for other students and the general public of Southern California. Apache elders had taught the student dancers, and they presented the sacred masks and headdresses—created in the proper manner prescribed by the wisdom keepers of their people—dance, and drumming in a culturally respectful and accurate manner so as to teach people an important element of their culture. Tribal elders allowed these students to shared dances and songs associated with *gaans*, but they did not perform the entire ceremony, which would be sacrilegious.[78]

On reservations, the *gaans* appear in the girl's puberty ceremony, or Naa'e'es.[79] Like all ceremony, customs, and belief systems of the Apache, the *gaans* follow laws of creation, as established by the creation stories that determine the *gaans*' roles and activities. Apache mask makers use black, red, white, and gray cloth or material on *gaan* masks. Most dancers wear black, which originally came from deer hides painted with sacred charcoal in a similar fashion as the paint used for the Navajo mask for Monster Slayer. Some dancers wear red cloth, and the clown, or Libaah'n (the Gray One), wears either a white or gray mask.[80] Mask makers cut holes for the eyes and mouth and tie the head mask around the neck. They make the crown or the headdress from

FIGURE 1.6. Apache students at the former Sherman Institute shared some of the Mountain Spirit songs and dances with fellow students wearing traditional regalia. Apaches call the dancers *gaans*, impersonating powerful mountain spirits living within the environment of Apache Country. Courtesy Sherman Indian Museum.

lightweight but durable yucca or sotol wood, painting the pointed headdress with a background of black or white and with numerous clan symbols, such as eagles, hawks, flowers, tobacco, lightning, and other cultural and environmental elements significant to Apache people.[81]

The number four, colors, and directions are important elements of Apache culture significant to medicinal religious ceremonies. They depict east in black, south as blue, west using yellow, and north through white. Mask makers have traditionally used natural elements for colors, such as white clay, mica, yellow and red ochre, and charcoal. They might adorn their masks or headdresses with turquoise (*yo'dotl'izhi*) and mirrors. *Gaans* nearly always appear four in number, and the clown wields a bullroarer, the voice of the gods. Like *yeis*, *gaans* do not speak but make sounds. They are spirits, manifested corporeally so that humans can see them. Apaches believe that at one time, *gaans* danced in ceremony among the first people, and mountain spirits watch over Apache dancers today to ensure they conduct themselves correctly in accordance to Apache sacred law. *Gaans* live in the mountains, but they come to humans when summoned, offering their help and support when engaged correctly. They link Apaches to the ancient past, just as *yeis* tie Navajos to their origins.[82]

Many scholars believe that Navajo and Apache masking traditions derive from Pueblo's masking traditions. Pueblo masked gods, or *katsinas* (kachinas), perform many of the functions found among the masked gods of the Apache and Navajo. They, too, are associated with sacred geography, the *katsina* living in the environment. Academics maintain that after the Pueblo Revolt of 1680, Pueblos dispersed into the mountains and valleys, where they lived among and intermarried with Apaches and Navajos, Athabascan-speaking people.[83] While the Pueblo cultures significantly influenced the tribes of the American Southwest, including the Navajo and Apache cultures, no one can gauge to what degree Pueblo people impacted Navajo and Apache masked gods or the belief that their spirits lived (and continue to live) in the environment.[84]

Yavapai-Prescott elder Ted Vaughn stated emphatically that his people believed in the *kakaka*, or mountain spirits, generations before the 1870s when Yavapais say they introduced the Apaches to masked gods.[85] Apaches and Navajos claim their masked gods originated from within their own cultures, dating back to the time of creation, using ancient stories and songs to buttress these claims. While all people learn from each other, often borrowing cultural ideas and elements, the Quechan, Apache, and Navajo had ancient beliefs in spirit beings of wisdom and power before interacting with Pueblos or Yavapais. However, there can be little doubt the rich Pueblo cultures influenced other Native American cultures in many ways, including their spiritual beliefs, material cultures, languages, foods, ceremonies, and other aspects of life. All Native American cultures say that many of their gods lived at the beginning of time, and that they live within the cultural landscapes today. Apache, Navajo, and Quechan have an intimate relationship with large Southwestern environments on and off their reservations. Mountains of the Southwest remain the home of spirit beings. Quechan, Navajo, and Apache—indeed, most or all tribal people of this vast region—consider certain mountains, rivers, lakes, buttes, caves, and valleys holy places, the homes of spirits that have long influenced the course of their histories, just as they influence people today. They believe that certain individuals, prophets, and holy people, have always had the ability to access power from spirits for health, curing, protection, and power in peace and war.[86] Spirits may be helpful or malevolent, but through song, prayer, ritual, and ceremony, wise men and women seek the aid of the wisdom spirits to provide positive, constructive, and healing influences to benefit themselves and their people.

NOTES

1. Keith Basso offered an important contribution in his book *Wisdom Sits in Places* (Albuquerque: University of New Mexico Press, 1996), 105, 71–103; Richard Stoffle, Richard Arnold, Kathleen Van Vlack, Larry Eddy, and Betty Cornelius, "Nuvagantu, 'Where Snow Sits': Origin Mountains of Southern Paiute," in *Landscapes of Origin in the Americas: Creation Narratives Linking Ancient Places and Present Communities*, ed. Jessica Christie (Tuscaloosa: University of Alabama Press, 2009), 32–44.

2. Clifford E. Trafzer, *Quechan Indian Historic Properties of Traditional Lands on the Yuma Proving Ground* (Riverside: California Center for Native Nations, University of California, Riverside, 2012), 23. Quechan Elder A, oral interview by Clifford E. Trafzer, July 24–26, 2012, Fort Yuma Quechan Indian Reservation.

3. John P. Harrington, "A Yuma Account of Origins," *Journal of American Folklore* 21, no. 82 (1908): 324–28. Harrington based the article on the oral histories of Joe Homer, 1907–1908. Papers of John P. Harrington, Microfilm Collection, Rivera Library, University of California, Riverside, Reel 161, Slides 202, 204. Hereafter cited as Harrington Papers, Reel, and Slide, respectively.

4. Gladys A. Reichard, *Navaho Religion: A Study of Symbolism* (New York: Bollingen Foundation, 1950), 11, 16, 24, 29.

5. Harrington, "Yuma Account of Origins," 324–28; Quechan Elders A and B, interview by Trafzer, May 26, 2011, June 2, 2011, June 21–23, 2012; and Quechan Elders A, B, and C, interview by Trafzer, October 22–24, 2012.

6. Quechan Elders A and B, interview by Trafzer, May 26–28, 2011, June 2, 2011, June 21–23, 2012, and October 22, 2012.

7. Ibid. Clifford E. Trafzer, ed., *Quechan Indian Voices: Lee Emerson and Patrick Miguel* (Riverside: California Center for Native Nations, University of California, Riverside, 2012), 39.

8. Quechan Elders A, B, and C, interview by Trafzer, October 23, 2012; Harrington, "Yuma Account of Origins," 324–28.

9. Quechan Elder A, interview by Trafzer, June 23, 2012; Harrington Papers, Reel 161, Slides 202, 204; Harrington, "Yuma Account of Origins," 328. In a version of this story found in John Harrington's notes, the anthropologist writes that Old Blind Man's name was Qama Akutar, but contemporary Quechan use the name Kweraak Kutar for Blind Old Man.

10. Harrington, "Yuma Account of Origins," 328.

11. Ibid., 329; Harrington Papers, Reel 161, Slide 203.

12. Harrington, "Yuma Account of Origins," 329.

13. Ibid.

14. Ibid.; C. Daryll Forde, "Ethnography of the Yuma Indians," *University of California Publications in American Archaeology and Ethnology* 28, no. 4 (1931): 106–7; Robert L. Bee, *Crosscurrents Along the Colorado: The Impact of Government Policy on the Quechan Indians* (Tucson: University of Arizona Press, 1981), xv–xvi. Quechan Elder A explained that Marxokuvek had a twin, and one represented positive and constructive action, while the other twin represented negative and destructive action. The Marxokuvek mentioned in this chapter is the positive, constructive creator. But the duality between positive and negative is a common thematic motif of the Quechan creation and other origin stories of various Native American cultures.

15. Harrington, "Yuma Account of Origins," 337.

16. Quechan Elder C explained that two intaglios of horses exist on the north (Black Horse) and south (White Horse) side of Pilot Knob, located on the southeast corner of California on the Colorado River. These represent spiritual horses that appear before a battle between the Quechan and Cocopa. If Black Horse appears, then the Cocopa win, but if White Horse emerges, the Quechan will triumph. The White Horse intaglio remains on the floor at the base of Pilot Knob near the international boundary with Baja California. See Leslie Spier, *Yuman Tribes of the Gila River* (Chicago: University of Chicago Press, 1933), 160–87.

17. Harrington, "Yuma Account of Origins," 330.

18. Ibid.

19. Quechan Elder A, interview by Trafzer, June 23, 2012.

20. Trafzer, *Quechan Indian Historic Properties*, 23. Kukumat created the Dark House with the help of ants that dug four holes into the earth. Using his thoughts, Kukumat brought about posts for the Dark House made of desert woods, perhaps cottonwood posts (*axavolypo*). Kukumat lived in the Dark House, but his influence and power flowed out from the center of the earth at Spirit Mountain to lands now part of the American Southwest and northern Mexico. In fact, the Creator's power permeated the universe and the entire earth. From the Dark House, Kukumat made his son, Kumastamho. In one version, Kumastamho emerged from his father's shadow. In another version, a woman came to the Dark House and sought Kukumat's help in creating a child. According to this version found in the papers of John Harrington, she wished to give birth to a boy who would become a doctor, since none existed on earth at the time. A doctor could help people when ill health came to them. She magically conceived a baby, most likely from Kukumat's thoughts. At the time of conception, Kumastamho, "already a wise doctor," grew inside her body. The baby instructed the woman to lie down. The baby made himself small "so that he would not cause the woman pain." In this way, she gave birth for the first time ever, but the baby grew remarkably fast as it was a god with power. It soon could walk and talk, and the infant reached manhood overnight. Kukumat named his son Kumastamho.

21. Harrington, "Yuma Account of Origins," 346.

22. George Bryant, interview by Trafzer, May 26, 2011, Fort Yuma Quechan Indian Reservation.

23. Harrington, "Yuma Account of Origins," 331–32.

24. Ibid., 332.

25. Ibid.

26. Ibid., 334–35.

27. Trafzer, *Quechan Indian Historic Properties*, 18. Sky Rattlesnake, as the Quechan called Ave in English, had two or four heads. Quechan Elders A and B told the author this story about the giant rattlesnake with multiple heads many times on journeys into the desert northeast of Yuma and the Quechan reservation. They say that when Kumastamho killed the monster, his blood poured out of his body, becoming gold, and his saliva spread widely, transforming into silver. In the late nineteenth and early twentieth centuries, non-Indian miners took large quantities of gold and silver from the mountains near the kill site. Rattlesnake's body left an imprint in the ground that runs from Castle Dome Mountain to the Colorado River, known today as the Yuma Wash. Kumastamho tossed his body toward the Pacific Ocean, creating the Pacific Coast Ranges. When his body settled near the ocean, Sky Rattlesnake's urine ran into the ocean, which is why the Pacific Ocean is salty.

28. Harrington, "Yuma Account of Origins," 337. According to Homer, Kukumat defecated on Avikwaxa (Cottonwood Mountain), located in present-day Yuma, Arizona, and known as Black Hill.

29. Ibid.

30. Ibid.

31. Ibid., 337, 340.

32. Ibid., 337. Quechan Elders A and B, interview by Trafzer, May 27, 2011.

33. Harrington, "Yuma Account of Origins," 338–39.

34. Quechan Elders A, B, and C and others, including John Jacob Norton, confirm that their creation stories and songs tell them their gods and people traveled great distances and have a cultural association with mountains in Arizona, Nevada, California, Mexico, and even South America. Quechan Elder A was emphatic about the Quechan association with South America.

35. Harrington, "Yuma Account of Origins," 338–39.

36. Ibid., 342.

37. Quechan Elders A, B, and C, interview by Trafzer, October 22–24, 2012.

38. Harrington, "Yuma Account of Origins," 342.

39. Ibid., 346–347.

40. Ibid.; Quechan Elders A, B, and C, interview by Trafzer, May 26–28, 2011, June 2, 2011, March 28–30, 2012, April 3–5, 2012, April 26–28, 2012, June 21–23, 2012, July 24–26, 2012, July 28–30, 2012, November 19, 2012.

41. Reichard, *Navaho Religion*, 13–25; James K. McNeley, *Holy Wind in Navajo Philosophy* (Tucson: University of Arizona Press, 1981), 6, 14–27; John R. Farella, *The Main Stalk: A Synthesis of Navajo Philosophy* (Tucson: University of Arizona Press, 1984), 69–93; Berard Haile, *Head and Face Masks in Navaho Ceremonialism* (St. Michaels, Ariz.: St. Michaels Press, 1947), 1–3. Some portions of this chapter first appeared in Ross Coates, ed., *Gods Among Us: American Indian Masks* (San Diego: San Diego State University Publications in American Indian Studies, 1989), 55–71. The authors encourage interested readers to consult a rare book produced on the Navajo Reservation by Navajo historian Ethelou Yazzie, *Navajo History*, vol. 1 (Tsaile: Navajo Community College Press, 1971).

42. Haile, *Head and Face Masks*, 1–3; Farella, *Main Stalk*, 73–78.

43. Haile, *Head and Face Masks*, 4–5.

44. Ibid., 6.

45. Reichard, *Navaho Religion*, 11, 16–17, 24, 29.

46. Ibid., 10, 12, 17, 53, 67, 75, 88, 122, 131, 153, 184–88, 198, 315, 322–23, 327–28, 330, 335, 386, 428, 664.

47. Washington Matthews, "The Nightway Chant, A Navajo Ceremony," *Memoirs of the American Museum of Natural History* 6 (1902): 10–11, 15–19, 24, 56, 60, 115, 443; Haile, *Head and Face Masks*, 17–18; Clyde Kluckhon, W. W. Hill, and Lucy W. Kluckhon, *Navajo Material Culture* (Cambridge: Belknap Press of Harvard University Press, 1971), 334–45.

48. Matthews, "The Nightway Chant," 10–11, 15–19, 24, 56, 60, 115, 443; Franciscan Fathers, *An Ethnologic Dictionary of the Navaho Language* (St. Michaels, Ariz.: St. Michaels Press, 1910), 386–91.

49. Matthews, "The Nightway Chant," 10–11, 15–19, 24, 56, 60, 115, 443.

50. Ibid. Before the Spanish introduced horses and horsehair to the Southwest, Navajo mask makers used cotton and other plant materials for hair on masks.

51. Ibid., 17–19; Haile, *Head and Face Masks*, 19.

52. Clifford E. Trafzer, "Masked Gods of the Navajo," in Coates, *Gods Among Us*, 58.

53. Haile, *Head and Face Masks*, 26–27; Matthews, "Nightway Chant," 9–10.

54. Matthews, "Nightway Chant," 15–17.

55. Ibid.; Farella, *Main Stalk*, 73–75, 85–86.

56. Matthews, "Nightway Chant," 15–17, 17–19; Haile, *Head and Face Masks*, 19.

57. Haile, *Head and Face Masks*, 11–13; Reichard, *Navaho Religion*, 56, 60, 93, 254, 438–39. Two types of Fringed Mouth masks exist, and the medicine man determines which one appears in a particular ceremony and inside the ceremonial hogan. The medicine man decides if he is performing the Midrock Branch of Nightway or the Water Bottom Branch of Nightway.

58. Trafzer, "Masked Gods of the Navajo," in Coates, *Gods Among Us*, 59.

59. Ibid., 61; Matthews, "Nightway Chant," 13–14; Haile, *Head and Face Masks*, 21–22.

60. Matthews, "Nightway Chant," 25–26; Haile, *Head and Face Masks*, 23–24.

61. Matthews, "Nightway Chant," 14–15, 26–29; Haile, *Head and Face Masks*, 22; Reichard, *Navaho Religion*, 17, 56–60, 71, 79, 90, 107–8, 156, 183, 205.

62. Trafzer, "Masked Gods of the Navajo," in Coates, *Gods Among Us*, 66; Matthews, "Nightway Chant," 14–15.

63. Matthews, "Nightway Chant," 14–15.

64. Ibid., 22–24; Reichard, *Navaho Religion*, 30, 55–59, 176–79, 192–98, 209–12.

65. Matthews, "Nightway Chant," 19–21; Haile, *Head and Face Masks*, 22–23; Reichard, *Navaho Religion*, 56.

66. Trafzer, "Masked Gods of the Navajo," in Coates, *Gods Among Us*, 61–63.

67. Matthews, "Nightway Chant," 19–24; Haile, *Head and Face Masks*, 22–23.

68. Matthews, "Nightway Chant," 104–12; Kluckhohn, Hill, and Kluckhohn, *Navajo Material Culture*, 226; Haile, *Head and Face Masks*, 50–53.

69. Trafzer, "Masked Gods of the Navajo," in Coates, *Gods Among Us*, 67.

70. Matthews, "Nightway Chant," 104–12.

71. Ibid.; Haile, *Head and Face Masks*, 50–53.

72. Matthews, "Nightway Chant," 104–12.

73. Ibid.

74. Quechan (and other Yuman people) hold the Keruk Ceremony periodically in an elaborate community gathering that involves a re-creation of the Dark House, a mock battle with bows and arrows between positive and negative forces, and community involvement with spirits and dead Quechan. Loved ones return in spirit to be with friends and kin. Navajo and Apache ceremonies also involve community participation with humans and spirits, but these involve Holy People, not their dead. In all cases, the tribes call on spirits to join in ceremony to strengthen community and individual health and protect against evil.

75. Philip G. Greenfeld, "Apache Masks," in Coates, *Gods Among Us*, 88. In addition to Western Apache, Jicarilla Apache also have a masking tradition.

76. Morris E. Opler, "The Apachean Culture Pattern and Its Origins," in *Handbook of North American Indians*, vol. 10, *Southwest*, ed. Alfonso Ortiz (Washington, D.C.: Smithsonian Institution Press, 1983), 748–52.

77. Greenfeld, "Apache Masks," in Coates, *Gods Among Us*, 93–96.

78. In the 1990s and early 2000s, Apache students, primarily from the San Carlos Reservation, participated in the Apache club at Sherman Indian High School (the former Sherman Institute). Young men and women in the club had their own dance team of Crown Dancers, portraying the *gaans* at social and school events on and off campus.

79. Louise Lamphere, "Southwestern Ceremonialism," in Ortiz, *Handbook of North American Indians*, 10:748–51.

80. Keith Basso, "The Gift of Changing Woman," *Bulletin of the Bureau of American Ethnology* 196, no. 76 (1966): 115–73, contains excellent information on this subject; Greenfeld, "Apache Masks," in Coates, *Gods Among Us*, 97.

81. Lamphere, "Southwestern Ceremonialism," 746.

82. Ibid., 748–49.

83. Ibid.; Greenfeld, "Apache Masks," in Coates, *Gods Among Us*, 88–93.

84. Ruth Underhill, *The Navajos* (Norman: University of Oklahoma Press, 1956), 41–57; Clyde Kluckhohn and Dorothea Leighton, *The Navaho* (Cambridge: Harvard University Press, 1946), 65–72, 85, 120, 126, 171, 193, 197, 238–40.

85. Ted Vaughn, oral interview by Clifford E. Trafzer, September 10–11, 2009, Yavapai-Prescott Indian Reservation; E. W. Gifford, "Southeastern Yavapai," *University of California Publications in American Archaeology and Ethnology* 29 (1932): 176–262; E. W. Gifford, "Northeastern and Western Yavapai," *University of California Publications in American Archaeology and Ethnography* 34 (1936): 308; Clifford E. Trafzer, *Historic Properties Inventory, Traditional Cultural Properties: Yavapai-Prescott Cultural Ethnography of Lands* (Riverside: California Center for Native Nations, University of California, Riverside, 2011), 67–70. Yavapai claim that their *kakaka* are the mountain spirits and that they introduced the Crown Dancers and the concept of mountain spirits to the San Carlos Apache after 1873, during the Apache Wars when General George Crook drove the Yavapai from western Arizona to San Carlos. Yavapai additionally maintain that they taught the Apaches about mountain spirits.

86. Morris E. Opler, "The Concept of Supernatural Power Among the Chiricahua and Mescalero Apaches," *American Anthropologist* 37, no. 1 (1935), 65–70; Keith Basso, *The Cibeque Apache* (New York: Holt, Rinehart, and Winston, 1970), 34–47.

2

MAIN POC

૨ई

Potawatomi Wabeno

R. DAVID EDMUNDS

MANY OF the Indian leaders who played prominent roles in the decades preceding the War of 1812 have attracted the attention of American historians. Most prominent, of course, is Tecumseh, whose attempts to form a political and military coalition among the tribes seemed logical and commendable, both to his white contemporaries and to more recent scholars. Other tribesmen, including Tenskwatawa, the Shawnee Prophet; Little Turtle of the Miamis; and even Pushmataha of the Choctaws are also familiar figures to most historians interested in this period. Yet there were other leaders who appear only as infrequent references in the vast amount of primary materials that focus upon these times—shadowy figures who remain hidden in the dusty archives of the United States, Britain, and Canada. Main Poc, a Potawatomi *wabeno* from the Kankakee River in Illinois, has been shrouded in such obscurity.

Among the Potawatomis (as among the Ottawas and Chippewas), wabenos were sorcerers of considerable, and sometimes malevolent, medicine. They were fire handlers, whose magical powers gave them the ability to hold hot coals, place their hands on campfires, and even to exhale flames from their mouths and nostrils. In a similar manner, they could thrust their arms into boiling water or vats of steaming maple syrup without any apparent injuries. Their medicine enabled them to transform themselves into living fireballs that could attack their enemies. They also had the power to assume the shape of animals and prowl the Potawatomi villages or the surrounding countryside after dark. Because so much of their medicine seemed to be related to fire, most of their ceremonies were performed at night, where constant contrast between the flames and their dark surroundings added dramatic effect to their performance. Often their rituals were accompanied by feasts that were "cel-ebrated with much noise and disturbance," for wabenos possessed certain songs that gave them access to the spirit world, and they accompanied their chants with special drums and rattles.[1]

A wabeno could use his power to do good. His medicine bundle (in addition to his knowledge of pharmacognosy) gave him the ability to cure diseases. He could also bring about changes in the weather and prepare powerful charms for his followers. Some of the charms promised success in hunting, while others were particularly effec-tive in winning lovers or obtaining sexual favors. Through their communication with the spirits, some wabenos could predict events and provide valuable advice to their adherents. Others used ventriloquism or "juggleries" (slight-of-hand tricks) to both amuse their followers and increase their influence over them.[2]

Such influence was quite extensive. Potawatomi society was considerably swayed by "medicine," and most tribe members were convinced that they were vulnerable to conjuration.[3] Personal misfortune such as illness, accident, or the loss of valued possessions was blamed upon evil medicine, and individual tribesmen often attached themselves to particularly powerful wabenos, hoping the shaman's power would protect them from less friendly conjurers. Indeed, almost all Potawatomis counted themselves within some wabeno's camp, and they relied upon the medicine man for his assistance against their enemies. Seeking out the wabeno, they asked him to place spells upon their foes and to cause misfortune to their rivals. In turn, they presented their protector with gifts of tobacco, liquor, or trade goods.[4]

In the first decade of the nineteenth century, Main Poc was the most powerful of the Potawatomi wabenos. The place and date of his birth remain unknown, but he probably was born in southern Michigan sometime during the mid-1760s. His father was a Potawatomi war chief of considerable reputation, and Main Poc grew to man-hood hating the Americans. Sometime after the Treaty of Greenville, he moved to Illinois, where he established a village at the junction of Rock Creek and the Kanka-kee River.[5] There he attracted other Potawatomis who also disliked the Long Knives, and his village became a springboard for raids against American settlements near Vincennes and St. Louis. During these years he also took several wives, most of whom were sisters. These unions produced a handful of children, including at least two sons who also aspired to influence among the Potawatomis.[6]

At first, much of Main Poc's power was based upon a deformity. He had been born with no fingers or thumb on his left hand (the source of his name means Crippled Hand) and Main Poc claimed that this accident of birth was a special sign of favor from the Creator. Indeed, according to Main Poc, although his hand was crippled, the Creator had given him special powers to compensate for the deformity. Not only could he communicate with the *maindog* (spirits), but he could also cast spells upon

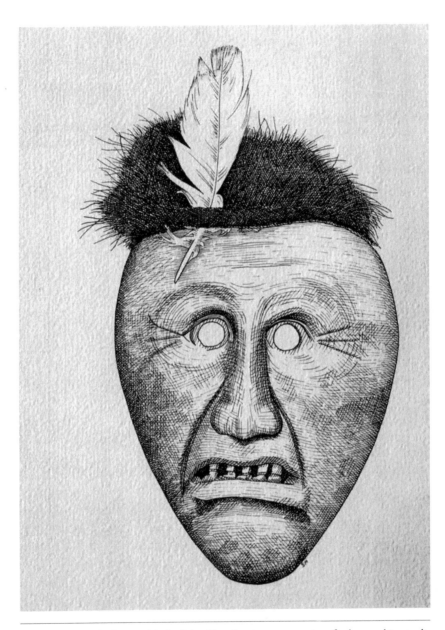

FIGURE 2.1. The Booger Mask of the Cherokee is representative of other masking traditions of the Eastern woodlands. The Booger represents negative spiritual forces, impersonated by people during ceremony. During a dance with an equal number of women, Boogers act aggressively, sometimes sexually chasing people. Main Poc and others of the Eastern woodlands knew of the Booger Masks, the dances associated with them, and the humor they caused within communities. Sketch by Sarah Moore. Editor's collection and photograph.

his enemies. Moreover, he could even protect warriors during battle, for he claimed to have the power to see bullets in flight and to avoid them.

Unquestionably, the Potawatomi wabeno was a figure of commanding presence. A huge, muscular man with long black hair, Main Poc had a "surly and brooding countenance," highlighted by dark, piercing eyes.[7] He also had a flair for the dramatic. After withdrawing to a solitary lodge in the forest, he would remain alone for a significant period before returning to the village. Upon his return, he would remain silent for several days, then assemble his followers to inform them of his latest revelations. Indian agents who knew him reported that he was an excellent orator with the ability to mesmerize his audience.[8]

Yet Main Poc had a darker side. As a young man, he had acquired a fondness for white man's whiskey, and as the years passed, the fondness became an obsession. In the decade preceding the War of 1812, the Potawatomi deteriorated into a notorious alcoholic whose drinking unleashed a violent temper. When in his cups, Main Poc's fury knew no bounds, and although he lashed out at both kinsmen and friends, women were particularly susceptible to his violence. While intoxicated, Main Poc frequently forced himself upon any woman who crossed his path, and the resulting rapes triggered intratribal bloodshed. Moreover, even sober, he was a dangerous adversary. Tolerating no rivals, he used his influence to destroy other wabenos, and if they failed to cower before his spiritual medicine, he sometimes resorted to poison.[9]

Main Poc was also a successful warrior. Claiming that his spiritual powers would give him victory over tribal enemies, Main Poc led large war parties of Potawatomis, Kickapoos, and Sacs and Foxes against the Osages. At first, the warfare was encouraged by the Spanish. During the early 1790s, Spanish officials at St. Louis had solicited the support of Main Poc and other warriors in the campaigns against the Osages in Missouri, but in 1794, the Spanish and Osages made peace, formally terminating their hostilities. Unfortunately for the Spanish, Main Poc and the northern tribesmen refused to abide by the treaty and continued their attacks with vengeance. In the decade preceding the Louisiana Purchase, Main Poc's warriors repeatedly crossed the Mississippi to strike at their ancient enemies. They also cut a wide swath of destruction among American settlements in southern Illinois.[10]

In October 1805, after Louisiana passed into American hands, officials at St. Louis brought Potawatomi and Osage leaders together in a futile attempt to stop the carnage, but Main Poc refused to attend the conference. The warfare continued. In November, less than one month after the conference ended, Main Poc led a large war party across the Mississippi and attacked a village of Little Osages near the juncture of the Osage and Missouri Rivers. Most of the Osage warriors were away hunting, and the Potawatomis killed thirty-four women and children in addition to capturing about sixty others. The prisoners were carried back to Illinois. Their faces painted black, the

Osages protested to American officials, and while some of the captives were returned, others were kept for several years in Main Poc's village.[11]

While Main Poc warred against the Osages, Shawnee tribesmen in Ohio and Indiana watched in dismay as the advancing white frontier poured around them. In the spring of 1805, when a former ne'er-do-well experienced a vision that promised deliverance, the Shawnee and neighboring tribesmen listened in wonder, then turned to the new holy man for a religious solution to their problems. At first, many Indians regarded Tenskwatawa, the Shawnee Prophet, as a charlatan, but when he successfully predicted an eclipse of the sun in June 1806, even many of the former scoffers were converted. Main Poc probably learned of the rapidly spreading new religion from the Kickapoos, who were among the prophet's first disciples, but as tribesmen from throughout the west journeyed to the Shawnee's village near Greenville, Ohio, the Potawatomi wabeno joined them. Evidence suggests that he did not regard Tenskwatawa as a rival, but he certainly was interested in learning more about deliverance.[12]

Main Poc arrived at Greenville late in October 1807 and spent almost two months conferring with Tenskwatawa. Although much of the substance of their conversations remains unknown, they were in marked agreement regarding their opposition to the Americans. Main Poc seems to have accepted certain parts of the prophet's doctrines, but he rejected others. He agreed that the Americans were children of the Great Serpent, or Evil Power, and evidently subscribed to Tenskwatawa's teachings that the Indians should use no products of American manufacture. Yet he adamantly rejected the prophet's denunciation of alcohol and refused to accept Tenskwatawa's doctrines that all Indians were brothers. In response, Main Poc informed the prophet that "the Great Spirit always told him that he must drink Spirituous liquor, that he must war [upon other Indians], otherwise his medicine would become weak and of no effect, and would be inferior to many Indians of the Nation." Although Tecumseh, the prophet's brother, especially discouraged intertribal warfare, Main Poc asserted that he would continue his campaigns against the Osages. He did agree, however, to assist in the spread of the prophet's new faith in the west and even suggested to the Shawnee brothers that they leave Greenville and relocate near the juncture of the Tippecanoe and Wabash Rivers. The new site, in western Indiana, was in a region holding more plentiful game and was less vulnerable to American military expeditions.[13]

Leaving Greenville in late December, Main Poc passed back through Fort Wayne. There, Indian agent William Wells spent considerable time and effort attempting to win him over for the United States. Informing his superior that Main Poc was "the greatest warrior in the west . . . the pivot on which the minds of all the Western Indians turned . . . , [and he had] more influence than any other Indians," Wells encouraged Main Poc to remain at Fort Wayne throughout the winter.[14] He provided the wabeno and those warriors accompanying him with ample stores of provisions and trade goods, believing that he could turn the Potawatomi against the Shawnee Prophet.[15]

Hoodwinking Wells, Main Poc willingly accepted the government's largesse. He remained in Indiana until April 1808, exhausting Wells' food supplies and causing the Indian agent to spend over $800.00 in government funds to support the Potawatomi and his followers. Meanwhile, he assured Wells that he would serve the American interest. According to Main Poc:

> You have caught me; like a Wild horse is caught with a lick of salt, you have Hobled me—that I can no longer range the woods as I please. You must now git [*sic*] a Bell and put [it] on my neck when I shall always be in your hearing, you must also put Bells on the neck of two of my war chiefs the will in able [*sic*] you to know at all times where the warriors of the west are and what they are about.

Yet he still refused to make peace with the Osages, and when Wells reminded him that several Potawatomi chiefs had signed the peace treaty in 1805, Main Poc laughed that the signatories where not men, but dogs, and they were "not fit to men his Mokissons [*sic*]."[16]

Main Poc's threats to reopen the war with the Osages prompted Wells to ask for permission to send the wabeno to Washington. Wells argued that if the Potawatomi could be taken to the capital and shown the power of the federal government, he would be more amenable to American influence. Accordingly, early in the fall of 1808, Wells asked Main Poc to accompany a delegation of chiefs who would assemble at Fort Wayne later in the fall and then journey to Washington. Main Poc accepted, and in November, he arrived at Fort Wayne accompanied by Siggenauk, war chief from the Chicago region, and one other warrior. These Potawatomi delegates also brought their wives. On November 5, 1808, in the company of Wells and several other Indians, the Potawatomis set out for the capital.[17]

The trip did not go as Wells had planned. The party proceeded to Wheeling, West Virginia, where they halted for several days so that the Indians could recover from an illness that they had contracted in Ohio. Main Poc remained uncooperative. En route to the capital, he secured a quantity of whiskey, and he remained intoxicated during the rest of the journey. Wells had hoped the trip through the East would intimidate the Potawatomi, but he was sorely disappointed. Main Poc openly avowed his dislike for the United States and informed all who would listen that the Americans should retreat across the Appalachians. The party arrived in the capital during mid-December, and although the other Indians spent several days touring the city, Main Poc remained in his hotel room, drinking whiskey and threatening those maids or waiters who ventured near him.[18]

During the Christmas holidays, he met personally with President Thomas Jefferson. Clad entirely in buckskin, his face painted in broad swatches of red and black, the Potawatomi informed Jefferson that he had no intention of making peace with the Osage. He reminded Jefferson that the government had asked Indians to remain neutral in any war between the United States and Great Britain; therefore, federal officials should also not meddle in the wars between the tribes. Although Jefferson reminded him that the Potawatomi warriors often killed American settlers or destroyed American property during their forays into Missouri, Main Poc was unabashed. He also rejected Jefferson's suggestions that the Potawatomis "cultivate the earth and raise domestic animals." Following the conference, the Potawatomi returned to his hotel room where he again fell victim to his whiskey.[19]

Late in December, the Indians left Washington and proceeded to Baltimore, where the dissipated Main Poc contracted a respiratory infection that kept him bedridden for several days. Finally recovering, he demanded that Wells escort the party back to Fort Wayne, where he would be free of the white man's maladies. As the party rode west, they stopped for several days at Ellicott's Mill, Maryland, where they met with a group of Quakers who were eager to establish a mission in the West. Once again, Main Poc was the center of attention. Unlike other Indians, he refused to participate in the conversations and spent the day roaming the surrounding countryside, gathering hickory nuts and persimmons. He also acquired another store of whiskey, for he threatened the lives of other members of the party. The Indian arrived back in Fort Wayne in early February. Exasperated, Wells complained to Secretary of War Henry Dearborn, "Main Poc exceeds everything I ever saw . . . his conduct is insufferable."[20]

Yet the trip to the East seemed to temporarily cow the wabeno, and he hesitated to renew his attacks upon either the Osages or the settlements in southern Illinois. In May, he returned to Fort Wayne, supposedly to meet with a delegation of Quakers he had so rudely snubbed in Maryland, but once again he "fell prey to whiskey; and on the day of the grand council, he sunk in inebriation." While the other Indians talked of peace and cooperation, Main Poc "walked about with rapid strides, his forehead wrinkled with terrible frowns, breathing vengeance and brandishing his war club in his hand." Following the conference, he returned to the Kankakee and spent the rest of the year renewing his ties to Tecumseh and the Shawnee Prophet, who had established a new village, Prophetstown, at the juncture of the Tippecanoe and Wabash.[21]

The serenity did not last. Although Tecumseh also championed a policy of peace among the tribes, Main Poc renewed his attacks upon the Osages. During the summer of 1810, he moved his village to western Illinois, where his followers first harassed the American travelers along the Mississippi, then skirmished with local militia units. Late in September, Main Poc led a large war party of Potawatomis, Sacs, and Kickapoos into Missouri, where they attacked an Osage hunting party. To his followers' amazement, in the resulting firefight, Main Poc was wounded. Frightened that their enemies had discovered some powerful new medicine that gave them hegemony over the wabeno, the northern Indians retreated, carrying Main Poc home in a canoe. The wabeno spent the winter of 1810–1811 recovering from his wounds at a camp near Portage des Sioux, Illinois. Meanwhile, he assured his followers that his medicine remained strong. He still could see the bullets fired by his enemies. He had jumped into the path of the bullet, which struck him only because it was aimed at his wife. He could have dodged the missile, but he had chosen to "sacrifice" his own safety through bravery and devotion to his family![22]

During the spring of 1811, his wounds mended, and after moving his camp from Traverse des Sioux to Crow Prairie, a site on the Illinois River north of Lake Peoria, Main Poc spent the following months traveling among the Potawatomis, Sacs, and Kickapoos, preparing them for battle. By the summer of 1811, Tecumseh's political and military confederacy had spread to many of the tribes of the Old Northwest, and the Indians knew the British and Americans were on the brink of war. Although Tecumseh cautioned against any provocations that might prompt Harrison to march against Prophetstown, Main Poc's followers ignored the warnings and repeatedly raided southern Illinois. Yet Main Poc did not take part in the incursions, for in late June, he left Crow Prairie and rode to Michigan, where he established a camp on the Huron River, south of Detroit, just opposite the British Indian agency at Amherstburg.[23]

Since Main Poc remained in Michigan throughout the winter of 1811–1812, he did not participate in the Battle of Tippecanoe. Yet he continued to exert considerable influence in opposition to the Americans. During the winter, he met with the Ottawa and Chippewa leaders from Michigan, urging them to strengthen their ties with the British. In the spring, he dispatched several riders to Illinois, informing the Potawatomis and the Kickapoos that the British had supplied him with many kegs of powder, and he would soon return to lead them against the Americans. But in early July, when news of the declaration of war reached the Detroit region, Main Poc abandoned his camp on the Huron River and crossed over into Canada. There he met with Tecumseh and assisted the Shawnee chief in the latter's efforts to persuade the Wyandots living near Brownstown, a village south of Detroit, to join the British against the Americans.[24]

At first they were unsuccessful. Anticipating the conflict, during July 1812, General William Hull and about two thousand Ohio volunteers reinforced Detroit, and when news of the declaration of war reached Michigan, they crossed over into Ontario, seizing Sandwich, the British settlement opposite Detroit, across the Detroit River. Hull then marched south toward Amherstburg, but his army was too small to both occupy the countryside and attack Fort Malden, the British military post at that location. The Americans advanced as far as the Canard River, where British and Indian possession of the bridges across the stream gave His Majesty's forces a decided advantage. Both Main Poc and Tecumseh took part in several skirmishes, and on July 19, Main Poc was again wounded, this time sustaining a gunshot wound in the neck. Although the injury was not serious, it was painful, and when the Americans retreated, Main Poc followed in their wake, hoping to take some scalps, which would help him save face and revalidate his medicine. Yet the Americans retreated so rapidly that the wabeno could find no stragglers. Unwilling to return to camp empty-handed, Main Poc encountered the body of a fallen British soldier, whom he scalped, and carried his trophy back to camp, where he claimed that the scalp had been taken from an American. Unfortunately, however, the hair on the scalp was bright red, and the soldier's friends recognized that it belonged to their former comrade. Not only did they denounce the wabeno, but several threatened his life, and although Main Poc denied their accusations, he became the laughingstock of the encampment.[25]

Main Poc spent the next six months trying to regain his influence. On August 9, he led part of the Potawatomis that accompanied Tecumseh and Brevet-Major Adam Muir in their unsuccessful ambush of American forces near Monguagon, a small Wyandot settlement south of Detroit. But in this encounter, events again did not go as Main Poc had planned. The Potawatomis became separated from their British and Indian allies by some underbrush, and in attempting to rejoin the British lines, they were mistaken by the Redcoats for Americans. British soldiers opened fire, and in the confusion, Main Poc and the Potawatomis returned the favor. Although the Potawatomis and their allies eventually recognized each other, the resulting disorder enabled the Americans to drive the British and Indians from the field. When the battle ended, Main Poc sought vengeance. He seized the first American captive whom he encountered and then tomahawked the hapless prisoner.[26]

Yet in the following weeks, the war turned in the British and Indians' favor. Although he remained in Michigan, Main Poc dispatched several messengers to the Potawatomis near Chicago, urging them to strike the Long Knives. On August 15, warriors from the Fox and Kankakee Rivers ambushed the garrison of Fort Dearborn as the Americans evacuated the post. The Potawatomi war party was led by Siggenauk, the chief who had accompanied Main Poc to Washington, and by Mad Surgeon, the wabeno's brother-in-law. Officials in Illinois blamed the incident upon Main Poc's influence.[27]

While his kinsmen were active near Chicago, Main Poc assisted British military commander of the region General Isaac Brock and Tecumseh in the capture of Detroit. He then accompanied Muir on an ill-fated expedition to support a Potawatomi siege of Fort Wayne. Yet William Henry Harrison and 2,200 militia reinforced the fort before the British left Michigan, and as Muir's forces ascended the Maumee Valley, scouts brought news that the Potawatomi siege had been broken. Moreover, the scouts also reported that General James Winchester was leading most of Harrison's army down the Maumee to attack Muir's expedition. At first the British and Indians decided to fight, but as Muir withdrew down the river, looking for an opportune defensives position, part of the Indians deserted. To his credit, Main Poc remained with the British and even informed Muir that he had experienced a vision, which promised a great British and Indian victory, but Muir was unimpressed and finally ordered a retreat. The expedition against Fort Wayne ended in failure.[28]

Following Muir's return to Amherstburg, Main Poc, Tecumseh, and the Shawnee Prophet journeyed to northern Indiana and Illinois, where they spent the winter of 1812–1813 recruiting warriors for a spring offensive. In January, Main Poc established a winter camp near the juncture of the Fox and Illinois Rivers, which he believed would keep "those troublers of the Earth, the Americans" from ascending the waterway and reoccupying Chicago. He spent the winter meeting with parties of the Sacs, Winnebagos, and Potawatomis, and in the following spring, he returned to Amherstburg, where he again joined with British and Indian forces in General Henry Procter's unsuccessful invasion of northern Ohio.[29]

The British and Indian retreat from Ohio in August 1813 marked a major watershed in the War of 1812. On September 10, Oliver Perry and the American fleet defeated the British in the Battle of Lake Erie, and in late September, Procter, Tecumseh, and most of the pro-British Indians abandoned Amherstburg and retreated up the Thames Valley. Main Poc did not accompany them. Instead, he led a large party of followers into Michigan, where they awaited the outcome of the upcoming battle in Canada. If the British won, the Potawatomi and his followers planned to fall upon the retreating Americans. If the Americans were victorious, Main Poc and his people could flee into the forests of Michigan. Meanwhile, they intended to live off the settlements in the Detroit region.[30]

On October 5, 1813, Harrison's army defeated the British and Indians at the Battle of the Thames, and the Indian cause was lost forever. At first Main Poc signed an armistice providing for a cessation of hostilities, but he feared American retribution, and early in 1814 he fled to the St. Joseph River in northern Indiana, where he tried to rally the remnants of Tecumseh's confederacy. Yet his efforts were in vain. Although he threatened American emissaries, he could not keep other Indians from coming to terms with the Long Knives, and in July 1814, he withdrew to a new village on the Yellow River in Indiana. There, surrounded by a handful of other hard-core hostiles, he raided a few American settlements on the Wabash, stealing horses and pilfering storehouses. More a nuisance than a threat, the aging wabeno watched in frustration as his remaining influence withered away. Aware of the changing times, most Indians now sought an accommodation with the Americans. Main Poc and his ways were passé. He belonged to a different era.[31]

When word of the Treaty of Ghent reached Indiana, Main Poc refused to believe that the British had made peace. In bewilderment, he journeyed to Mackinac, where early in 1815 he learned that the rumors were true. Embittered, he returned to western Michigan but refused to sign the treaty, which formally ended the hostilities. Still denouncing the Long Knives, he established a lonely camp near Manistee, on the eastern shores of Lake Michigan, where, dissipated by alcohol and now grown deaf, he died in the spring of 1816.[32]

Although Main Poc was a leading figure among the tribes of the Old Northwest during the first two decades of the nineteenth century, he has escaped the notice of historians for several reasons. Unlike Main Poc, Tecumseh has so attracted the attention of white scholars that they have maximized his role during this period. In turn, the Shawnee war chief's shadow has shrouded many of the Indians who also played important parts in the struggle against the Americans. In this instance, Main Poc's obscurity is shared by other important leaders such as Blue Jacket of the Shawnees and Round Head of the Wyandots. All of these warriors were pivotal figures in the decades surrounding the War of 1812, yet they are rarely mentioned in modern histories of that period.

Main Poc also suffers when he is compared with the other major Indian religious figure of these decades: the Shawnee Prophet. Although Main Poc originally exercised more influence than Tenskwatawa, the Shawnee's rapid rise to prominence, his reputed ability to predict eclipses and perform miracles, and his association with Tecumseh gave him a notoriety with white historians that Main Poc lacked. Unquestionably, the wabeno's religious influence was never as widespread as the prophet's, but it may have been more pervasive among the tribes of northern Illinois.

Main Poc has also escaped notice because the historical references to him are scattered through a myriad of widely dispersed documents. Indeed, references to the wabeno are so sporadic, and usually so brief, that they discourage any serious investigation. In addition, there is considerable confusion regarding his name. Not only is Main Poc presented in at least one dozen different spellings, but he is also known by at least two other Potawatomi names: Winibiset and Wapake, and perhaps several others. And finally, when his more common name is translated into English, it also is translated into several different variations (i.e., "Lame Hand," "Withered Hand," "Left Hand," "Crippled Hand," etc.). Because most historians have been unaware of the different names, they have often discussed Main Poc as two or more different Indians.

In summary, there is little about the old wabeno to endear him to anyone. Described by his white contemporaries as "a monster who was distinguished by a girdle, sewed full of human scalps, which he wore around his waist, and strings of bear claws and the bills of owls and hawks, round his ankles," he remains as far removed from the image of the "noble savage" as can be imagined. He possessed few of those qualities admired by most Americans of either the nineteenth or twentieth century. Yet in the decades surrounding the War of 1812, he emerged as a pivotal figure in Indian-white relations in the Old Northwest. William Wells may have exaggerated when he called Main Poc "the greatest warrior in the west . . . , [with] more influence than any other," but the old wabeno certainly was the focal point of much of the government's Indian diplomacy.[33] And yet, ironically, his actions probably were detrimental to the Indian cause. His refusal to curtail his raids against southern Illinois goaded Harrison into attacking Prophetstown, and the resulting Indian defeat seriously weakened Tecumseh's attempts at a red confederacy.

In many ways Main Poc resembles the old "Berserkers" of the Norse sagas, men whose whims and emotions governed their lives. His death in 1816 marked the end of an era. Indian leaders who followed him in Illinois and Indiana held their positions through their ability to accommodate Americans. Main Poc possessed some interesting traits of character, but flexibility and accommodation were not among them.

NOTES

1. The George Winter Papers, Tippecanoe County Historical Society, Lafayette, Indiana; John Tanner, *A Narrative of the Captivity and Adventures of John Tanner During Thirty Years Residence Among the Indians in the Interior of North America* (New York: G. C. H. Carvill, 1830), 287–88; William H. Keating, *Narrative of an Expedition to the Source of the St. Peters River* (London: George B. Whittaker, 1825), 163–64; Ruth Landes, *The Prairie Potawatomi: Tradition and Ritual in the Twentieth Century* (Madison: University of Wisconsin Press, 1970), 51–52; Robert E. Ritzenthaler and Pat Ritzenthaler, *The Woodland Indians of the Western Great Lakes* (Garden City, N.Y.: American Museum Science Books, 1970), 102–4.

2. A. Irving Hallowell, *The Role of Conjuring in Saulteaux Society*, Publication of the Philadelphia Anthropological Society 2 (Philadelphia: University of Pennsylvania Press, 1942), 53; Landes, *Prairie Potawatomi*, 51–52, 89; Ritzenthaler, *Woodland Indians*, 102–4.

3. Thomas Forsyth to T. Rhea, March 10, 1812, M221, Roll 48, 2771, Main Series, Letters Received (LR), Records Office of the Secretary of War (OSW), National Archives Building, Washington, D.C. (NA); statement by Thomas Forsyth, 8YY57 (microfilm), Tecumseh Papers, Draper Manuscripts, State Historical Society of Wisconsin, Madison, hereafter cited as Tecumseh Papers.

4. Hallowell, *Role of Conjuring in Salteaux Society*, 62–64; Landes, *Prairie Potawatomi*, 27–29, 46–48, 51–52, 55–60. Mary B. Black, "Ojibwa Power Belief System," in *The Anthropology of Power*, ed. Raymond Fogelson and Richard Adams (New York: Academic Press, 1977), 141–50.

5. Mary B. Black, "Ojibwa Power Belief System," in *The Anthropology of Power*, ed. Raymond Fogelson and Richard Adams (New York: Academic Press, 1977), 141–50.

6. Statement by Forsyth, 8YY57, Tecumseh Papers; Draper's Notes, 26S90, Draper Manuscripts.

7. *Life of Elisha Tyson* (Baltimore: B. Lundy, 1825), 70; Hopkins, *Mission to the Indians*, 187; statement by Forsyth, 8YY57, Tecumseh Papers.

8. William Wells to Henry Dearborn, January 16, 1809, M221, Roll 33, 1317; *Life of Elisha Tyson*, 70–71; statement by Forsyth, 8YY57, Tecumseh Papers.

9. Northern Indians to Zenon Trudeau, 1793, in *Spain in the Mississippi Valley, 1765–1794*, ed. Lawrence E. Kinnaird, vol. 3 of Annual Report of the American Historical Association for 1945 (Washington, D.C.: American Historical Association, 1945), 110–11; Trudeau to Baron de Carondelet, March 2, 1793, in *Before Lewis and Clark: Documents Illustrating the History of Missouri, 1775–1804*, ed. A. P. Nassir (St. Louis: Historical Documents Foundation, 1952), 1:167–68; Trudeau to Carondelet, April 30, 1795, in Nassir, *Before Lewis and Clark*, 1:322; Trudeau to Gayaoso de Lemos, December 20, 1797, in Nassir, *Before Lewis and Clark*, 2:528; Henry Vanderburgh to Winthrop Sargent, April 2, 1797, Winthrop Sargent Papers, Massachusetts Historical Society, Boston, Mass.; secretary of war to Harrison, April 2, 1802, M15, Roll 1, 205, Letters sent (LS), OSW, NA.

10. "A Treaty Between Tribes," in Carter, *Territorial Papers*, 13:243–44; James Wilkinson to Dearborn, November 26, 1805, Donald J. Berthrong Collection, University of Oklahoma, Norman; Wilkinson to Dearborn, December 3, 1805, Donald J. Berthrong Collection; Dearborn to Jouett, October 13, 1806, M15, Roll 1, 205.

11. R. David Edmunds, *The Shawnee Prophet* (Lincoln: University of Nebraska Press, 1983), 3–62 passim.

12. Forsyth to William Clark, January 15, 1827, 9T53–54, Thomas Forsyth papers, Draper Manuscripts; statement by Forsyth, 8YY57, Tecumseh Papers; Wells to Dearborn, January 7, 1808, M221, Roll 5, 4881.

13. Wells to Dearborn, January 7, 1808, Potawatomi File, Great Lakes–Ohio Valley Indian Archives, Glen A. Black Laboratory of Archaeology, Bloomington, Ind.; Wells to the Secretary of War, April 20, 1808, in Carter, *Territorial Papers*, 7:555–60.

14. Wells to Dearborn, April 2, 1808, Potawatomi File, Great Lakes–Ohio Valley Indian Archives.

15. Wells to the Secretary of War, April 20, 1808, in Carter, *Territorial Papers*, 7:555–60.

16. Wells to Dearborn, April 2, 1808, Potawatomi File, Great Lakes–Ohio Valley Indian Archives; Wells to Dearborn, September 30, 1808, M221, Roll 33, 1199, NA; also see Paul Woerhmann, *At the Headwaters of the Maumee* (Indianapolis: Indiana Historical Society, 1971), 189.

17. Wells to Dearborn, December 24, 1808, M221, Roll 33, 1257; Hopkins, *Mission to the Indians*, 186; Woerhmann, *At the Headwaters of the Maumee*, 189.

18. Jefferson to the Potawatomi, Potawatomi File, Great Lakes–Ohio Valley Indian Archives; Hopkins, *Mission to the Indians*, 186–88.

19. Wells to Dearborn, December 29, 1808, M221, Roll 33, 1272; Wells to Dearborn, January 16, 1809, M221, Roll 33, 1317; Hopkins, *Mission to the Indians*, 190–91.

20. *Life of Elisha Tyson*, 70–71; Woerhmann, *At the Headwaters of the Maumee*, 137–40.

21. Weeks to Ninian Edwards, June 1810, in Carter, *Territorial Papers*, 16:116; Deposition by James Moredaugh, August 17, 1810, Ninian Edwards Papers, Chicago Historical Society, Chicago, Ill.; Deposition by Stephen Cole, September 21, 1810, Ninian Edwards Papers; Clark to William Eustis, January 1811, Potawatomi File, Great Lakes–Ohio Valley Indian Archives; statement by Forsyth, 8YY57, Tecumseh Papers.

22. John Lalime to Clark, May 26, 1811, in *Messages and Letters of William Henry Harrison*, ed. Logan Esarey (Indiana Historical Commission, 1922), 1:511; Clark to Eustis, May 24, 1811, Potawatomi File, Great Lakes Indian Archives; Lalime to Clark, June 2, 1811, in Logan, *Messages and Letters of William Henry Harrison*; Levering to Edwards, August 12, 1811, in Carter, *Territorial Papers*, 16:175–79; Forsyth to Rhea, March 10, 1812, M221, Roll 48, 2771.

23. Speech by the Ottawas to the Secretary of War Relating to Indian Affairs, National Archives, M271, Roll 1, 651; Josiah Snelling to William Henry Harrison, January 18, 1812, Potawatomi File, Great Lakes–Ohio Valley Indian Archives; Ninian Edwards to Eustis, March 3, 1812, in Carter, *Territorial Papers*, 16:193–94; Matthew Elliott to Claus, July 14, 1812, Wyandot File, Great Lakes–Ohio Valley Indian Archives.

24. Elliott to Claus, July 26, 1812, Record group (RG) 10, Volume 28, 16394–16395, Public Archives of Canada; Milo M Quaife, ed., *War on the Detroit: The Chronicles of Thomas Vercheres De Boucherville and the Capitulation by an Ohio Volunteer* (Chicago: Lakeside Press, 1940), 81–84, 246–49; William F. Coffin, *1812: The War and Its Moral: A Canadian Chronicle* (Montreal: John Lovell, 1864), 199–200.

25. Procter to Brock, August 11, 1812, in *Collections of the Michigan Pioneer and Historical Society* (Lansing, Mich.: Thorp and Godfrey and others, 1874–1929), 15:129–30; Hull to the secretary of war, August 13, 1812, in Ernest Cruikshank, ed., *Documents Relating to the Invasion of Canada and the Surrender of Detroit* (Ottawa: Government Printing Bureau, 1912), 139–41; Alexander C. Casselman, ed., *Richardson's War of 1812* (Toronto: Coles Publishing, 1974), 33–42; Quaife, *War on the Detroit*, 90–92.

26. Forsyth to Howard, September 7, 1812, in Carter, *Territorial Papers*, 16:261–65; Milo M. Quaife, *Chicago and the Old Northwest, 1673–1835* (Chicago: University of Chicago Press, 1913), 220, 393; Robert McAfee, *History of the Late War in the Western Country* (Lexington, Ky.: Worsley and Smith, 1816), 101; Edmunds, *Potawatomis*, 186–88.

27. Hull to Eustis, August 26, 1812, *Collections of the Michigan Pioneer and Historical Society*, 40:460–69; Unknown to secretary of war, September 8, 1812, in Casselman, *Richardson's War of 1812*, 296–300.

28. Procter to Shaeffe, January 13, 1813, *Collections of the Michigan Pioneer and Historical Society*, 15:215–15; Forsyth to Clark, July 20, 1813, Potawatomi File, Great Lakes–Ohio Valley Indian Archives; Chambers to Freer, April 25–May 5, 1813, *Collections of the Michigan Pioneer and Historical Society*, 15:289–91; McAfee, *History of the Late War*, 264–77.

29. Harrison to the secretary of war, September 30, 1813, Potawatomi File, Great Lakes–
   Ohio Valley Indian Archives; MacArthur to the secretary of war, October 6, 1813, *Collections of the Michigan Pioneer and Historical Society*, 40:535–36; Wallace Brice, *History of
   Fort Wayne* (Fort Wayne, Ind.: D. W. Jones and Sons, 1868), 269.

30. "Terms of an Armistice with the Indians," in Esarey, *Messages and Letters*, 2:577–79;
   Cameron to Elliott, March 25, 1814, *Collections of the Michigan Pioneer and Historical
   Society*, 16:524, "Report from the Indian Department," Spring 1814, *Collections of the
   Michigan Pioneer and Historical Society*, 16:553; Kinzie to Cass, September 22, 1814, in
   Carter, *Territorial Papers*, 10:489–90; Thomas Posey to the Secretary of War, November 12, 1814, in Esarey, *Messages and Letters*, 2:665.

31. "Minutes of a Council," January 29, 1815, *Collections of the Michigan Pioneer and Historical Society*, 23:469–71; McDonall to Bugler, February 26, 1815, *Collections of the Michigan Pioneer and Historical Society*, 23:489–92; "A Treaty Between the United States and
   the Indians," September 8, 1815, in Charles Kappler, ed. *Indian Treaties, 1778–1883* (New
   York: Interland Publishing, 1972), 2:117–19; statement by Forsyth, 8YY57, Tecumseh
   Papers.

32. McAfee, History of the Late War, 298.

33. Wells to Dearborn, January 7, 1808, M221, Roll 5, 4881.

3

KENEKUK,
THE KICKAPOO PROPHET

☙

JOSEPH B. HERRING

THE MOST FAMOUS AMERICAN INDIANS of the nineteenth century were Sitting Bull, Geronimo, and other gallant war chiefs who led their people in defense of their lands and way of life. Those who chose peaceful means to help their people to adjust to a new and distasteful, but unavoidable, way of life are for the most part forgotten. Kenekuk, "prophet" of a small band of Kickapoos and Potawatomis, displayed exceptional leadership in helping his four hundred followers make the outward adjustment to white society in order to retain their lands in Kansas without losing their identity as Indians.[1] Because Kenekuk represented a band of peaceful Kickapoo and Potawatomi farmers living in the Vermillion River valley of southern Illinois, rather than a force of warriors, his achievements have been largely neglected.[2] Yet the leadership of this Native American shaman turned religious prophet was astute, and his positive influence over the lives of his followers persisted well beyond his death.

Although information on his early years remains scant, it seems that Kenekuk was born about 1788 near the confluence of the Wabash and Vermillion Rivers, not far from the present Illinois-Indiana border.[3] He was likely of mixed tribal heritage, with his father being Kickapoo and his mother Potawatomi; although undoubtedly fluent in both tribal languages, Potawatomi was apparently his primary tongue.[4]

Kickapoo tribal folklore indicates that Kenekuk's father was an alcoholic who was held in low regard by his band and not recognized as a leading man. For this reason, and because the Kickapoo and Potawatomi tribes both maintained patrilineal-clan social structures, Kenekuk never held formal status as a headman or chief in either tribe.[5] He was politically astute, however. Like many of his Potawatomi relatives, he was a polygamist, and by the 1830s, he was married simultaneously to the daughters of the headmen of the Kickapoo and Potawatomi factions on the Kansas reservation.[6]

Kenekuk was no ordinary man. At an early age he began displaying shamanistic abilities, and he had his first shamanistic vision, or trance, when he was about sixteen years old. During that experience, he ascended to heaven to meet with the Great Manitou, the Creator, who told him to forsake traditional Indian ways for the customs and religion of the whites.[7]

The young Indian was confused and frightened by this episode, and instead of obeying the vision's mandate, he soon descended into a life of hard drinking, debauchery, and violence. Tribal lore says that the young Kenekuk proved so unruly that he was cast out of the band and forced to seek handouts in the frontier settlements of Indiana and Illinois. Eventually, a priest took him in, cared for him, and taught him Christianity and the ways of white society. Under the priest's tutelage, Kenekuk began to change his ways. He had been, he later recalled, "like a bird in a hollow tree slowly recovering from torpor by the warmth of spring." Then, at age twenty, he experienced yet another vision, traveling again to heaven to see the Creator, who instructed him to return to his people with a new doctrine of salvation. His return journey proved long and difficult. After soaring above the earth for a long time, he finally happened upon a blue opening in the sky, descended through it, and managed to get back to his people at their village along the Vermillion River.[8]

After his second vision, Kenekuk's religious views expanded and evolved. Scholars have demonstrated that shamanism among Native Americans often merged with more formal, prophetic manifestations, which developed in response to the long-term efforts by missionaries to convert Indians to Christianity. Catholic and Protestant missionaries had interacted with sundry bands of Kickapoos and Potawatomis since the 1660s. Although most Kickapoos had successfully resisted the overtures, many Potawatomi bands welcomed and even embraced the preachers. Long before his experience with the priest, Kenekuk had likely learned about Christian teachings from his mother and her Potawatomi relatives. The young Indian's innate shamanistic talents, then, combined with his long-term exposure to Christian teaching, allowed a maturing Kenekuk to become a religious prophet among his people and even earned him the respect of many outside observers.[9]

In addition to his shamanistic and priestly abilities, Kenekuk proved to be a savvy political leader. Although never considered a true chief by his own people, the headmen of the Kickapoo and Potawatomi factions often deferred to him in dealings with outsiders, and he eventually became well-known even in the white world. At meetings similar in style and flamboyance to the foremost white revivalists of the day, Kenekuk implored followers to obey God's commands, for sinners were damned to an afterlife "filled with fire for the punishment of all wicked and ill men; all professed drunkards, tattlers, liars, and meddling bodies." The true path, Kenekuk intoned, was blazed by Jesus, who "brought his soul here to live in the flesh; he brought his blood too, to wash away our sins. . . . He has made a very good road for people to travel in; it is a happy road and leads to heaven."[10] All who rejected evil and led religious lives, he proclaimed, would be saved.

Kenekuk's zeal and energy, however, went beyond saving souls. In an era when whites constantly demanded and took Indian lands, the prophet devised a strategy to protect his people's interests. By blending evangelical Protestantism, Catholic ritual, and traditional tribal ceremonialism, he helped create a new Indian society. His unlikely religious synthesis was a pragmatic accommodation to the dominant culture, and it revitalized and strengthened the band's societal bonds. Far from causing the erosion of Indian ways, it enabled members to adjust to rapidly changing conditions and to resist repeated attempts to dispossess them.[11] When the band was forced, reluctantly, to emigrate from Illinois to Kansas, Kenekuk's people survived adversity and overcame the pressures caused by the flood of buckskin-clad whites who inundated their territory.

In Kansas from 1833 until his death in 1852, Kenekuk astutely protected his people's rights by strengthening their social and cultural integrity. He effectively resisted efforts by Indian agents and missionaries to force his people to profess Christianity and accept standardized schooling, and resisted schemes to divide tribal lands into individual allotments. Other tribes that followed such designs to uplift them from "savagery" to "civilization" lost both their will to resist and their Kansas lands in the 1850s and 1860s. But the two small bands of Kickapoos and Potawatomis held out, even after their prophet's death. They owed their survival to their devotion to Kenekuk, and especially to his religious tenets stressing peace and temperance, his belief in land retention, and his insistence that the men farm the fields, which was a departure from the usual custom that consigned women to most farm labor.

At the height of his power and influence in the 1830s and 1840s, Kenekuk evoked a religious fervor and pious faith in his people, who considered him the messenger of God. It was his own unique version of God's teachings, however, that he brought to the people. Kenekuk's message departed significantly from conventional Christianity and contained an implicit cultural nationalism that merged with, rather than contradicted, traditional Indian beliefs. Yet many visitors among the combined Kickapoo and Potawatomi band assumed the Indians were Catholics. Presbyterian missionary William Smith, stopping at their village on the Missouri River in the summer of 1833, remarked that their religion bore a "striking resemblance" to Roman Catholicism.[12]

On the surface, such an assessment was accurate. Kenekuk's followers believed in heaven, hell, and purgatory, just as they worshiped Jesus, the Virgin Mary, and the saints. They attended church services on Sundays and holy days. They publicly confessed their sins on Fridays, but unlike most Roman Catholics, they demanded physical evidence that God had cleansed their souls, and wrongdoers willingly submitted to the whip. One white visitor saw Kenekuk's adherents voluntarily accepting "lashes on their bare backs, so well laid on as to cause the blood to run freely. Many of them bore visible scars on their backs, caused by former flagellations." After the ordeal, penitents shook hands with their flagellators and declared themselves "relieved of a heavy burden." A visiting minister reported that men carried long rods at religious assemblies "to keep order among the children and dogs, and to see that each person was in his proper place."[13]

While such practices strengthened tribal unity and enabled Kenekuk to maintain discipline, his emphasis on both abstinence and peaceful coexistence with whites was even more important. Realizing that frontier settlers might accept peaceful and sober Indians as neighbors, he railed against violence and alcoholism. He commanded his followers to love their neighbors and to turn the other cheek when wronged, and he warned drunkards that they would "go into a place prepared for the wicked, and suffer endless days and nights of grief."[14]

To provide ritual structure to his services, the prophet provided disciples with "prayer sticks"—twelve-inch wooden boards on which three sets of five figures were carved. To outsiders, the devices superficially resembled the Roman Catholic rosary, and contemporary witnesses reported that Indians often wept while manipulating the sticks. William Smith wanted to learn more about these fascinating implements being used in prayer like the "Roman beads." Baptist missionary Isaac McCoy heard the oft repeated chants rendered "in a monotonous sing-song tone"; in his ethnocentric mind "the repetitions were exceedingly frequent . . . and all apparently unmeaning." After attending one service, English traveler Charles Augustus Murray was most intrigued by the "carved symbols, which answered the purpose of letters, and enabled them [adherents] to chime in with the prayer or hymn of the preacher." A Catholic missionary noted depictions of a house and tree branches on some of the prayer sticks. He assumed that the Indians did not know the meaning of these figures, which, he observed, helped supplicants determine the number of repetitions for each prayer. "They put a finger upon the character, as in saying the Rosary," the priest wrote. "They know nothing of baptism; yet there is a cross on the *pentecote* [prayer stick], and they know that the master of life died for love of us."[15]

Presbyterian minister Cyrus Byington provided the most thorough description of the prayer sticks:

At the head of the upper end of the paddle is a crude picture of a house with four trees in front of it. The house represents heaven. The forth tree is a small one, and is designed to represent the tree on which our Savior was crucified. Then follow below the house and the trees, three sets of five distinct characters. One character represents man's heart, the second his flesh, the third his name, the fourth his life, the fifth his kindred. Below these

FIGURE 3.1. Kenekuk led a group of Kickapoo that lived along the Vermillion River in east-central Illinois before removing to Kansas. In 1831, before the removal of the Kickapoo to Kansas, then part of Indian Territory, George Catlin painted this portrait of the Kickapoo Prophet. Courtesy of the Kansas State Historical Society.

characters are lines drawn, which represent the "broad and narrow ways," and a left hand way, which leads down to destruction. In repeating their prayers, [Kenekuk's adherents] begin at the characters just above the lines, which mark the two ways, and repeat them in an ascending series, till they reach the house on top.[16]

Although their use of prayer sticks and other new worship forms indicated that the prophet's followers were religiously innovative, and although they had also abandoned some of their traditional customs—discarding their Algonquin medicine, or clan, bundles, and discontinuing the use of face paint—these Indians never lost sight of the fact that they were a tribal people. Most were bilingual, fluent in Kickapoo and Potawatomi, and, although many spoke or understood some English, they would prefer their native languages well into the late nineteenth century. Their religion, moreover, remained thoroughly in harmony with traditional beliefs, and they continued to perform their Native music and dances. At Sunday services, moreover, menstruating women were forbidden from entering the village medicine lodge, indicating that the traditional menstrual taboo was still rigorously enforced.[17]

Such practices disturbed federal officials and missionaries, and the band's reverence of their prophet-shaman instead of a priest or minister rankled and frustrated the missionaries. The Presbyterian Smith, for one, noted that while Kenekuk ruled "in a manner which would reflect honor on an enlightened statesman," his teachings "would be impossible to break down." In their report to fellow religionists in the East, Quakers John D. Lang and Samuel Taylor allowed that although Kenekuk possessed "some talent," he was in reality an "arch deceiver." Reverend N. Sayre Harris of the Protestant Episcopal Church was not pleased when the prophet supposedly insisted that Jesus may have been the savior of the whites, but that he, Kenekuk, was the messiah of the Indians—he "was the Jesus Christ of the red man."[18]

Whether Kenekuk was a latter-day messiah or not meant little to his people in the long run. What mattered were the prophet's religious teachings, which reinforced tribal sovereignty and solidarity and gave followers not only the courage and conviction to defend their rights but also the wisdom to avoid violence against the more powerful settlers. For many years, Kenekuk and his followers managed to hold on to their eastern Illinois homeland. Their efforts failed only because of the combined pressures of President Andrew Jackson's Indian Removal Act and the Black Hawk War, which broke out along the Illinois-Iowa border in 1832. Although Kenekuk's people remained neutral during that conflict, angry Illinois citizens demanded the expulsion of all Indians. Government officials insisted, therefore, that Kenekuk take his people west of the Mississippi. Although a violation of the Creator's stricture against selling tribal lands, the prophet realized it was the prudent course to follow, and in October 1832, he signed the Treaty of Castor Hill, ceding all claims to Illinois lands. It was the only time that Kenekuk ever sold any territory.[19]

Early in 1833, Kenekuk and approximately four hundred Kickapoos and Potawatomis settled on the west bank of the Missouri River, just a few miles north of Fort Leavenworth. Their arrival immediately attracted missionaries who thought the prophet's religion so closely resembled Christianity that the Indians were ready for conversion. While the Indians seemed to accept the preachers with open arms, appearances were deceptive. In fact, they hoped to reestablish their accustomed way of life in the new land, and they knew that missionaries could be useful intermediaries to a government slow in providing the money, food, and farming tools promised in the recent treaty.[20]

About one mile upriver from the Kenekuk's village lived the Prairie Kickapoos, recent arrivals from Missouri who had also ceded their lands in the Treaty of Castor Hill. Long-standing differences aggravated by their new proximity resulted in frequent bickering and strife. While men from the prophet's village tended to their fields, the prairie band steadfastly clung to traditional customs, shunning agriculture, white civilization, and Christianity. They also rejected Kenekuk's religion, preferring their own manitous, clan bundle rites, and traditional religious ceremonies. They were often away from their village hunting or trading, and many enjoyed drinking, gambling, and carousing. Some were also accused of physically assaulting Kenekuk's sober followers, who feared that the women could be accosted while the men worked in the fields.[21]

Into this environment ventured a succession of optimistic but naïve advocates of Indian social change.[22] In May 1833, Baptist missionaries made plans to build a school among Kenekuk's hardworking and sober people. Their hopes were dashed, however, for the Indians maintained a "remarkably uniform" attachment to the prophet. Abandoning the project, disgruntled Baptist Isaac McCoy admitted that the Kickapoos and Potawatomis displayed a few good ethics, but he uncharitably portrayed their religion as "a step from savage blindness into greater absurdity."[23]

On the heels of the Baptists came Harriet Livermore, the forty-four-year-old daughter of a New Hampshire congressman and likely one of the most colorful characters ever to preach in Indian country. As a young woman, Livermore had enjoyed dancing, card playing, and sundry other frills. In 1811, however, she renounced her carefree ways to start anew. "I drew up a resolution in my mind to commence a religious life," she recalled. In an age when professional women were rare, she became an itinerant preacher, and by the 1820s was famous in the eastern states for her rousing sermons. In 1827, she warned a congressional audience (which included President John Quincy Adams) to repent, for the end of the world was at hand.[24] Following that presentation, Lucy Johnson Barbour, wife of the secretary of war, described Livermore as an attractive, powerful woman, whose "tremulous" but "eloquent" oration brought many in the audience to tears. Most others simply thought Livermore daft. John Greenleaf Whittier would later immortalize this "erratic" woman—a dichotomous blend of "vixen" and "devotee"—in his poem "Snow-Bound: A Winter Idyl."[25]

In 1832, with the end of the world still in the offing, Livermore journeyed west to take her message to the Indians—"the poor sheep in the wilderness." She arrived at Fort Leavenworth sometime the following year, expecting "to pitch my tent with the prophet's band of the Kickapoo nation." That August she informed Kenekuk that Napoleon Bonaparte had risen from the dead as the Antichrist and would soon rule the world in a reign of terror. The Rapture, she proclaimed, was imminent! There was little call for worry, however, for the prophet Elijah would reappear on September 4 to carry her and the Kickapoos off to heaven.[26]

Special Indian Commissioner Henry L. Ellsworth was furious that this "deranged" woman actually had official government sanction to pursue her calling among the Indians. Lacking the authority to evict her, he urged that she leave Indian Country quietly, reminding her that the recent Black Hawk War had demonstrated "the bad influence of Indian dreamers." After proclaiming that she would go only in irons, Livermore finally left the region on perhaps an even more preposterous endeavor— she would go to Jerusalem and spread Christ's teachings among the Jews.[27]

Other attempts to Christianize the Kickapoos followed. Arriving at Kenekuk's village for a brief visit in November 1833, Jesuit Father Benedict Roux found the prophet away and unable to return in time to meet him. Roux was undismayed, for the Indians treated him with reverence. "I was received by them as an angel sent from heaven," he wrote. He was deeply impressed that the sober and industrious Indians refrained from lying, stealing, and fighting. Since Kenekuk's two "docile" sons appeared to desire religious instruction, the Jesuit thought that "mighty conquests" would be won "if God would call one of the sons to the priesthood."[28]

The Kickapoo people from the Vermillion band had good reason for trying to make a favorable impression on missionaries. They knew that their economic security would be enhanced if the government lived up to its treaty commitments and provided money, farm tools, food, and other supplies. Since repeated requests for the promised aid had gone unheeded, Kenekuk decided it was to their advantage to allow preachers, who could help loosen federal purse strings, to come among them. Although he realized that they would try to undermine his authority, the advantages outweighed the risks. He had enough confidence in his religious powers to allow competition from outsiders.

Throughout their early years in Kansas, efforts to convert the prophet's followers intensified. Missionaries, thinking Kenekuk's religion to be halfway between Christianity and paganism, reasoned that with some proper instruction, the Kickapoos and Potawatomis would submit to conversion. Soon after Father Roux departed, Methodist missionary Jerome C. Berryman ventured into the village. Pleased by the Indians' apparent piety, Berryman was encouraged when, after an initial coolness, Kenekuk allowed him to preach. Before long, the Methodist had baptized more than four hundred Indians, including the prophet himself. Kenekuk's baptism "would have been attended to sooner," Berryman explained, "but the prophet had two wives, and we were unwilling to administer the sacraments to a polygamist." The minister was so optimistic about his prospects for winning converts that he engaged Kenekuk as an assistant at an annual salary of $200.00. Despite many promises, however, the wily Kenekuk stayed married to both wives; he had children by both women, and divorce might offend the influential father of whichever wife he abandoned. He had, however, seen the "error" of his ways and would henceforth preach against the practice of polygamy.[29]

Berryman thought that Isaac McCoy had made a "great mistake" in implying that the prophet knew little of Christian doctrine. More perceptive than McCoy, the Methodist knew that the Kickapoos and Potawatomis had been without religious guidance so long that "their theory and practice of religion would be imperfect," and he observed that although they had many "peculiarities foreign to Christianity," the Indians were "truly pious" and "united with us." He became convinced of Kenekuk's devotion when the prophet raised Bible in hand and told his followers to learn the tenets of Methodism from Berryman.[30]

But Berryman's expectations were not fulfilled, for Kenekuk rarely allowed him to officiate at religious ceremonies. The prophet promised to ease his followers gradually into Christianity, but Berryman remained dubious. There was room for hope, however. Despite the fact that Kenekuk's "peculiar" methods, including the use of flagellation, considerably hindered mission work, Methodist superintendent Thomas Johnson remained optimistic. Johnson admitted that while they had encountered some difficulties, these were being overcome, and he thought the "prospects of ultimate success are as good as they have been."[31]

Such hopes were severely dampened when another Jesuit arrived to study the feasibility of establishing a mission among the Kickapoos and Potawatomis. Little concerned about Methodist competition, the priest was confident of success, for the black-robed Jesuits had several advantages over their Protestant counterparts. Their church bureaucracy organized and mobilized missionaries on a grand scale, and their well-rounded classical educations gave Jesuits a facility in languages that Protestant ministers generally lacked. In addition, priests were unhindered by family affairs or financial worries, and Indians appreciated their continence. Experience had taught them, moreover, to make concessions to local customs and to begin serious proselytizing only after mastering Indian languages and understanding traditional folkways. While others condemned traditional dancing, games, and festivals, Jesuits tolerated such practices.

Rather than eradicate existing Indian ceremonies, they sought to remold and reorient them to fit Catholicism. By giving Christian meaning to traditional ritual, however, the priests inadvertently helped to create a cultural blend dominated by the Indian contribution rather than the European.[32]

While such a cultural synthesis often served to enhance Jesuit conversion efforts with other tribes, the religious syncretism of the Kickapoos and Potawatomis reinforced their society and protected it against subtle pressure to accept unwanted change. Their moral code already approximated that of the Jesuits, and they were satisfied they had found the true path. As one Kenekuk disciple put it, "We are happier and more flourishing here . . . it is only a few years since we learnt [God's] will and commands" through Kenekuk, but if we "obey Him, we shall daily grow wiser and happier."[33] The Indians' devotion to Kenekuk was complete; his charismatic hold over them bordered on omnipotence, a situation that even Jesuits could not fathom.

As Father Charles Van Quickenborne approached Kickapoo Country in July 1835, he had only the faintest inkling of the difficult task ahead. He had come to investigate the glowing reports of the Indians' piety and to facilitate their conversion. Van Quickenborne met Kenekuk and, following an exchange of pleasantries, the two began discussing theology. When Kenekuk asked for an explanation of Catholicism, the priest replied that "every man must believe in God, hope in God, love God above all things, and his neighbor as himself; those who do this will go to heaven, and those who do not will go to hell." When he added that biblical prophets proved through miracles that God had spoken to them, Kenekuk interrupted to say that he had also performed miracles. "I raised the dead to life," he explained, relating how he had once breathed new life into a woman and a child on the brink of death. The Jesuit retorted that Kenekuk had only helped restore the sick to health; there was nothing miraculous about that. At first Kenekuk was taken aback, irate that a stranger dared contradict him. After a few minutes, his vexation eased, for he saw the futility of arguing religious matters with this mulish Jesuit. Moreover, he knew that with both Catholics and Methodists stationed on their lands, the missionaries would have to compete for the Indians' favor. He decided to take a neutral approach. "I realize," he told the priest humbly, "that my religion is not a good one: if my people wish to embrace yours, I will do as they say." With this assurance, Van Quickenborne set out for Washington to seek government aid in starting a mission.[34]

After Van Quickenborne left, rivalries between Kenekuk's followers and the traditional Kickapoos intensified. The prophet disapproved of the Prairie Kickapoos' conduct, and he held Pashishi, one of their headmen, responsible for their drinking, gambling, and ill-mannered ways. Kenekuk threatened to invoke supernatural powers to punish the "sinners" and vowed that if Pashishi refused to repent, he would "blow into a flame that would not be easily smothered" and cause his rival's death.[35] But Pashishi paid little heed to the prophet's bluff, and when word of the Seminoles' triumph over American troops in Florida reached the Kickapoos, the prairie band staged a boisterous dance. Consuming several casks of whiskey, they rejoiced that "the time was near at hand when the white people would be subdued, and red men restored again to their country." As drunken Indians rode through the village, harassing women and destroying property, Kenekuk rushed to Fort Leavenworth to seek aid from the soldiers.

Outraged by the Indians' celebration of an American defeat, officials brought charges against Pashishi, who wondered why there had been such a fuss about a simple religious ceremony. Asserting that it was "the right of all people to dance, the white as well as the red man dance," the unrepentant headman denied that his people had caused any serious damage. The white men, after scolding the Indians for their alleged bad behavior, agreed to let the rival bands settle differences in their own way.[36]

Father Van Quickenborne returned in June 1836 with three assistants and began conversion efforts in earnest. But winning Native souls proved difficult, for it was "one thing to come to the Indian mission and another to convert the Indians." Kenekuk, angry because of the favoritism the priests showed to Pashishi's band, ordered followers to shun the black robes. When the Jesuits pressured the Prairie Kickapoos to reform, they, too, rejected Catholic demands. "We want no prayer," they announced; "our forefathers got along very well without it and we are not going to feel its loss." Despite such obstinacy, the Jesuits remained hopeful. "With the help of God and with patience," thought Van Quickenborne, "we can go far."[37]

In the following years, however, the missionaries did not "go far" with regard to converting the Kickapoos and Potawatomis. The Catholics and the Methodists had built schools on reservation lands, but attendance was light at both of these institutions. The Methodist Berryman assumed that the "detrimental influence" of the prophet kept children out of the classroom. School discipline was impossible to maintain because children "abscond and go home with impunity." Berryman branded Kenekuk a "savage politician" whose appeal rested on the gullibility of his followers, and he warned that such men "must be held in check by counteracting influences of popular virtue, or they will in time barbarize the world."[38]

The Jesuits also resented Kenekuk's influence and indirectly acknowledged his effectiveness by blaming him for their failure to win converts. As they closed their mission's doors for the last time in 1841, Father Nicholas Point, a visiting priest, condemned the prophet, whose "cool effrontery and persevering industry" had "palsied" Catholic efforts. Ignoring the Kickapoos' acceptance of basic Christian morals, Point was outraged that they refused to accept Catholicism. He grieved that the mission "had been plunged into the deepest abyss of moral degradation by the scandalous conduct of people who pretend to civilization." The well-traveled Jesuit Pierre-Jean De Smet called Kenekuk a "false prophet." Curiously, De Smet, ignoring the fact that none of the traditional Kickapoos had become Catholic, praised Pashishi as "a man of good wit and good sense, who needs only a little courage to become a Christian." Since Kenekuk had successfully thwarted them, De Smet attempted to rationalize the fact that one man, and an illiterate Indian at that, had prevented highly educated priests from converting unschooled "heathens." For want of a better reason, he decided that the prophet was too "profoundly ignorant of Christian doctrines" and that his followers were more "densely ignorant" of sin, confession, and penance than the "rudest savages."[39] The black robes left Kickapoo Country to reap souls among less obstinate Indians.

Kenekuk ignored such barbs as the expressions of frustrated men. Following the closing of the missions in the 1840s, his followers prospered unhindered by meddling preachers. Under the prophet's guidance, Kickapoo and Potawatomi men worked hard to clear and plow the fields, and their farms provided a secure living. Indian Agent Richard Cummins noted in his annual reports that they raised a substantial surplus of corn, pumpkins, potatoes, cattle, and pigs, which they sold to white settlers for a considerable profit.[40]

Many admired Kenekuk's disciples because they adhered to a Protestant-like work ethic. Methodist minister Nathaniel Talbott noted that they "raise more corn than any other Indians in this country," and even the Baptist McCoy conceded that "the Prophet's influence has made them more industrious." A government-employed teacher found the children intelligent, "their memory quick and retentive, their morals good, their manners pleasant, and they are remarkably active and industrious." A trader called Kenekuk's Potawatomi converts "the best Indians we have: industrious, sober, and most of them religious." Agent Cummins glowingly reported that Kenekuk's band almost equaled whites in government, farming, and religion. They "evince a determination [and] perseverance; they are at this time truly in the spirit of work, if they continue to progress ... they will be ahead of any of the Indians in this section of the country."[41]

Fortunately the continued prosperity among the Kickapoos and Potawatomis strengthened the bonds that Kenekuk's religion had initially forged, for by 1850, white settlement had encroached upon Indian Country, and outbreaks of smallpox touched off panic among other tribes in the region. The prophet's followers managed to escape unscathed when, in 1851, numerous Sacs and Foxes succumbed to the disease.[42]

The Kickapoo Prophet died sometime in 1852, but whites initially ignored this event. The agent reported merely that the Indians had "lost Keu-e-kuck, their principal chief," but no cause of death or date was given. Like many who had known Kenekuk, the agent had ambivalent feelings about him. He praised the prophet for exerting "a most beneficial influence over a great portion of that tribe for some years before his death, in restraining, by all means in his power, the introduction and use of spirits." In his brief eulogy, however, the agent also noted that Kenekuk "was notorious for his superstitious quackery—a conjurer of the first water—and regarded by most of his people as possessing supernatural powers."[43]

Although this was a jaundiced view of Kenekuk, it contained some measure of truth. Nevertheless, it is clear that the prophet played a vital role in the tribe's determined efforts to survive. Even after his death, his followers continued to farm intensively and to abstain from drinking, gambling, and other "vices" that could have eroded tribal solidarity. Their agricultural endeavors and religious unity proved a bulwark in their struggle against encroachments on their lands. If the prophet's band sometimes diplomatically showed signs of accommodating the dominant culture, they never capitulated to the pressure. Instead, they skillfully used their adaptive culture and flexibility to resist outside threats. To the dismay of missionaries and government agents, they steadfastly rejected Christianity, formal education, and schemes of individual land allotment.

During the late 1850s and early 1860s, thousands of settlers flooded onto surrounding lands. Kansas became a state and war began. Settlers, not wanting Indians among them, managed to force most of the tribes out of the region after the Civil War. Unified by Kenekuk's religion and teachings, the Kickapoos and Potawatomis were able to defend a portion of their remaining land, and by the turn of the twentieth century, they were among the few Indians left in the state. The vast majority of Kansas tribes that agreed to accept Christianity and white ways were quickly forced to move, but not Kenekuk's followers. They never forgot they were Indians, and their acceptance of white culture stopped short of assimilation. Today the Kickapoo reservation, one of only four small Indian reservations in the state, suggests that Kenekuk's religion was proof against all schemes to "civilize" the Indian.[44]

NOTES

1. The name Kenekuk (also spelled Kanakuk, Kanekuk, Kannekuk, Kennekuk, etc.) apparently translates as "putting the foot upon a fallen object." Details on the prophet's family life remain sketchy. Evidently, his first wife, Sakeetoqua (or So-ke-tok-wa), died before the Kickapoo and Potawatomi bands removed to Kansas. Sakeetoqua was the mother of Kenekuk's son Pahkahkah (or John Kennekuk). The prophet had another son who reached maturity, Wapautuck (or Wappatuk); however, little is known about him. Kenekuk's second wife, Ahsameeno-Tenwaqua (or Asameno Ten-wak-wa), was the daughter of a Kickapoo headman named Mecina. She gave birth to three girls: Kachasa (or Kaseetha), Netinapee, and Kwatheet; the latter two died during childhood. The prophet next married a Potawatomi woman named Aquona, who died shortly thereafter. His last wife was a Kickapoo named Wainetukoosh, who also preceded him in death. His

daughter Kachasa lived to maturity, rearing three children, Wawawsuk, Wapoatek (John Winsee), and Opsukkee (Commodore). See Milo Custer to George W. Martin, December 10, 1906, History—Indians—Kickapoo, Manuscript Division, Kansas State Historical Society (hereafter KSHS), Topeka. Also see Joseph B. Herring, *Kenekuk, the Kickapoo Prophet* (Lawrence: University Press of Kansas, 1988); Joseph B. Herring, *The Enduring Indians of Kansas: A Century and a Half of Acculturation* (Lawrence: University Press of Kansas, 1990), 4–5, 29–46; and Alfred A. Cave, *Prophets of the Great Spirit: Native American Revitalization Movements in Eastern North America* (Lincoln: University of Nebraska Press, 2006), 225–43.

2. In 1851, Kenekuk's Kickapoos and Potawatomis signed a "national compact," officially coming together under one social-political structure. See "National Compact Between the Kickapoos and Potawatomis," May 9, 1851, History—Indians—Potawatomi, Manuscript Division, KSHS; and David D. Mitchell to the Commissioner of Indian Affairs, October 25, 1851, *Senate Executive Documents*, 32nd Cong., 1st sess., 1851, (serial 613), 323. See also Herring, *Enduring Indians of Kansas*, 122–24.

3. In October 1838, a correspondent to a Congregational newspaper—the *Christian Mirror* of Portland, Maine—visited the Kickapoo village in Kansas and reported that Kenekuk was then fifty years old; see correspondence reprinted in the *New York Evangelist*, October 20, 1838.

4. In November 1833, a messenger delivered a speech that Kenekuk had dictated to him in Potawatomi; the messenger subsequently translated the prophet's words for listeners into Kickapoo and French. See Louise Barry, *The Beginning of the West: Annals of the Kansas Gateway to the American West, 1540–1854* (Topeka: Kansas State Historical Society, 1972), 253.

5. Kenekuk was identified in an 1816 Kickapoo treaty as the "Drunkard's Son"; see Charles J. Kappler, ed., *Indian Affairs: Laws and Treaties* (Washington, D.C.: Government Printing Office, 1904), 131.

6. Methodist missionary Thomas Johnson thought that Kenekuk was mixed Kickapoo and Miami. Although mistaken about the prophet's parentage, Johnson was one of many preachers who noted the Indian leader's practice of polygamy; see Johnson to the secretary of the Methodist Missionary Society, February 27, 1837, *Christian Advocate and Journal* (New York), April 28, 1837. Apparently, polygamy among the Kickapoo tribe was rare; it was far more common among the Potawatomis. For information on traditional Kickapoo culture, see Charles Callender, Richard K. Pope, and Susan M. Pope, "Kickapoo," in *Handbook of North American Indians*, vol. 15, *Northeast*, ed. Bruce G. Trigger (Washington, D.C.: Smithsonian Institution, 1978), 656–67; and Arrell M. Gibson, *The Kickapoos: Lords of the Middle Border* (Norman: University of Oklahoma Press, 1963), 1–51. For information on the Potawatomis, see James A. Clifton, "Potawatomi," in Trigger, *Handbook of North American Indians*, 15:725–42.

7. Shamans served as intermediaries between the physical and spiritual worlds. A typical shaman could fall into a deathlike trance, consult with spirits in the netherworld, and then regain consciousness with solutions to problems or instructions on how people should lead their lives. For an excellent description of shamans and their ability to interact with the spirit world, see Amanda Porterfield, "Shamanism: A Psychosocial Definition," *Journal of the American Academy of Religion* 55 (Winter 1987): 721–39.

8. For accounts of Kenekuk's youth and his early religious experiences, see the *New York Evangelist*, October 20, 1838; Nicholas Point, *Wilderness Kingdom: Indian Life in the Rocky Mountains, 1840–1847: The Journals and Paintings of Nicholas Point, S.J.*, trans. and ed. Joseph P. Donnelly (New York: Holt, Rinehart, and Winston, 1967), 23–24; and James H. Howard, "The Kenakuk Religion: An Early 19th Century Revitalization Movement 140 Years Later," *Museum News* 26 (1965): 4–5.

9. Handsome Lake of the Senecas, the Shawnee Prophet, Tenskwatawa, and other Indian religious leaders, writes Amanda Porterfield, "adapted prophetic and priestly activities from Judeo-Christian traditions as means of defending their cultures against Christian imperialism"; see "Shamanism," 729–30.

10. For the texts of two Kenekuk sermons, see Gurdon S. Hubbard, "A Kickapoo Sermon," *Illinois Monthly Magazine* 1 (October 1831): 472; and Jerome C. Berryman to secretary of the Methodist Missionary Society, April 18, 1837, *Christian Advocate and Journal*, May 26, 1837.

11. Kenekuk and his followers had begun a revitalization of their Native culture and society. Revitalization movements have long been analyzed by anthropologists and historians. For descriptions of such movements, see Fred W. Voget, "The American Indian in Transition: Reformation and Accommodation," *American Anthropologist* 58 (April 1956): 249–63; and Anthony F. C. Wallace, "Revitalization Movements," *American Anthropologist* 58 (April 1956): 264–81. Scholar Michelene E. Pesantubbee points out that while the numerous nineteenth-century Indian revitalization movements may have shared similar characteristics, such movements varied in complexity and substance and should not all be lumped under the same rubric. Each of these movements was unique; some, Pesantubbee notes, were "apocalyptic, others restorationist or millennial." See "When the Earth Shakes: The Cherokee Prophecies of 1811–12," *American Indian Quarterly* 17 (Summer 1993): 301–17.

12. William D. Smith to Reverend E. P. Swift, July 3, 1833, in *American Indian Correspondence: The Presbyterian Historical Society Collection of Missionaries' Letters, 1833–1893*, (Westport, Conn.: Greenwood Press, Inc.), microfilm box 3, vol. 1, letter 5.

13. See Jerome C. Berryman, "A Circuit-Rider's Frontier Experiences," in William W. Sweet, *Religion on the American Frontier, 1783–1840*, vol. 4, *The Methodists: A Collection of Source Materials* (Chicago: The University of Chicago Press, 1946), 538; Isaac McCoy, *History of Baptist Indian Missions* (Washington, D.C.: W. M. Morrison, 1840), 458; and Thomas

Forsyth, "The Kickapoo Prophet," in Emma Helen Blair, ed., *The Indian Tribes of the Upper Mississippi Valley and Region of the Great Lakes* (New York: Arthur H. Clark, 1911), 280–81. Flagellation was hardly a departure from Kickapoo custom; it had long been used to keep order within the traditional tribal bands.

14. Howard, "Kenakuk Religion," 22. For Kenekuk's quote, see Hubbard, "Kickapoo Sermon," 474.

15. Smith to Swift, July 3, 1833, in *Presbyterian Missionaries' Letters*; McCoy, *Baptist Indian Missions*, 457–58; and Charles Augustus Murray, *Travels in North America During the Years 1834, 1835, and 1836*... (London: Richard Bentley, 1839), 2:78–79. For the observations of the unnamed Catholic priest, see "Extract from a Manuscript Journal," *Catholic Telegraph* (Cincinnati, Ohio), July 21, 1832.

16. For a detailed description of the Kickapoo prayer sticks, see Byington's letter to the *Cincinnati Journal*, reprinted in the *Boston Recorder*, October 24, 1834.

17. See Herring, *Kenekuk*, 27–36.

18. See George J. Remsburg, "Some Notes on the Kickapoo Indians," *Philatelic West* 36 (1907): 325–26; Howard, "Kenakuk Religion," 22; Murray, *Travels in North America*, 2:78; John D. Lang and Samuel Taylor Jr., *Report of a Visit to Some of the Tribes of Indians Located West of the Mississippi River* (Providence, R.I.: Knowles and Vose, 1843), 19; and N. Sayre Harris, *Journal of a Tour in the "Indian Territory," Performed by Order of the Domestic Committee of the Board of Missions of the Protestant Episcopal Church* (New York: Daniel Dana Jr., 1844), 41.

19. The treaty was concluded October 24, 1832; see Kappler, *Indian Affairs*, 365–67. This was the only land cession treaty ever signed by Kenekuk, who believed that selling tribal land violated the laws of God. Scholars have confused the 1816 peace treaty with an 1819 land cession agreement and they state, incorrectly, that Kenekuk's signature appears on the land cession. Milo Custer was the first to make this mistake; see "Kannekuk or Keeanakuk: The Kickapoo Prophet," *Illinois State Historical Society Journal* 2 (1918): 48. Others have followed Custer's lead; see, for example, George A. Schultz, "Kennekuk, the Kickapoo Prophet," *Kansas History* 3 (1980): 38–39.

20. Over the following two decades, these Indians frequently sought help from missionaries when dealing with federal officials slow in complying with treaty provisions. See, for example, Lang and Taylor, *Report of a Visit*, 20.

21. For reports on the strife that erupted between the two groups, see Agent Richard Cummins to Commissioner of Indian Affairs Elbert Herring, September 30, 1835, and Capt. Matthew Duncan to Col. Henry Dodge, May 23, 1835, M234, Roll 300, Letters Received by the Office of Indian Affairs, Fort Leavenworth Agency, National Archives and Records Administration, Washington, D. C., (hereafter cited as LR, NARA, with appropriate agency and microfilm numbers). See also "Council with the Kickapoo," June 13, 1836, and Duncan to Gen. Henry Atkinson, June 14, 1836, M234, Roll 751, St. Louis Superintendency, LR, NARA.

22. Robert F. Berkhofer Jr. discusses the typical missionary plan for Indians in *Salvation and the Savage: An Analysis of Protestant Missions and American Indian Response, 1787–1862* (New York: Atheneum, 1976), 1–15.

23. McCoy, *Baptist Indian Missions*, 456–57.

24. For information on Livermore's life, religious philosophy, and commitment to what scholars call "biblical feminism," see Catherine A. Brekus, *Strangers and Pilgrims: Female Preaching in America, 1740–1845* (Chapel Hill: University of North Carolina Press, 1998), 1–19, 190–93, 199–200, 204; Catherine A. Brekus, "Harriet Livermore, the Pilgrim Stranger: Female Preaching and Biblical Feminism in Early-Nineteenth-Century America," *Church History* 65 (September 1996): 389–404; and Elizabeth F. Hoxie, "Harriet Livermore: 'Vixen and Devotee,'" *New England Quarterly* 18 (1945): 40–45.

25. For Lucy Barbour's description of Livermore's sermon before Congress, see *Scioto Gazette* (Chillicothe, Ohio), April 5, 1827. For Whittier's comments on his poem's depiction of Livermore, see the poet's letter to James Thomas Fields, October 3, 1865, in *The Letters of John Greenleaf Whittier*, ed. John B. Pickard, 3 vols. (Cambridge: Harvard University Press, 1975), 3:101.

26. Samuel T. Livermore, *Harriet Livermore, the "Pilgrim Stranger"* (Hartford, Conn.: Lockwood & Brainard, 1884), 123–26; Harriet Livermore, *Millennial Tidings* (Philadelphia: privately printed, 1839), 5; Harriet Livermore, *The Harp of Israel to Meet the Loud Echo in the Wilds of America* (Philadelphia: J. Rakestraw, 1835), 3–4; and Henry L. Ellsworth to Elbert Herring, August 19, 1833, M234, Roll 921, Western Superintendency, LR, NARA.

27. Ellsworth to Herring, August 19, 1833, M234, Roll 921, Western Superintendency, LR, NARA; Livermore, *Millennial Tidings*, 5; Harriet Livermore, *Addresses to the Dispersed of Judah* (Philadelphia: L. R. Bailey, 1849), 233.

28. Roux quoted in Gilbert J. Garraghan, *Catholic Beginnings in Kansas City, Missouri: An Historical Sketch* (Chicago: Loyola University Press, 1929), 49–54. On July 16, 1839, one of Kenekuk's sons, Wapautuck, became inebriated and killed a government blacksmith named Andrew Potter. He was convicted of manslaughter and sentenced to eighteen months in the St. Louis jail. He was set free in June 1841 following a presidential pardon. The prophet's other son, Pahkahkah, or John Kennekuk, later became a government-recognized chief, signing the Kickapoo treaties of 1854 and 1862. Unfortunately, Pahkahkah died of alcohol poisoning sometime in the late 1870s. For details on Wapautuck's trial, conviction, and subsequent pardon, see *Daily Missouri Republican* (St. Louis, Mo.), April 10 and June 18, 1841; *New-York Spectator*, April 28, 1841; *Boston Courier*, April 29, 1841; and Barry, *Beginning of the West*, 253–54, 375. For information on Pahkahkah's death, see Milo Custer to George Remsburg, May 25, 1908, Remsburg Papers, Collection 78, Box 4, Manuscript Division, KSHS.

29. Berryman, "Frontier Experiences," 538; and Berryman, "Missionary Intelligence," May 10, 1837, *Western Christian Advocate* (Cincinnati, Ohio), June 16, 1837.

30. Berryman, "Frontier Experiences," 523–25.

31. Thomas Johnson to the corresponding secretary of the Methodist Episcopal Church, June 16, 1835, in Sweet, *Religion on the American Frontier*, 4:516–18.

32. Edward H. Spicer presents an excellent account of Jesuit attitudes in *Cycles of Conquest: The Impact of Spain, Mexico, and the United States on the Indians of the Southwest, 1533–1960* (Tucson: University of Arizona Press, 1962), 308–24. For the Jesuit approach to mission work, see Peter A. Dorsey, "Going to School with Savages: Authorship and Authority Among the Jesuits of New France," *William and Mary Quarterly* 55 (July 1998): 399–420; Jerry E. Clark, "Jesuit Impact on Potawatomi Acculturation: A Comparison of Two Villages in the Mid-Plains," *Ethnohistory* 26 (Autumn 1979): 377–95; James P. Ronda, "The European Indians: Jesuit Civilization Planning in New France," *Church History* (1972): 388–93; and Peter Duignan, "Early Jesuit Missionaries: A Suggestion for Further Study," *American Anthropologist* 60 (1958): 725–32.

33. Quoted in Murray, *Travels in North America*, 2:80.

34. Van Quickenborne wrote about his journey to Kickapoo country in "Relation d'un voyage fait chez les tribus indiennes situées a l'ouest du Missori," September 24, 1835, *Annales de la propagation de la foi* 9 (September 1836): 99–101. Also see Gilbert J. Garraghan, "The Kickapoo Mission," *St. Louis Catholic Historical Review* 4 (1922): 27–28.

35. "Council with the Kickapoo," June 13, 1836, and Duncan to Atkinson, June 14, 1836, M234, Roll 751, St. Louis Superintendency, LR, NARA.

36. Dale Van Every describes the Seminole victory in *Disinherited: The Lost Birthright of the American Indian* (New York: Avon Books, 1967), 196–97. For Pashishi's comments, see "Council with the Kickapoo," June 13, 1836, and Duncan to Atkinson, June 14, 1836, M234, Roll 751, St. Louis Superintendency, LR, NARA.

37. Van Quickenborne to McSherry, June 29, 1836, and July 10, 1836, in Garraghan, "Kickapoo Mission," 32–33, 37–40; and "Council with the Kickapoo," June 13, 1836, M234, Roll 751, St. Louis Superintendency, LR, NARA.

38. Berryman to Cummins, October [n.d.], 1839, M234, Roll 751, St. Louis Superintendency, LR, NARA; Berryman to Cummins, August 15, 1842, *Senate Executive Document* 1, 27th Cong., 3rd sess. (serial 413), 488–89; and Berryman, "Frontier Experiences," 537–39.

39. Point is quoted in Garraghan, "Kickapoo Mission," 48–49. The letters of De Smet are in Hiram M. Chittenden and Alfred T. Richardson, eds., *Life, Letters, and Travels of Father Pierre-Jean De Smet, S.J., 1801–1873* . . . (New York: Kraus Reprint Co., 1969), 1:150–51, 162; 3:1085–86.

40. For reports on the Indians' farming, see Cummins to Superintendent of Indian Affairs David D. Mitchell, September 12, 1842, *Senate Executive Document* 1, 27th Cong., 3rd sess. (serial 413), 431; and Cummins to Mitchell, October 1, 1843, *Senate Executive Document* 1, 28th Cong. 1st sess., (serial 431), 404.

41. For reports on the Indians' work habits, see Talbott to Spencer, January 28, 1843, M234, Roll 302, Fort Leavenworth Agency, LR, NARA; McCoy, *Baptist Indian Missions*, 458;

Kinnear to Cummins, September 30, 1838, M234, Roll 301, Fort Leavenworth Agency, LR, NARA; Mason to Mason, December 26, 1849, M234, Roll 303, Fort Leavenworth Agency, LR, NARA; Cummins to Clark, January 31 and May 16, 1838, and Cummins to Harris, September 25, 1838, M234, Roll 301, Fort Leavenworth Agency, LR, NARA.

42. For reports on smallpox in Indian country, see Agent John R. Chenault to Commissioner of Indian Affairs Luke Lea, September 17, 1851, and Agent William P. Richardson to Mitchell, September 26, 1851, *Senate Executive Document* 3, 32nd Cong., 1st sess. (ser. 613), 328–29, 361; and Chenault to Lea, October 3, 1852, *Senate Executive Document* 1, 32nd Cong., 2nd sess. (ser. 658), 381.

43. Richardson to Mitchell, September 30, 1852, *Senate Executive Document* 1, 32nd Cong., 2nd sess. (ser. 658), 361.

44. A small but hearty group of adherents still meets for services at the Kennekuk Church, located just west of Horton, Kansas.

4

MASKING AND EFFIGY IN THE NORTHEASTERN WOODLANDS

❧

TROY R. JOHNSON

T HE TRADITION OF MASKING has historically been widespread among Native American tribes in North America and has great cultural significance in
the lives and histories of these peoples. Masks and effigies connected people to the
spiritual world, and specialized individuals handled and wore or used the sacred
material items. These tribes included the Mixtec of Mesoamerica, who created jade
masks that date as early as 1350–1300 BC; the driftwood and walrus ivory masks
of the Alaskan Inuit; and the masks of the Northwest coast Natives and Kwakiutl
Hamatsa dancers. These double and triple masks opened and closed to reveal mythical characters in the Northwest religious cosmology, and depict a wide and illustri-
ous spectrum of spirit, human, and land and sea creatures.

Mask forms have a variety of meanings to Native people. Masks depicted human
ancestors, supernatural spirits, visions revealed in dreams, healing forces, and effigies
that the person to whom the mask was revealed was commanded to re-create and imitate for the remainder of their lives. In some societies, such as the Iroquois, masks were
considered to be living forces, and special people of power treated them with great
care, including the offering of tobacco, lest the mask owner become seriously ill. Iroquois masks are not designed to disguise the identity of the wearer. In fact, the wearer
is of no importance when compared to the *orenda*, or power, that is represented and
present in the mask.[1] Traditional masks had a variety of sizes, shapes, and forms. They
were made from carved wood or cornhusks. Other types of materials were used to
decorate the masks, such as human or horsehair, ribbon, yarn, tobacco ties, stones,
animal teeth, brass, tin, and semiprecious stones used to replicate eyes. Masks were
used to tell stories, re-create tribal histories, and attract supernatural power forms and
forces; to frighten, amuse, instruct, instill proper behavior, and admonish those who

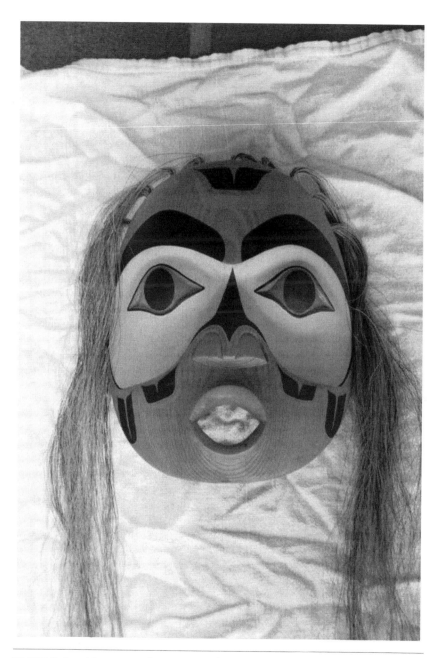

FIGURE 4.1. Master artist D. Dannis made this Tlingit Shaman Speaker mask. Northwest Coastal people conduct ceremony and storytelling events using masking. Masks represent different characters known in stories, songs, and creation narratives. Editor's collection and photograph.

misbehaved; and, among the Northeast woodland tribes, for medicinal purposes such as healing.

The Northeast woodlands of the United States provide perhaps the quintessential example of masking and effigy in North America, rivaled only by that of the Haida and Kwakwqkq'wakw (formerly Kwaikutl) of the Northwest coast. It is in the Northeast woodlands, however, where we see the evolution of the curative or medicine societies with their rich display of masks and their rich association with Native cosmology. If we are to understand the sacredness of masks, masking, healing, and Native religion, we must first understand the people and their relationship with nature and the universe. The Native religious cosmology is far different than anything encountered in the non-Native mind, and the failure to understand the existence of a sophisticated cosmology has caused cultural misunderstanding, warfare, and the death of millions of Native people. Therefore, if we are to arrive at an understanding of just one piece of this cosmology, we must address the whole. To understand the Native cosmology, it is perhaps easiest to begin with the simplest form and then add the layers that are unseen but permeate and make whole the reality. The easiest way is to begin with the concept of the sacred hoop, or Mother Earth. If one were to envision in the mind's eye an unbroken circular hoop, one would have a beginning point. With this simplistic hoop in mind, transform the hoop into the cosmology of passage of time in a continuum, moving around the hoop endlessly.

For the non-Indian world, the passage of time is linear, moving from a point of creation, such as the Big Bang theory, to some point in the future when the linear passage is completed and the world is destroyed or mankind itself destroys the world and stops the linear clock. The passage of time is not necessarily tied directly to the other concepts of life except perhaps as a way to categorize, make reference to, or create a chronological record of important events and how they are viewed. An example might be the chronological concept of history. In the non-Indian world, history is studied in a direct chronological timeline with specific markers. One popular way that this is done is by dating the linear passage of time by connecting history with the various wars that have taken place. Thus one can trace the passage of time by its connection to the American Revolution, the War of 1812, the Mexican-American War, the Civil War, World War I, World War II, and up to the conflict taking place in the Middle East at the present time. Using the linear passage of time, one can study any particular subject such as culture, religion, forms of government, the recording of history (writing), art, music, or the development of medicine without reference to the other attributes of humanity. The studies are perhaps endless, but one does not have to understand the whole in order to study the part.

In the Native world, everything is interconnected, and the sacred hoop connects together all things. First, and of intrinsic importance, is that the hoop is a continuum of the passage of time. There is no beginning or ending as the Western world under-stands the concept. Time simply continues unabated. This is not to imply that Native people believe in reincarnation, even though some do; it is the concept that there was no one beginning and there is no definitive end. The sacred hoop, then, is the meta-physical concept around which all else in the Native world is intertwined. Rather than it being possible to take a particular concept out of the Native cosmology and understand it, one must understand the whole. Woven around and intertwined with all else are the same concepts I have mentioned above for the non-Indian world (the attributes of humanity such as culture, religion, forms of government, art, music, lan-guage, etc.). What is absolutely necessary to understand, however, is that these are interconnected and cannot be studied in a linear way. They cannot be removed from within themselves. All things are part of the sacred hoop, and therefore all things are sacred. For the Native person, the religious experience begins when they arise in the morning and progresses through their day, when they go to sleep, and as they sleep. Their religion is embedded within the cosmology and within themselves. It is part of the sacred hoop and is intertwined with the rest of the person's life. Thus it is so that one person's life affects the whole. We can see this in the founding principles of the major masking group in the Northeast woodlands—the Iroquois.

The Iroquois are not a tribe but rather a league or confederation consisting of a number of separate but independent tribes. Although there were a number of tribes in the Northeast woodlands, there were six competing nations in what we see today as New York State—the Huron, Mohawk, Oneida, Onondaga, Cayuga, and Seneca Nations. The tribes were traditional enemies and competed over access to fur-bearing animals that fueled the trade between Indian tribes, the French, the Dutch, and the English. The member nations of the Iroquois League controlled more than one mil-lion square miles of fur trapping territory from the Atlantic Ocean west past the Great Lakes, and from Canada south to approximately the Jamestown settlement in the present-day state of Virginia. Warfare and death were common occurrences as the six tribes vied for access to additional trapping areas that were often in the traditional territory of one of the other tribes. A deeply imbedded rule of blood feud or death vendetta resulted in a cycle of retaliation that was so destructive that it ultimately forced the Huron north of the Great Lakes, where they developed an extensive fur-trapping empire of their own. In 1570, the League of the Iroquois was formed from the five remaining tribes. The Tuscarora tribe that was located far to the south was decimated in raids by the Iroquois and was forced to join in 1772. At that point, the league became known as the Six Nations or, more correctly, the Haudenosaunee, or People of the Longhouse.

The creation of the Haudenosaunee is tied directly to the religious cosmology of the Six Nations people and is imbedded in the historical narrative of Deganawida and

Hiawatha. Deganawida was most likely an Onondaga even though some say he was a Cayuga. Deganawida was a spiritual person who was in the possession and control of rituals that removed grief and eased troubled minds. Hiawatha met Deganawida while mourning the death of his daughter Mnihaha. Deganawida spoke words of condolence, and Hiawatha's sorrow was relieved.[2] From the removal of Hiawatha's mourning came Deganawida's message to the five nations that were at war with one another. Deganawida's message included an admonition to stop the blood feud and to join together in a peaceful confederation. "When men accept it," Deganawida said of his message, "they will stop killing, and bloodshed will cease from the land." Hiawatha and Deganawida spread the good news to the Five Nations, and the Great League of Peace of the Haudenosaunee was founded.[3]

The origin of the masking tradition of the Haudenosaunee lies in the sacred truths of creation of the Five Nations and in the ecosystem in which the Creator placed them at the time of their creation. As with most Native oral histories, there is no "universal" that is the only narrative or necessarily the true narrative. This is true among the member nations of the Haudenosaunee. There are some twenty-six versions of the creation of the original Five Nations. The origin of the False Face masks is included in most all of the versions in some form, and a representative text is provided here in a condensed version. In the beginning of time, the world was divided into a sky world and the earth below. The sky world was inhabited by humans and was a world of plenty. Game abounded, as did fish and birds. The agricultural fields were rich with corn and vegetables. People harbored no grudges or ill feelings toward one another. No one went hungry or thirsty, and there was no illness. The earth below was covered by water, with no human life.

At an undisclosed point in time, in the sky world a pregnant woman asked her husband to bring her food that could only be found on the root of a great tree that stood in the middle of the sky world. The Creator had instructed the people that no one was to touch the tree. The husband, wishing to make his wife happy, scraped away soil from the root of the tree in order to gain access to that particular food. He could now see down into the lower world. The man invited his wife to look into the underworld, at which time she fell through the hole. As she fell, she grasped plants to stop her fall. Included were the strawberry and tobacco plants. As she fell toward the earth, a flock of loons flew up to slow her descent and helped transport the woman as she fell. A hurried conference took place on the earth world, and it was decided that the woman should be placed on the back of the great sea turtle. At the same time, the beavers began diving deep into the water, bringing up soil that they placed on the back of the turtle. With the assistance of the loons, the woman landed softly on the back of the great sea turtle and began planting bits of roots and plants she had brought from the sky world.

The soil then began to expand, ultimately creating the earth where humans would live. Sky Woman set out to build a home and settled into her new surroundings. Soon Sky Woman gave birth to a daughter who herself became pregnant in a supernatural way. The father is not identified in all of the creation stories but in some versions is identified as the "West Wind." The father placed two arrows on the chest of Sky Woman's daughter, and she delivered twin boys. While in the womb, one of the boys was peaceful while the other was impatient to leave the womb. A quarrel took place that resulted in one twin being born in the normal fashion and the other bursting out from beneath his mother's left armpit, resulting in her death. The twins buried their mother, who became Corn Mother, source of corn, beans, and squash—the Three Sisters of the Iroquois. Throughout their early life, the twins competed as they created the animals and plants. They clearly represented different ways of living: good versus evil, light versus dark, peace versus warfare. The right-handed twin created the light, calm weather, beautiful hills, plants, and gentle animals. The left-handed twin created darkness, storms, thorns, boulders, arid soil, cactus, and predator animals.

Ultimately the twins faced off in a duel over power. The evil twin wanted to rule the earth and create hardship for the people. The peaceful twin wanted to promote peace and harmony among all people. The evil twin challenged the peaceful twin to a duel that would decide who was the most powerful and who would rule the world. The twins sat down facing the east with their backs to the west. The challenge was for each twin to demonstrate his power by moving a mountain that was to the west of them. The left-handed twin sang, chanted, and called upon all of his power to draw the mountain closer. When he had completed his efforts, he looked and the mountain had not moved. The right-handed twin now took his turn. He sang, chanted, and called upon all of his power to draw the mountain closer. Unbeknown to the twins, the mountain moved up close behind them. The left-handed twin, now anxious because of his failure to move the mountain, turned around quickly and hit his face on the mountain. As a result, his nose was broken and bent, his mouth was distorted, and his eyes bulged out. The right-handed twin had won the contest. The penalty for the left-handed twin was that he had to cease his evil ways and to use his powers as a healer and a sacred medicine person. The result was the founding of the False Face society of the Iroquois. The masks of the False Face represent the distorted face of the evil twin and are assigned to treat the ill and comfort the dying, helping them transition to the spirit world.[4]

A second belief is that false faces or "flying heads" have been present in Iroquoia since time immemorial. A Tonawanda Seneca chief, Barber Black, recalled that this is closely associated with the ecosystem of the land.[5] Prior to European contact, the land was covered by forests of deciduous and coniferous trees, including oak, pine, hickory, spruce, birch, beech, maple, hickory, ash, and basswood. It was from these trees that the Iroquois constructed houses, containers, canoes, bows and arrows, and ritual and subsistence equipment. The forests were also home to much of the game hunted by the Native peoples: bear, wolf, fox, moose, deer, and forest buffalo. These were the forests that Europeans called the forbidding wilderness and the Iroquois called home. At some unidentified time past, an Iroquois man was hunting game when he saw a strange face peering at him from behind a tree. Chief Black states that this was a Ga-go-sa, or False Face. The False Face spoke to the hunter, telling him, "I will help you during your lifetime if you put the tobacco on the fire and speak, asking for my help." The False Face then instructed the man to "make white corn-meal mush and use it whenever someone is sick."[6] He told the man that if the people would make a mask similar to his and give him offerings of tobacco and corn mush, "They too would have the power to cure disease by blowing of hot ashes."[7] A variation on this origin story focuses on a good hunter and his encounter with the False Face while in the dark forest. The hunter is usually a person who is obliged to overcome adversity in his life. The hunter goes into the forest, where he is confronted by a False Face that is described as "having only faces—no bodies or limbs—and anyone who sees them could become paralyzed."[8] Another group of masked supernatural spirits are the Husk Faces (Gajesa), or Bushy Heads. The spirits are earthbound and are believed to have taught the Iroquois the skills of agriculture and hunting. The Seneca believe that the Bushy Heads live on the opposite side of the earth in great canyons where they perfected the creation of the Three Sisters (corn, beans, and squash) that provide the major food groups for the Haudenosaunee. Unlike the False Faces, however, the Husk Faces or Bushy Heads cannot speak and require a speaker.[9]

False Face masks are most commonly carved from a live basswood tree, but other wood such as white pine, maple, poplar, and willow may be used in the absence of access to basswood. In most instances, the person who will wear the mask is the carver. If an individual is unable to carve, then he may hire a False Face society member to carve for him. The design for each mask is individualistic to the person who will wear it. The design for the mask is usually given to that person in a dream or vision. Once the face is dreamed or envisioned, the person must carve the mask, or have it carved, or he will become severely ill. The most common occurrence is that a tribal male member of one of the Iroquois tribes will become ill. During the illness, he will have a vision in which a False Face appears to him and he is instructed to call for the False Face healing society to perform a curative ceremony. Once the person is healed, he becomes a member of the False Face society and must carve the mask he saw in his vision.

The carving of the mask begins with the search for the basswood tree. The most common practice is for the carver to request the assistance of members of the False

Face society or men who are well respected in the tribe for their strict moral practices. As a group they go into the forest to areas that are known to house basswood trees, seeking a mature tree with a large carving area. Once a suitable tree is located, a fire is built at the base of the trunk. Prayers are offered to the tree and to the False Face spirits. The carver then offers a tobacco offering to the tree for the cutting and carving that is about to take place. The carving then begins in the living tree while it is standing. First, the mask is roughed out on the surface of the tree. A notch is made above the area that will become the mask and a notch is made below that area. This is to keep the mask from splitting during carving and to keep the tree from dying. Some carvers believe that if the tree remains alive, the mask will take on the power imbedded in the tree itself.[10] During all of this time, pinches of tobacco are being thrown into the fire as an offering. Much of the actual carving of the mask occurs while it is still attached to the tree. Once the main features of the mask are developed, the mask is removed as a block of wood from the living tree, taken home, and completed. As the mask is carved, it is rubbed with sunflower oil to appease the spiritual power of the mask, and tobacco offerings are made to ensure the spiritual connection between the carver and the spirit world. The final accoutrements added are the eyes and horsehair that has been treated with deer brains.[11] The rubbing of sunflower oil and offering of tobacco will be a life-long requirement to ensure that no harm comes to the mask or mask owner. Masks, once completed, are treated as if they were alive. They are prayed to, talked to, and informed when they are going to be moved, used, or perhaps traded. Masks are painted red if the tree from which they are cut was selected in the morning and black if the tree was selected in the afternoon or night. Masks are most frequently stored in a trunk or box designed specifically for that purpose. A turtle-shell rattle is placed in the box with the mask, along with ties of tobacco. The mask itself is wrapped in a cloth and placed facedown. If a mask is hung, it must be hung with the face to the wall or it must be covered. Tobacco offerings must be made to masks on an ongoing basis or it is believed that the offended mask can cause illness or trouble. The tobacco offering is generally contained in tiny cloth pouches (ties) that are attached to the mask. Miniature masks that are similar in design to the larger mask are common among the False Face society. These masks are one to two inches in height and represent the same spirit of the original. They are often attached to the hair of the larger mask and "ride along," or are kept in the home of the mask owner as personal guardians. Among the Seneca, the miniatures are referred to as "the child" of the larger mask.[12]

As previously mentioned, the individual design of the mask is given to the carver in a dream or vision and may take many shapes. In his book *Iroquois False-Face Masks*, Robert Ritzenthaler states, "The two basic types of wooden masks are the crooked-mouthed, broken-nosed, heavily wrinkled style that represent the first False-faces . . . and the Common faces that are both nameless and varied in terms of facial treatments."[13]

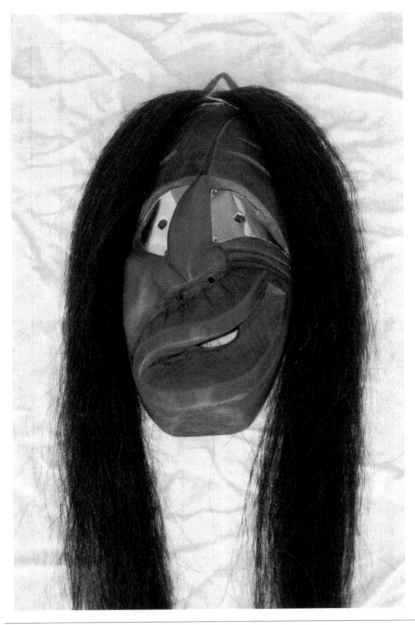

FIGURE 4.2. Broken Nose is the grandfather of the False Faces of Iroquoian people. On-ondaga artist Gowahen'da.we, She Has Been Given a Wager, carved this mask from pine. She is a member of the Wolf clan. Mask wearers are healers, helping others seek harmony and health. Only members of the Iroquoian Nations wear False Face masks. Others should not wear the masks. Editor's collection and photograph.

William Fenton is much more definitive and, using the mouth of the mask as the most variable feature, identifies twelve mask types. The most striking feature of the mask is the mouth and nose. The mouth is almost universally crooked or twisted, and the masks have deep-set eyes made more dramatic by arched brows, metal sconces, and deep wrinkles. This may or may not be accompanied by a crooked or broken nose. These features relate directly to the battle over power between the right- and left-handed twins. As the left-handed twin turned to check the location of the mountain, he smacked his face into the mountain, which had been moved directly behind him and distorted his face. One corner of the mouth is generally pulled up or forced down; the nose is pushed sideways. This is generally accompanied by heavy wrinkling of the facial features. Another style of face is recognizable by distended, rather than crooked, lips. The mouth is often open; the lips are enlarged and pulled forward. The eyes on these masks are generally large, giving the mask a startled expression that would also reflect the right- and left-handed power struggle.

The Seneca have a variation of the straight-lipped face whereby the lower lip is larger and extended. These faces, called spoon-lipped masks, represent a Seneca belief that the left-handed twin is forced to officiate at False Face healing ceremonies as doorkeeper in the round dance and as impersonator of wind and disease spirits.[14] Another variation of the "mouth theme" is the hanging-mouth mask found among the Onondaga. On this mask, the corners of the mouth are turned down and hanging.[15] A number of masks are classified as protruding-tongue masks. The tongue generally protrudes from the center of the distorted or straight lips and hangs downward. This mask is found most generally among the Onondaga people and is meant to demonstrate the pain of the left-handed twin as his face struck the mountain behind him. Other types of masks include the smiling mask, the whistling mask, the divided mask, the longnose mask, the horned nose mask, the animal mask, the pig mask, and the blind mask. The smiling mask features thick puckered lips, leering eyes, puffy cheeks, and wrinkled and distorted skin associated with the twins' power struggle. The smiling mask is often described as the "beggar mask" or "dancing beggar mask" of the Seneca, and the Onondaga people likely used it in curing ceremonies.[16]

Fenton describes the whistling mask also as having a puckered mouth and wrinkled skin. The mask is also called the "blowing spirit mask" or the Whistling God.[17] As mentioned earlier, False Face masks are painted either red or black, depending upon what time of day the tree from which they were carved was found. One exception to this is the divided mask, or "his body is split in half." Half of the mask is painted red and half black. The mask is clearly associated with the left- and right-handed twins' battle for power and is most common among the Cayuga and Onondaga tribes.[18] The Haudenosaunee probably used the longnose or thin-nose mask as a tool to frighten unruly children. Also known as *hadondes*, the mask represented a cannibal spirit or bogeyman-type entity that allegedly carried off truculent or ill-behaved children in his basket. The longnose mask was originally made from buckskin but joined the basswood carving tradition at some undisclosed time.[19] The horned mask is perhaps the most recent of the False Face masks to be added to the Iroquois pantheon. Jesse Cornplanter, a Seneca mask carver from the Tonawanda reservations, states that the mask "was derived as recently as 1900. . . . Since that time, masks of this character have acquired power and usurped the role formerly reserved for the so-called 'doctor' masks. Some of these horned masks were possibly intended as caricatures of the missionaries' versions of the devil."[20]

The Husk Face (also known as Ga-go-sa, Gagohsa, or Gajesa) masks, also known as the Bushy Heads, are a second type of common mask found in the Iroquois Confederacy. These masks were traditionally made by the Iroquois women and worn by the men. The masks were most commonly made from coils of braided cornhusks sewn together. Fenton states that the Husk Face masks "look like door mats, the only difference being that the masks have holes for the eyes and mouth."[21] A ragged maize fringe of hair was usually added to complete the mask. The origin of the Bushy Heads is not connected with the right- and left-handed twins tradition but represents a parallel class of earth-bound supernatural beings that formed a pact with the Indians of the Southeastern woodlands and taught them the arts of hunting and agriculture. The Bushy Heads also participate in False Face healing ceremonies in the longhouse. They were often called upon to participate in the actual healing, to offer gifts of tobacco, or to serve as guards stationed outside the longhouse to prevent interruption of the ceremony. Today, craftswomen of the Onondaga Nation continue to make Husk Face masks for ritual purposes, but they have also begun to produce cornhusk dolls of mothers and children for exhibition and sale, intended primarily for the amusement of children.[22]

The introduction of the pig-head mask into the Iroquois pantheon represented a change in the availability of the bear as the principal society feast food at the medicine men's healing ceremonies among the Seneca and the Cayuga. The Cayuga believed the *orenda* residing in the pig mask to have extraordinary power and the ability to effect miraculous cures when the mask was worn by one of the False Face society members.[23] Frank Speck records that the pig-head mask was used to cure those who had been injured "by violence, falls, accidents, or wounds. . . . The members of the Medicine Men's healing society perform over the patient by singing the songs of the different animals in a room or apartment where they are secreted with the patient."[24] No outsiders were permitted to view the ceremony, and there were restrictions regarding the cooking of food, the use of salt, and the requirement that a cornmeal mush be served. The room where the healing was to take place was kept as dark as possible, and tobacco was burned as an offering. One of the most important parts of this healing ritual was the "passing around among the members present a cooked pig's head."[25] The pig's head was eaten with no utensils being used. Speck also reports that the secrecy of the society served as a shield against full disclosure of the healing ceremony. It is believed that originally a bear's head had been passed around and consumed but that had been replaced by the pig's head at some unspecified time.[26] Pig face mask wearers have also been reported as doorkeepers in the Delaware skin-beating dance and as having served as longhouse doorkeepers among the Iroquois midwinter festival to be discussed later.[27]

Three extant Cayuga pig masks still exist. They were carved from a maple or elm tree in the facial likeness of a common pig. One mask has a goat's hair, another has a horse's tail or mane, and the third has a tuft of curly wool. The upper portions of the masks are painted black while the forehead, face, and snout are painted white. Two of the masks have brass or tin plates inset as eyes while the third lacks eyes. All three of the pig masks have teeth set into the mouth made either of wood or actual teeth.[28]

At this point it is important to place the False Face, the Husk or Bushy Heads, and other masking traditions to be discussed in the context of the Native American cosmology mentioned at the beginning of this chapter—specifically that the practice of healing, spirituality, and the daily life of the people cannot be separated. They are intertwined and inseparable. Spirituality and healing, spirituality and agriculture, spirituality and life make up the essence of the existence of the Longhouse People. Of particular importance to the Iroquois (as with many other Native people) was the vision or dream. Simply stated, to ignore or oppose a message or vision sent from the spirit world was to court almost-certain illness, disaster, and possibly madness. If the proper ceremonies and instructions given in the dream were carried out, dreams could help cure disease and disorders of the mind, restore balance within the community, and meet needs and desires. The dream was seen as a direct interaction with the spirit power, or *orenda*—a force to be reckoned with—and as a mechanism for fulfilling the secret longings of the soul.

Perhaps the most commonly known appearance of False Faces have been at midwinter ceremonies or healing ceremonies. It is in this context then that we must explore the founding of the False Face society, the function of the society, and membership in the society. Following the power struggle between the left-handed and right-handed twins, the left-handed twin abandoned his evil ways and became a healer and a medicine person. His responsibility was to develop a healing society whose members would have curative power and would wear carved wooden masks with distorted faces such as his. Membership in the society would be restricted to those healed by the left-handed twin, and participation in the rites of the society became limited to its members. The existence of the False Face society was known by the various tribes of the Iroquois League, but the people generally did not know the membership of the secret society.

The secrecy of the society's membership is practiced by some tribes but not by others. William Fenton, in his book *The False Faces of the Iroquois*, states that the society's "membership is known to most persons in the community."[29] The Seneca believed that "the society was to be a most secret one and only for a qualified numbers ... the Company was to have no outward sign and members were to recognize one another only by having sat together in a ceremony."[30] Becoming a member of the False Face society was the result of contact with the spirit world through a dream or vision. When a member of the Iroquois League became sick with an illness that came within the range of powers of the society and dreamed or had a vision in which he saw a false face, this was interpreted to mean that the healing was to be done by a member of that society. The sick individual or a relative immediately contacted a woman of the False Face society and asked that a healing ceremony be performed. Preparations were then begun for the offering of tobacco and a feast. The longhouse was cleared of everyone except the sick individual. Deerskins were used to cover all windows and doors. Iroquois dimly lit the longhouse with three smoke holes placed above the living areas. A fire was started in a fire pit, and the sick person sat and waited. Once the longhouse was properly prepared, the False Faces entered single file in a line that curved and moved like a giant snake, weaving back and forth. Each member wore a False Face mask that he had most likely carved himself, wore tattered blankets draped over his shoulders, and carried turtle-shell rattles that were hundreds of years old. The healing ceremony could now begin.

The first thing that occurred was for a member of the False Face society to stir the ashes in the fire that had been prepared. Members of the False Face society had the ability to handle hot ashes without being burned. Hot ashes were taken from the fire by hand and then sprinkled over the patient until the head and hair were covered. It was not uncommon for a member of the Bushy Heads to also participate in the placement of ashes. As some members of the society sprinkled the ashes, others took hands full of hot ashes and blew them onto or over the part of the body where the particular illness was manifest. During all of this time, the other False Face members danced, sang False Face healing songs, and shook their turtle-shell rattles, which themselves were imbued with great *orenda*. The patient was then invited to join with the False Face members in a dance, after which the ceremony inside of the longhouse was completed. The celebration, however, was carried outside and to other longhouses, where private feasting continued.[31] The cured person now became a member of the False Face society. It was now his responsibility to acquire an appropriate mask. While Robert Ritzenthaler states that this could be done through inheritance, individuals often carved masks themselves or hired someone to carve it for them.[32] The design of the mask generally came to the new society member in a dream or vision. In some instances, the image might not have been clear, and a seer may have been called upon to interpret the dream. Once the design had been determined, then the new society member selected an appropriate tree and began the carving process described earlier in this chapter. Ritzenthaler also informs us that some individuals may have commissioned a carver to "duplicate or simulate a certain mask in the community," and that "it is not a prerequisite of society membership to own a mask and there are many members at Grand River [Ottawa] without them; indeed, the borrowing of masks is very common."[33]

A turtle-shell rattle completes the False Face regalia. The typical rattle is made from the shell of the mud turtle (but sometimes a snapping turtle). The turtles are generally obtained in the late spring before the summer heat damages the shell. The rattle maker (often the same person who carves the mask) cuts off the turtle's tail, severs the jugular vein, and hangs the shell to drain. After a period of time, the carver cleans the inside of the shell and sews up the apertures. He then inserts three hickory splints in the sternum and lateral splints in the back of the shell. Cherry pits, pebbles, or kernels of corn are inserted into the shell to provide the necessary rattling sound. The artisan next binds the splints to the neck with basswood fiber using rawhide, basswood fiber, or inner elm bark. Once completed, the rattle is sealed and laced in the ashes at a healing ceremony and is thus purified and becomes permeated with *orenda*.[34]

The second most commonly known appearance of False Faces occurred during the midwinter ceremony. Each of the individual tribes within the Iroquois League celebrated midwinter in its own way, and it is impossible to present a description of each of these in this chapter. To complicate matters even further, there are differing versions of the telling of the midwinter ceremony within each tribe. Elisabeth Tooker, in her book *The Iroquois Ceremonial of Midwinter*, provides four historical versions of the Seneca midwinter ceremony, beginning with the ceremonial at the Cornplanter settlement of the Seneca Nation, near the Allegheny River in present-day New York (ca. 1799), and concluding with changes introduced into the midwinter ceremonial during the nineteenth and twentieth centuries.[35] The midwinter ceremonial begins at dawn on the fifth day of the first or second new moon following the winter solstice. Tooker's description of the midwinter ceremonial celebrated at Squakie Hill in the Genesee Valley, near present-day Mt. Morris, New York, in 1816 and 1819 is paraphrased below as an example of one such ceremony.[36] The ceremonial began on the morning of February 7 with the sacrificing of a white dog. The dog, which was unblemished, was brought to the council house and strangled. Particular care was taken to ensure that no bones were broken or any blood was shed. The dog was then hanged on a post. The body was striped with red paint, and five strings of purple beads were fastened about the neck, as was a stem of hedgehog quills. Various brightly colored feathers and red and yellow ribbons were attached to the dog's legs. A tobacco offering was placed below the now-sacred body. The remainder of the day was spent in speeches and dream-telling. Near nightfall, two tribal members appeared wearing bearskins. Long braids of corn husks adorned their ankles and heads. These individuals, accompanied by singing tribal members, visited each longhouse in the village, where they pounded the benches inside and the sides of the house to drive out any evil spirit dwellers. Their arrival at the longhouses announced the feast of dreams that marked the new year.

The second day's events began with the arrival of five tribal members who appeared with long wooden shovels and began to scatter fire and ashes until the council house was filled with dust and smoke. Accompanied by personal chants, the Indians repeated the same ritual at each longhouse several times during the day. The False Faces made their first appearance of the midwinter ceremony at dusk on the second day. The participation of the False Faces increased with each following day, culminating with the appearance of the Husk Faces on the evening of the sixth day. The largest gathering of False Faces actually occurred at a special celebration for the False Faces that took place on the weekend after the midwinter ceremony. At that time, all masks were assembled, and those masks not worn were carried and bound together by men in a procession that included the keeper of the False Faces.[37]

The third day of the ceremony was marked by speeches, reciting of dreams, and personal chants, and at about noon, participants repeated the fire shoveling with increased vigor. Once that was completed, the people changed their clothing, adorned their heads with feathers, and painted their faces. Women wearing calico short gowns and blue broadcloth petticoats, ornamented with beadwork and a profusion of silver brooches, joined with the dancers. The dancing began at the council house and was repeated at every longhouse during the day. The bowl game was played inside all of the longhouses. This gambling game consisted of a wooden bowl decorated with four clan symbols—the bear, wolf, turtle, and deer. Six nuts were colored on one side and placed into the bowl. The bowl was struck, and if all six nuts came up the same color, the player scored and took another turn. The first player to reach ten points won the game.

On the fourth day of the ceremony, a Husk Face entered the longhouse and selected one man to go with him outside. There he taught the man a speech and brought him back into the longhouse to repeat it. The speech, which was repeated to an old woman, the leader of the Husk Faces, generally instructed the women to go to a specific location where they were to plant squash, corn, and beans. Other women were instructed to remain home to care for the children. The Husk Face then requested to participate in a series of social dances in the longhouse, and that request was always granted. Following the social dances, tobacco was collected and taken to participants outside of the longhouse.[38] In the evening of the fourth day, a party of dancers visited each of the longhouses. They would enter into the longhouse, soon to be followed by a False Face draped in a bearskin. The dancers acted as if afraid and escaped to the next longhouse, where the ritual was repeated.

The next day began with the appearance of the False Faces at each of the longhouses, where they approached every person, expecting a gift. Only small gifts were expected—an apple, plug of tobacco, or a few coins. Tribal members dressed as bears followed the False Faces, who went from house to house pretending to destroy furniture and other possessions. Other tribal members now appeared carrying guns and drove the bears from the village. On the evening of the fifth day, three tribal men appeared in deerskins and rags, one of who impersonated the evil twin. He was chased from longhouse to longhouse, where he would fall down, roll on the ground and into the fire pit, and then dig out the ashes and scatter them about the house. The day closed in the council house with community dancing.

The sixth day began with the appearance of the False Face beggars and other False Faces arriving at the council house, where they entertained the spectators with their dancing. An aged female brought participants cornmeal mush and provided a noon meal for everyone in attendance. In the afternoon, the community was encouraged to participate in the dances. In the early afternoon of the sixth day, preparations began for the burning of the white dog. This was a respectful and solemn sacrifice (no longer practiced) that represented a thanksgiving for the new crops. The dog was taken down from the post where he had been hung on the first day and laid upon a pile of dry wood. More wood was then placed around and over the dog. The mood within the council house was now somber and respectful. A tribal elder lit the fire and, as it burned, he walked around the pyre in a circle, talking to the spirit of the dog. When the speaking was completed, everyone left the council house and adjourned for a general feast that consisted of bread, squash, corn, beans, pumpkins, and venison. The remainder of the evening was filled with singing and dancing, in which everyone participated. The formal ritual part of the midwinter ceremony ended.

The seventh and last day of the midwinter ceremony began with the gathering together of all the members of the tribe in a ceremonial house and the singing of the Ah-do-weh.[39] This was a song of celebration sung in an extemporized style. The participants sat against the walls in an unbroken line, each holding a rattle that emitted different tones according to the conches placed inside them and the holes bored in them.[40] Each participant was afforded the opportunity to sing an Ah-do-weh and invited the other tribal members to join in. The singing, which might go on for hours, was followed by the peach-stone game that marked the end of the midwinter ceremony. The peach-stone game symbolized the game played by the right- and left-handed twins as they competed at the creation of the earth. The game was one of chance, much like dice or flipping a coin.[41] Tooker informs the reader that the seventh day was spent mostly in petty gambling and feats of strength.[42] The midwinter ceremonial was then complete.

The practice of masking still continues in the twenty-first century among member tribes of the Iroquois League, and they remain highly connected to the sacred. Every aspect of the creation, use, and performance of the masks remain tied to spiritual power. Members of the False Face and other medicine societies call on the spirits to help individuals and groups of people, asking for power to be transferred from the other world to people on earth. Of course, much has changed over time, but the connection between the masks and the Iroquois in their religious cosmology remains the same. It remains strong and highly significant. In the course of the creation of the Smithsonian's National Museum of the American Indian, representatives of the Haudenosaunee traveled to Maryland to bless and recover the museum's collection of False Face masks. The museum handed them over because of the Native realization of their sacred place within the spiritual world of the Iroquois. The Iroquois consider it sacrilege to sell, publicly display, or mimic a sacred False Face mask, and have petitioned numerous museums to remove these masks from their exhibits and to return them to the tribes. This is a reciprocal responsibility. Throughout Indian Country, people recognize and respect the sacred and the cosmology of other nations. In order to live in harmony, balance, and peace, Native Americans believe they must act toward and handle masks in proper ways, as taught through ancient songs and stories about the arrival of the first masks.

NOTES

1. Dean R. Snow, *The Iroquois* (Cambridge: Blackwell Press, 1994), 105.
2. Daniel K. Richter and James H. Merrell, *Beyond the Covenant Chain: The Iroquois and Their Neighbors in Indian North America, 1600–1800* (New York: Syracuse University Press, 1987), 15–17.
3. Ibid., 17.
4. This creation story is taken from a number of sources, including Demus Elm and Harvey Antone, *The Oneida Creation Story* (Lincoln: University of Nebraska Press, 2000), 11–26; and William N. Fenton, *The False Faces of the Iroquois* (Norman: University of Oklahoma Press, 1987), 95–106. The Oneida creation story contains comparative versions from various sources.
5. Quoted in Fenton, *False Faces*, 137.
6. Ibid., 121–22.
7. Snow, *Iroquois*, 104.
8. Robert Ritzenthaler, *Iroquois False-Face Masks* (Milwaukee: Milwaukee Public Museum, 1969), 14–15.
9. Fenton, *False Faces*, 383.
10. Ibid.
11. Ibid.
12. Fenton, *False Faces*, 60; Ritzenthaler, *Iroquois False-Face Masks*, 19–20.
13. Ritzenthaler, *Iroquois False-Face Masks*, 23.

14. Gertrude P. Kurath, *Iroquois Music and Dance: Ceremonial Arts of Two Seneca Longhouses* (New York: Courier Dover Publications, 2007), 14.

15. Harold Blau, "Function and the False Faces: A Classification of Onondaga Masked Rituals and Themes," *The Journal of American Folklore* 79 (October–December 1966): 572.

16. Arthur C. Parker, "Secret Medicine Societies of the Seneca," *American Anthropologist* 11 (April–June 1909): 167.

17. Fenton, *False Faces*, 35.

18. Elisabeth Tooker, ed., *An Iroquois Source Book*, vol. 3, *Medicine Society Rituals* (New York: Garland Publishing, 1986), 226–27.

19. "A Haudenosaunee Pantheon," accessed on April 20, 2008, http://web.raex.com/~obsidian/HaudPan.html.

20. Jesse Cornplanter, quoted in Fenton, *False Faces*, 39.

21. Tooker, *Iroquois Source Book*, 411.

22. *Realm of the Iroquois* (Alexandria, Va.: Time-Life Books, 1993), 36–37.

23. Frank G. Speck, *Midwinter Rites of the Cayuga Longhouse* (Philadelphia: University of Pennsylvania Press, 1949), 104–5.

24. Ibid., 106–7.

25. Ibid.

26. Ibid.

27. Fenton, *False Faces*, 48.

28. Tooker, *Iroquois Source Book*, 227.

29. Fenton, *False Faces*, 140.

30. Ibid., 140–42.

31. Lloyd M. Morgan, *League of the Ho-de-no-sau-nee or Iroquois*, vol. 1 (New York: Burt Franklin Press, 1901), 158–60.

32. Ritzenthaler, *Iroquois False-Face Masks*, 17.

33. Ibid.

34. Fenton, *False Faces*, 424–25.

35. Tooker, *Iroquois Source Book*, 123–53.

36. Ibid., 132–34.

37. Fenton, *False Faces*, 363.

38. Tooker, *Iroquois Source Book*, 62–63.

39. Morgan, *League of the Ho-de-no-sau-nee*, 199–213.

40. Richard Wallaschek, *Primitive Music: An Inquiry into the Origin and Development of Music* (New York: Longmans, Green, and Company, 1893), 51–52.

41. "Iroquois Midwinter Ceremony History," accessed on May 3, 2008, http://www.brownielocks.com/iroquoisceremony.html.

42. Tooker, *Iroquois Source Book*, 134.

5

SPIRITUAL TRADITIONS
OF THE GREAT PLAINS

૨૬

TROY R. JOHNSON

SINCE THE BEGINNING OF TIME, mankind has performed ceremonies and rituals that have kept the world in balance. They have performed world renewal ceremonies, first salmon ceremonies, and green corn ceremonies that ensured that the Great Spirit, or the spirit of the fish, game, and crops was appeased and the world would be renewed; life would be revitalized. No one has ever explained this better than the Pulitzer Prize–winning author Dr. N. Scott Momaday, a Kiowa. In the movie *In the White Man's Image*, Momaday tells the story of an old Kiowa holy man who, every day of his life, arose before dawn, went from his house, faced to the east, extended his arms outward, and prayed the sun up into the sky. Thus the world was once again renewed; the Kiowa were revitalized.[1]

The world renewal ceremonies have taken various forms, and practitioners that oversaw the ceremonies have been known by various names. Most common on the Great Plains was the shaman, or holy person. These people represented the contact between the tribe and individual Indian people and Wakan Tanka, the Creator, or the Great Mystery. The position of shaman or holy man may in some cases have been hereditary, but in most cases it was because these people (almost always men) had received a vision or revelation from Wakan Tanka that provided them with special powers and special access to the Creator. The position entailed a tremendous amount of responsibility as the well-being of the nation was often entrusted to them and their advice. Holy men who followed tradition would be known as revitalization prophets and peyote roadmen. All of these sacred people attempted to address pressures that proved to be insurmountable.

As Americans crossed Indian homelands in large numbers, destroying and straining the ecosystem, it was not uncommon for an Indian person to receive a message of survival from the Great Spirit. This message might be delivered in a dream, but it more commonly came during a vision quest. It was through this experience that a person acquired a spiritual power helper (a spirit power that could be called upon for guidance by the individual).

There is no single example or description of the vision quest. Most every horse-mounted, buffalo-hunting, and warring tribe of the Great Plains had its own sacred right-of-passage vision quest ritual or ceremony. Among the Gros Ventre (or A'ani) Indians of the northern plains, for instance, the vision quest took place when a young boy reached the approximate age of twelve. In preparation for the vision quest, a medicine person would have instructed the youth to go alone to a distant place where in the past successful vision quests had taken place. Snake Butte, on the Fort Belknap Indian Reservation in present-day Montana, is one such place. The young boy would take nothing with him to eat or for comfort. The vision quest generally lasted from one to four days, during which the participant fasted or "cried" for a vision. Alone, hungry, and in tune with the spiritual world, the seeker usually had a vision or dream in which a spirit person, animal, or supernatural force was made known to him. This would be his spirit helper throughout his life and could be called on in time of need. Religious leaders often participated in numerous vision quests and had a number of spirit helpers.[2]

A Cheyenne vision quest is best described as a fast in a lonely place where one petitions the spirits for indulgence and spiritual aid. This is sometimes referred to as "crying for a vision." If favored by a spirit, the person would receive a blessing, along with instructions on how to prepare power objects (such as amulets), how to paint himself, and what songs to sing to release the power. Visions and supernatural powers also came unsought in times of trouble. The individual Cheyenne who wished to become in tune with the animistic powers (animism being the belief that all things in nature have souls independent of their physical being in the universe) did it through fasting, vision seeking, and sacrificial offerings. Pledging to participate in a ceremony such as a Sun Dance is one such offering.[3]

The Sun Dance (Wiwanyag Wachipi, or Dance Looking at the Sun) was one of the best known and most misunderstood religious ceremonies conducted by American Indian people. It was practiced in some form among most of the tribal groups of the Great Plains regions, including the Arapaho, Arikara, Blackfeet, Comanche, Crow, Gros Ventre, Kiowa, Mandan, Plains Creek, Plains Ojibwa, Shoshone, and Ute. The Sun Dance has many variations, however; for most tribes, the sacred ceremony was held to pray for the renewal of the people and the earth, give thanks for help in battle, fulfill a pledge made to Wakan Tanka, or to protect the people from danger or illness.[4]

For some tribes, but not all, the Sun Dance was an annual event, with its timing determined by natural events such as when certain berries began to ripen, when the trees were in leaf, or when the buffalo returned, generally in July. It began with sweat

FIGURE 5.1. Native Americans of the northern and southern plains had a masking tradition for humans and horses, which included face and body painting. For masks, they often used tanned buffalo, pronghorn, and deer leather, which represented various spirits, characters, and clowns. The illustration provides one form of Plains Indian masking conceived by David Whitehorse. Sketch by Sarah Moore, author's collection.

lodge purification by those who would search for a Sun Dance pole that would be placed in the center of the dance circle. Indian men who had pledged to participate in the dance would be purified in a sweat lodge and receive instructions regarding the protocol to be followed.[5]

Preparation for the Sun Dance ceremony began with the selection of a tree that would become the center point in the ceremony. The Sun Dance chief, or intercessor, accompanied by a holy man, a group of followers, and an Indian woman who was a virgin, went into the forest to select a tall tree (preferably a cottonwood) that was straight and without blemish; some tribes used straight poles with forked limbs at the top. The virgin woman was representative of White Buffalo Calf Woman, who had given the Sun Dance to the Lakota.[6] Once the tree was selected, the young Indian woman made the first cut on the tree.[7] Often a noted warrior would then make a tobacco offering and "count coup," or touch the tree. The tree was then chopped down, and as it fell, it was caught so that it never touched the ground. Offerings of tobacco and other religious items were often made to the fallen tree as it was carried

FIGURE 5.2. Comanche healer Kenneth Coosewoon made the small tobacco bundles and the two medicine bundles presented in this photograph. He wraps tobacco ties while praying for patients and places them on the willow ribs of the lodge. He gives patients beaded bundles to wear, filling them with sacred plants, his blue medicine, and prayers. He smudges people with the feathers. Editor's photograph.

back to the village. The tree was then trimmed and taken to the Sun Dance arena and placed upright in a hole in the center of the arena. Before raising the pole, a sacred pipe and buffalo tallow were placed in the hole, and a buffalo skull and buffalo hide were fastened to its top.[8] Some tribes decorated the pole with long banners of cloth that represented the four sacred directions and with green and blue banners representing Mother Earth and Father Sky.[9]

The Sun Dance arena was a sacred area where only those who would participate in the ceremony, accompanied by the holy men, could enter. Wooden arbors were often built on the fringes of the arena in which tribal elders, noted warriors, and observers could stand or sit. Decorated buffalo skulls were often placed around the edge of the arena as well. The Sun Dance pole stood at the center of the arena, and from it hung leather or buckskin ropes. The dancers and holy men entered the arena, accompanied by the beating of a sacred drum, and saluted the sun. At that time, those who would participate in the dance might choose to show their devotion to the Creator by cutting small strips of skin from their arms or legs. The holy man then pierced the muscle on the upper left- and right-hand side of the chest in two places, about one inch apart. A bone skewer was passed through the cuts on each side of the chest, and the ropes were tied to the skewers. Once all of the participants had thus been pierced, they moved backward to the full extent of the ropes, stared up into the sun, and leaned backward in order to break the skewer through the muscle and chest skin.

During this time, the dancers held an eagle-bone whistle in their mouths. They did not speak, but rather they used the whistles to carry their message to the Creator that they had fulfilled their pledge. If a dancer had difficulty breaking free of the skewer, the holy man might assist by piercing the muscles on the dancer's back and attaching buffalo skulls as added weight. In some tribes, the sun dancers, once they had been pierced and attached to the ropes, were raised into the air and remained suspended until the skewer was pulled through the chest muscles. Buffalo skulls might be attached to the dancers' backs if necessary to break free. Traditionally, Indian women did not participate in the Sun Dance; however, that changed over time. They did not pierce but rather, if they pledged, stood along the edge of the Sun Dance arena and lacerated their arms by cutting away small strips of skin.

The Sun Dance was outlawed in the United States and became a punishable offense under the Courts of Indian Offenses in 1883. Indian tribes moved the sacred ceremony back into the far reaches of Indian reservations and continued the dance on a sporadic schedule. The Crow held a Sun Dance in 1875, the Gros Ventre in 1884, the Kiowa in 1890, and various Lakota bands in 1881, 1882, and 1883.[10] The Sun Dance survived into the twenty-first century, and many of the tribes of the Great Plains continue to carry out the Sun Dance, although in altered form. The overall significance of the Sun Dance involves the spiritual renewal of participants and their relatives and the revitalization of Mother Earth. This revitalization theme is evidenced by the Cheyenne, who call the structure in which the ritual now takes place the New Life Lodge. This term expresses the idea that the Sun Dance "is supposed to recreate, reform, reanimate the earth, vegetation, [and] animal life" and hence is a ceremony of revitalizing all things on earth.[11]

This was true not only for the Cheyenne but also for most Plains Indian tribes. The Lakota are an excellent example as well. The Lakota received their sacred ceremony and instruction from White Buffalo Calf Woman. There are numerous oral histories and recordings telling of White Buffalo Calf Woman's visit from the spirit world. They vary only slightly in their recitations. The following version is taken primarily from the voice of Black Elk and from Ed McGaa but incorporates other tellings as well.[12]

Many, many years ago, two hunters of the Sans Arc band of the Lakota Nation were sent to scout for buffalo for the people. When the scouts reached the crest of a hill, they looked to the north where they saw an image. As the image came closer, they noted that it was a beautiful woman dressed in white buckskin, carrying a bundle wrapped in buffalo hide, and she appeared to be floating above the ground. As she moved, she sang out, "Behold me, behold me, for in sacred manner I am walking." She repeated the song several times as she walked toward the men. In her hands she carried a large bundle and a fan of sage leaves. One of the men, beholding the beauty of the young woman, thought evil thoughts and spoke them to the other scout. His companion told him that this was surely a sacred woman and that he should throw all bad thoughts away. The men approached the woman, who could read their thoughts; she told the evil thinker, "You do not know me, but if you want to do as you think, you may come." As he approached her, a cloud of white smoke surrounded them. When the smoke cleared, the beautiful young woman came out of the cloud, and all that remained of the man was his skeleton, covered with worms. Some versions state that lightning instantly struck the man and burned him up, so that only a small heap of black bones remained.[13] After emerging from the cloud, White Buffalo Calf Woman instructed the remaining man to return to his camp, gather the leaders, and wait for her. She instructed him to have a large tipi built for her in the center of the nations and instructed him further to send runners to the distant bands of the Sioux Nation and to bring in the many leaders, the medicine people, and the holy men and holy women.

After a period of time, White Buffalo Calf Woman appeared in the village and went into a tipi, where she sang, "With visible breath I am walking. A voice I am sending as I walk. In a sacred manner I am walking. With visible tracks I am walking. In a sacred manner I walk." She then walked in a clockwise direction, stopping before the leader. White Buffalo Calf Woman took a bundle form her back and removed a pipe and round stone. She then began her sacred teachings. Beginning with the pipe, she explained its meaning and the significance of each of its components. She told the people that the pipestone bowl represented the earth and that the wooden stem represented all the earth's growing things. She said that the buffalo calf carved on the bowl represented the earth and all four-legged creatures, and that the pipe's twelve feathers, from the spotted eagle, represented the sky and all winged creatures. The old woman also instructed the people regarding the stone, explaining that the seven circles on it stood for the seven sacred rites of the Lakota people. She presented the first rite, the Ghost-Keeping or Soul-Keeping ceremony, and told them that the remaining six ceremonies would be made known to them in visions and that the sacred pipe was to be used in each of them.[14] She sang again, walked in a clockwise direction around the tipi, and then went out. As she started to leave, she reminded them to remember how sacred the pipe was and to treat it in a sacred manner.

The people watched as she walked some distance away from them. As she walked over the ridge of a hill, she sat down. When she rose, she had been transformed into a white buffalo calf. She then walked farther away, bowed to the four sacred quarters of the universe, and disappeared.[15] White Buffalo Calf Woman's sacred bundle was left with the people, and to this day, a traditional Sioux family, the Keepers of the Sacred Bundle, guards the bundle and its contents on the Sioux reservation.

Frank Fools Crow followed in the tradition of White Buffalo Calf Woman and became a revered Sun Dance intercessor, *yuwipi* (mediator between the people and the spirit world) man, and *waive* (healer) for over sixty years. He was born in the Porcupine community of the Pine Ridge Reservation in South Dakota shortly after the Wounded Knee tragedy of 1890. He was the son of Black Elk, another noted Lakota holy man, and is considered by many to be the greatest Native American spiritual leader of the past century. His spiritual mentor was a well-known Lakota holy man named Stirrup.[16] Fools Crow experienced his first vision quest in 1905 at the age of fourteen. His experience is typical of a Lakota vision quest experience. Two tribal elders, Daniel Dull Knife and Grady Dull Knife, assisted Frank Fools Crow. The place where he quested was at Yellow Bear Creek, near present-day Kyle, South Dakota. Daniel Dull Knife and Grady Dull Knife went early in the morning to the spot where the quest was to take place to prepare for the four-day ceremony. On the afternoon of the first day, Fools Crow and his attendants participated in a purification ceremony held in the sweat lodge.

The sweat lodge was a sacred structure constructed from bent tree limbs in a domed style and covered by buffalo, deer, or other animal skins. A flap was placed across the entrance so that total darkness could be achieved. The purpose of the sweat lodge was to cleanse and to purify. The cleansing process was not just a physical cleanse of "sweat," but also a spiritual, emotional, and mental cleanse through this ritual process. The lodge also served as a place for worship, healing, and celebration of events or achievements.[17] As the sun was going down, the vision quest preparations continued. A black cloth hood was placed over Fools Crow's head so that he could not see where the men were taking him. He was led to a questing pit that was about two feet wide, four feet deep, and six feet long. Sage had been spread on the bottom to purify the pit and to make a bed. Fools Crow remained in the vision quest pit for four days and nights without food or water, praying for a vision. On the fourth day, he received his first vision. The following day he was escorted back to camp, where he related what he had seen in the vision to the Lakota holy man, Stirrup, about the vision.[18] Stirrup instructed him to keep the meaning a secret because the Great Spirit would not want him to reveal everything that he saw. Fools Crow went on his second vision quest in 1914, at which time he received the most profound secrets that he would need to know to begin his career as a holy man.[19] Fools Crow maintained the secret of the Great Spirit's teachings and served as a holy man and ceremonial leader for the Lakota until his death in 1978.

The vision quest of Hohonaiviuhk (Stone Forehead) provides another cogent description of a vision quest experience. Stone Forehead was a highly respected Cheyenne holy man who served as keeper of the Sacred Arrows of the Cheyenne Nation from 1849 until his death in 1876. Stone Forehead was noted for possessing extraordinary spiritual powers.[20] He could call to him his *maiyu* (spiritual helpers), and he could converse with the spirit world. In one demonstration of his connection to the spirit world, Stone Forehead's spirit helper called out "Make a light!" And after the fire had blazed up, Stone Forehead had disappeared, although his rattle could be seen and heard moving along through the air, as if shaken by a person.[21] On other occasions, Stone Forehead would demonstrate his spiritual power by dancing through the camp, carrying a pole in one hand and a drum in the other. He would throw the drum in the air, and it would fly a long way, then suddenly turn and fly back, coming to an end on the pole where the drum would then slide down into Stone Forehead's hand.[22]

Stone Forehead demonstrated his connection with the spirit world in other ceremonies as well. One such ceremony was performed when many people were present. Traditional singers were invited into Stone Forehead's lodge, where he unwrapped his sacred bundle that contained personal power items given to him in dreams or during vision quests. As Stone Forehead opened his medicine bundle, the singers sang their spiritual songs, and the fire was permitted to die out until the lodge was dark. Before the fire was out, and before he began to call for his spirit helpers, Stone Forehead was tied with four bowstrings. Each finger of each hand was tied separately to the next finger in a hard knot, and the ends of the bowstrings were tied together on each hand and then bound behind his back so that his hands were tightly secured. His feet were bound together in the same manner, each toe being tied to the next one in a hard knot, and the feet bound together by the bowstrings. Once he had been tied securely, Stone Forehead was placed at the back of the lodge and tied to one of the lodge poles.[23]

After the fire had gone out, the lodge began to shake as if blown by a strong wind as Stone Forehead's spirit helpers entered the lodge. The poles creaked and bent, and suddenly Stone Forehead heard voices talking to him. The participant had likely called

FIGURE 5.3. Many Native Americans of the Great Plains and American Southwest conduct ceremonies honoring the American bison. This sketch by famous artist Richard A. Kern depicts a Zuni Indian buffalo dancer. Many tribes admired the great animals and hunted them for food. Editor's collection, Captain L. Sitgreaves, *Report of an Expedition Down the Zuni and Colorado Rivers* (Washington, D.C.: R. Armstrong, 1853).

on the spirit helper to ask the location of buffalo or enemies of Cheyenne people. The spirit helpers could also assist in locating missing people or even tell where lost horses might be found. After Stone Forehead's spirit helpers had gone and a light had again been made, he was found to be untied and the bowstrings used to bind him were lying in the door. It was believed that his spirit helpers had untied him.[24]

During the period when Stone Forehead served as keeper of the Sacred Arrows, the Cheyenne people and their traditional way of life increasingly came under attack as the federal government pushed them to surrender their homelands. In 1851, Stone Forehead became one of the signers of the Treaty of Fort Laramie. Approximately ten thousand Cheyenne, Sioux, Crow, Arapaho, Assiniboine, Gros Ventre, and Arikara Indians had met with U.S. treaty officials at Horse Creek near Fort Laramie in Wyoming Territory. The treaty included provisions establishing territorial boundaries and rights of way as well as pledges of peace and friendship between the U.S. government and the Native nations. The Plains Indians defined their territories and promised to stop further hostile acts. In return, the United States pledged to protect the tribes from trespass and depredations by American citizens and to pay compensation for any damages suffered.[25] The United States also promised tribes an annual distribution of annuity goods for a ten-year period. Failure of the United States to comply with its obligation under the Treaty of Fort Laramie precipitated twenty-two years of intermittent warfare that culminated in the 1876 Battle of the Little Bighorn and the demise of Lieutenant Colonel George Armstrong Custer and 266 soldiers of the Seventh Cavalry.[26]

In 1869, Lieutenant Colonel Custer smoked the sacred pipe with Stone Forehead and other Cheyenne elders in the Sacred Arrow lodge and pledged not to fight against them. Stone Forehead warned Custer that the outcome of any treachery would result in the death of Custer and his entire command. Stone Forehead then put ashes from his pipe bowl on Custer's boots and warned Custer that Maheo, the Creator, would destroy him if he went against his words spoken while smoking the sacred pipe. The Cheyenne people remembered Stone Forehead's prophetic warning to Custer after he and the Seventh Calvary were defeated at the Battle of the Little Bighorn.[27]

Moving into the western edge of the southern plains (southern New Mexico and eastern Arizona), the life of Geronimo, a famous and highly respected holy man, provides an example of the spiritual traditions of the Chiricahua Apache Indians. Geronimo, or Goyathlay, was born in 1829 and raised near the headwaters of the Gila River in present-day Arizona.[28] His father was Taklishim, a full-blooded Chiricahua Apache. His mother, Juana, was also a full-blooded Apache, and had been held captive among the Mexicans for a period of time. Geronimo was the fourth child in a family of eight children, four boys and four girls. While a young child, Geronimo was taught the sacred traditions of his people. He was taught the relationship of the Apache to the sun and sky, the moon and stars, and the clouds and storms. His mother taught him to kneel and pray to Usn (the Creator) for strength, health, wisdom, and protection. Geronimo's father told him of the brave deeds of Apache warriors, the pleasures of the hunt, and the glories of the warpath.[29]

Geronimo came to be considered a holy man by his people because of his gift of power—the ability to influence people and events. Geronimo also had war medicines, such as a gun ceremony that he used to make himself invincible to bullets. It was reported that he also had the ability to control daylight. An unidentified informant once stated that when Geronimo was on the warpath, he had the ability to control the sunrise so that morning would not come too soon. He did this by singing sacred songs that had been given to him in a vision. It was also believed that Geronimo had the magic of "far seeing"—to see in advance the results of a battle—and because of this he came to be depended upon as a war leader.[30]

As a shaman, Geronimo had many special powers. For healing, he had ghost powers and coyote medicine. The coyote was a very powerful spirit, difficult to kill and with the ability to shape shift in times of emergency.[31] His ghost medicine allowed him to call upon assistance from the spirit world to heal people who had become ill as the result of contact with evil spirits from the ghost world or inflicted by evil shamans seeking increased powers. Despite his ability to heal and to influence people and events, Geronimo could not stop the advance of non-Indians into Apache lands. His spiritual powers proved to be of little effect against rapid-fire rifles and cannon.

In 1894, following the Indian wars of the plains, the United States Army transferred Geronimo and other Apache warriors from Florida and Alabama to Fort Sill, Oklahoma, where the army retained them as prisoners of war. In his new home, Geronimo took up farming and was active in the Dutch Reformed Church until his death in 1909.

Wolf Chief, a Hidatsa shaman (born ca. 1830), was a contemporary of Geronimo. He acquired most of his medicine power from his father, Small Ankle, who had received his powers from a shaman named Missouri River. Some of Wolf Chief's medicines included a medicine pipe, two human skulls, a buffalo skull, and a turtle shell. The medicine pipe was approximately twenty inches long and made of hickory and was his most sacred possession. The keeper of the medicine pipe was regarded as a person of great stature, and Wolf Chief was highly honored to have this responsibility. One power the pipe contained was war medicine. Its proper use protected the user and those in his company from harm during battle. When an enemy approached, Wolf Chief took the pipe from its sacred bundle and rolled it on the ground toward the enemy. While carrying out this ceremony, he sang a medicine song that had been given to him by his father. This power of the pipe, coupled with the ceremony, caused the enemy to become frightened and to flee.[32]

The two human skulls proved equally important. During a drought, the skulls were placed on a bed of pennyroyal. Pennyroyal, a member of the mint family, was highly regarded because of its sweet smell. Water was sprinkled on the skulls and the pennyroyal, and songs were sung to bring rain. Pennyroyal was also placed in water before the skulls and then rubbed on an ailing person to heal him or her.[33] Hidatsas considered the buffalo sacred, and Wolf Chief used the buffalo skull as part of his medicine pipe ceremony. When buffalo became scarce and could not be found, the medicine pipe was filled and rubbed with buffalo fat. It was then placed before the buffalo skulls and a sacred song was sung to the buffalo. The location of the buffalo was then made known to Wolf Chief in a dream or vision. Wolf Chief observed his father successfully perform both the buffalo and rain ceremony, and Wolf Chief earned the respect of the Hidatsa people with his ability to emulate his father's successes.[34]

Tavivo, a Northern Paiute Indian (born ca. 1835) was a contemporary of both Geronimo and Wolf Chief. Tavivo was born near Walker Lake in present-day Esmeralda County, Nevada, and is considered by many to be the first revitalization prophet of the Great Plains area. Revitalization prophets generally arose during times of great physical, cultural, and spiritual distress, such as the Wounded Knee Massacre and the forced confinement of Indians on reservations. Revitalization prophets arose to bring a millennial message that they had received from the Creator. The message provided hope to a beleaguered people. The prophets related that they had communicated with the Creator in a vision or dream and were told to teach the people songs, dances, and a return to traditional values. If they carried out the dictates of the Creator, the white man would disappear, the buffalo would return, and they would be reunited with those who had died or been killed. Tavivo was one such prophet.

Tavivo rose from obscurity to become a dreamer-prophet, leader of the Paiute community, and a well-known shaman and visionary who was said to have the power to affect the weather. He was known as a dreamer-prophet because he communicated with the Great Spirit while in a dream state. He also received visions while dreaming.[35] Tavivo insisted that the only real world was the dream world, and that it was while in this state that the spirits of the dead talked freely to the chosen, such as him. During one such revelation, Tavivo was instructed to have his followers attain a state of trance by dancing a traditional circle dance that would become a centerpiece of both the Ghost Dance religion of 1870 and the Ghost Dance religion of 1890. Although Tavivo is often credited with being the founder of the Ghost Dance religion of 1870, whether or not this claim is true is unclear. It is clear, however, the he was associated with that religion, and his teachings had a strong influence on his son, Wovoka, who founded the Ghost Dance religion of 1890.

Among the Paiute, there had always been a strong belief in communicating with the Great Spirit to ensure success in the food quest and to maintain the precarious balance with nature. It is possible that Tavivo may have been a shaman at an early age based on his close relationship with the supernatural powers of nature and the Creator. He practiced hand magic (healing by placing a hand on the infected area) and spoke of a spirit world yet to come. Tavivo prophesied about a time to come when the lands of the Great Plains, the Southwest, and the Great Basin regions would once again be green with grass and rich with game. It would be a pleasant world where the Paiute would be a happy race. They would never again argue or draw the bow to make war.

Tavivo was described as a talented orator. He was said to have possessed *bbooha*, or power, and on at least one occasion was accused of being a witch because he treated a woman who subsequently died.[36] Following the destruction brought about by white migration during the California gold rush of 1849, Tavivo experienced a series of visions concerning the destiny of all Indians and the white invaders. After a period of solitude in the mountains, he received a vision from the Great Spirit and was told that the white invaders would be destroyed in one great earthquake. Indians alive would be spared and would repopulate a restored and prosperous land. The Great Spirit appointed Tavivo as the visionary who was to carry forth this teaching to his people that revitalization was at hand. Tavivo journeyed back to the mountain, where he received a second vision. He returned to his people and prophesied that the coming earthquake would kill not just whites, but all humans. After a given period of time, however, Indians would be returned to life and would live in a restored land of plenty. Tavivo also claimed a third revelation. He related to his people that the Great Spirit would punish Indian people because of their lack of faith, and only Indians who believed Tavivo would be resurrected. Those Indians that doubted, along with whites, would be sentenced to eternal punishment.[37]

Tavivo's popularity waned as the number of settlers encroaching onto the Great Plains increased. The slaughter of the buffalo and the unceasing warfare carried out by the United States Army decimated the population. When Tavivo's Ghost Dance prophecies did not come to pass, his followers were dispirited. Many were killed, and many were captured and placed on Indian reservations. The Native people looked for a new religious prophet and found that revitalization message in Wovoka, son of Tavivo.[38]

Wovoka was a Paiute Indian born about 1856 near Walker Lake in present-day Esmeralda County, Nevada. He grew up in the area of Mason Valley, Nevada, near the present Walker Lake Reservation.[39] Wovoka's vision became the basis of the 1890 Ghost Dance religion, which was based on the belief that there would be a time when all Indian people—the living and the dead—would be reunited on an earth that was spiritually regenerated and forever free from death, disease, and all the other miseries that had recently been experienced by Indian people. Word of the new religion spread quickly among Indian peoples of the Great Basin and Great Plains regions.[40] Indian people representing more than thirty tribes traveled great distances to visit Wovoka and to learn more of his teachings, often returning home filled with messages of hope for their people. Many Indian people who had undergone severe cultural and physical attacks eagerly accepted the teachings of Wovoka. The United States Army's scorched-earth military policy carried out by Generals William T. Sherman and Phillip Sheridan, the destruction of the buffalo, confinement on reservations, and epidemics of strange and lethal European-introduced diseases set the stage for the acceptance of Wovoka's message of revitalization.[41]

As the religious movement spread, it took on features unique to individual tribes. When the Ghost Dance reached the Lakota, they added the wearing of a Ghost Dance shirt to the religion. The Ghost Dance shirt, it was believed, would be impervious to the white man's bullets. Non-Indians now became alarmed by reports of what they perceived to be warriors performing a strange new war dance. The wearing of the Ghost Dance shirt thus transformed Wovoka's religious movement into a warrior movement.[42] The 1890 Wounded Knee Massacre of 250 Lakota men, women, and children occurred because of a fear by the United States Army that American Indian people who were adherents of the Ghost Dance religion were preparing to go to war in protest of the continuing loss of land and the enormous loss of Indian lives to European-introduced disease and warfare.[43] Government agents and missionaries opposed the Ghost Dance, and in 1890, the army outlawed the practice of the Ghost Dance on Indian reservations. Tensions intensified between the Lakota and the soldiers as Indian people left the reservations without permission to participate in the Ghost Dance ritual out of sight of the army. Sitting Bull, a highly respected Lakota spiritual leader, was blamed for the unrest. The army was now concerned about the number of Indian men, women, and children who were leaving the Cheyenne River, Pine Ridge, and Standing Rock Reservations to practice the new dance. It was feared that the Indian wars were about to begin anew.[44] In addition to Sitting Bull, who the army had conspired to murder, a prominent chief of the Miniconjou Sioux, Big Foot, was reported to be en route with some three hundred warriors to join the Ghost Dancers. The report was in error; in fact, Big Foot was on his way to the Pine Ridge Reservation to encourage the Indian people to return to their reservation. Chief Big Foot, fearing danger from the army, had accepted an offer from Chief Red Cloud to join him and his band on the Pine Ridge Reservation and to help in negotiating a peace before any warfare began.[45] Unfortunately, Chief Big Foot was sick with pneumonia and had only reached Porcupine Butte when Major Samuel Whiteside and the recently reconstructed Seventh Cavalry intercepted him and his followers—men, women, and children—on December 28, 1890, and demanded their surrender. Of the 365 persons arrested, only 116 were men, and they were poorly armed and represented no threat to Major Whiteside and his men.[46] Major Whiteside, now under orders from General John Brook, had Chief Big Foot and his followers escorted to Wounded Knee Creek in present-day South Dakota. Later that day, Colonel James Forsyth arrived and assumed command of the Seventh Cavalry and Chief Big Foot's Miniconjou encampment.[47]

Upon arrival at Wounded Knee Creek, Chief Big Foot and his followers were instructed to camp in an area that had been prepared by the army. Major Whiteside demanded that Chief Big Foot and his warriors turn over twenty-five rifles that he believed had been taken from the bodies of Lieutenant Colonel Custer's men following the Battle of the Little Bighorn. Big Foot agreed to the demand, but no timeline was established for the surrender of the weapons. Chief Big Foot posted a white peace flag over his tipi, and he and his followers settled down for a restless cold night's rest.[48] Colonel Forsyth was unsure of the ability of his troops to disarm Big Foot and his followers and called for reinforcements. The new troops arrived during the night of December 28 and joined with the solders of the Seventh Cavalry encamped on a small hill northwest of the Indian camp. Hotchkiss cannons were positioned on the hill, aimed at the Indian encampment.

The morning of December 29, 1890, broke clear and cold on the Dakota plains. A hint of snowfall was in the wind. Colonel Forsyth was now intent on a quick disarmament of the Indians and on their incarceration at the army post at Gordon, Nebraska. The warriors would then be separated from the women and children and transferred by train to the army headquarters in Omaha, Nebraska, where they would remain until the Ghost Dance threat was destroyed.

Colonel Forsyth now ordered Chief Big Foot and his followers to surrender all of their weapons. A small group of Indian men brought a small cache of old rifles from their tipis and stacked them in front on the solders. None of the weapons were new enough to have come from the Custer battlefield. Soldiers, intent on finding the Custer rifles, then went into the Indian tipis and searched through bedding, clothing, and sacred bundles, but no additional weapons were found. Black Coyote, a deaf Lakota holy man, came forward, however, with a rifle held in his hands. A struggle to disarm Black Coyote ensued, and the rifle discharged. A volley of firing from the soldiers followed the shot, including the use of rapid-fire howitzer cannons.[49]

The firing at the Indian encampment lasted only about ten minutes, while the firing at the adjacent ravine lasted for about an hour and a half. Most of the Indian warriors died in the initial onslaught, while the Hotchkiss guns of the Seventh Cavalry mowed down Indian women and children running or hiding in the ravine. By the end of the firing, the slight snowfall had turned into a blizzard. The Seventh Cavalry left the dead and injured on the battlefield to freeze and to die.[50]

On January 3, 1891, troopers escorted a civilian burial party to Wounded Knee, where 146 dead and frozen bodies were taken from the snow, loaded onto wagons, and buried in a mass grave near the Pine Ridge Episcopal Church. Some survivors, families, and friends had removed some of the dead and dying before the burial party arrived. Seven Indians wounded in the massacre died at the church that had been converted into a field hospital. The total number killed at Wounded Knee Creek will never be known, as no accurate record exists. What is clear, however, is that the Wounded Knee Massacre ended the Ghost Dance revitalization movement among the Lakota and quashed the millennial expectations of the Great Plains Indian people.[51]

As the influence of individual revitalization prophets decreased in the years following the Wounded Knee Massacre, another important sacred ceremony, centered on the ancient use of the peyote plant, increased. One of the most influential figures in the peyote church was Quanah Parker. Quanah Parker was born between 1845 and 1850 to Peta Nocona (also referred to as Noconi, meaning "Wanderer"), chief of the Quahada (or Kwahadi) band of Comanche Indians, and Cynthia Ann Parker, a white woman who had been captured in May 1836 along with her nine-year-old brother, John. While in his teens, Parker was left without parents following the death of his father in about 1866 or 1867.[52]

Parker grew to manhood at a time when continuous warfare and European-introduced disease were taking a heavy toll on all Indians. As he matured, he became a war leader to claim and maintain control of Comanche hunting and warring. He became a war chief among the Kwahadi band of the Comanche by around 1867. It was at this time that he also became one of the most important peyote roadmen, or leaders of the early peyote religion in Indian Territory (present-day Oklahoma).[53] The roadman is the leader of the all-night peyote ceremony. The "road" is the peyote road, or a line laid out along the crest of the altar on which individuals concentrate in the belief that the peyote and the road will lead their thoughts and prayers to the supernatural.[54]

Peyote was originally one of the offerings made to the gods in Aztec temples, where the button of this small hallucinogenic cactus plant was ritually consumed. Peyote flourished in other regions of Mexico and in South Texas. The Comanche frequented South Texas and northern Mexico in the early nineteenth century, where Lipan Apache were reportedly using peyote in spiritual ceremonies. As Parker was born just before 1850, it is reasonable to assume that he was familiar with peyote throughout his lifetime and perhaps used it in his power quests (a quest that included fasting and isolating to acquire a spiritual helper). Parker obtained his power through mystic visitations, a dream phenomenon, or hallucinatory experience.

Peyote is a small, turnip-shaped cactus grown primarily in the arid Rio Grande Valley of northern Mexico and southwestern Texas. Indian people ate the bitter, dried tops, or "buttons," to induce heightened perceptions of sound and color. Peyote could also be ground and smoked or made into peyote tea. It enhanced concentration and highlighted religious truths with vivid imagery during ceremonies. Its use among the

Great Plains tribes during the 1800s was different from the organized Native American Church that developed later.[55]

Peyote use was first used by the Lipan Apache, who taught its use to the Kiowa, Comanche, and other tribes.[56] As a religion, peyote use spread rapidly from Texas into Oklahoma and the Great Plains. Peyote offered its adherents a means of religious expression by which they could maintain a positive identity as Indian people at a time when the Native population had reached its lowest point: hungry and defeated, they were confined to reservations as conquered people, their traditional way of life was destroyed, and Native religions were outlawed.[57]

The traditional peyote ceremony was held in a lodge, tipi, or other dwelling space under the direction of the roadman or road chief. Inside the space, a crescent moon altar was created using sand or earth so that it was six to eight inches above the ground. The crescent began in the south and ended in the north. The line from north to south cut the altar in half, giving it a half-moon appearance and thus the name Half-Moon Ceremony. At the center of the north-south line was the space where the sacred fire was kindled and kept burning for the duration of the ceremony. The roadman sat in the west, directly opposite the door. A drummer sat at his right and a cedar person on his left. The cedar man was responsible for starting a cedar fire and maintaining it throughout the nightlong ceremony. Next came the most sacred part of the ceremony; the largest peyote button, Chief Peyote, was taken from the roadman's cedar box and placed in the center of the crescent. The lodge or tipi was now fully a sacred place. Other forms of peyote were then introduced—dried and ground peyote, green peyote buttons, and peyote tea. These were blessed by being passed through the cedar smoke. The roadman and the drummer then ate some of the peyote and announced that the ceremony had begun. A sacred staff, sage wand, gourd rattle, and feather were then passed from person to person in a clockwise direction. As the sacred objects were passed around, the participants had the opportunity to sing, speak, or make requests for prayer or intercession on their behalf. Throughout the remainder of the night, the cedar fire was kept burning. Water was periodically sprinkled on the fire to produce a sacred smoke that carried the petitioners' prayers to the Great Spirit. Throughout the night, the various forms of peyote were passed around the circle in the same manner as the sacred objects. Peyote was eaten, smoked, or drunk. Everyone was encouraged to participate in some form even though it was not required; women and new initiates usually began with peyote tea.

The traditional peyote ceremony lasted from sundown to sunrise. A break was allowed at midnight, at which time participants were allowed to leave the ceremony for personal comfort, to drink water, or to talk to other participants. After the midnight break was complete, the ceremony began anew and continued to daybreak. Following the ceremony, it was common for the roadman to provide a breakfast meal.[58]

Parker's involvement with peyote began in 1884 after he sustained a serious wound when a Spanish bull attacked him. A burning fever quickly set in, as did serious blood poisoning. Parker was treated with *woaui*, or peyote juice. When he recovered, he attributed his cure to peyote. This made him a convert to the peyote religion, and he embarked upon a lifelong pursuit to spread the practice of the peyote religion among Native peoples.[59] His position as a respected and influential chief contributed to the spread of peyotism by attracting followers to his beliefs. Parker was responsible for spreading the peyote religion to members of the Delaware, Caddo, Cheyenne, Arapaho, Ponca, Pawnee, Osage, and other tribes.[60]

Parker defended Native use of peyote against powerful opponents and incorporated some Christian elements into the religion. Parker is reported to have said, "The White man goes into his church house and talks about Jesus, but the Indian goes into his tipi and talks to Jesus."[61] Parker fought for the right of Indian people to practice the peyote religion at a time when the religion was increasingly threatened by government efforts to make the use of peyote illegal. He and other peyotists successfully defended their rights to the religious use of peyote before the Medical Committee of the Oklahoma State Constitutional Convention in 1906–1907, where they convinced the committee that peyote was not harmful and was a sacrament necessary in their Indian religious services.[62] Legal battles followed in the wake of the Oklahoma convention, and many states passed laws that prohibited the use of peyote or the transport of peyote across state lines. Court battles ensued at both the state and federal levels. In 1978, the U.S. federal government issued the peyote exemption for use of peyote in the Native American Church and passed the 1978 American Indian Religious Freedom Act, which authorized the use of peyote as a sacrament in the Native American Church. Some states, such as Arizona and Texas, initiated federal appeals based on the premise that the legal possession of peyote was not covered by the freedom of religious practices act. Those appeals were rebuffed by the Supreme Court as a violation of the Free Exercise Clause of the First Amendment to the United States Constitution and were in conflict with the intent of the Supreme Court's ruling that the use of peyote as a sacrament within the Native American Church is uniquely supported by the legislative history.[63]

Quanah Parker and John Wilson (a Delaware) are often credited as the spiritual founders of the Native American Church movement that began in the 1880s and formally incorporated in 1918.[64] The church incorporated the elements of the peyote religion and Christian beliefs and practices. This includes communicating with the Creator through spirit forces by means of peyote-induced visions. The articles of incorporation for the Native American Church state that the church is formed to "foster and promote religious believers in Almighty God and the customs of the several tribes of Indians throughout the Unites States in the worship of a Heavenly Father and to promote morality, sobriety, industry, charity, and right living."[65]

The role of the peyote roadman in the Native American Church is analogous to the role of the shaman or holy man in the halogen days of Native American life on the Great Plains and to the priest or pastor in Western religious ceremonies. The Native American Church and the use of peyote as a holy sacrament continue to this day.

NOTES

1. See N. Scott Momaday in the documentary "In the White Man's Image," *American Experience*, season 4, episode 12, directed by Christine Lesiak, aired February 17, 1992 (Boston: WBGH Production). For more information on Native Americans of the Great Plains, see N. Scott Momaday's presentation in the documentary film *More Than Bows and Arrows* (New York: Baseline Studio Systems, 2008).

2. Kathleen Margaret Dugan, *The Vision Quest of the Plains Indians* (Lewiston, N.Y.: Edwin Mellen Press, 1985).

3. Ruth Fulton Benedict, "A Vision in Plains Culture," *American Anthropologist* 24 (1922): 17.

4. Sam D. Gill and Irene F. Sullivan, *Dictionary of Native American Mythology* (New York: Oxford University Press, 1992), 291–92.

5. Arlene Hirschfelder and Paulette Molin, *The Encyclopedia of Native American Religions* (Logan: Utah State University, 1996), 284.

6. Ed McGaa (Eagle Man), *Mother Earth Spirituality: Native American Paths to Healing Ourselves and Our World* (New York: Harper & Row Publishers, 1990), 85.

7. Ibid.

8. Ibid., 286.

9. Ibid., 86.

10. Hirschfelder and Molin, *Encyclopedia of Native American Religions*, 284.

11. Hugh Lenox Scott, "Notes on the Kado, or Sun Dance," *American Anthropologist* 13 (1911), 347.

12. John Neihardt, *Black Elk Speaks: Being the Life Story of a Holy Man of the Oglala* (Lincoln: University of Nebraska Press, 1961), 3–6; McGaa, *Mother Earth Spirituality*, 3-6.

13. Richard Erdoes and Alfonso Ortiz, *American Indian Myths and Legends* (New York: Pantheon Books, 1984), 48.

14. John Redtail Freesoul, "The Native American Prayer Pipe: Ceremonial Object and Tool of Self-Realization," in *Shamanism: An Expanded View of Reality*, ed. Shirley Nicholson (Wheaton, Ill.: Quest Books, 1987), 204–10.

15. Gill and Sullivan, *Dictionary of Native American Mythology*, 337.

16. Thomas E. Mails, *Fools Crow: Wisdom and Power* (Tulsa, Okla.: Council Oaks Books, 2001), 184.

17. Ibid., 165.

18. Ibid.

19. Troy Johnson, *Distinguished Native American Spiritual Practitioners and Healers* (Westport, Conn.: Oryx Press, 2002), 86–87.

20. Hirschfelder and Molin, *Encyclopedia of Native American Religions*, 282–83.

21. George Bird Grinnell, *The Cheyenne Indians: Their History and Ways of Life* (Lincoln: University of Nebraska Press, 1972), 1:113–14.

22. Ibid., 1:127.

23. Hirschfelder and Molin, *Encyclopedia of Native American Religions*, 284.

24. Ibid., 347–48.

25. George Bird Grinnell, *The Fighting Cheyenne* (Norman: University of Oklahoma Press, 1915), 265.

26. Ibid., 100.

27. Frederick F. Van DeWater, *Glory-Hunter: A Life of General Custer* (Lincoln: University of Nebraska Press, 1988), 216–17.

28. Johnson, *Distinguished Native American Practitioners and Healers*, 93.

29. Ibid., 94–96.

30. William S. Lyon, *Encyclopedia of Native American Shamanism: Sacred Ceremonies of North America* (Santa Barbara, Calif.: ABC-CLIO, 1998), 91.

31. Ibid., 89–90.

32. Ibid.

33. Ibid.

34. Duane Champagne, ed., *The Native North American Almanac: A Reference Work on Native North Americans in the United States and Canada* (Detroit, Mich.: Gale Research, 1994–1995), 567–68.

35. L. G. Moses, "'The Father Tells Me So!': Wovoka: The Ghost Dance Prophet," in *American Indian Prophets: Religious Leaders and Revitalization Movements*, ed. Clifford E. Trafzer (Newcastle, Calif.: Sierra Oaks Publications, 1986), 98.

36. Michael Hittman, *Wovoka and the Ghost Dance*, ed. Don Lynch (Carson City, Nev.: The Grace Danberg Foundation, 1990), 17–32.

37. Ibid.

38. Robert H. Lowie, *Primitive Religion* (Chatham, UK: George Routledge and Sons, 1924), 193.

39. Champagne, *Native North American Almanac*, 677.

40. James Mooney, *The Ghost-Dance Religion and the Sioux Outbreak of 1890* (Chicago: University of Chicago Press, 1965), 62–63.

41. Robert M. Utley, *Frontier Regulars: The United States Army and the Indian, 1866–1891* (New York: Macmillan Publishing, 1973), 144–45.

42. Ibid., 82–83.

43. Ibid., 403.

44. Ibid., 404–5.

45. Mooney, *Ghost-Dance Religion*, 127.

46. Ibid., 114.

47. Ibid.

48. Ibid., 115.

49. Ibid.

50. Ibid., 115–18.

51. Champagne, *Native North American Almanac*, 1162–63.

52. Gill and Sullivan, *Dictionary of Native American Mythology*, 100–101.

53. Omer C. Stewart, *Peyote Religion: A History* (Norman: University of Oklahoma Press, 1987), 60.

54. Ibid., 68–69.

55. Ibid., 36.

56. The first use of peyote in the present-day United States is unknown. While the first reported use in the United States was in the 1870s, peyote was being used in Mexico as early as the Spanish contact in the 1500s and reportedly as early as 1000 BCE. It is likely that the indigenous people of today's states of Texas, New Mexico, and Arizona were acquainted with the enlightenment offered by the use of peyote as early as the 1500s.

57. Champagne, *Native North American Almanac*, 674–75.

58. Roland Wagner, review of *Peyote Religion*, by Stewart, *American Anthropologist* 90 (1988): 704–5.

59. Omer C. Stewart, *Peyote Religion: A History* (Norman: University of Oklahoma Press, 1987) 72.

60. Jay Fikes, "A Brief History of the Native American Church," *Council on Spiritual Practices*, accessed May 12, 2008, http://www.csp.org/communities/docs/fikes-nac_history.html.

61. Johnson, *Distinguished Native American Practitioners and Healers*, 163.

62. Michael Katakis, *Excavating Voices: Listening to Photographs of Native Americans* (Philadelphia: University of Pennsylvania Museum of Archaeology, 1998), 23.

63. Bernadette Rigal-Cellier, *The Peyote Way Church of God* (Bordeaux, France: University Michel de Montaigne, 2004), 13.

64. Champagne, *Native North American Almanac*, 673–75.

65. Ibid., 675.

6

SMOHALLA, WASHANI, AND SEVEN DRUMS

&

Religious Traditions on the Northwest Plateau

CLIFFORD E. TRAFZER AND RICHARD D. SCHEUERMAN

FOR THOUSANDS OF YEARS, Salish and Sahaptin people of the Columbia Plateau have had a deep and abiding relationship with the creative spirit that put their world into motion and established the laws by which tribes and families functioned. Spiritual beliefs of the people have played a central role in the history of the Northwest and continue to influence the course of Northwestern tribes today. In addition to the older Washani faith, people of the Northwest have attended worship ceremonies of the Indian Shaker Church; Waptashi, or Feather religion; and Christianity. The Washani has become known as the Seven Drums religion or Longhouse religion. It remains a powerful religion today on the Columbia Plateau. Over the years, several religious leaders led their people in song, ceremony, and dance. Since ancient days, Indian youth sought their spirit power during their vision quests, and communities met in midwinter ceremonies to honor their personal power, often referred to as *tah*.[1]

Plateau people did not live in a utopia, but they lived with predictability until the coming of non-Indians, which forever changed their lives. In response to the invasion of their lands and the British and American takeover of various aspects of their lives, Plateau people responded in many ways, including a realignment of their religious beliefs. Some Native Americans became Christians, influenced by Protestant and Catholic missionaries.[2] Some participated in Christian and Native religious ways, but others grew stronger in their Native spiritualism, following the teachings of prophets and holy ones who urged the people to hold on to and strengthen the old beliefs by formalizing ritual and ceremony.

During the mid-nineteenth century, non-Indian settlers from the United States moved in ever-increasing numbers into the Northwest, many following the Oregon

Trail across the Blue Mountains through the lands of Cayuse, Umatilla, Walla Walla, and others. Settlers traveled down the Columbia River to the Willamette Valley of Oregon Territory, where they colonized the region, reestablishing their forms of government. They soon moved north of the Columbia River into Washington Territory, where they built homes, businesses, and set up governments. Colonization of the Northwest significantly harmed Native Americans, who had enjoyed full sovereignty for years without the influences of newcomers. Other sojourners came by boat to the Columbia River and later to Puget Sound. They brought new religion, government, law, economics, and culture, often contrary to those of Native Americans. New governments financed militia forces, which territorial governments used to expand the influence, property, and resources of settlers. Without Native permission, settlers and colonial governments took indigenous resources and lands, which cost the lives of untold numbers of First Nations people of the Northwest. Unintentionally, settlers introduced smallpox, measles, influenza, common colds, and other diseases that killed unknown numbers of Indian men, women, and children.[3] Predictability of life disintegrated for the people, and various degrees of chaos emerged after settlers colonized areas of the Northwest. The degree of chaos and change depended on the amount of contact Indian families and individuals had with newcomers, their actions, and their introduced sicknesses. Social, economic, legal, and cultural ways of newcomers conflicted with those of Native Americans, and tensions arose between people. Christian newcomers and missionaries considered themselves superior to American Indians and their heathen beliefs, and tensions arose from this cultural conflict, resulting in a realignment of spiritual ways among Indian people. Some people sought deeper association with their old religion, and others gravitated to Protestant or Catholic religions.[4]

American Indian people of the Columbia Plateau had long practiced their own faith. Many Plateau Indians practiced the Washani religion, with slightly different variations from place to place and tribe to tribe. The central tenets of the Washani remained consistent. The heart of the religion emerged from creation accounts. At the time of origins on earth and in the universe, creators placed power on the earth, concentrating it in certain places and enabling individuals to access power to heal, counsel, teach, lead, fight, produce art, and excel in other areas of life.[5] Everyone had the ability to access power, but some individuals had superior ability or gifts to gain more power than others. Plateau Indians based their religions and many of their tribal laws on the many creation narratives handed down to them by past generations. The stories taught the people correct behavior and the consequences of violating tribal laws. From these stories, the people learned about *tamánwit ku súkat*, the spirit and the law.[6]

For generations, Plateau people honored the old laws and attempted to pattern their lives on the ancient teachings, or *tamanwit*. The laws taught the people their relationship with animate and inanimate things on earth and in the heavens. The people believed that during the first creation, plants, animals, and places in the environment interacted in grand dramas known to humans through songs and stories. After the first beings put the earth into motion, then humans came into being and learned proper behavior, respect, and understanding of life on earth through stories. Several beliefs grew out of *tamanwit*, including the belief in spiritual power or *tah*. People used their sacred knowledge to access *tah* through ritual, song, and ceremony. Boys and girls received their personal power through vision quests and carefully guarded their power source, except when they shared their experiences with elders and medicine people who helped them interpret the sacred event.[7]

During the winter months, Plateau people conducted a ceremony in their villages to celebrate their spiritual power, sometimes reenacting the power that had visited them. During the late nineteenth century, Nez Perce warrior Yellow Wolf received his power during a vision when a yellow wolf and white thunder imparted power to the young boy of eleven or twelve. He used his *tah* to guide his violent actions against the United States during the Nez Perce War of 1877 and survive the bloody conflict and forced removal to Eekish Pah (Indian Territory). In similar fashion, Texanap, a young Wenatchi and Yakama girl, received her power in the Wenatchee Mountains of central Washington, a medicine power consisting of water and black water bugs that skirt across the water. Mary Jim, a tribal elder of Snake River–Palouse descent, received her *tah* on the Columbia Plateau, or present-day Washington State, where a fog enveloped her and she saw birds flying without wings and other birds flying without feathers.[8]

Young people shared their visions with elders in the sweat lodge, a sacred dwelling. Elders helped young people interpret the meanings, but people protected the details of their visions, and they did not generally share their experiences and meanings. Some people believed they could lose their power or invite harm to come to themselves and their kin. During the centuries before the twentieth, some Indian people of the Greater Columbia Plateau shared hints of their power by dancing in the winter ceremony. During midwinter ceremonies, people of all ages had an opportunity to act out their power through dancing. In accordance with tribal *tamanwit*, people told others little about their visions and power. Only occasionally, and then for specific purposes, they shared their visions with medicine people or displayed their *tah* in ceremonial dances. Plateau people shared their powers during the winter ceremonies when individuals sang songs they had learned during their vision quests. They also acted out their power through dances.[9]

During war and healing ceremonies, people sometimes summoned their power through spirit songs. Medicine people, particularly, called on their *tah* for help in healing, fighting, loving, and gambling. Power songs belonged to individuals, and Plateau Indian law prohibited others from using those songs, except by permission. The old songs and Native American spiritual ways had developed over the course of hundreds of years before the arrival of Christian missionaries during the 1830s. Protestant and Catholic missionaries discouraged traditional songs, ceremonies, and worship. The arrival of Christians split Indian communities into those believing in the new religion and those embracing the old faith. The introduction of Christianity often caused turmoil within some American Indian villages and put a strain on the spiritual structure of Plateau Indians. Christianity divided families, friends, and groups of people. This contributed to profound changes that affected the history of Northwestern Indians and to the continuance of some difficulties between Indian people today.[10]

Within many different tribes and villages, new spiritual leaders emerged who countered the impact of Christian missionaries with revitalization movements intended to strengthen Native culture. Smohalla, the Wanapum Prophet, had the broadest impact of any Northwestern Indian religious leader during the nineteenth century, and his teachings and innovations influenced Indians throughout the Northwest from the mid-nineteenth century to the present. During the early nineteenth century, sometime between 1815 and 1820, a Wanapum woman living at the village of Wallula, located on the eastern bank of the Mid-Columbia River, gave birth to a boy. That boy would one day become known as Smohalla, after his adult vision quests when he sought his own power through isolated visits to Lalac, a mountain near the Columbia River known today as Rattlesnake Mountain. Most likely he experienced his first visitations in the late 1820s or early 1830s, when he was about eleven years of age. Limited sources suggest that Smohalla grew up to be an unusual boy with a hunchback and little ability as a warrior. Instead, he became a boy of exceptional intelligence and oratory ability. Specific information about Smohalla's youth has not come to light through documents or oral histories, but like other Indian children, he lived with his family, traveling by horseback on seasonal rounds to the root fields in the early spring, fishing areas during the summer, hunting grounds in the fall, and a permanent village on the Columbia River in the winter. Smohalla followed the Washani faith of his ancestors but would add formality to the old faith.[11]

Smohalla lived during a time of rapid change. He was born shortly after the expedition of Meriwether Lewis and William Clark and the arrival of fur traders, missionaries, and Oregon settlers. In the 1840s, he lived through the killing of Marcus and Narcissa Whitman and the Cayuse Indian War. Smohalla grew up during a turbulent era, when events unfolded quickly for Native Americans of the Northwest as non-Indians moved into the region, bringing new ways of life, governments, religions, and dangerous and devastating diseases—like measles, smallpox, influenza, and cholera—that killed many Native Americans.[12] Also menacing, the government of the United States sent surveyors and soldiers to study areas for future growth, a condition new to American Indians of the Northwest but one known by them through the oral accounts

FIGURE 6.1. Smohalla and his priests, 1884. The Wanapum Prophet revitalized the old Washani faith, known today as the Seven Drums religion. Indigenous people throughout the Columbia Plateau met in longhouses like this one and followed the precepts, songs, ceremonies, and protocols taught by Smohalla. Courtesy of Yakima Valley Libraries.

of Iroquois and Delaware Indians working for the Hudson's Bay Company. Indians of the Columbia Plateau knew about American expansionism into Indian Country in the eastern parts of the United States and of the forced removal of Eastern Indians to Indian Territory located in present-day Oklahoma and Kansas. New local and territorial governments in the Northwest threatened every aspect of Native American life and culture.[13]

Settlement patterns of newcomers from the United States into Indian Country threatened Indian religions, root grounds, fisheries, hunting areas, families, and villages. White settlements compromised the free movement of Native Americans across the landscape that held their economic lifeway. Eventually, the settlers, colonial governments, Indian policies, reservations, and removals destroyed all the Native economies of the Pacific Northwest. These and other factors—including the presence of non-Indians and continual immigration by white settlers—influenced the everyday lives of Native Americans. Indian people responded to the newcomers in several different ways, including requests to the Creator to preserve the people, their culture, and their relationship with the earth's bounty. Some Indians moved away from the newcomers, while others remained in their homelands and tried to live in the midst of an ever-growing non-Native population. Some Indians gravitated to trading posts and Christian missions to learn the ways of the newcomers, trading with white settlers or working with them in many enterprises. Others rejected Christianity and tried to separate themselves from settlers. But regardless of their reaction to newcomers, the presence of *suyapo*, or white people, threatened Indians with "walking diseases" (traveling or moving diseases, or infectious diseases).[14] Non-Indian immigration to the Northwest created instability among Indian people and brought an end to life's predictability.

In such a state as this, Smohalla sought refuge on the mountain called Lalac (Rattlesnake Mountain) west of the Columbia River, where he prayed, meditated, and sang. He asked for *tah*, the basis of understanding within his world. According to Smohalla and others, the future prophet had a revelation while he fasted, prayed, and sang on Lalac.[15] As a child of eleven, he had an earlier vision when he sought his *tah* or *wayakin* power during his childhood vision quest. No known record of his first visions has survived to indicate his original spiritual power. However, his vision on the mountain of Lalac changed the course of Northwestern Indian history, as it began Smohalla's revitalization movement and regular meetings on Sundays to sing, dance, and drum in the longhouse. He became deeply involved in preaching the continuance of the Washani religion with new forms of structure, dance, songs, and protocols.[16]

Smohalla used the Washani as the fundamental belief of the religion. He added to the number of songs by sharing those the Creator gave him, and he brought a new dance to earth, the *washat*. The Creator, he reported, gave him the vision on Lalac that began a process leading to revitalization of the Washani religion. His vision also led to a greater focus of indigenous religion by Native Americans generally living on the Columbia Plateau. During the course of his revelation on Lalac, Smohalla traveled to the "land in the sky," where he neared the land of the dead, but because he was still alive, the keepers of this kingdom of the dead refused to allow him to enter, saying he must go back to his people and tell them to return to Native ways and reject the culture and religion of non-Native newcomers. Smohalla said he had learned from Naamii Piap (Creator, Our Elder Brother) that Indian people should reject many aspects of the settlers and their agents, particularly their materialism, modes of labor, and religion that drew people away from *tah* and *tamanwit*. The Creator in the land in the sky told Smohalla to become a preacher, teacher, and messenger for the holy people and spread the Creator's teachings.[17]

According to Smohalla's nephew, Puck Hyah Toot, Smohalla had died on Lalac but had returned to life to inform Plateau Indians about how to respond to the white invasion of the Northwest. After the vision, Smohalla came down from the mountain, then changed his name to Shmoquala (Shouting Mountain), a name that has evolved into Smohalla. His name came to have other meanings, including preacher, teacher, and dreamer.[18] In a real sense, Smohalla's death and rebirth compare similarly to that of other American Indian prophets, including Neolin, Tenskwatawa, and Wovoka. Smohalla's life also mirrored the many adventures of Speelyi (Mythic Coyote), who often experienced death and rebirth. In many traditional stories of the Columbia Plateau, Speelyi died, learned lessons, and returned to life. While Plateau people portray Coyote as a trickster figure in their oral traditions, they also speak of Speelyi as a creative force who planted all the foods. In one account, Coyote destroyed a dam on the Columbia River and led the salmon into the inland Northwest.

By way of his heroic actions, Coyote the Creator helped the people in many ways, and he established many of the laws by which the people lived, and by which some still live today.[19] Like Coyote, Smohalla did live to enhance his own ego or enlarge his popularity. He lived to serve the Indian communities of the inland Northwest and acted for the benefit of all people. Smohalla's revelations from the sky above brought him a new reputation, one he had not enjoyed before the mid-nineteenth century. One reporter wrote that, as a young man, Smohalla was "a rather undersized Indian with a form inclining toward obesity." Another person claimed his head to be "large and well-shaped." His head was described as "almost Websterian . . . with deep brow over bright intelligent eyes."[20] Non-Indians considered Smohalla to be "peculiar" and "not prepossessing at first sight." He was born a hunchback, and he did not fit the American view of a great Native American leader. Still, he was a persuasive speaker who could "spellbind" his audiences with "his magic manner." He could arouse a crowd because his oratory was "full of fire." Added to this, Smohalla reportedly could predict future events, call the weather, locate lost objects, and "read" or understand people through his psychic ability.[21]

Smohalla lived during a turbulent era of Northwestern history, an era of rapid change brought by settlers and colonists of the United States. Army and navy expeditions and missionaries made their way onto the Columbia Plateau, encouraging immigration into the Native Northwest. In 1837, during Smohalla's youth, a few Cayuse Indians ordered Dr. Marcus Whitman to leave his mission at Waiilatpu (Place of the Rye Grass). Whitman had settled in the Walla Walla Valley without permission from Cayuse leaders. In the 1840s, a measles epidemic swept across the plateau, killing many Indian people. Some Indians believed Whitman had unleashed the contagious disease, and they ordered him several times to abandon his mission. But Whitman felt he was on a mission from God and refused to leave. Indians warned him that his life was in danger, but he refused to leave. Finally a few Cayuse warriors lost their patience. They attacked and killed the missionary, his wife, and others. This triggered the Cayuse War, but only a few warriors participated in the tragedy, and all Cayuse

FIGURE 6.2. This photo of Andrew George was taken around 1940. George was a famous *towat* or *twati*, holy man and healer. Throughout his adult life, he led Washat ceremonies on the Northwest Plateau. George was a highly spiritual man who followed the precepts of Smohalla. George's daughter, Tillie George Sharlo, shared this photograph. Courtesy of Richard D. Scheuerman.

had not sanctioned the killings. Non-Indians hanged four Cayuse men for the killings, and the entire affair still hangs over the Northwest like a dark cloud.[22]

Smohalla did not participate in the Whitman affair, but he knew of the troubles in the Cayuse homelands. Smohalla preached nonviolence, not war, and he wanted as little contact with settlers as humanly possible. He also refused to participate in the treaty proceedings of the Walla Walla Council of 1855 that produced the Yakama, Nez Perce, and Umatilla Indian Reservations. Negotiations resulted both in treaties and in an enormous amount of indigenous animosity against the government agents and miners who moved onto Indian lands without permission. The Plateau Indian War from 1855 to 1858 resulted from these events, but Smohalla did not advocate war or participate in the ugly conflict that forever changed life for Native Americans in the Northwest. Nevertheless, Smohalla's teachings about the old faith had a profound influence on Plateau Indian people at the time and influenced future events caused by the non-Native invasion of Indian lands. Smohalla also preached against the political, economic, and "legal" takeover of the Northwest by settler-colonists. Smohalla and his followers practiced nonviolence, finding security and predictability in their religion and ceremonies. Followers of the Washani and Washat sought peace at their home sites, where they drummed, prayed, and sang for the ability of Indian people to cope with and survive the rapid changes facing them. Born at Wallula on the Columbia River, Smohalla began his ministry at the same site but ultimately moved his village upriver to Priest Rapids.[23]

While Smohalla lived at Wallula, he attained a small following. Some people living nearby on the banks of the Columbia River listened to the *yanchta* (teacher) and lived in a traditional way of life away from white people. Others followed Homli, a village chief and rival of Smohalla. Sometime between 1858 and 1860, Smohalla moved his followers and their village north along the Columbia River adjacent to hard, dark basalt rock walls in a canyon that became known as Priest Rapids, named after the Wanapum *yanchta*. At Priest Rapids, on the west side of the Columbia River, Smohalla built P'na, a small, vibrant village of A-framed mat lodges. This is the site of the Wanapum village today on the middle Columbia River near Wanapum Dam, Washington. The people today carry on the teachings and worship taught by Smohalla, making the Washat or Seven Drums religion a living faith. The prophet lived in the ceremonial lodge and held ceremony just north of the village. The village also included a fenced-in ceremonial space where a long wooden flagpole flew Smohalla's flag. Smohalla explained his flag to Major MacMurray, saying it "represents the world." During Smohalla's vision quest, the Creator told him that his village would be the center of the four cardinal directions. The red spot on the flag represented Smohalla's heart, and the yellow represented yellow bunch grass on the hills. The green in the flag was the boundaries of the earth, while the blue was the sky.[24] The stars, moon, and sun played significant roles in the prophet's symbols. Above the flag, Smohalla placed a wooden carving of Wawshukla, an oriole and sacred bird. The bird represented a power figure that visited Smohalla during his vision quest. The prophet believed the bird called the salmon to continue their journeys each year up the Columbia River. Wowshuxkluck also "awakened" the roots, berries, deer, and fish to come alive to feed the people in accordance with *tamanwit*.[25]

During worship services, Smohalla paid homage to the Creator, who had given the people a beautiful place on earth beside the great Columbia River. Naamii Piap gave the people many varieties of roots, berries, moss, deer, salmon, and other Native foods. During ceremony, Smohalla and worshipers gave thanks for the foods that nourished their bodies and provided them survival on earth. They also thanked Naamii Piap for water and ritually drank *kuus* before they ate and at the conclusion of feasts. The people sang to the beat of the bell and of seven hand drums, and rows of females danced on the balls of their feet as they stood in place. Worshipers of the Washat believed in the power of the seven-pointed star, and as a result, they required seven drummers. Over the years, the people began calling the Washat the Seven Drums religion or Longhouse religion.[26] Three was also a sacred number as it represented the sun, moon, and stars, all part of the universe within which the people lived. Throughout the ceremony, worshipers sang and chanted words of thanksgiving. People often held their hands on their hearts and raised them at times toward heaven, sending their prayers to the Creator, and received power back by holding their hands with fingers spread toward the sky at the end of prayers. The also turned their bodies in a complete circle from right to left, audibly saying, "I-ah."[27]

The longhouse (ceremonial house) became the center of village activities at P'na, the site where the people gathered to pray, sing, and give thanks to the sacred foods the Creator had given them through Speelyi's sacred creations. During the decade of the 1860s, non-Natives recorded that Smohalla had ten wives. At the time, he had only one child, a daughter. He was training this girl to be his successor. Smohalla considered her a special child, and he chose her to carry on his teachings. However, during her vision quest in which sought her *tah*, she became ill with an unknown disease.[28] Smohalla and his people could not identify the disease the girl contracted. Smohalla tried to save her life using his own medicine. When she did not improve, Smohalla called on other *twati*, or medicine people, to attempt a cure. No one could help the girl, and she died. Her death was a terrible blow to her father, friends, and relatives at Priest Rapids.[29]

In his grief, Smohalla participated in the all-night wake of his people, praying and singing in the mat-covered A-framed longhouse. The women dressed the girl's body in white deerskin and ritualistically dealt with her hair and face. The people offered her grave goods to be buried with her. The Wanapum Indians of Priest Rapids and many others from near and far participated in the funeral service. For three days, the people sang and prayed, mourning her death. They prepared her coffin, made of a dugout canoe that they had cut in half, placing the body inside one half of the canoe and inverting the other end to form a lid of her coffin. They buried Smohalla's daughter not far from their village, singing and praying all the while. The *yanchta* remained at the grave all day and night. He mourned for his child for days. He could not be

FIGURE 6.3. Alex Jim and Mary Jim, Naxiyamtáma (or Snake River-Palouse Indian) followers of the Washani faith of the Northwest. They raised their children on Snake River in the old faith, taking them to Priest Rapids, where Puck Hyah Toot taught them traditional medicine ways. Throughout the year, they held ceremonies to honor all their indigenous foods, including salmon, deer, roots, and berries. Courtesy of Carrie Jim Schuster.

consoled, so his family and friends left him alone at the grave, but after a few days, they returned to find their leader dead. The people now grieved for Smohalla, taking his body to the longhouse and preparing it for a funeral. The women washed his body and dressed him in buckskin clothing. After washing his hair, the women braided his hair and placed long strips of fine otter fur in his long gray hair. The women painted his face yellow and prepared the longhouse for the second funeral in a few days. They assembled the people, and the leaders began the funeral service.[30]

Men gathered on one side of the longhouse and women assembled on the other. The leader used a handbell, much like those used by schoolteachers in the nineteenth century, to call the Spirit. He prayed, using the bell to keep time, and the service began. The men used hand drums called *kookoolots* to accompany the songs. The men sang a verse and women sang in response. The congregation sang funeral dirges long into the night. Early in the morning, Smohalla's body moved, and participants witnessed the unbelievable event. First, his hand twitched, and then he moved his hand to remove the buckskin sheet covering his face. Smohalla opened his eyes and rose to his knees, but said nothing. The participants ran from the sacred place and scene in fear of his awakening. They filed outside, where they awaited word of Smohalla's condition. Two days later, Smohalla asked one of his wives to assemble his followers on the Columbia River at Water Swirl Place, not far from the village. In the interim, news of Smohalla's resurrection spread across the plateau, and many Indians visited Priest Rapids to witness the miracle. At Water Swirl Place, Smohalla addressed the crowd and told them of his new experiences in the land in the sky. Smohalla reported he had messages from Naamii Piap.[31]

Smohalla preached about his revelations to the people, giving them the word as reported to him from the Creator. According to the *yanchta*, the Creator wanted the people to follow the Washani and live by the old laws, or *tamanwit*. Through the oral traditions, Plateau Indians had practiced the old Washat faith since time immemorial. Through traditional stories, the people learned how to deal with each other, plants, places, animals, and the spirit world. Smohalla emphasized that Naamii Piap wanted the people to continue to bless each other and the first foods that sustained life. The Creator wanted Indian people to give thanks by continuing to hold root, berry, salmon, and deer ceremonies. At these sacred events, people gave thanks to Naamii Piap for the foods, and they gave thanks to the foods for surrendering their lives so Indian people could survive life on earth. The Creator provided food, water, and air, and the prophet and other religious leaders emphasized the people should be forever thankful for these gifts, without which humans would perish. Smohalla instructed the people to thank the Creator for his many blessings, including life itself and the lands upon which they drew their livelihood. Smohalla said the Creator wanted the people to continue to sing songs of the Washat and add to them the new songs He had given the prophet Smohalla. The Creator wanted to hear the beat of seven drums, the heartbeat of the earth and all creation. The drums vibrated the longhouses and were (are) symbolic of life. According to Smohalla, Naamii Piap said, "Teach the Wanapum and others to be good, do good, and live like Indians. Give them this song and show them this dance."[32]

> Sound of the bell
> Sound of the heart
> My Brothers
> My Sisters
> I am meeting you
> I am meeting you at the dance[33]

Smohalla told the people that Naamii Piap wanted them to follow a new procedure in worship and to meet each week to pray and sing. The Creator had taught Smohalla a special dance accompanied by seven *kookoolots*. Smohalla instructed his followers to use a *qualal qualal* (brass bell) when they prayed and sang, the bell representing the heart and timing of life. The voices of the people represented the breath of life, and their movement offered a reminder that life was about movement. At the meeting at Water Swirl Place and at subsequent ceremonies, Smohalla reminded the people that the Creator had made the earth, heavens, and all things, and the people had a holy obligation to give thanks to Naamii Piap for life, land, resources, and people. The Creator had "called forth all animals, birds, and plants" for the benefit and continuance of life. Smohalla reported that salmon was first among all animals, and the Creator had made the huckleberries last. As a result, Smohalla pointed out, "It is in this order that salmon and food roots are taken as Communion at the feasts of thanksgiving to the Creator." Thus during First Foods Celebrations of salmon, roots, and berries, the people give thanks to the Creator and foods, following prescribed rituals of prayers and presentation of sacred foods. Smohalla taught the people not to "taste the first food without performing the first-food ceremonies." To remind the people of their deep relationship with the earth, plants, and animals, Smohalla taught the people to meet every seventh day to worship, perhaps an outgrowth of Christians meeting on the Sabbath.[34]

Smohalla was not the first or last prophet and holy person to emerge within the tribal communities of the Northwest plateau. Several Indian people received prophetic teachings from the Creator, but Smohalla's teachings had long-term and profound consequences. His people at Wanapum Village near Priest Rapids and other followers of the Washat remember the Wanapum Prophet and his teachings. The *yanchta* changed the course of history and affected the spiritual life of thousands of

FIGURE 6.4. Mary Jim and daughter, Carrie Jim, are shown after returning from gathering camas root, which they used in First Foods Ceremonies. Both women, followers of the Seven Drums faith, have been members of the Longhouse all their lives. Courtesy of Richard D. Scheuerman.

FIGURE 6.5. Today, most followers of Smohalla's principles call their religion Seven Drums. During services and ceremonies, men use thunderous hand drums, which shake the lodges or rooms wherever used. Master photographer of the Northwest John Clement took this photograph of drummers and singers during a First Foods Ceremony. Courtesy of John Clement Galleries.

Plateau Indians, past and present. He initiated changes to the Washani that influenced the dance and ceremony that people perform and the teachings practiced today, with their emphasis on ritual, ceremony, and reverence for the earth's bounty.[35] Over the years, other spiritual leaders emerged among the Plateau tribes. Some of the notable religious leaders of the Northwest included Shuwapsa, Lishwailait, Husishusis Kute, Toohoolhoolzote, Skolaskin, John Slocum, Mary Slocum, Titcam Nashat, and others. All of these spiritual leaders, like Smohalla, emphasized the relationship of the people to the Creator and creation, particularly the celebration of foods, singing of prayer songs, respect for plants and animals, and protection of land the Creator had made for the people.

Mary and John Slocum created the Indian Shaker Church, which was not associated with the Shaker Church known in the eastern part of the United States. The Indian Shaker Church had a direct association with Christianity, but it maintained a strong Native American foundation and continues that tradition today. On the Northwest plateau, often followers of the Indian Shaker Church also incorporate other spiritual ways in their everyday lives. Northwestern Indians, past and present, might attend Seven Drums Ceremonies, First Food Ceremonies, Feather Ceremonies, and Christian churches. Many maintained their strong Native foundation, even while attending

Christian services.[36] Unlike Christians that would not stray from their dogma, some Native American "converts" did not forsake *tamanwit* or precepts of the Washani faith but blended different doctrines without forsaking the old traditions.

The Wanapum Prophet explained that he had not created the revitalization of the old Washani religion. Naamii Piap had created the revitalization and had instructed Smohalla about new additions and specific rituals, songs, and ceremonies. The Creator had taught Smohalla the *washat* with exact instructions about the construction of the dance floor inside the longhouse and dancing techniques. Naamii Piap had explained the meaning of all these things to the prophet. Smohalla said he was only the messenger, but he became a significant force among many diverse tribes and influenced people across the Northwest. Other spiritual leaders among Sahaptin- and Salish-speaking Indians used portions of his revitalization and added to his teachings. Smohalla formalized the Washani faith and brought structure to the ancient religion. He incorporated traditional beliefs into the instructions provided by the Creator. Smohalla drew on traditional beliefs to support the additions he brought to the belief system of Plateau people. The prophet always emphasized the sacredness of the earth, plants, animals, and places. He preached the preservation of Native lands, laws, and ceremonies.

All of Smohalla's new protocols, use of instruments, dances, songs, prayers, and procedures coincided with the old faith, so he did not take a wide turn from tradition but built on the old ways to energize the religion as a holy and peaceful way of coping with radical changes brought by non-Natives. The use of the old ways has resulted in the longevity of Smohalla's teachings, songs, and ceremonial ways. Smohalla preached nonviolence and a devout commitment to the old faith that made it a "sin" to surrender land and natural resources to settlers and agents of American colonialism. He had no interest in the work ethic of Christian missionaries, business interests, or agents of the Bureau of Indian Affairs. His laws came from the Creator, not man, and he preached adherence to *tamanwit*, the ancient laws of Washani followers. Smohalla opposed treaties, reservations, homesteads, and new labor systems introduced by white people.[37]

Smohalla's teachings provided military and civilian policy makers a justification to remove Indians forcefully from the so-called public domain and force them to reservations where white agents of the Bureau of Indian Affairs could monitor and control "Dreamers."[38] Whites believed Smohalla threatened Christianity and American civilization. The Wanapum Prophet appeared to white Christians as the embodiment of Satan—a backward, primitive, and evil being that stood as a counterimage to God, Christ, and American civilization. Although agents and army officers targeted Smohalla as an enemy of the United States, many Plateau Indians gravitated to him and his teachings, especially because his teachings coincided with their own spiritual beliefs

FIGURE 6.6. Wilson Wewa is a medicine person living on the Warm Springs Reservation of Oregon. He is a ceremonial leader and healer, well-known by Native Americans in the Northwest. He has spent his life serving others and preserving the spiritual ways of indigenous people of the Columbia Plateau. Courtesy of Richard Scheuerman.

and interest in returning to the ancient ways to preserve the laws, land, resources, and beliefs of the people.

Officials within the War and Interior Departments of the United States feared Smohalla and his teachings. Smohalla's doctrines ran contrary to Christianity, Manifest Destiny, and mission. Many officials pointed out contradictions between the Washani and Christian faiths. Settlers and soldiers found Smohalla a threat, as he refused Christianity and preached against American values of capitalism, cheap labor, land division, and policies toward American Indians, including treaties, reservations, and forced removal. Some Indian people became Christians. Some Christian Indians saw similarities between their old faith and the Old Testament, as well as the teachings of Jesus. The ancient laws of Plateau Indians and some teachings of the Judeo-Christian faith emphasized love of humans and the earth, cooperation, kindness, sharing, and spiritual power. But non-Indians feared Smohalla's teachings. As a result, settlers denigrated the prophet and his religious beliefs.[39]

By the 1850s, when the United States had taken political control over the Northwest, American governmental officials brought a well-developed policy to the region that called for treaties, liquidation of Indian land titles, confinement of Indians onto reservations, limitations of Indian rights, regulation of the Indian trade, rights of way through Indian lands for roads (later railroads and highways), and control of Native Americans through agents, superintendents, and commissioners of the Office of Indian Affairs and soldiers of the United States Army.[40] In addition, the Oregon Territory received support of the State Department, which organized territorial government and militias. Before the 1850s, American Indians of the Columbia Plateau had interacted with explorers, trappers, traders, missionaries, and some soldiers. Native Americans had no unified policy like that of the United States. Instead, they organized by villages and bands and had a variety of civil, military, medicine, and spiritual leaders, with each village and tribe determining its own policies, although inter- and intratribal councils took place formally and informally. Still, during the 1850s, Plateau tribes had no unified policy, which helped representatives of the United States divide the tribes and pressure them for land cessions.

Smohalla understood the overall agenda of settler-colonists in the Northwest. He viewed them and their various levels of government as threats to Native American religion on the plateau, and he fought against Americans through his faith, urging Indians to follow his teaching to preserve Native American sovereignty through their religious practices of nonviolence. In order to wrest lands from the tribes, Washington Territorial governor Isaac Stevens had his secretaries draft treaties with groupings of tribes living in certain regions. Stevens drafted treaties before treaty councils and browbeat several tribal leaders into surrendering their lands. Then he turned his sights east, onto the Columbia Plateau.

In 1855, Stevens acted as the superintendent of Indian Affairs for Washington, while Joel Palmer served as the Oregon superintendent of Indian Affairs.[41] Together they met several tribes at the Walla Walla Council in May and June 1855. The Nez Perce, Yakama, Cayuse, Palouse, Walla Walla, and Umatilla sent representatives to the great council, and leaders from other groups from the region attended the conference to listen and learn. No record exists to suggest that Smohalla attended the council, but he knew of the gathering and disapproved of negotiating with the Americans. In spite of his absence, Smohalla's spiritual concepts and those of the Washani religion emerged as the central theme at the conference. Indigenous leaders meeting at Walla Walla spoke eloquently from their hearts in a futile attempt to explain their spiritual beliefs to Stevens, Palmer, and other non-Indians. The indigenous leaders framed their arguments around the Washani religion and the religious revitalization movement then sweeping the Columbia Plateau. Their responses to proposals set forth by Stevens and Palmer reflected a deep commitment to Washani doctrines and new reassertion of indigenous sovereignty. Nearly all of the Indian leaders attending the Walla Walla Council spoke of the creation and *tamanwit*, the ancient laws, although interpreters cast the ideas involving ancient Native American laws into the English language in ways that made sense to Americans. Rather than using the word *Naamii Piap* or other indigenous words to refer to the Creator, interpreters used the term *God*. When the Indian leadership learned that the Americans wanted them to surrender their lands and move onto designated areas called reservations, the leaders responded using teachings of the Washani and beliefs they shared with the Wanapum Prophet. Cayuse chief Stickus spoke many times at the council, and he often illustrated his points with examples reflected in the Washani faith.[42]

When asked to give up nearly all their tribal land, Chief Stickus responded by equating the earth with one's own mother. His response mirrored teachings common among Plateau people and Smohalla's views: "If your mothers were here in this country who gave you birth, suckled you and while you were sucking some person came and took your mother and left you alone and sold your mother, how would you feel then?" Chief Owhi of the Yakama responded in a similar fashion when he reminded Governor Stevens that the Creator had "looked one way and then the other and named our lands for us." According to Washat beliefs and Smohalla's teachings, the Creator had created the land for Native Americans of the plateau and "he made it to last forever. It is the earth that is our parent [and] it is God who is our elder brother [Naamii Piap]." Owhi feared making a decision at the Walla Walla Council that might be contrary to the old law, since he was "afraid of the rights of the Almighty." The earth and its bounty belonged to the Creator, not to Indians, so Owhi asked, "Shall I steal this land and sell it? Shall I give the lands that are part of my body and leave myself poor and destitute? Shall I say I will give you my lands? I cannot . . . I am afraid of the Almighty."[43] Cayuse leader Young Chief drew on *tamanwit* when he addressed the council: "I wonder if this land has anything to say; I wonder if the ground is listening to what is said. I wonder if the ground would come to life and what is on it; though I hear what this earth says, the earth says, God has placed me here." Young Chief reminded the others that the Creator had "named the roots that he should feed the Indians on: the water speaks the same way: God says feed the Indians upon the earth; the grass says the same thing."[44]

Smohalla agreed with all these lines of reasoning, since all things were of the earth, born of the earth by Naamii Piap. For Smohalla, the Creator intended life to be closely interwoven and tied to nature so that humans would continually give thanks and remember their sacred relationship with plants, places, animals, and the Creator. Smohalla refused to surrender the earth and its bounty to the newcomers, and he preached against removal to reservations. Most of the leaders attending the Walla Walla Council opposed treaties and removal to reservations, but they felt they had little choice but to sign the Umatilla, Yakama, and Nez Perce treaties or lose all their land. Iroquois and Delaware Indians living with the Plateau tribes warned the leaders to make a deal with the United States or lose everything. Thus, in 1855 Indian leaders signed treaty agreements they believed were permanent, like their laws.[45]

To Smohalla and the other Indians, Naamii Piap had intended life to remain connected to the Spirit. The Wanapum Prophet refused to negotiate with whites or to move onto a reservation, despite the fact that Stevens had included the Wanapum in the Yakama Treaty of 1855. Smohalla steadfastly refused to remain on a reservation, and he spent his life urging others to follow *tamanwit*, not the law of the United States. The prophet taught that Naamii Piap had "commanded that the lands and fisheries should be common to all who lived upon them; that they were never to be marked off or divided." Smohalla further stated that "God said he was Father and the Earth was the Mother of mankind; that nature was the law; that the animals, and fish, and plants obeyed nature, and that man only was sinful." Smohalla followed the old law and Washani faith that formed the foundation of his teachings. As for those Indians who signed the treaties or moved onto the reservations, the Creator would punish them.[46]

In spite of Smohalla's message and the teachings of other spiritual leaders, many Plateau Indians lived on or moved to reservations. Some people became Christians. Thus, divisions occurred over time within the Indian communities as Christian, reservation, treaty Indians stood in marked contrast to non-Christian, nonreservation, and nontreaty Indians. The most glaring example of this social schism emerged with the Nez Perce bands, particularly after 1863, when a part of the tribe signed a treaty relinquishing 6,932,270 acres of their reservation to the government. Of the fifty-two

FIGURE 6.7. During ceremonies, Smohalla raised this carved spirit bird, a Bullock's oriole, which first came to him during a vision quest on Rattlesnake Mountain in eastern Washington. Smohalla's followers say that the bird called out to the salmon, urging them to migrate upriver, and to spring buds, urging them to open. The carving turned upon a pole on top of the longhouse. Courtesy of Richard D. Scheuerman.

Indians who agreed to the "Thief Treaty," all were either Christians or openly sympathetic to Christians and Chief Lawyer. However, not one of the antitreaty Indians signed the treaty of 1863, which created a new Nez Perce reservation one-tenth the size of the original one negotiated in 1855. The actions of the treaty between Nez Perce, government agents, miners, and ranchers put the Nez Perce on a course leading to war and bloodshed.[47]

In response to the extreme pressures of governmental policies, white expansion, and tribal factionalism, many Nez Perce and their Palouse and Cayuse neighbors turned inward to embrace their traditional spiritual beliefs. To some degree, Smohalla's teachings and revitalization movement influenced other Native Americans that practiced derivatives of the Washani faith, categorized by whites as the Dreamer religion. Representatives of the government characterized Washani religious followers as practicing the "new-fangled religious delusion." Settlers called Indians that followed the precepts of the so-called Dreamer religion subversive "wizards" and "magicians."[48] Tension between the Indian traditionalists and government agents reached an impasse in 1876, after the Battle of the Little Bighorn, when General Oliver O. Howard and Nez Perce Agent John B. Monteith ordered nontreaty Nez Perce, Palouse, and Cayuse onto the Nez Perce Reservation. In 1876 and 1877, Native American leaders met General Howard at Lapwai, Idaho. Howard ordered the Indians to move onto the much-reduced Nez Perce Reservation. Indian leaders responded by enunciating again the precepts of their religion. Surrendering the earth—the soil that held the bones of their ancestors—was a violation of the Washani and *tamanwit*. The Creator had given Indians the earth and its bounty, and the earth was sacred and could not be divided or sold. The topic of the earth was a spiritual matter, and the Nez Perce, Palouse, and Cayuse shared a belief system with other Plateau Indians that had a direct influence on many people. However, Smohalla never advocated violence, war, or an Indian confederacy. The prophet would have concurred with Nez Perce that Native Americans should never sell their lands that included Indian burials, fisheries, hunting grounds, and gathering areas. These were tied to the sacred and a gift from the Creator never to be alienated from the tribes. But he never prepared for war or urged Indians to fight the United States.[49]

At the Lapwai Council of 1877, nontreaty Indians asked Toohoolhoolzote to represent them when they met with General Howard. The general believed Indian religious leaders were "fanatics" and that the "dreamers, among other pernicious doctrines, teach that the earth being created by God complete, should not be disturbed by man, and that any cultivation of the soil or other improvements to interfere with its natural productions, any voluntary submission to the control of the government, any improvement in the way of schools, churches, etc., are crimes from which they shrink."[50] He correctly perceived the basic ideology of Smohalla and others like Toohoolhoolzote, but "the Christian General" did not understand or value these "pagan Indian" beliefs about land, property, religion, and government. In the end, the Nez Perce and Palouse chiefs agree to relocate to the reservation to avoid war, even though Smohalla's teachings had widespread appeal. In the words of the Prophet:

> You ask me to plow the Ground! Shall I take a knife and tear my mother's bosom? Then when I die she will not take me to her bosom to rest.
> You ask me to dig for stone! Shall I dig under her skin for her bones? Then when I die I cannot enter her body to be born again.
> You ask me to cut grass and make hay and sell it and be rich like white men! But how dare I cut off my mother's hair?[51]

Although Smohalla did not attend the Lapwai Councils of 1876 or 1877, Joseph, Toohoolhoolzote, Husishusis Kute, and others attended and shared the views of the Wanapum Prophet. When General Howard announced at the first Lapwai Council that the nontreaty Nez Perce would have to give up the Wallowa area of northeastern Oregon, Chief Joseph explained, "The Creative Power, when he made the earth, made no marks, no lines of division or separation on it." The chief explained that the Indians were "of the earth and grew up on its bosom," since the earth was "Mother and nurse, was sacred to his affections, too sacred to be valued by or sold for silver or gold."[52] Joseph refused to surrender his lands, perhaps remembering his father's words: "This country holds your father's body. Never sell the bones of your father and your mother."[53] At the second Lapwai Council, in 1877, Palouse leader Husishusis Kute related ideas that he shared with many Plateau Indians. Howard labeled Husishusis Kute "the oily, wily, bright-eyed young chief, who could be smooth-tongued or saucy as the mood seized him." More important was the aged Nez Perce, Toohoolhoolzote, whom Howard called "the cross-grained growler."[54] Toohoolhoolzote and Palouse chief Husishusis Kute were followers of Smohalla's teachings. Howard characterized them as followers of the "new religious people" who used "a drum to beat in his worship [Seven Drums]."[55] Husishusis Kute had learned the fundamentals of his religion from his father, "who was an outstanding Dreamer Prophet, and spiritual man."[56] He had also learned a great deal from Smohalla, whose band often traveled, hunted, and gathered roots with Palouse bands. When the Indians camped together, they often worshiped together, singing, praying, and conducting ceremony.[57]

At the Lapwai Council, Husishusis Kute "was held in high esteem by all the Dreamer tribesmen" and was selected to speak second after Toohoolhoolzote.[58] He never had an opportunity to speak, though, because an argument escalated between Toohoolhoolzote and Howard. As the general put it, Toohoolhoolzote made "the usual long preliminary discussion about the earth being his mother, that she should not be disturbed by hoe or plough, that men should subsist on what grows of itself."[59] When reminded of the treaty of 1863, Toohoolhoolzote said that the document was "born of to-day" and that it was not the "true law at all."[60] In every meeting, Toohoolhoolzote spoke of the "chieftainship of the earth" and explained that Indian law revolved around the reverence of the land that could not be bought, sold, or traded.[61]

Toohoolhoolzote explained, "White people get together, measure the earth, and then divide it." The Indians, he said, could not do this, because it was contrary to *tamanwit*. "The earth is part of my body," he announced, "and I never gave up the earth."[62] The discussion between Toohoolhoolzote and Howard became hostile. Howard ordered his soldiers to seize Toohoolhoolzote and jail him. Toohoolhoolzote told Howard he was "trifling with the law [*tamanwit*] of the earth." Howard created a volatile moment that might have erupted. The chiefs hesitated, surrounded as they were with armed guards. With Toohoolhoolzote in jail, Howard threatened the Plateau people with war unless they relocated to the reservation. He pressed each chief for an answer: Would they move to the reservation or not? As Chief Joseph said years later, "We were like the deer. They were like the grizzly bear." The nontreaty Nez Perce, Cayuse, and Palouse agreed to move onto the reservation.[63]

While the Nez Perce and Upper Palouse prepared to move onto the reservation, Howard traveled to the Lower Snake River to council with a number of Indians, including Smohalla and his close friend, the Palouse headman Thomash. Howard feared a general rebellion among the Indians because of "a craze that spread from tribe to tribe, and swept many of the peaceable and friendly Indians from the moorings of common sense and prudence."[64] Howard and other officers accused Smohalla of teaching a "fanaticism" that was "calculated to appeal to the Indians and stir them up against the whites, and unite them in rebellion." Rumors had spread within the white communities that Smohalla and a host of "dreamers, and prophets" contemplated "a general uprising" that would spread across the land "like wild fire."[65] In late May 1877, Howard met with Smohalla and representatives from the Palouse, Cayuse, Wanapum, and Walla Walla tribes in an attempt to quiet hostilities, explain the government's position, and end rumors.

Howard camped near Smohalla's first home at Wallula and invited the chiefs to visit him. Smohalla entered Howard's camp "bedecked with paint and feathers."[66] The prophet's "cavalcade filed in with all the pomp and circumstance characteristic of Indian conceit."[67] Howard later wrote that Smohalla "could not be exceeded by any earthly potentate in assumption of power or importance of manner." The Wanapum Prophet stated that he wanted peace with the whites, but he wished for his band the right "to roam at large whenever and wherever they pleased."[68] Smohalla caused no trouble during his conference with Howard, but Thomash "was wild and fierce to the last."[69] Palouse chief Thomash, from the village of Sumuyah, chastised Howard for "sending troops to Wallowa, and denounced the actions and wishes of the United States government in unmeasured terms."[70] Thomash left the council angry, but like Smohalla and other indigenous leaders, he met with Howard again on June 8, 1877, at the Fort Simcoe Council in the Yakama Country.

At the council, Howard announced that the government required that all Indians "shall all come on this [the Yakama] or some other of its reservations." None of the leaders liked this talk, and Smohalla reportedly "seemed to be out of his place and was ill at ease."[71] The prophet reportedly appeared nervous when he spoke, and he perspired profusely as he explained his position centered on the Creator and *taman-wit*. According to Dr. G. B. Kuykendall, a physician in attendance and stationed at the fort, "Smohallah's talk was quite rambling . . . aimed to impress those present that he was a great teacher and leader."[72] Smohalla knew that Howard wanted the Indians to move onto the reservation, despite his objection to doing so. Howard reported that Smohalla reportedly agreed to move onto the Yakama Reservation and Thomash onto the Umatilla Reservation. Smohalla probably agreed to move onto the reservation as a delay tactic, since he knew that trouble was brewing in the Nez Perce country. On June 13, 1877, three young warriors triggered the Nez Perce War. After the war commenced, Smohalla, Thomash, and other followers of the Washani abandoned any idea of relocating to the reservation, knowing that troops would be committed to the Nez Perce theater of war. Smohalla returned to his home on the Columbia River, and Thomash traveled to his home on Snake River.[73]

When the Nez Perce War began, Husishusis Kute abandoned the nonviolent precepts of Smohalla, sending emissaries to many tribes on the plateau, requesting that they join the war. The Palouse religious leader rode north of Snake River to rally a large gathering of Sahaptin- and Salish-speaking Indians then gathering roots near the present-day Washington-Idaho border. At the request of the Catholic missionaries and Christian Indians, most of the Indians moved to a place called Elposen, nine miles west of the Coeur d'Alene Reservation. Neither Smohalla nor the Wanapum relocated to Elposen, but several hundred Indians met at the site to discuss their course of action. Those Indians who did not support the Nez Perce labeled Husishusis Kute and the Indians supporting him "pagan Dreamers." Christian Indians were "much bothered" by Husishusis Kute's "unruly" Indians.[74]

Husishusis Kute and his emissaries rode through Indian communities speaking out against the Christian faith and white men. Catholic missionaries blamed Husishusis Kute for attempting "to turn the good feelings of our Catholic Indians," and Father Joseph Joset blamed Husishusis Kute for stirring up hostilities against the United States. Despite his efforts to incite noncommitted Indians, Husishusis Kute failed to enlist many warriors or gain needed men to fight the United States Army. Except for some Upper Palouse under Chief Hahtalekin, few Palouse Indians joined

Husishusis Kute and the warring Nez Perce and Cayuse.[75] Unfortunately for Smo-halla, many whites felt that Husishusis Kute, Toohoolhoolzote, and other religious leaders had acted on Smohalla's instructions. This false rumor inflamed settlers and harmed the prophet's reputation in the Indian and white communities. Nevertheless, Smohalla stood by his nonviolent position and retreated to Priest Rapids.[76]

Husishusis Kute had contacted Smohalla and Thomash asking for assistance, but neither leader supported the Nez Perce War, although some of the young men in the village may have joined the fight against the United States. Smohalla main-tained strict neutrality and never joined the war efforts, primarily because he adhered to nonviolent religious precepts.[77] Nevertheless, agents, soldiers, settlers, and ranch-ers suspected "that Smohalla had been in back of a great deal of disquietude and unrest among the 'wild' Indians."[78] Although Smohalla was innocent of inciting the tribes, a group of white men formed a lynch mob and planned to hang the Wanapum Prophet while he camped on the Yakama Reservation. Smohalla wisely left the reser-vation under cover of darkness and hid in the mountains along the Columbia River.[79] Furthermore, General Howard feared that Smohalla would lead a religious crusade against the settlers, while others argued that the "treacherous deceptive old rascal" busied himself "secretly helping to keep up the strife . . . sending his young men out on the war path, while he was skulking in the mountains." White settlers accused Smo-halla of "harboring all the renegades and disaffected of all the surrounding tribes," but no historical evidence exists to support this assertion.[80] Such public statements encouraged defamation and rumors that created anger, hate, and racism against Smohalla and his followers. These false perceptions about Smohalla and the other Washani followers created an image that non-Christian Indians constituted a real threat to white security, offering settlers a just cause to remove nonreservation Indi-ans and steal their land. This is a reoccurring theme in American history—accounts glorified in textbooks portraying the benefits of Manifest Destiny as a contribution to the winning of the West and building of a nation. Settlers and government agents believed Indians should all be removed and forced onto reservations, which would serve to protect citizens of the territory and provide an opportunity for Indians to become civilized and Christianized.

Following the Nez Perce War in October 1877, Smohalla "resisted all inducements offered by the government to settle on some reservation."[81] The Wanapum Prophet urged people to practice peaceful resistance and to place their lives in the hands of Naamii Piap, who promised he would deliver those who danced and sang the Washat ceremony. On the Lower Snake River, Thomash followed the precepts of Smohalla, and he taught these beliefs to his family, including the parents of Harry and Mary Jim.[82] However, Thomash and Smohalla disagreed about the application of the Indian Homestead Act of 1874, which offered Indians title to 160 acres on the public domain. In 1878, Thomash filed a formal claim to his land on the Snake River where his family and his ancestors had resided for years and where his family continued to reside until the early 1960s, when "the law" moved Mary Jim and her family from their home on Snake River to the Yakama Reservation.[83]

Much to the chagrin of Smohalla, some of his other followers filed for homesteads. In 1878, Big Thunder, chief of the Palouse at the confluence of the Snake and Palouse Rivers, told General Howard that "they wished to remain where they were" and to take up lands in severalty. Howard urged Big Thunder to file a homestead claim, as "it was right to do so, and that was just what the great father in Washington wanted all Indians to do."[84] Smohalla opposed the Indian homesteads. To accept a homestead, he argued, constituted severing the sacred relationship of people with Naamii Piap. Homesteads ran contrary to *tamanwit*. Therefore, the very policies advocated by President Rutherford B. Hayes ran contrary to the old Washani faith and *tamanwit*. Times had changed rapidly for Native Americans, and some of them considered using the Indian Homestead Act to secure their homelands near the rivers of the inland Northwest.

According to Smohalla, Naamii Piap had told the prophet "lands were never to be marked off or divided." Smohalla preached, "Those who cut up the lands or sign papers for lands will be defrauded of their rights and will be punished by God's anger."[85] Thus, Indians who filed homesteads broke a fundamental law of the Creator. Added to this, Indian homesteaders were required to improve their lands and pay their taxes, which Smohalla said violated God's law. Around 1890, Captain E. L. Huggins visited the prophet and reported that Smohalla stated, "My young men shall never work. Men who work cannot dream, and wisdom comes to us in dreams."[86] Despite the protests of the Wanapum Prophet, Thomash, Big Thunder, Harlish Washomake (Wolf Necklace), Poween, Fishers, and other followers of the Washani filed claims for homesteads. They filed homesteads after Major J. W. MacMurray visited these families. General Nelson A. Miles had ordered MacMurray to meet with Plateau Indians and inform them of the Indian Homestead Act. MacMurray made a strong effort to reach nonreservation Indians and encourage them to file for homesteads as a way of protecting their property. Many Plateau Indians signed on to accept a homestead so they could remain in their traditional homes along the Columbia and Snake Rivers.[87]

In 1884, the year Congress passed the second Indian Homestead Act, MacMurray had considerable success among the Lower Palouse registering their land claims, but the officer had no success convincing Smohalla that the Indian Homestead Act offered Indian people an alternative to Indian removal and reservation life. MacMurray met the Wanapum Prophet in 1884 when the major journeyed to "the fountainhead" of the Washani faith at Priest Rapids, Washington Territory, on the Columbia

River. The huge dark basalt bluffs looming over the Wanapum village must have impressed the major. Today, the massive rock formation continues to cast an evening shadow over the Wanapum village. The Columbia River ran east of the village, proving a constant song as the rushing waters passed over the rocky stream. Smohalla lived at this important village site, and his decedents and followers remain in this secluded village today.[88]

MacMurray recognized that Smohalla was an "orator and natural leader of men" whose influence was widespread, even among "villages quite distant" where many "people believe in his inspiration." The major called Smohalla the "inventor of a New faith (or rather remodeler of several old ones)" who had, through the Washani, "upturned the religious convictions of [many] tribes of Indians . . . [including] the Nez Perce." At Smohalla's request, MacMurray explained the Indian Homestead Act using a checkerboard to depict the division of land into parcels.[89] Smohalla and his people listened patiently as MacMurray made his presentation, which an interpreter translated into Wanapum. Then the prophet addressed the people, explaining that the idea of dividing lands into parcels, homesteading, private ownership, and farming were contrary to *tamanwit*. He urged his people not to take up lands in severalty, and he admonished Thomash, Wolf Necklace, and others for having done so. MacMurray's visit to Smohalla did nothing to further the application of the Indian Homestead Act among Smohalla's people, but it provided the major a rare opportunity to meet the prophet and later to write of his experiences.

Despite the fact that Smohalla never filed claim to his land on the banks of the Columbia River, he remained on the "public domain" and refused to move to the Yakama Reservation. Under the terms of the Yakama Treaty, the government was required to pay the Indians for any improvements before forcing the people to surrender their property and resources. Thus, Yakama Agent and reverend James Wilbur never succeeded in forcing Smohalla and his band onto the reservation. Smohalla continued to reside at his village at Priest Rapids until his death in the 1890s. During all of that time, he never wavered from his beliefs and the ceremony given to him by Naamii Piap. He passed on his religion to his son, Yoyoni, and his nephew, Puck Hyah Toot, who in turn passed on the faith to other followers of the Washani religion, like contemporary leader Rex Buck.[90]

Smohalla was one of many religious leaders in the inland Northwest during the turbulent era of the late nineteenth century, but he was the most important *yanchta* in the region.[91] Yet far more important than Smohalla or the changes he brought to the old religion was the influence of the Washani faith on the course of history. In response to white expansion and the pressures of a new economic, political, social, and religious order, the Plateau Indians sought security and sovereignty through their own faiths and belief systems. Smohalla's afterlife experiences and his beliefs about land, animals, and spirits made little sense to nineteenth-century white Americans.

But since Smohalla built his faith on the precepts of the old Washani, they made sense to thousands of Plateau Indians, and many still sing to the beat of the thunderous seven drums used in ceremony. Chiefs Joseph, Toohoolhoolzote, Thomash, Husishusis Kute, and others shared Smohalla's beliefs and articulated them in public, so that these doctrines influenced hundreds of indigenous people across the Northwest. Smohalla made a profound impact on the course of Northwestern history, and today remains a highly significant figure within many Native American communities of the Greater Columbia Plateau.

NOTES

1. Trafzer published his first essay on Smohalla with Margery Ann Beach, "Smohalla, the Washani, and Religion as a Factor in Northwestern Indian History," in *American Indian Prophets: Religious Leaders and Revitalization Movements*, ed. Clifford E. Trafzer (Sacramento, Calif.: Sierra Oaks Publishing, 1986), 71–86. See also Margery Ann Beach, "The Waptashi Prophet and the Feather Religion: A Derivative of the Washani," in Trafzer, *American Indian Prophets*, 87–95; and for Indian Shakers, see Robert H. Ruby and John A. Brown, *John Slocum and the Indian Shaker Church* (Norman: University of Oklahoma Press, 1996), 3–10; and Robert H. Ruby, John A. Brown, and Cary C. Collins, *A Guide to the Indian Tribes of the Northwest* (Norman: University of Oklahoma Press, 2010), 131, 244, 298, 318. For an early study of prophecies in the Northwest, see Leslie Spier, *The Prophet Dance of the Northwest and Its Derivatives: The Source of the Ghost Dance*, General Series in Anthropology 1 (Menasha, Wis.: George Banta Publishing, 1935), 43–44. For several original documents on Smohalla and his revitalization movement, see the many documents in the Relander Collection, Yakima Valley Regional Library, Yakima, Washington (hereafter cited as Relander Collection).

2. For a Native American interpretation of early Christian missionaries, see Alan P. Slickpoo Sr., *Noon Nee-Me-Poo (We, The Nez Perces)* (Lapwai, Idaho: Nez Perce Tribe of Idaho, 1973), 67–86. Also, see Ruby and Brown, *John Slocum and the Indian Shaker Church*, 3–21.

3. Robert Boyd, *The Coming of the Spirit of Pestilence: Introduced Infectious Diseases and Population Decline Among Northwest Coast Indians, 1774–1874* (Seattle: University of Washington Press, 1999), 116–71.

4. Clifford E. Trafzer and Richard D. Scheuerman, *Renegade Tribe: The Palouse Indians and the Invasion of the Inland Pacific Northwest* (Pullman: Washington State University Press, 1986), 21–30; Spier, *Prophet Dance*, 41–46.

5. Clifford E. Trafzer, ed., *Grandmother, Grandfather, and Old Wolf: Tamánwit Ku Súkat and Traditional Native American Narratives from the Columbia Plateau* (East Lansing: Michigan State University Press, 1998), 23–24; Richard D. Scheuerman and Clifford E.

Trafzer, eds., *River Song: Naxiyamtáma (Snake-River Palouse) Oral Traditions from Mary Jim, Andrew George, Gordon Fisher, and Emily Peone* (Pullman: Washington State University Press, 2015), 4–7, 10–11, 20–28, 40–41; George B. Kuykendall, "Smohalla," Box 55, Folder 16, Relander Collection; James Mooney, "The Ghost Dance Religion," in *Fourteenth Annual Report of the Bureau of Ethnology* (Washington, D.C.: Government Printing Office, 1896), 716–19.

6. Scheuerman and Trafzer, *River Song*, 21–27; Clifford E. Trafzer, "Tamanwit at the Treaty Council," in *Wiyaxayxt/Wiyaakaa'awn/As Days Go By: Our History, Our Land, Our People—The Cayuse, Umatilla, and Walla Walla*, ed. Jennifer Karson (Seattle: University of Washington Press, 2015), 77–79.

7. Scheuerman and Trafzer, *River Song*, 20–21.

8. Ibid., 26; L. V. McWhorter, *Yellow Wolf: His Own Story* (Caldwell, Idaho: Caxton Press, 2000), 27–29.

9. Clifford E. Trafzer and Richard D. Scheuerman, eds., *Mourning Dove's Stories* (San Diego, Calif.: San Diego State University Publications in American Indian Studies, 1991), 8–11; Clifford E. Trafzer, "Learning the Love Medicine," *Fiction International* 20 (1991), 142–56. The author reprinted the essay in a book, Clifford E. Trafzer, ed., *Looking Glass* (San Diego: San Diego State University Publications in American Indian Studies, 1991).

10. Trafzer and Scheuerman, *Renegade Tribe*, 22–24; Clifford E. Trafzer, *As Long as the Grass Shall Grow and Rivers Flow: A History of Native Americans* (Fort Worth, Tex.: Harcourt, 2000), 179–82.

11. Virginia Beavert, *The Way It Was* (Olympia, Wash.: Consortium of Johnson O'Malley Committees, Region IV, 1974), x–xii; Click Relander, *Drummers and Dreamers* (Caldwell, Idaho: Caxton Printers, 1956), 50–68.

12. Boyd, *Coming of the Spirit of Pestilence*, 116–71; Trafzer, *As Long as the Grass Shall Grow*, 181; Trafzer and Scheuerman, *Renegade Tribe*, 116–71.

13. Trafzer and Scheuerman, *Renegade Tribe*, 50.

14. Maureen Lux, *Medicine That Walks: Disease, Medicine, and Canadian Plains Native People, 1880–1940* (Toronto: University of Toronto Press, 2001), 3–19; Clifford E. Trafzer, "Medicine Circles Defeating Tuberculosis in Southern California," *Canadian Bulletin of Medical History* 23 (2006): 477–98.

15. Relander, *Drummers and Dreamers*, 70.

16. Ibid., 71–71; Trafzer and Scheuerman, *Renegade Tribe*, 23–24, 105–10; Robert H. Ruby and John A. Brown, *Dreamer-Prophets of the Columbia River: Smohalla and Skolaskin* (Norman: University of Oklahoma Press, 1989), 41–64.

17. Ruby and Brown, *Dreamer-Prophets*, 40–44.

18. Mooney, "Ghost Dance Religion," 717; Cora DuBois, *The Feather Cult of the Middle Columbia*, General Series in Anthropology 7 (Menasha, Wis.: George Banta Publishing, 1938), 5.

19. Trafzer, *Grandmother, Grandfather, and Old Wolf,* 89–106; Stella I. Crowder, "The Dreamers," *Overland Monthly* 62 (1913): 606–9; Spier, *Prophet Dance,* 42; Edward S. Curtis, *The North American Indian* (Norwood, Mass.: Plimpton Press, 1911), 7:10–11; "Smohalla Services at Yakima Village of Pa'Kiut," Box 60, Folder 10, Relander Collection; Frank Buck's speech, June 2, 1962, Box 55, Folder 6, Relander Collection; "Yakima Notes," Box 18, Folder 2, Relander Collection.

20. Works on Smohalla necessarily draw on the writings of Major J. W. MacMurray and Captain E. L. Huggins. MacMurray's account is found in "Reports of the August 26 and September 19, 1884 to the Acting Assistant Adjutant General, Department of the Columbia, National Archives, Washington, D.C., Record Group 94; hereafter cited as MacMurray, "Reports to the Department of the Columbia." Mooney used this material in "Ghost Dance Religion." Also see J. W. MacMurray, "The Dreamers of the Columbia River Valley, in Washington Territory," *Transactions of the Albany Institute* 2 (1887): 244; E. L. Huggins, "Smohalla, the Prophet of Priest Rapids," *Overland Monthly* 17 (1891): 212.

21. Huggins, "Smohalla," 212; MacMurray, "Reports to the Department of the Columbia"; MacMurray, "Dreamers of the Columbia River," 244.

22. Ruby and Brown, *Dreamer-Prophets,* 21, 25.

23. Ibid., 25–27; Relander, *Drummers and Dreamers,* 75–79; Mooney, "Ghost Dance Religion," 718–19; Spier, *Prophet Dance,* 13–14, 17, 21–22.

24. Ruby and Brown, *Dreamer-Prophets,* 41–42.

25. Ibid.

26. Ibid., 45–46, 48.

27. Ibid., 48.

28. Relander, *Drummers and Dreamers,* 75–78.

29. Ibid.; Ruby and Brown, *Dreamer-Prophets,* 25.

30. Relander, *Drummers and Dreamers,* 77–79; Spier, *Prophet Dance,* 17–21, 43–44; Beach, "Smohalla," in Trafzer, *American Indian Prophets,* 71–73.

31. Relander, *Drummers and Dreamers,* 77–79; Spier, *Prophet Dance,* 17–21.

32. Relander, *Drummers and Dreamers,* 81–86; Mooney, "Ghost Dance Religion," 719–22; Huggins, "Smohalla," 212–15.

33. Huggins, "Smohalla," 212–15.

34. "Smohalla," Box 25, Folder 12, Relander Collection; Relander, *Drummers and Dreamers,* 27, 84.

35. Ruby and Brown, *Dreamer-Prophets,* 41–49.

36. Ibid.; Ruby and Brown, *John Slocum and the Indian Shaker Church,* 36–39.

37. Ruby and Brown, *Dreamer-Prophets,* 31–32. Beach, "Smohalla," in Trafzer, *American Indian Prophets,* 78.

38. Ruby and Brown, *Dreamer-Prophets,* 52–55.

39. Ibid.

40. Trafzer, *As Long as the Grass Shall Grow*, 183–88, 259–65.

41. Ibid.

42. Walla Walla Council Proceedings, 1855, "Documents Relating to the Negotiations of Ratified and Unratified Treaties With Various Indian Tribes, 1801–1869," Microfilm T-494, Reel 5, Record Group 75, National Archives, Washington, D.C. (hereafter cited as Walla Walla Council Proceedings, 1855); Trafzer and Scheuerman, *Renegade Tribe*, 46–59.

43. Walla Walla Council Proceedings, 1855.

44. Ibid.

45. Ibid.; to read the full texts of the Yakama, Nez Perce, and Umatilla treaties, see Charles J. Kappler, *Indian Affairs, Laws and Treaties*, 2 vols. (Washington, D.C.: Government Printing Office, 1940).

46. MacMurray recorded these statements by Smohalla and they are found in Mooney, "Ghost Dance Religion," 721.

47. Alvin M. Josephy Jr., *The Nez Perce Indians and the Opening of the Pacific Northwest* (New Haven: Yale University Press, 1965), 479. By means of the treaty of 1863, the government stole 784,996 acres from the Nez Perce Reservation negotiated in 1855.

48. "Report of the Civil and Military Commission to the Nez Perce Indians, Washington Territory and the Northwest," in *Annual Report of the Commissioner of Indian Affairs, 1877* (Washington, D.C.: Government Printing Office, 1877), 213.

49. Ibid., 607–9.

50. Ibid., 609. Members of the commission included D. E. Jerome, Oliver O. Howard, William Stickney, and A. C. Barstow.

51. MacMurray recorded this statement by Smohalla. See Mooney, "Ghost Dance Religion," 721. Richard Scheuerman, Lee Ann Smith, and Trafzer learned about these Washani beliefs from Andrew George, a Palouse *twati* and holy man, during an interview with George on November 15, 1980, author's collection.

52. "Report of the Civil and Military Commission to the Nez Perce," 212.

53. Young Chief Joseph, "An Indian's View of Indian Affairs," *North American Review* 128 (1879): 55.

54. Oliver O. Howard, *Nez Perce Joseph* (Boston: Lee and Shepherd, 1881), 63–64.

55. Document 213 B/70, McWhorter Collection, Washington State University Library Special Collections, Pullman, Washington. Hereafter cited as McWhorter Collection, WSU. Also see L. V. McWhorter, *Hear Me, My Chiefs* (Caldwell, Idaho: Caxton Printers, 1952), 172–73.

56. McWhorter, *Hear Me, My Chiefs*, 172–73. Also see Document 213/B37, McWhorter Collection, WSU.

57. McWhorter, *Hear Me, My Chiefs*; Howard, *Nez Perce Joseph*, 58–67.

58. Howard, *Nez Perce Joseph*, 58–67.

59. Ibid.

60. Ibid.

61. Ibid.

62. Ibid.

63. Joseph, "Indian's View of Indian Affairs," 57.

64. Kuykendall, "Smohalla," Box 55, Folder 16, Relander Collection.

65. Ibid.

66. Oliver O. Howard, *My Life and Experiences Among Our Hostile Indians* (Hartford, Conn.: A. D. Worthington, 1907), 259–60, 263–64.

67. Ibid.; Beach, "Smohalla," in Trafzer, *American Indian Prophets*, 80.

68. Howard, *My Life*, 259–60, 263–64.

69. Ibid.

70. Ibid.

71. Ibid., 271–79; Kuykendall, "Smohalla," Box 55, Folder 16, Relander Collection.

72. Kuykendall, "Smohalla," Box 55, Folder 16, Relander Collection.

73. Beach, "Smohalla," in Trafzer, *American Indian Prophets*, 80.

74. Ibid., 81; Verne E. Ray, "Native Village Groupings of the Columbia Basin," *Pacific Northwest Quarterly* 27 (1936): 132; Robert I. Burns, *The Jesuits and the Indian Wars of the Northwest* (New Haven: Yale University Press, 1966), 392.

75. Sgalgalt to Howard, June 21, 1877, Giorda Papers, Gonzaga University; McWhorter, *Hear Me, My Chiefs*, 171–73; L. V. McWhorter, *Yellow Wolf: His Own Story* (Caldwell, Idaho: Caxton Printers, 1940), 36n.

76. Beach, "Smohalla," in Trafzer, *American Indian Prophets*, 81.

77. Ibid.

78. Andrew Pambrun, *Sixty Years on the Frontier in the Pacific Northwest* (Fairfield, Wash.: Ye Galleon Press, 1979), 128–29.

79. Beach, "Smohalla," in Trafzer, *American Indian Prophets*, 81.

80. Kuykendall, "Smohalla," Box 55, Folder 16, Relander Collection.

81. Pambrun, *Sixty Years on the Frontier*, 128–29.

82. Congress passed two Indian Homestead Acts, on in 1875 and the other in 1884. See Beach, "Smohalla," in Trafzer, *American Indian Prophets*, 83.

83. Trafzer and Scheuerman, *Renegade Tribe*, 140; Scheuerman and Trafzer, *River Song*, 55.

84. George Hunter, *Reminiscences of an Old Timer* (Battle Creek, Mich.: Review and Herald, 1889), 412–23.

85. MacMurray in Mooney, "Ghost Dance Religion," 721.

86. Huggins, "Smohalla," 213.

87. MacMurray, "Dreamers of the Columbia River," 246.

88. Ibid., 241–48; Mooney, "Ghost Dance Religion," 716–23, 725–27.

89. MacMurray, "Dreamers of the Columbia River, 241–48.

90. "Yakama Treaty, 1855" in Kappler, *Indian Affairs*, 2:698–702; Relander, *Drummers and Dreamers*, 238–39.

91. Relander, *Drummers and Dreamers*, 149–61, 275–85; Beach, "Smohalla," in Trafzer, *American Indian Prophets*, 83–84.

7

TOLOWA INDIAN SHAKERS

※

The Role of Prophecy at Smith River, California

AL LOGAN SLAGLE

I N THE 1880s, the Prophet Dances and the Indian Shaker Church enjoyed increasing influence in the Pacific Northwest, eventually spreading into California. These movements fulfilled the "need for powerful helpers and human fathers; North American messiahs and prophets of crisis cults were all cast in the mold of the old Indian Shamanistic god-man and culture heroes."[1] The Shaker Church was organized as an association on June 7, 1892, at Mud Bay, Washington, and incorporated June 20, 1910, at Olympia.[2] Weston La Barre wrote, "Every prophet is at once revivalist and modernist, . . . [and each] . . . movement finds its own culture-hero or prophet. His genius is communication, particularly in his ability to establish similar subjective states in others."[3] John Slocum, a Nisqually Indian of Mud Bay, Washington, and his wife, Mary Johnson Slocum, received the basic inspirations of the Indian Shaker religion in 1882. Like the Native American Church, this syncretic religion incorporated elements of Christian theology with traditional Indian religions. On June 25, 1893, at Tacoma, Washington, James Wickersham, the Shakers' attorney, recorded John Slocum's deposition regarding the incidents and prophetic insights that led to the founding of the new religion. Church records include the few reasonably authenticated direct statements of John Slocum in his capacity as founder-prophet of the new religion.

Like many other Indian prophets, Slocum reportedly died and was resurrected. After Slocum contracted a serious illness that made him "weak and poor," and after five Indian doctors had tried unsuccessfully to revive him, his "soul would die two or three hours at a time," and though Shakers disagree as to whether he "died" in the usual sense, they believe his soul was out of the body. Slocum may have believed that he in fact had died, because he said he "saw a shining light—great light—trying my soul. I looked and saw my body had no soul—looked at my own body—it was dead." Then Slocum returned and spoke to an assemblage of his friends, saying "When I die, do not cry." At that point he died a second time: "Angels told me to look back and see my body. I did, and I saw it lying down." According to the Shaker Prophet, his "soul left [his] body and went up to judgment [*sic*] place of God." Slocum's experience continued as he saw "a great to light in [his] soul from that good land; [he acquired an understanding of] all Christ wants us to do." The prophet reported that he spoke to angels, who told him to "go back and turn alive again on earth." His work on earth had not been completed, so his soul returned to his body.[4]

Slocum offered these reflections on the role as an Indian prophet following his afterlife experiences: "When I came alive, I tell my friends, good things in heaven. God is kind to us. If you all try hard and help me, we will be better men on earth." The prophet believed that bad people could not reach heaven and that he and others should "believe in God" the Almighty, the source and provider of light and truth. Tolowas say this latter idea was aboriginal to them. "They know in heaven what we think. When people are sick, we pray to God to cure us. We pray that he take the evil away and leave the good." Slocum taught that this was the "good road for us to travel" and that Indians should worship when "their body and heart feel warm." He urged all Indians to "do good and sing good songs . . . [as for us] Christ said, he sends power to every believing soul on earth." Slocum cautioned about prophets and cult phenomena with a test for predicting fakery. For those individuals who "start religion here on earth," God must help begin the faith, and, "if God helps, we know it." An inner "voice" tells believers to "do good." Through the Spirit, the Indians learned to help themselves or others in sickness by kneeling in prayer and asking for help to cure, and, "If we do not learn to help him, we generally lose him."[5]

The single most important element of practice in the faith was healing through the power of the Holy Spirit, very broadly defined to mean working through prayer to restore the health and balance of everyone and everything. The faith reflected the belief systems of various bands and tribes of Indians and attracted an enthusiastic following among desperate and socially dislocated and disenfranchised people. The prophet's creed was simple, required no understanding or familiarity with Western Christianity or the Bible, and held out enormous hope. Indeed, on August 11, 1984, the bishop of the Indian Shaker Church, Harris Teo, addressed the Smith River Shaker Convention and reaffirmed that Bibles were not to be used or directly quoted in any Shaker Church. From its roots at Mud Bay, the Shaker religion spread throughout the Pacific Northwest. The Indian Shaker Church and prophetic tradition of the faith enjoys a major following in the Pacific Northwest and northern California, including the congregation at Smith River Rancheria, California, site of a Tolowa stronghold since precontact times. From 1850 to the present, it is possible to trace a continuous

FIGURE 7.1. Indian Shakers met in many dwellings, including mat lodges. The image depicts the skeleton of a mat lodge. Women wove heavy mats to cover this lodge, which was waterproof and warm once parishioners lit small fires inside. Courtesy of Richard D. Scheuerman.

line of leadership in the religious growth and life of the Tolowa people. Indeed, the Tolowas have a rich religious tradition, which is evident in the Indian Shaker Church at Smith River. During the 1850s, non-Indians created a climate of warfare, pestilence, and ruin that virtually decimated the tribal towns of the Tolowa Nation. Within a few years, much of the surviving population had been scattered and moved from one reservation to another, from Siletz and Grande Ronde to Hupa and Klamath River. They tried to resume their old life on their remaining village sites. The culture revived, though much was lost. A large portion of their knowledge dissipated, Tolowa religious culture persisted fairly intact through the period of the Ghost Dance (1870s).[6] Tribal and religious leaders who survived to that period were all active in the Tolowa Ghost Dance.

Tolowas continued to believe in Indian medicine, however, and to some extent, as the result of the Ghost Dance, in the resurrection of their dead. Wearing their best finery and valuables, carrying elkhorn purses and dentalium money, the Tolowa Ghost Dancers hoped that if they danced with their valuables, including dresses and money, they would not lose their wealth when the dead returned looking for wealth. Anyone could participate. Some entered a trancelike state, and shamanistic curing was an important part of that experience.[7] About 1880, the Tolowa leaders abandoned the

Ghost Dance and only conducted the Nay Dosh (Ten Night Dance) and other ceremonial activities. Indeed, in 1927, having taken over the Methodist Indian Mission at Smith River (now Gushchu Hall, site of the Del Norte Indian Welfare Association), the Tolowas held modest Feather Dances, World Renewal and Ten Night ceremonies there. The last great Ten Night Dances prior to a 1934 federal ban occurred at the homes of Frank Hostler (Howonquet) and Longhair Bob (Smith Island). Following a twenty-year hiatus, the autumnal Feather Dances and Ten Night Dances of the Tolowas resumed early in the 1950s, though many of the original four hundred or more songs had been forgotten.[8] Significantly, Frank Hostler also hosted early Indian Shaker meetings. Thus, until the advent of the Shaker Church, Christianity in its usual forms made little lasting progress among the Tolowas, perhaps because Tolowas perceived Christianity as the non-Indians' state religion, and therefore, offensive. However, acculturative demands of the Indian Shaker Church were perceived as palatable, since the doctrine came from the words and example of Indian kin. Tolowa leaders joined the Shaker Church at Smith River as readily as their forebears had taken up the Ghost Dance, while maintaining secular authority and leading the tribal dances. The original leaders of the Smith River Indian Shaker Church always have been traditional Tolowas.[9]

Amelia Brown (July 4, 1868–March 25, 1979) exemplified traditionalists at Smith River who embraced the new dispensation and assumed leadership of the Shaker Church. Her honored life's work contributed greatly to the survival of Tolowa culture before and after the advent of the Shake. After Amelia Brown's mother died from postpartum complications, her father took her into the men's sweathouse at Cushing Creek, where he raised her among men while assuring that she learned all the arts and responsibilities of Tolowa women. She became a smoke doctor and herb woman. Embodying all the women's prerogatives, she acquired enhanced power and respect in the community, using her special knowledge and authority as a prophet/shamaness when she became a Shaker at the age of seventy. She converted after testing the Shakers' power against her own as a smoke doctor.[10] She attended services once, with her tobacco-medicine pouch in her blouse, and sat in the rear. Ellen LaFountain, working "under power," detected the bag and retrieved it. From that day, Amelia was a Shaker.[11] Amelia perceived the accommodation between the old shamanism and the Shaker Church, for the work of Shakers was similar to that of the old-time Indian doctors in the area. Indeed, Jimmy Jack Hopell, the first Shaker in the area, "used to heal people." The "sick people used to come to church," and Jimmy Jack "would work on 'em. . . . Just like Indian Doctor."[12]

Jimmy Jack Hoppel (1884–January 15, 1969), a Yurok with Tolowa relations, lived at Siletz, Oregon, from 1919 until his conversion in 1926 because of differences with his family. Jack returned to Requa at Klamath to minister to the Yurok and demonstrate shaking. Tolowas became deeply involved in the religion, and in 1932, some figured prominently in the Hupa conversions to the church.[13] Thus by the early 1930s, the Tolowas assumed significant roles in church activities but were willing to continue to do so only if they could validate their own cultural heritage. One Tolowa was sufficiently committed to the religion to lead an assault against an Indian devil. The *tetnagi* was disturbing a healing meeting for John Charley, a Hupa who had been medically treated for Bright's disease, without success:

> To the Tolowa man it was revealed that an "Indian devil" was lurking about the meeting house and must be driven away. Impelled by the vividness of his vision, he rushed into the darkness in pursuit of the fleeing devil. . . . A straggling of fascinated spectators brought up the rear. An erratic chase led the crowd through a neighboring field, and ended at the foot of a large oak tree. The Tolowa man had seen the devil climb the tree, and he continued the pursuit up the trunk and out on a large limb. At that point the devil somehow got away. . . . As it happened, he "shot" the Tolowa man with his "poison" and made him very sick the next day.[14]

One Shaker says the Tolowa man, only recently deceased, was an early convert from Smith River, raising suspicions among some Shakers because he was so amazingly adept at nosing out *tetnagis*. At his death, the man, who had stayed away from church for years, requested a Shaker funeral.[15]

Initially, the majority of Tolowas were reluctant to accept the Shaker religion, but in 1929, under the leadership of Norman George (No'-Mun of Howonquet), several Tolowas went to Requa to learn about the faith from Jimmy Jack. Norman George (who died in 1942) was the first Tolowa to get the power. With Jimmy Jack and "Ery" Turner (actually, Ira, husband of Carrie, who today is in her nineties and a noted basket weaver), George organized the congregation at Smith River. In 1930, Norman George, Alex Billy of Sixes River, Frank Hostler (Yutl'-Hosch-Setl) of Howonquet, Donny Flannery (Me-Jes'-No) of Ta-At-Tun, Ben White (Yutl'-No-Dest-Wet) of Achulet, Maggie-Charley Seymour Billy (Num-Ni'-No) of Mels-Tetl-Tun (Pebble Beach), and other Tolowas constructed the still-existing buildings in Smith River on a flat, keyhole lot on North Indian Road, formerly part of Indian reservation land.[16] As early as 1928, services were held at the home of Frank Hostler at Howonquet and others. Evelyn Whipple also recalls that the Tolowas invited Oregon Shakers and others for Shaker services at Frank Hostler's and a traditional Tolowa Ten Night/World Renewal Dance (Nay Dosh) in which the Oregon Shakers enthusiastically participated, even dancing in borrowed Tolowa regalia. Tolowas accepted the Shaker prophets and their new religion in part because the Shaker promised to alleviate the dangers of the old, decaying Indian religion without requiring the Tolowas to abandon their culture and identities as the white missionaries had required.

Tolowa Shakers decided on their own what in their culture was worth preserving and what was expendable. Some stopped making new regalia and burned up attics full of fine goods. Some sold them either to show their total fidelity to the new faith or to exorcise "bad medicine."

The Tolowas of the 1920s had been liberated to a degree from their own harsh and increasingly irrelevant laws; but, reluctant to endanger what remained of their heritage, they felt that religion must serve social needs, not reflect psychoses or stem from foreign cults. Traditional Tolowas who received healing songs had always been obligated to treat them as public property. Likewise, when the Tolowas received Shaker blessings, most felt obligated to welcome the new gifts in order to enhance their benefits for the whole community. Most Tolowas were "chosen" and received the Shake en masse. To this day, Tolowa Shakers scorn the invidious notion that Tolowas were the victims of false prophets. Their inferences about the implications in the Tolowas' adoption of the Indian Shaker religion are consistent with La Barre's rule for distinguishing between cult and culture.

In diagnosing or prophesying, the Tolowa Shakers set out early to assert their own culture was their Old Testament. They heartily embraced the view that their people had suffered only because they were incomplete without the "grace of Jesus Christ," as given through the Shaker Church. Many Tolowas practiced their culture, preserved their language, and carried on their traditional arts as devotional Shaker acts. Indeed, the ability of some Tolowa Shakers to identify and treat troubles caused by aboriginal agents occasionally has raised suspicions about their using "the wrong side of power." The general result has been that members have prayed for the person in question. Human judgment, Shakers say, is supposed to be suspended in such matters and left to God, for confusion, quarrels, accusations, and backbiting are "the work of our Enemy." It is not for humans, say the old Shaker leaders, to excommunicate for sorcery or heresy, for whom God calls to be a Shaker will be a Shaker forever. God will correct and guide. One may elect to avoid attending services or leave the Shake, perhaps permanently, to return to "the World," thus attempting to excommunicate oneself. One may come back and express "contrition" by submitting to the process of being "relit," or "cleaned off," in a special ritual conceived for that purpose. Having suffered the oppression of non-Indians and their missionaries who wanted all Indians to become like white men, Shakers have been loath to impose in the same manner on their fellows.

Interestingly, it appears the Tolowa Shakers feel their aboriginal ideas about health and spiritual medicine were "proven" in their personal experiences as Shaker healing workers. They still sometimes ignore their non-Californian coreligionists' explanations for disease, favoring their own models. None of the concepts of illness held by non-Tolowas appeared to "prevail among the California Shakers," for whom

> any incomprehensible sickness is caused by the presence of "pains" in the body—the aboriginal theory. The presence of the pain entity explains any disorder of mind or body. As with "sickness" in Washington, it must be removed, and by the same means. But it differs in being conceived of as a thing and not as a state or condition, although it may produce exactly comparable symptoms. Pains can be felt in the hand, and a patient feels them being drawn out. They are visible but not to everyone. Some Shakers can see them; others cannot, but their hands are led to them and they can extract them. A person under power can take pains out of his own body.[17]

However, Homer Barnett's claim that Tolowa Shakers he knew only worked on aboriginal "pains," though perhaps true forty years ago, puzzles contemporary members. Their Shaker forbearers of the 1930s also attributed disease to other factors. For instance, since the 1930s, the "alcohol demon" has been exorcised repeatedly, and yet they do not classify alcohol abuse as the result of a "pain." While Tolowas retained aspects of aboriginal world view, they generally recognized and internalized their experience in the church as a means of adapting to fearful alien conditions and ideas, as a part of their daily Shaker "walk." While accepting clinical diagnoses of conditions, however, they still believe that demons are at the root of any suffering: aboriginal "pains" simply compose one class of demons Tolowa Shakers recognize and treat. On the other hand, Barnett says one Indian doctor flatly contradicted Jimmy Jack's claim that Shakers could remove "pains":

> This shaman, a woman, appears to have been genuinely interested in Jack's pretensions to power: and she once suggested to him that the two of them treat a certain sick man in order to see what kind of pains each of them took out of him. Jack refused, saying that her presence would "spoil his power." Later, when another sick person came to this same shaman for help, she "saw hands playing over his body and felt slime on it." She did not know what this meant, but she was able to take several pains out of his body. Afterwards she learned that the Shakers had previously treated him, so she concluded that whatever kind of pains they claim to get out of a sick person they are not the same as those she extracts; otherwise they would not have left the ones she found in this man's body.[18]

However one Tolowa, on my reading aloud this passage, wryly remarked that the Indian doctor could have installed her own pains and then removed them after the Shakers worked in order to hurt Jimmy Jack's credibility. He reported that people often come to Shaker meetings just to "play with their power, or pit their power against the God of the Shakers."[19] He also pointed out that many people feel that the old doctoring and deviling powers that challenge Shakers have been in part exorcised from Tolowa territory due to years of Shaker work.

The Shakers incorporated in California on March 18, 1932. As members of a state-recognized church, members could practice their religion without molestation. California Shakers had state and local officers who controlled the local work and property. Tolowas recognized the Indian Shaker Church as a part of tribal traditions. Richard A. Gould said, "In terms of history and location the position of the Smith River Shaker Church is peripheral to the principal center of Shaker activity in western Washington." It was not surprising "to find some difference between the ceremonies of our California Shakers and those described for Washington."[20] However, no Shaker Church is "peripheral to" any other simply because the California congregations are distant from the "mother church," despite the regard for "one-mindedness." Some northern Shakers consider non-Washington Shaker congregations "peripheral," but any such sense of superiority is repeatedly declared antithetical and discordant. Local cultural differences inevitably affect each church. Thus, Tolowas attribute disease to "pains" according to their own traditions.

Major schisms have opened over the use of Bibles in church. Although Bible use is condoned outside actual services, no Bibles are used in church, and none lay on altars, since Shakers insist their own church was a direct inspiration to Indians, as was the ancient inspiration to medicine men. "A good Shaker," it is said, "is a good medicine man." Besides, says the current bishop, Harris Teo, contentions over interpretation have bred dissension close to bloodshed; for instance:

> When Kitsap was Bishop, he did not keep records, and failed to convene yearly conventions. He was invited to speak about Shaking all around Puget Sound, even to San Francisco. They began to pay him great money to speak. Eventually he received quite a group of groupies that followed him around. Then he and his non-Shaker "groupies" began to change the Shake Religion. They would come to church and preach from the Bible until ten p.m., and then they would say, "Have your Shake." By that time all the patients had left. They were too sick to just sit around. This really was taking the Shake away from its purpose. Finally, at Concrete in Jamestown, the minister stood up and put a stop to his actions. From that time they outlawed the Bible and receiving money for doing the Lord's work. At that time the Shake split into Independent and Original 1910 Shakers. There was court over the name as well. The 1910 won out. Once you whip your brothers and sisters with the Word, it is no good.[21]

Shakers are very careful about proselytizing, preferring to show by example—living an exemplary life, if possible—and following their call, thereby allowing people to seek the Shake for themselves. Still, the Shaker Church has missionaries, persons who have the responsibility for organizing and maintaining congregations and who can convene or take over local church meetings anywhere to settle disputes that cannot be resolved internally. Shakers compare their missionaries and ministers to the evangelists and missionaries of the early Christian church. Prophetic utterances of missionaries can be more influential than their experience of knowledge of church teachings, since the Shake still is an oral tradition lacking written canons rather than a constitution and bylaws.

Shakers conduct church business through licensed local church officers and missionaries. Ministers, assistant ministers, and missionaries are appointed for life, during good behavior. Officers must maintain faith, and even more than that, always conform to conventional morality, since morality is supposed to follow faith, and if one's life is right, unrighteousness is eliminated. Chief elders manage statewide business, while local ones attend to the local congregation. Vocation and faith lead members to answer calls for medical and spiritual help, and if they are active, they are encouraged to become missionaries.

The bishop and church officers view idiosyncrasies in the individual churches' services and practices with careful tolerance in order to avoid schisms in the relatively small communities. A teaching or prophetic insight must withstand tests of prayer and debate at its origin and thence among other congregations before it can be generally accepted. Dissemination is generally by word of mouth.

Thus the wearing of collarless, floor-length, smock-like white garments came into general use through a prophecy, then gradual acceptance, rising to gradual standardization so that most are adorned with an appliquéd dark blue cross on a simulated necklace. The wearing of these is not universal, is only at Sunday morning services, and is not required for full membership. Northern Shakers protest that Sunday morning service (10:00 a.m.–12:00 p.m.) is "only" for glorification, for "that is when God opens the doors of Heaven and hears our praise to Him," but some Californians have replied that "God's work is done anytime," and that Christ also healed on Sunday. Thus the use and meaning of the garment can vary, and, hence, the interpretation of the original prophetic insight that led to garment wearing.

Garment making is the work of those with a special calling, but one can become a garment wearer, or the candidate for a garment, through a personal vision or by being the subject of a garment wearer's vision. Acquiring a garment is a heavy undertaking, for the wearer must be especially careful to avoid error: "Garments are a passport to Heaven. The wrong you do clings to the garment and is visible." One possible inspiration for these garments is the Ghost Dance shirts of the late 1800s, except that they fend off error and evil in general instead of literal bullets. Those without garments are blessed off as if they had them. No one is left out of the blessing of the "Garment

Songs" of Sunday service. There can only be communal sharing of such things, as in the case of all other Shaker gifts, including prophetic ones.

Prophecies warn, teach, direct, or reinforce the Indian Shaker faith. That direct revelation and spiritually inspired teachings are the most practical and reliable sources of instruction remains a fundamental Shaker tenet. True prophecies are called "gifts" or "teachings" of God, and substitute for written literature. A proto-Shaker prophetic tradition in the Puget Sound predicted the advent of a new Indian religion, thus laying the groundwork for John Slocum's early success. Prophecies of discord in the movement led churches to avoid internal contentions, abjure "challenging spirits," and address complacency, doubts, or neglect of the faith. An "inappropriate spirit" speaking can always come into a community to "devil" the people, whose only defense is prayer and fasting.

During one legal controversy of the Smith River Church, the congregation believed their church building was under supernatural assault, as various Shakers had detected while under the influence of the prophetic shaking power. Margaret Moorehead Brooks placed a candle under the altar in the 1960s during a period of change, and its presence there grew into a tradition. In that period, pictures, flowers, and even an innocuous water bucket were banished from meetings. Though members who installed them almost all eventually stopped attending services, their reforms became permanent. Assaults continued until a prominent Canadian Shaker, Herman Seymour, came to a service and discovered "something" hiding under the altar. Aided by other workers, Seymour wrestled the thing out onto the floor. Various workers "saw" tentacles and random parts of a menagerie. They supposed that the protean apparition was a sea monster, called an Ing'-Let-Stin, perhaps the sort that once had plagued the Tolowa. Seymour, witnesses recall, was thrown all around the church and slammed against walls as he wrestled the beast. Gifted with the spiritual uses of candles, Seymour finally stalked his prey to the floor with a cruciform configuration of eleven burning candles (combining the sacred numbers seven and four). Lacking any anchoring, the candles bounced without falling as over a score of dancers feverishly pounded the floor. Seymour collected the candles and placed them in a galvanized bucket of water. The candles began to swim and soon formed a snake, which wriggled all over the bucket, trying to escape. Workers "canned" the beast in a quart jar and buried it (in accordance with a practice still largely confined to California Shakers). Afterward, Seymour underscored the importance of having a candle in the center of the space beneath the prayer table during services to prevent it from being used as a lair for any demons that jealous Indian devils might place in the church.

The church at Ukiah, California, has taken up the practice for similar prophylactic reasons (because a young boy saw a "spider" under the altar), though no doctrine required the addition. Generally, the candle under these altars now provides a visual reminder to heed their prophets, to remain attentive and prayerful, and to avoid contentions, since faults attract nuisances. Few churches display candles, but it is one example of a particular variance specific to California Shakers.

Old tribal prophecies are occasionally purified and co-opted into the Shaker canon. At Smith River, the minister, Charley Bighead, sometimes interjects accounts of the prophecies of Creek/Seminole Stomp Dance tradition from Oklahoma, using them in testimony to illustrate the nature of prophecy or directly incorporating them into his "walk" as a Shaker. For Bighead, Shaker prophecy has displaced the use of Indian medicine to divine or analyze trends, situations, and events. Bighead is an alcoholic who recovered through the Shake.

Bighead believes that he personally received a revelation that the old Indian religions were prophetic forerunners of the Shake. He explained that, prior to his conversion, he was standing in the yard of the Smith River Shaker Church during services. He vacillated over whether or not to go inside until he heard the congregation singing what he recognized as a Cherokee Stomp Dance song, and accepted that event as a personal sign for him.

Bighead directly analogizes his old tribal religion and the teachings and prophecies of Christianity. In one Shaker meeting in 1984, Mr. Bighead recalled that in his youth, the elders in his tribe predicted that a great famine would follow destructive storms and a long drought. He said that the trouble would come when a sign appeared in the form of a row of four rainbows. Bighead opined that the old people's insight was as divinely inspired as anything in the Bible.

Bighead is not alone in subscribing to the idea that the old Indian religion has been validated in part by the Shake. For instance, the Indian prophet Big Bill, of the Puget Sound, foretold the coming of John Slocum and the advent of the Shake in his community. Also, the Tolowas believe that a white race once lived in their land as a subservient minority and disappeared, only to return in the California gold rush— an opinion held by their Ghost Dance messenger, Depot Charlie. Furthermore, the Tolowas believe that the Spirit manifested in their communities with the arrival of the Tolowa Ghost Dance in the 1870s. The best of the spirit of the old Tolowa religion also flourishes in Shaker Christianity, which Tolowa Shakers believe genuinely helped to preserve, revitalize, and complete their cultural foundation. They feel that their spiritual gift must be shared with others. California Shaker Kathleen Cooley (Yurok/Tolowa) received a message early in August 1982 that the Shake would expand to more California Indian communities. Her vision included a belief that the Shaker Church would one day exist throughout California.

Cooley's prophecy is just one of many examples of messages Indian Shakers have received. Significantly, many types of prophetic gifts exist in the Church, including nine essential Shaker gifts of power. There are subsidiary powers and categories that overlap into divination and prophecy. It may be that the concept of nine gifts simply reflects the Shaker affinity for using sacred numbers for mnemonic purposes, because other churches enumerate different gifts! The nine gifts of Shaker power include the following:

1. healing per se, the primary gift
2. ringing bells in services (bells are the only musical instruments Shakers use)
3. singing/dancing
4. praying (silently or audibly)
5. leading the church after accepting election or appointment to some official post, such as bishop, elder, missionary, minister, or organizer
6. preaching and evangelizing
7. passively receiving messages, answers, and guidelines for others (in which case the worker may not comprehend the message himself but, as a medium, receives and passes it on)
8. receiving and sending messages or commands that may have limited impact but serve immediate needs (in which case the worker usually understands the message and is taught how to use it by helping spirits)
9. prophesying and interpreting signs, dreams, and visions that affect the whole congregation, community, or world (in which case the worker warns and admonishes the audience, preparing them for a sequence of events that may be avoidable if proper action is taken)

Obviously, most of these gifts involve communication between and among mortals and immortals. They are not ranged in order of relative importance, because it seems that no ranking is attached to these gifts, and no greater prestige attaches to having one or more of them. The Shaker ideal is to receive these gifts and act as a clear medium. Since the gifts come and go "as God has His way," church members must avoid pride and a sense of "owning" the gifts. Most important, the gifts are the primary benefits of the faith and the accepted means for carrying it on.

Two of the gifts of power the Shaker Church enumerates in the usual nine are the ability to receive revelations or prophecies regarding a particular individual and any group or community or even the world. The distinction between these categories is not fixed, and is indeed tenuous. A Shaker is obligated to announce a received vision, but it is the duty of the subject person to accept or reject the prophecy. A seer has no duty to do more than reveal and pray for the vision.

A novice Shaker is always cautioned not to take what anyone says in any trancelike prophetic testimony as a valid judgmental comment directed at him or her simply because the speaker appears to be making the testimonial statement while under the influence of the Shake. Shakers constantly remind one another, "Not every message is for everyone. Take everything to heart, but be careful not to take things too personally." Likewise, Shakers learn to avoid adverting directly to others' behavior and its effects, present or hypothetical, in open services, regardless of how much trouble the transgressions of another may cause. Serious dissensions about public accusations in the churches have given rise to such aphorisms as, "Our mouths are the biggest enemy we have," and "If you point a finger at somebody else, remember you're pointing three back at yourself." Thus, if one divines that someone in the congregation has a problem but does not know who that person is, one is duty bound to reveal the vision. If, however, one can specifically identify the person who has a spiritual need, unfulfilled duty, or problem—such as an addiction to tobacco—one has the duty to convey the information discreetly and directly to the individual, preferably outside of services.

On the other hand, the congregation or individual recipient of a prophetic message is obligated to listen prayerfully. The hearer must consider foundational questions: What is God using the speaker to say? Are these remarks intended for a general audience or a specific one—namely, for me? If I know or discover a person to whom these remarks might apply, how can I help this person? Whether these remarks apply to me or not, what can I do, besides pray for help for myself or for the affected person(s)?

The members of the congregation often feel the further duty, as recipients of a prophecy, to testify in the event the prophecy comes true. Often, signs, prophecies, or gifts of power that come to distinct individuals appear to link together, as if to emphasize the deliberateness of Providence. Signs and gifts may be shared or may have changing import depending on the viewer and circumstances. The author witnessed the testimony of a woman whom an older member had divined to have a smoking dependency. The addict wrestled with the problem for months, smoking furtively and trying to quit, until once at a beachside doctoring place adjacent to Smith River Church, she received a sign when waves returned (three times) a box of a certain brand of cigarettes she was trying to throw away forever. She reported that, later, she had to try to stop smoking three more times before she could finally quit.

Later, another woman who had been in the congregation listening to this testimony wondered what day it was those cigarettes went out to sea. It seems that later that same afternoon, the second woman (who at the same time also was trying to quit smoking, without much resolve or success) was standing at the water's edge with her grandsons when a wave tossed up a new box of that same brand of cigarettes, leaving it high and dry. She had taken that event as a sign to stop. Thus, seeing the box in the tide had carried a different significance to each of the two women, depending on its behavior and their separate circumstances. The first woman, whose smoking had not yet affected her health, learned that her earnest struggle to quit smoking would have to fail twice, while the latter, who was sickly from smoking, received what she took for an ultimatum that she had to stop smoking in order to live. These testimonies did not necessarily lead others in the congregation to decide to change any personal habits.

Just as in the case of diagnoses or person- or group-specific prophecies, one is supposed to lend a critical ear when witnessing prophetic utterances of a generalized or even global nature. Such caution is always appropriate since Shaker prophecies almost invariably are calls for some kind of action. Shakers have become wary of self-fulfilling prophecies.

Shaker revelations and prophecies are so numerous and frequent among the congregations that two examples should suffice. The author witnessed both being received and acted upon on a single occasion. During a Sunday evening Shaker service at Smith River in the summer of 1982, Bighead announced that he had received two visions, and that these should be prayed for so that the congregation could receive help in understanding them. He asked the congregation to pray in order to prepare for, or possibly to avert, the chain of events that he saw coming. In the first, Bighead saw the death of a neighbor in a fiery accident. In the second, he saw a picture of a smoking, bombed city with a beach and what looked like a burned, rusty Ferris wheel, which he said was an image of some war-torn port city in the Middle East. The small congregation then rose and huddled together at the altar, though Shaker teaching concerning prophecies reflects an acceptance that there might be no way to avert foreseen disasters "except through prayer and fasting." In little more than a week, the prophecies became reality with the death and funeral of the accident victim and the stunning Israeli air assault of Beirut, which appeared on televisions around the world. Though any Shaker, not just a leader or elder, is presumed capable of receiving the gift of any sort of prophecy at any time, some are deemed specially talented (Bighead is known for finding lost objects and bodies), and living an exemplary Shaker life is thought almost essential in retaining the gift. Accounts of the central prophecies and prophets of the Indian Shaker Church have been handed down through the families of original members, such as the present (Skokomish) bishop, Harris Teo. The author received an account of the prophecy surrounding the founding of the Indian Shaker Church through Loren Bommelyn of the Smith River Church from Bishop Teo. According to Teo, prior to the coming of the Shake, Indians in Washington had a tradition stemming from the Prophet Dance tradition that a new dance and religion would replace all that went before with a "new dispensation." A particular proponent of this prophecy was a man named Big Bill, who was influential to John Slocum and later an enthusiastic supporter of the Shaker Church. Teo added that when Mary Slocum got the shaking power and John Slocum built his church, all the Indians within the range of its influence—including the dance leaders in Teo's family, who knew and believed in the prophecy of Big Bill—burned all their old dance dresses and regalia and joined the Shake.

The Tolowas, as indicated above, had taken up the Ghost Dance and had prophecies of some "new dispensation" long before the advent of the Indian Shaker Church. According to one authority, the Ghost Dance was characteristic of many indigenous societies under duress and threat of destruction. The Shaker Church at Smith River began as a localized instance of a wider movement to address the grief felt generally among the Indians over the destruction of their cultures. The Smith River Church has remained under Tolowa leadership and numerical dominance since its inception, retaining an exclusively Indian clergy. It was dedicated by a Tolowa on land reclaimed by Tolowas from swampland, and built by Tolowa hands, including Donny Flannery, Frank Hostler, Norman George (probably the original Tolowa Shaker Prophet), Dewey Billy, Ben White, Maggie Seymour Billy, Alex Billy, and Nellie May. The Indian Shaker Church at Smith River continues to be the most significant constant religious influence in the community; and its practicing members are living remnants of Tolowa divinatory and prophetic tradition.

There is a well-defined genealogical line of religious and secular leaders in the Tolowa communities, flowing from the precontact period to the present. Authority lies primarily in lifelong, or in formerly active, Shakers. Authority is also held by persons who have used the old Tolowa powers as shamans and dance leaders but who later became Shakers. In every case, the secular power and most religious authority descend from the headmen and leaders of the tribe.

Basic forms and doctrines are well set in most congregations. However, dissatisfaction and a spirit of autonomy led the California Shakers to separate from the main body of the Shakers at the insistence of dissatisfied Tolowa members who touted a prophetic vision of an autonomous California Indian Shaker Church with its own bylaws and bishop from 1948 until the mid-1960s. The Tolowa Shakers, with other Californians, through the efforts of Ellen White LaFountain, have since rejoined the mainstream of their church. Smith River Shakers still vary in their personal attitudes about the use of the Bible outside the church meetings, and much is left to individual conscience, which suggests a very significant point about the effect of the Shake and its prophetic tradition on Tolowa culture.

By the time of the advent of the Shake at Smith River, the Tolowas were losing their sense of being a people their Creator had blessed. The Shake emphasized the transformation of the society, through "chosen" individuals, into a new spiritual community in the best spirit of their old culture. Through the Shake, many Tolowas gradually regained the sense of being a chosen people whose individual culture bearing was significant. Thus, people like Amelia Brown saw their prestige as Tolowa leaders, prophets, and medicine men increase by joining the Shaker Church. If the Shake was a widespread manifestation of emotional collapse, it was also a means of recovery. Indeed, in communities where "shamans are few or nonexistent," many Indians find that "the emotional experience of shaking is a healing instrument. It *is* a medicine, the fulfillment of a prophecy for the afflicted and the oppressed, an unmeasured gift to the faithful."[22]

The Shaker Church in California, particularly that at Smith River, enjoys some important distinctions from other regions of the country. Among the Tolowa Shakers, there is a clear association between their activities as Shaker workers and the arts of the traditional shaman prophets, curers, and Indian doctors: "Some of the older participants see a direct connection between the activities of the old 'Indian Doctor' [that is, shaman] and the Shaker Church."[23]

Tolowa Shakers generally consider the ceremonial life of the Smith River Indian Shaker Church to be an expression of Tolowa traditionalism. Actually, the influences of many different tribes and Christian sects are apparent in Shaker ceremonialism, even at Smith River. However, the Smith River Indian Shaker Church's ceremonial activities and repertory of songs reflects Tolowa traditions of healing and sickness—for example, that Tolowa Ten Night Dance songs such as Naydosh Ceyney, "When You Hear Sickness Is Coming from the South," were used during Shaker services in the early 1960s. Gould and Furukawa suggest that "similar native antecedents exist for all or most of the others [Indian Shaker Churches]."[24]

Loren J. Bommelyn leads Tolowa ceremonial activities such as the Feather Dances. Lineal descendant of tribal religious and secular leaders, he is California Organizer for the Indian Shaker Church and Chairman of the Nelechundun band of Tolowa Nation. In an interview for Debra Webster, religion editor of the *Times Standard Eureka*, Bommelyn described factors that distinguish Indian Shakerism from the religious beliefs and practices of other sects:

> By adhering to the Shake faith, Native Americans were "brought back in touch with God through Jesus Christ," whom they believe to be the son of God. However, one key difference between the Shakers and traditional Christians is their stance regarding the Bible.
>
> "We only depend on the Holy Spirit . . . not on the Bible," Bommelyn said. Shakers look to "direct revelation" through the Holy Spirit and do not seek guidance through written testimony as do many Christians . . .
>
> He believes that the Shaker faith will eventually have a unifying effect on the tribes if it is allowed to blend with the more traditional aspects of Native American customs and is not seen as a competition. . . .
>
> "I would be the first to blame Christendom for the death of some 12 1/2 million Native Americans," he said, referring to early American history. However, Bommelyn

now views being a Christian as "walking like Christ," rather than associating the name with settlers armed with their "manifest destiny" attitude.

[Bommelyn] continues to "walk a fine line" between the traditional aspects of his culture and his new-found faith in Jesus Christ.[25]

The Shaker religion arose among Washington Indians of the 1870s who, in profound distress, were ripe for a promised Ghost Dance prophet and new religion. In California, the faith came to the Tolowas when their culture was at a very low ebb, having suffered eighty years of cultural disintegration at the hands of aggressive strangers armed with an incredibly rapacious technology. After abandoning some of their ancient culture to accommodate needs and conditions of the time, the Tolowas, ravaged by depression, poverty, famine, and disease, still longed for something more than mere survival. They wanted to keep their identity as Indian people, and as many Ghost Dancers had done before, they found new hope through religion.[26]

Since the old Tolowa culture and religion had failed to defend them from the whites or their Christian God, the Tolowas embraced the Shaker Church as God's spiritual gift and hope to the Indians. One authority suggests, "Each ghost dance is a failure in the secular adaptiveness of a society from which later men must extricate themselves."[27] For the Tolowa Shakers, their New Testament, the Indian Shaker religion, despite all its apparent conservatism and formalism, afforded some chance to adapt to their conditions. The Tolowas of the 1930s vividly recalled that their ancestors had made written treaties with non-Indians in good faith to buy a chance for survival in nominally Christian America. The Americans had ignored these contracts with impunity. Possibly, some Tolowas thought that since the God who had first come to the whites had served America's wishes so well, surely Indians could do no worse by serving Christ. However, Christian missionaries had proselytized in Del Norte County with little lasting effect, while the Shaker Church emerged from Indian roots and through an Indian prophet. Indian evangelists brought Slocum's prophetic message of a special Indian dispensation to the Tolowas, explaining that the Christian God had finally offered something tailored to their own needs.

As Cora DuBois discovered, when the Ghost Dance arrived in the 1870s, the Tolowas had accepted its Spirit, but on their own terms. They had hoped that the Ghost Dance would preserve their culture, if not in this world, then surely in the next. Though they eventually lost interest in the Ghost Dance and returned to their old rites, they embraced the Shake as the fulfillment of the hope that the Ghost Dance had offered.[28] Tolowas of the 1930s identified with the shaking power, the Shakers' ways of doing medicine, worship, and communion. They believed that since the Shake was American Indian in origin, organization, and content, the Shake offered a process of enculturation—a means of completing and preserving Indian culture.

Tolowas could join with dignity, knowing that they could thereby contribute their own cultural strain to a Christian community. This was something they could not hope to do as members of any other Christian sect. Thus, Loren Bommelyn rankles at the charge that the Shaker religion is "non-traditional." He insists on the appropriateness of the Tolowas' enthusiastic acceptance of the new religion, explaining that it "came through the Spirit and not through some preacher coming down here and laying the law down; it was the Spirit that led the people."[29] He believes that the Spirit of the Shake came to the Tolowas through the Ghost Dance, and if the Shake was replaced "within the cultural construct of the society, it's taken the place of the Kick Dance, a doctoring dance," which a shaman, generally female, performed with her singers. Bommelyn recognizes that the Kick Dance was subsumed into the Shake, along with many of its elements. The "old ways" are the Old Testament, represented by a lighted candle on the left side of the church altar, while the Shake is the New Testament, represented by another candle on the right side of the altar. "All the old powers are there," says Bommelyn, "except now, through the power of Jesus Christ, we are set free from the Old Testament, the old religion."[30] The old remains the foundation. Perhaps another Tolowa Shaker, Betty Green, put it best when she commented, "Why give up our old ways? That's giving up the acorns and the basket making, and yet God put all of this on this earth, for his children."[31]

In recent years, some Indians have criticized the Shaker Church, claiming that the religion is Indian. Bommelyn dismisses this as a frivolous charge by "the Johnny-Come-Lately-Indians that just found their roots here the last fifteen or twenty years. They did not live through the cultural migrations. When they return, they are looking for some pre-contact Indian."[32] Bommelyn and other Shakers hold no grudges against their uninformed critics, realizing that not everyone is expected to be a Shaker. However, Shakers also believe that if one participates in a ceremony, one does so through the power of the Holy Spirit, and any whom the Spirit touches can receive the gifts of the Shake, including prophetic powers. At the same time, the movement reaches out through its members, who have an obligation to proselytize, not so much by evangelizing as by praying for healing and living exemplary lives. Nelson Lukes, a Shaker missionary and director of the Nespelem Community Center of Nespelem, Washington, on the Colville Indian Reservation, succinctly expressed the sense of the role of Shaker workers and prophets in the secular Indian reality. "Shakers do not go around dragging people to church," he said "but, prayers are for you. If you belong to a church in town or the Longhouse or to the Medicine dance, Shakers are praying that you will do all possible to save your people." Whether a person works "on the reservation or on the business council, or in office dealing with people, Shakers are praying for you and the decisions that you make that somehow you may listen to the spirit in you."[33]

FIGURE 7.2. John and Mary Slocum started the Indian Shaker Church at Mud Bay, Washington. The church emerged among many indigenous groups, including the Tolowa. An unknown artist for the *Mason County Journal* made this sketch of John Slocum praying with his right hand raised to heaven. Courtesy *Mason County Journal*, December 10, 1897.

Thus the power and influence of the Shake is broader than one might expect, as Shakers reach out to the wider spectrum of the Indian community through their extended families, affinal relationships, and acquaintances. Indeed, within a few years after its appearance, almost the entire local Indian population had attended or joined the Shaker Church. There are members of the church on all the Tolowa trust lands, including the Elk Valley and Smith River Rancherias and the Nelechundun village (Jane Hostatlas allotment). Of the original allottees at Elk Valley, Maggie Seymour Billy, George and Ben White, and Deleliah Charley were dance leaders and Shakers. Today, Lila James Moorehead, Fred Moorehead, Eunice Bommelyn, Betty Green, Cornelius and Irene Natt, and Elsie Napoleon are Shakers. At Smith River Rancheria, many Tolowas have been members of the church. Loyette and Mary Bartow are active members of the church, and Mary Bartow is an elder (and a former dancer).

The Shaker Church at Smith River received its Spirit with the advent of the Ghost Dance in the 1870s and became an important element in the history of the Tolowas in the 1930s. The Smith River Shake has the unique distinction of holding on to many of the tenets of the old Indian ways while embracing the precepts of the greater Shaker Church. The tie to traditional methods, procedures, and beliefs is apparent in the Tolowa Shake, as is the link between traditional tribal leaders and today's Shaker leaders at Smith River. Indeed, according to two scholars who studied the Shaker Church among the Tolowas, the religion would "provide the most tangible focus for the identity of the 'Indian' in the face of American culture in this area of northwestern California."[34] Like the Tolowa worshippers themselves, they understood the moving Spirit and social significance of the Indian Shaker Church at Smith River.

NOTES

1. Weston La Barre, *Ghost Dance: Origins of Religion* (New York: Dell Publishing, 1972), 199.

2. State of California, "Articles of Incorporation of the Indian Shaker Church of Washington," *Domestic Corporations*, Book 92, No. 29212, 1932, p. 243.

3. La Barre, *Ghost Dance*; for a study of the religion before 1940, see Homer G. Barnett, *Indian Shakers: A Messianic Cult of the Pacific Northwest*, 2nd ed. (Carbondale: Southern Illinois University Press, 1972).

4. See full text in Barnett, *Indian Shakers*, 35–38. In addition, see "John Slocum" in the Calendar of the Indian Shaker Church of Washington, a church document titled, "Celebrating 100 Years of Existence," (Olympia, Wash.: Indian Shaker Church, 1982).

5. Barnett, *Indian Shakers*, 35–38.

6. Tolowa Shaker, oral interview by author, field notes, 1984, author's files, Native Healers in Alcoholism Treatment Project, Grant # 2ROIAA04817–01, 2, 3, 4 from the National Institute of Alcoholism and Alcohol Abuse (hereinafter cited as oral interview).

7. Tolowa Shaker, oral interview, 1982.

8. Alex Billy, son of Sixes Billy, was an important Tolowa dance leader in the early 1900s. Alex Billy's mother, Liza Billy, had important connections, since she was a daughter of Drey-Ding-Tlting, who was a son of Yut'tl-De-Yun of Chit (Chetco). Yut'tl-Gho-Sutl of Stundossun's son, Joe Hostler, was an important Howonquet leader. Joe's son, Frank, succeeded him, and Frank's son, Fred, succeeded him. Fred's successors were Betty Green and Elmer and Frank Hostler. Frank Hostler was an important leader of the early 1900s at Howonquet. With Norman George and Alex Billy, he formed a critical link of political and ceremonial leadership running, in particular, to Sam Lopez. Sam and Ed Lopez, and Joe and Maggie Seymour, sons of John and Etta Lopez, succeeded Captain Tom (Gylish of Howonquet, son Yut'tl-De-Yun of Chit). Lagoon Ben of Achulet (Lake Earl) was another recent leader, and Ben White and his daughter, Ellen White LaFountain, were his successors.

   Most political and ceremonial leaders in the modern period became Shakers after 1932, except for Jasper James and Sam and Mandy Lopez. Sam Lopez was a member of the Foursquare Church and held church meetings of his own near Howonquet for many years, but late in life decided that ancient Tolowas had also known God, and so set about reviving the dances.

9. Modern dance leaders have included Edward Lopez Sr.; Sam Lopez; Amelia Julia James Brown (a Chu-My-Yusth-Shre, or female herbalist, a smoke doctor and singer, later a Shaker); Amelia's daughter, Berneice Brown Humphrey; Lena Lopez; Ed Richards Sr.; Ed "Gobel" and Walter Richards; Lila James Moorehead; Ellen LaFountain; Ernest Scott; Kenneth Billy; Betty Green; Jasper James; Frank and Fred Moorehead; Ben White; and Loren Bommelyn. Bommelyn, the youngest, was the successor of Sam Lopez and descends from Billy Henry and Alice Charley.

   Tolowa dance leaders at discovery and during conquest were Fred Yontocket (of Yontocket), Yut'tl-De-Yun/Gylish of Chit (through an advantageous political marriage with Howonquet-Trey of Howonquet), Tosno of Achulet, Yut'tl-Gho-Sutl of Howonquet, Kearney of Gasquet, Kweltl-Ne-Son of Yontocket, John Flannery (To-Mo-Tre-Mu of Chit), Wharf Charley (or Toch-Tring-Gus of Pebble Beach), and Son-Dos of Yontocket. Leaders in the 1850s who participated in the Ghost Dance included Pyuwa (son of Son-Dos of Yontocket), Captain Tom or Gylish of Howonquet and Longhair Bob (sons of Drey-Ding-Tlting of Chit), Joe and Bob Smiley (sons of Tos-No of Achulet). Other important leaders included John Grimes Yontocket; Donny Flannery, son of John Flannery (To-Mo-Tre-Mu of Chit); and Pyuwa of Ench-Wo. Pyuwa's son was John White, a dance leader, who was succeeded by his son, George; his son-in-law, Willie Scott; and his daughter, Jennie White Scott. Jasper James (son of Gasquet Jim, grandson of Kearney of Gasquet) was succeeded by a son, Leonard.

Original Tolowa Shaker Church officers at Smith River included Norman George (minister), Ellen LaFountain (full-blood Tolowa, Nay Dosh dance leader, then assistant minister), Etta Richards (secretary), Maggie Seymour Billy (treasurer), Frank Moorehead (a Nay Dosh dance leader, then first elder), Frank Hostler (a Nay Dosh leader), Ben White (a Nay-Dosh leader), Amelia Julia James Brown (a Nay Dosh leader), Lydia George, Ida Bensel, Ed Richards Sr. (Nay-Dosh leader), Alice Henry, Laura Scott Coleman, and Fred Scott.

10. Tolowa Shakers (for whom it is a favorite anecdote), oral interviews, 1982–1984; see also Austin D. Warburton and Joseph F. Endert, *Indian Lore of the North California Coast* (Santa Clara, Calif.: Pacific Pueblo Press, 1966).

11. Tolowa Shakers, oral interviews, 1982.

12. Richard A. Gould and Theodore P. Furukawa, "Aspects of Ceremonial Life Among the Indian Shakers of Smith River, California," *Kroeber Anthropological Society Papers* 31 (1964): 51–67. Helen Williams observed Amelia Brown's healing power at a Shaker service in 1964. Amelia, who sat on the opposite side of the church from her, gazed at Williams, then

> she arose, and with a gentle smile on her face, she flitted across the candlelit room to where I sat on the bench against the wall. Tenderly she touched me, whispering words I could not translate but which I understood. Her beautiful hands glided over my back and shoulders as she searched for the pain she knew I was experiencing . . .
>
> I actually did feel better, but I am sorry I never did tell her I had come to the service straight from the emergency room of Seaside Hospital [in Crescent City], the excruciating pain of a wrenched shoulder alleviated slightly by medication but sufficiently bearable to allow me to drive my car.

Obituary, "Amelia Julia Brown, Born July 4, 1868, Died March 25, 1979," *People's Exchange* (Crescent City, Calif.), April 1980, 5.

13. Barnett, *Indian Shakers*, 80–81.

14. Ibid., 80.

15. Tolowa Shaker, oral interview, 1984.

16. Ibid.; Helen M. Williams, "'The Indian Shaker Church," *People's Exchange* (Crescent City, Calif.), August 1979. Williams used pieces from her personal journal to write this account.

17. Barnett, *Indian Shakers*, 171.

18. Ibid., 172–73.

19. An anonymous consultant shared this information with the author.

20. Gould and Furukawa, "Aspects of Ceremonial Life," 31.

21. An anonymous consultant shared this information.

22. Barnett, *Indian Shakers*, 353.

23. Gould and Furukawa, "Aspects of Ceremonial Life," 54.

24. Debra Webster, "The Indian Shaker Church," *Times Standard* (Eureka, Calif.), November 27, 1982, 6.

25. Ibid. Loren Bommelyn is a prominent contemporary Tolowa singer and ceremonial leader.

26. Tolowa Shaker, oral interview, 1982.

27. La Barre, *Ghost Dance*, 635.

28. Tolowa Shaker, oral interview, 1982; Cora DuBois, *The 1870 Ghost Dance*, Anthropological Records 3 (Berkeley: University of California Press, 1939), 1.

29. Tolowa Shaker, oral interview, 1982.

30. Ibid., the anonymous consultant said, "When a doctor got her power, the singers would sit around her in a circle and kick their foot on the floor. What happened when the Spirit would come into her body was, they would jump off the floor that eighteen feet high.... The abalone in the dance dresses would ring, if you would pick that up, like a bell as used in Shaker meetings. And then, that cross on the altar with the candles is the dance-fire. The Indians always prayed with that in the old religion. When they danced, they had a fire and the candles in Shake that represents the fire of God."

31. Ibid. Statements by the anonymous consultant.

32. Bommelyn interview, 1982.

33. Ibid.

34. Ibid.

8

"THE FATHER TELLS ME SO!"

⸙

Wovoka, the Ghost Dance Prophet

L. G. MOSES

THE HEBREW PROPHET JOEL, in a time of great distress, warned the Israelites to turn away from sin. A plague of locusts was ravaging the land; the day of the Lord's wrath was approaching. If the people gathered, repented, and renewed their covenant with the Almighty, however, Joel assured them that bounty would again reign in Zion. God, speaking through this early surrogate, warranted that for the chosen people, having returned to righteousness, "I will pour out my spirit upon all flesh; and your sons and your daughters shall prophesy, your old men shall dream dreams, and your young men shall see visions."[1] Prophets, dreams, and visions were very much a part of the Judeo-Christian tradition, and both Old and New Testaments are replete with direct divine guidance to mortals. The same was true among American Indians, who, like the Israelites, suffered from great distress. Prophets emerged among many Indian groups, and by far one of the most important was Wovoka, the Ghost Dance Prophet.[2]

The Ghost Dance, one of the largest social and religious movements among American Indians during the nineteenth century, developed as a result of many factors. The tribes had been defeated militarily, concentrated onto reservations, removed from their homelands, and forced to accept new laws directed by the government of the United States. Broken treaties, land encroachment, depletion of game, and assimilationist programs of the Bureau of Indian Affairs had demoralized the tribes to such an extent that they awaited deliverance from their depression and sorrow. Indeed, by 1880, Indians in the American West retained small hope of ever challenging the white man's government. Consigned either through persuasion or force to reservations, Indians were subjected to government-sponsored programs of assimilation. Commissioner of Indian Affairs Thomas J. Morgan bluntly stated, "The Indians must conform to the 'white man's ways,' peaceably if they will, forcibly if they must."[3] Government agents encouraged Indians to abandon their tribal affiliation, to accept allotments of land, and to lead, in the opinion of Indian-policy reformers, productive lives as citizen-farmers. "This civilization may not be the best possible," wrote commissioner of Indian Affairs Thomas Jefferson Morgan, "but it is the best the Indians can get." Their children were forced to attend reservation day or boarding schools or distant boarding schools such as the Carlisle Indian Industrial Training School in Pennsylvania. They were to become educated and white-like, abandoning forever their Indianness. It was the hope of white reformers that, within a generation, Indians would cease to be Indians, and, for the allotted tribes, that individual freeholds would have provided them with the means of livelihood, independence, and a respect for private property.[4]

Indians had difficulty adjusting to the new order created by the reservation system, and many Indians turned inward toward their religions in search of divine help in their demoralized state. Throughout the ages, frightened and oppressed humans have longed for deliverance, and Wovoka's message of renewal, rebirth, and revitalization offered hope for many Indian people. Like many prophets, Wovoka "died" and was reborn, returning from heaven with divine messages about how to live and worship. Furthermore, God gave Wovoka specific instructions about a sacred dance and ceremony that the prophet was told to bring back to the Indians. The ritual and dance became known by many names but is best remembered as the Ghost Dance. Wovoka believed that all Indians—living and dead—would be reunited in a world paradise, where Indians would be eternally free from poverty, disease, and death. Wovoka prophesied a great cataclysm whereby whites and their ways would be swept away, inaugurating an Indian millennium. All of this would be hastened by the continual performance of the Ghost Dance, a religious movement that spread rapidly among numerous western tribes.[5]

The leader of the Ghost Dance was born around 1858 near the Walker River in Mason Valley, Nevada. Wovoka (the Cutter) was a full-blood Paiute Indian who was born during an era of radical change for the Paiutes and other Indians in the West. Little is known about Wovoka's mother, but his father, Tavivo (White Man), helped shape the life of the future prophet. Tavivo followed the teachings of a spiritual leader named Wodziwob, who was a part of the first Ghost Dance movement of the 1870s and taught that the world would soon end and whites would be destroyed. Tavivo himself was a prophet and visionary with great spiritual power, and both he and Wodziwob shaped the beliefs and values of young Wovoka. As a boy of twelve or fourteen, Wovoka learned about the great cataclysm prophesied by Wodziwob and others, and of the new religious wave that was rolling across the plains, mountains, and deserts of the West.[6] "The prophetic claims and teachings of the father," wrote James Mooney, the renowned anthropologist who studied Wovoka's religion, "the reverence with which he was regarded by the people, and mysterious ceremonies which were doubtless of frequent performance in the little tule wikiup at home must have made early and deep impressions on the mind of the boy, who seems to have been by nature of a solitary and contemplative disposition, one of those born to see visions and hear still voices."[7] But Wovoka is equally remembered as Jack Wilson, "stepson" of David Wilson.

As a youth, Wovoka worked at the ranch of David Wilson, who in 1863, with his brothers William and George, had preempted tablelands along the southern rim of Mason Valley, land wooded in juniper and scrub pine but otherwise ideal for running cattle.[8] David Wilson, a devout Presbyterian, and his sons gave Wovoka his anglicized name, provided him steady work, and introduced him to Christianity.[9] So it appears that Tavivo, Wodziwob, the Wilsons, and their seemingly incompatible religions shaped the youth of a man who would become one of the most significant of the Indian prophets.

In the twenty years that separated the Ghost Dances of the 1870s with those of the 1890s, Wovoka grew to adulthood. Those twenty years also marked the military conquest of the Plains and Great Basin tribes. Apparently, at the age of eighteen, Wovoka ended his association with the Wilsons, gravitating to his father and the ritual life of the Paiutes.[10] "For two years," wrote Wovoka's only biographer, Paul Bailey, Wovoka, "shunned his white brothers, and wrestled with a hate for the whole white race that all but consumed him."[11] The documentary evidence upon which the author based the remark is nonexistent, but the biblical allusion is inescapable. The seeker, the prophet, the "messiah," withdraws into the wilderness—of his own making, in this instance—to search his soul for answers to questions that throb in his brain. At the end of his exile, he beholds his vision and begins his public ministry.[12]

By the time Wovoka was twenty, he stood nearly six feet tall. He married a Paiute woman to whom he gave the name Mary, in honor of David Wilson's wife, a fact that belies little of the self-consuming hatred for whites alluded to by Bailey.[13] Wovoka may also have visited the states of the Pacific Coast. Bailey, using the reminiscences of E. A. Dyer, for many years a friend of Wovoka and a storekeeper in Yerington, Nevada, claimed that the prophet traveled extensively in California, Oregon, and Washington. Dyer, in the transcription of his memoir edited by his son, stated simply that not much "is known of his activities as a young man, except that he did considerable wandering about this state and neighboring California." Regarding his travels he was never "loquacious." Paiutes were hired as pickers in the hop fields of Sonoma and Mendocino Counties in northern California. But elsewhere in his account, Dyer equivocates that probably "young Jack Wilson also traveled to the California hop fields."[14] Bailey inferred that Wovoka traveled widely and therefore came into contact with other Indian messianic or millennial religions, particularly the Washani, or Dreamer, religion and the Indian Shakers of John Slocum. Given certain similarities in beliefs, James Mooney also wondered if these Indian religions of world renewal had influenced Wovoka.[15]

In 1892, Mooney learned that two Indian Shaker missionaries had traveled throughout the Willamette Valley and other parts of Oregon. "It is said among the northern Indians that on this journey those apostles met," Mooney wrote, "a young man to whom they taught their mysteries, in which he became such an apt pupil that he soon outstripped his teachers, and is now working even greater wonders among his own people. This man can be not other than Wovoka." The only question that troubled the anthropologist was whether the story told among the Columbia tribes was legend based on vague rumors of a great prophet to the south or whether Wovoka actually derived his knowledge from these northern apostles. Mooney knew from his survey of correspondence in the files of the commissioner of Indian affairs that Plateau Indians from the Warm Springs Reservation in Oregon, as well as people from other areas of the inland Northwest, occasionally visited and worked in the Mason Valley and nearby Walker River Reservation. These Indians, often followers of the Washani faith or the Indian Shaker Church, shared their beliefs with the indigenous people of California and Nevada. They had also learned about the Ghost Dance religion from Native Americans in these states. Wovoka had told Mooney and, even earlier, Arthur Chapman, that the Ghost Dance Prophet had never wandered far from his home. Thus, we may accept that Wovoka knew about Wodziwob, John Slocum, Smohalla, Jesus of Nazareth, and perhaps even the revelations of Joseph Smith. Mormons had labored among the Lamanite descendants in Nevada, spreading the message of the Church of Jesus Christ of Latter Day Saints to Indian people.[16]

Wovoka probably began his public ministry as a weather prophet and healer in the mid-1880s, but it was not until January 1, 1889, according to Mooney's calculations, that Wovoka experienced his major revelation. Wovoka had been hearing voices for about two years, when on New Year's Day, 1889, he lay ill with a high fever in his wickiup. The day was marked by an eclipse of the sun, and on this day Wovoka "died" and journeyed to heaven. According to Wovoka,

> He saw God, with all the people who had died long ago engaged in their oldtime sports and occupations, all happy and forever young. It was a pleasant land and full of game. After showing him all, God told him he must go back and tell his people they must be good and love one another, have no quarreling, and live in peace with the whites; that they must work, and not lie or steal; that they must put away all the old practices that savored of war; that if they faithfully obeyed his instructions they would at last be

reunited with their friends in this other world, where there would be no more death or sickness or old age. He was then given the dance which he was commanded to bring back to his people. By performing this dance at intervals for five consecutive days each time, they would secure this happiness to themselves and hasten the event. Finally God gave him control over the elements so he could make it rain or snow or be dry at will, and appointed him his deputy to take charge of affairs in the west. . . . He then returned to earth and began to preach as he was directed, convincing the people by exercising the wonderful powers that had been given him.[17]

Wovoka had already introduced a dance two years before, but it was apparently nothing more than his version of the Paiute Round Dance.[18] Following his revelation, however, the ceremony, staged at the appropriate intervals as commanded by God, became the Ghost Dance, where, in their exhaustion and delirium, the participants communicated with the dead.[19]

There has been a tendency among certain authors who write about Wovoka to interpret his revelation as entirely self-serving. Many have relied on Bailey's account, wherein Wovoka, seeing so many of his people defer to him, is swept up in the masque. But it may be simpler to explain. Wovoka believed himself to be a prophet ordained by Providence with a special mission to the American Indians. So intense was this conviction that he elicited the assistance of the farmer-in-charge at Walker River Reservation. In February 1890, James O. Gregory wrote Indian Superintendent of the Nevada S. S. Sears, stationed at the Pyramid Lake Reservation, admitting that "you will doubtless be amazed at the letter you will have received from Jack Wilson the prophet." Gregory confided that Wovoka "has got the Indians all wild at this wonderful command of the Elements" because the prophet had apparently convinced the people "that he alone is responsible for the storms of this season." Wovoka had written Sears to learn if the government believed "in him and will acknowledge him as a prophet." Gregory reported that well over two hundred men, women, and children had turned out to see and hear the prophet, despite a driving snowstorm. Indeed, the crowd talked "of nothing but Jack Wilson and the miracles he performs," and they took up a collections of twenty-five dollars, which they presented to the holy man. According to Gregory, Wovoka wanted "to come on the reservation to farm and guarantees the Indians that if the government gives him permission to come he will cause lots of rain to fall and they will never lose a crop again."[20] Wovoka and the other Indians expected the government to answer the letter, but Sears never forwarded the correspondence. There is no reason to suspect that he would have, once confronted with the fantastic claims of, as far as he was concerned, an ignorant and superstitious people. The letter is only remarkable in retrospect, and takes on added significance when one considers the response of the

FIGURE 8.1. During the course of his life, many people took photographs of Wovoka. Often he appeared wearing a big black hat, one of his trademarks. Indians and non-Indians sought out the Ghost Dance Prophet for consultations. He was well-known in Nevada, California, and other western states and territories. Courtesy of the Nevada Historical Society.

government to the Ghost Dance. It is part of the tragedy that the first information received by the Bureau of Indian Affairs about the religion spoke not about an apocalyptic religion of peace and fraternity, but rather of a possible rebellion among disaffected Sioux.[21] Gregory's letter is equally noteworthy because it supports the implication that Wovoka took his mission seriously. In addition, corroborating testimony appears in the correspondence of the commissioner of Indian Affairs. From the Indian Territory seven months later, Cheyenne and Arapaho Agent Charles F. Ashley wrote that a letter had recently arrived from the Wind River Reservation in Wyoming, telling that the "messiah" had written to the "Great Father in Washington" to ask that he remove within two years all whites from the western United States, lest they be destroyed.[22]

Following his New Year's revelation, Wovoka's renown increased throughout 1889, first among Paiutes and later among western and southwestern tribes who heard the good news of the prophet. In March of that year, Sarah Winnemucca, daughter of a Paiute headman, reported to the editor of *The Daily Silver State* that "a prophet has risen among the Indians at Walker Lake and is creating some excitement among the ignorant and more credulous Piutes [*sic*]. He says the spirits of all the Piute [*sic*] warriors who have died . . . are to return to earth and resume their old forms. They have condemned the whites and the Indians who write and speak their language or adopt their customs, and will exterminate them from the earth."[23] *The Walker Lake Bulletin* reprinted the article first published in *The Daily Silver State*, thereby spreading the news about the Ghost Dance to non-Indians. By the summer of 1889, news about Wovoka had reached distant Plains tribes who learned not about a prophet who foretold wondrous things but instead about the "Indian Messiah" himself. Elaine Goodale, teacher at the White River Industrial School on the Great Sioux Reservation, reported that while camping with a hunting party on the evening of July 23, she met Chasing Crane, a Sioux just returned from the Rosebud Agency. He had a wonderful story to tell. "God," he explained, had "appeared to the Crows across the Stony Mountains."[24] The appearance of an Indian "Christ" among the Crows, as Goodale described Wovoka, suggests both the rapidity with which Wovoka's doctrine had spread and his transformation from prophet to messiah. Rumors of an Indian messiah traveled pell-mell from reservation to reservation across the western part of the United States, growing more fantastic with each retelling. News of the Ghost Dance messiah also fueled apocalyptic expectations by Native nations suffering from the invasion of their homelands by settlers, miners, and soldiers.[25]

Although Wovoka would have disavowed the honor of being the Indian Messiah, his identity underwent a metamorphosis in the minds of the faithful from the Paiute Prophet to the Indian Messiah, and finally to the inviolate Christ.[26] By the time the Plains tribes began their investigation of the new religion, Wovoka had ascended to such spiritual heights that his visitors, by some accounts, approached him with averted eyes.[27] Wovoka, however, never said he was the messiah, claiming only to be a prophet of God. Indeed, this fact was recorded by John S. Mayhugh, former agent at the Western Shoshone Reservation in Nevada and the allotment officer of the Nevada tribes. Mayhugh, who knew Wovoka, wrote that the prophet foretold the coming of a messiah who would appear on Mount Grant near the Walker River Agency. Mayhugh's accurate message never became the prevailing view, and even today Wovoka is usually referred to as the Indian Messiah.[28]

Wovoka's message spread quickly from the Paiute wickiups huddled around Walker Lake southward to the Hualapais and eastward to the Bannocks, Shoshones, Arapahos, Crows, Cheyennes, Caddos, Pawnees, Kiowas, Comanches, and Sioux. To learn more about the doctrine, tribal delegates traveled westward to Mason Valley to sit at the prophet's feet. They then returned to their tribes with written instructions. Engaged in research among the Southern Cheyennes, Mooney obtained what he called a "Messiah Letter." His free rendering appears here in its entirety.

When you get home you must make a dance to continue for five days. Dance four successive nights, and the last night keep up the dance until the morning of the fifth day, when all must bathe in the river and then disperse to their homes. You must all do in the same way.

I[,] Jack Wilson, love you all, and my heart is full of gladness for the gifts you have brought me. When you get home I shall give you a good cloud which will make you feel good. I give you a good spirit and give you all good paint. I want you to come again in three months, some from each tribe there [from Indian Territory].

There will be a good deal of snow this year and some rain. In the fall there will be such a rain as I have never given you before.

Grandfather says, when your friends die you must not cry. You must not fight. Do right always. It will give you satisfaction in life.

Do not tell the white people about this. Jesus is now upon the earth. He appears like a cloud. The dead are all alive again. I do not know when they will be here; maybe this fall or in the spring. When the time comes there will be no more sickness and everyone will be young again.

Do not refuse to work for the whites and do not make any trouble with them until you leave them. When the earth shakes do not be afraid. It will not hurt you.

I want you to dance every six weeks. Make a feast at the dance and have food that everybody may eat. Then bathe in the water. That is all. You will receive good words again from me some time. Do not tell lies.[29]

Wovoka gave this message, or one very much like it, to all the delegations that visited him. The first Sioux delegates, for example, left their reservations in the fall of 1889, and after many adventures, returned in the early spring of 1890.[30] By summer, Ghost Dances had been organized at a number of reservations scattered throughout the West. The government's response was premised, however, on the hostility of a religion as practiced among the Sioux that promised the destruction of whites through whatever means.[31]

When the Western Sioux, then among the most populous tribes in the United States and popularly recognized as the most warlike and recalcitrant Indians, embraced the religion, the Ghost Dance conjured images of half-crazed "savages" ready to follow lives of rapine and slaughter.[32] During the fall and early winter of 1890, newspaper accounts from the Dakotas sustained the prevalent image of the Indians as erstwhile predators.[33] For all the years the Sioux had huddled around the agency—lulled into submission by rations and gimcracks—they were now portrayed as demonic killers. Mythical stories about treacherous Sioux, joined by other "hostiles" in a grand Indian conspiracy, overshadowed the actual story of Wovoka and his religion of peace and love. Dancing, peaceful Indians awaiting their divine redemption did not sell newspapers, so journalists surfeited the country with stories about Indians dancing themselves into frenzies as they awaited reinforcements from the risen dead. No journalist and no official of the Indian service ever traveled to Mason Valley to hear the prophet's unadorned message.[34] Instead, misunderstanding of Wovoka's religion significantly contributed to the Dakota disaster that ended at Wounded Knee, South Dakota.

On the cold morning of December 29, 1890, Big Foot's band of Minneconjou Sioux were attacked by troopers of the famed Seventh Cavalry. The Indians were encamped at Wounded Knee, and most of them were followers of the Ghost Dance, a religion that had been banned by agents on the Sioux Reservations. Fighting had erupted after the soldiers decided to search the camp and some of the Sioux had refused to submit. The camp of tipis was raked by the bullets of Hotchkiss guns, and at least 150 Indians—men, women, and children—were killed, while many others were wounded. Wovoka's vision of an Indian world filled with peace, restoration, and brotherly love crumbled that bleak December day. Three days after the tragedy at Wounded Knee, a burial party interred in a mass grave the frozen corpses of the Sioux, and it buried something else as well. In the words of Black Elk, an Oglala Sioux holy man who had witnessed part of the slaughter, a dream was buried with the slain Sioux. That dream was of a redeemer who would "drive out the usurper and win back for his people what they had lost." For a few short seasons, Wovoka's dream had flourished, but his religion of hope died with the Sioux on the snow-swept plains surrounding Wounded Knee.[35]

When Wovoka learned about Wounded Knee, he understandably feared that he would be blamed. He counseled the delegates, whose ardor still sent them to Nevada seeking news of the millennium, that they should return to their respective tribes and stop the dances. The Indian resurrection had been postponed. For the nation, the Ghost Dance soon retreated into memory as the "Last Indian War." As one historian has noted, the Sioux died at Wounded Knee at the end of the same year in which the superintendent of the census announced the closure of the frontier.[36] Thus, Wovoka, his religion, and Wounded Knee have become a metaphor for a nation in transition from the wilderness to a modern industrial state.[37]

Transition was equally an appropriate element of Wovoka's life, especially during that period after Wounded Knee: although his promise of an Indian millennium was not fulfilled, he still inspired devotion among followers beyond his own Paiutes. That devotion represented, in part, a continuing desire for a better life. Burdened by the present and discomfited by a future that offered little hope, many Indians sought succor in a restored past. For his followers, Wovoka served as a last link in a chain that bound them to individual ways of life, separate and distinct from mainstream American society, which stood poised on the threshold of a new century. Through relentless government programs, Indian societies had been undermined, their leaders had been dishonored—sometimes imprisoned or killed for their recalcitrance—their traditional means of subsistence had been destroyed, their lands had been expropriated or considerably reduced, their religions had been harassed, and their children in many instances had been taken from them and sent to the white man's schools. The government, with the assistance of a legion of well-intentioned reformers, had decreed that Indians should be like other Americans. They should lead useful and productive lives. For some tribes, the Dawes Act divided tribal lands into 160-acre parcels upon which Indians would farm and grow independent. Once independent, the reformers and government agents believed anachronistic tribalism would retreat, giving way to "civilization." The favorite aphorism of Richard Henry Pratt, a contemporary of Wovoka and a proponent of Indian education, was "kill the Indian and save the man."[38] It is little wonder that for thousands of Indians, Wovoka offered solace and a sense of continuity with the past in an alien world. [39]

Although Wovoka did not preach his religion as extensively after 1891, he continued to serve the Paiutes as a holy man and healer, and for erstwhile Ghost Dancers, as an object of continued veneration. Wovoka has been most criticized for the latter capacity, with charges that the prophet personally gained from his celebrity. Indeed, some claimed that Wovoka connived with local storekeeper Dyer to create a lucrative business in Ghost Dance memorabilia. For years after the demise of the Ghost Dance, Wovoka received letters of supplication from the faithful. Many asked for sacred objects, such as the red clay paint used in the dance. Very few of these letters have been preserved, but Dyer reported that Indians asked for Wovoka's "garments, particularly shirts," which they believed held "miraculous powers." In fact, anything "he had worn, owned, touched, looked upon or simply just thought about" reportedly had powers. "In time a great many requests were for hats, specifically for those which he had personally worn. I was very often called upon to send them his hat which he would remove forthwith from his head on hearing the nature of the request in a letter." In return, Wovoka reportedly expected and got twenty dollars for such a gift. Dyer and others criticized Wovoka for conducting "a steady and somewhat profitable business in hats." Wovoka also sold "magpie tail feathers and red ochre," but his critics remarked that the prices were "on a par with those asked for similar 'war-paint' and geegaws in our modern salons."[40] That Wovoka "sold" objects or received money for services is only significant if one disregards the traditions of Paiute shamanism and gift giving among most Indian peoples. Objects such as feathers, hats, or paint were signs of individual power—analogous in a broad sense to the use of sacramentals, such as holy water or blessed medals, by Roman Catholics. Wovoka transmitted signs of his power, and occasionally their efficacy, by giving them to his followers, who returned the favor with a gift or offering.[41]

Yet Wovoka could also demur. Johnson Sides, a Paiute who liked to call himself the "peace maker" and who was for years Wovoka's enemy, reported that the prophet refused a gift of forty silver dollars dumped at his feet by a Pawnee delegate who happened to be in the service of the Bureau of Indian Affairs. The money represented a collection taken by the tribe for the prophet. Sides explained that Wovoka feared the money was tainted and that he might be killed through witchcraft.[42] Sides may have been telling the truth, but were Wovoka as grasping and as calculating as is often suggested, why should he refuse such a handsome gift? A charlatan with his eye on a chance to gain would never have refused. Clearly, not all Paiutes were enamored with Wovoka, but for many he was held in respect, his advice sought on matters pertaining to the people at Walker River and his powers over the weather and disease invoked. On communal rabbit hunts, for example, his position was always one of honor; he rode in a wagon. He had no need to shoot his own game. Every member of the hunt shared his prizes with him.[43]

By one account, Wovoka remained on the Wilson ranch until 1920, whereas another holds that between 1912 and 1932, he lived in the Paiute colony at Yerington, Nevada.[44] Sometime before 1920, he traveled to Idaho, Wyoming, and twice to Oklahoma, where his former followers feted and presented him with many gifts that he treasured for the remainder of his life.[45] In the spring of 1919, Grace Dangberg, an aspiring ethnologist and historian, learned that Wovoka's sight and hearing were failing. At the invitation of Carrie Willis Wilson, wife of James Wilson, Wovoka's boyhood companion, Dangberg retrieved some letters from the basement of the ranch house in Nordyke, Nevada, where Wovoka had once lived. These twenty-one letters and fragments, deposited at the Nevada State Historical Society, were written between 1908 and 1911 and indicate the esteem people held for Wovoka. The letters are all that remain of the many hundreds the prophet received. Dangberg hoped to interview Wovoka, but at the last moment, he refused. She did not press the issue.[46]

Later in the 1920s, Wovoka agreed to speak to Colonel Tim McCoy, the only non-Indian, except James Mooney, to speak to the prophet specifically about his religion. In the winter of 1924, the actor and showman was serving as technical director for the filming of *The Thundering Herd* on location in Bishop, California. McCoy had been a longtime friend of former Ghost Dancers among the Northern Arapahos. He hired a few of them as extras for the film. McCoy knew that he was within easy distance of the Ghost Dance Prophet and decided to make a "fool's errand" in search of him. McCoy recorded that he drove to Yerington, where he found Wovoka and persuaded him to visit Bishop the following day. Three decades after the end of the Ghost Dance, Wovoka found the Arapahos deferential. But McCoy commented, "Whatever he was to the Arapahoes, Wovoka was still a Paiute Medicine Man to me and I would not put out of my head the story that some years before, after prophesying an early winter, he had directed a flunky to dump blocks of ice into the river near his home."[47] The story of the floating ice, repeated in numerous accounts of the prophet, may have been that "miracle" witnessed by E. A. Dyer on the banks of the Walker River. Wovoka had told a group of Paiutes that he would make ice fall from the heavens despite the mid-July heat. According to Dyer, Wovoka probably secreted a block of ice high on the limbs of a cottonwood tree, whereupon, after sufficient melting, it dropped to the ground, shattering and thereby amazing a hundred Paiutes gathered around their holy man.[48]

Another story, the one alluded to by McCoy, tells of Wovoka having caused ice to float down the river in mid-July. The "flunky" that McCoy refers to was actually two people, the Wilson boys, who served as the prophet's confederates in a ruse to awaken credulity among the Paiute congregation. This story is repeated by Bailey, who used as his source Beth Wilson Ellis, daughter of William Wilson. That McCoy knew of this episode at the time he met Wovoka is doubtful. He probably learned about it from Bailey, who had interviewed him for the biography of Wovoka.[49] Dyer himself had heard this story a number of years after he witnessed the ice "miracle." But of the ice-in-the-river incident he wrote, "Whether that was a distortion of what I witnessed or a separate affair I can't state."[50] McCoy also told Bailey during the author's research that the prophet "appeared to have the impression that he would never die."[51] In his memoirs, however, McCoy writes that, just before leaving the movie set at Bishop, Wovoka turned to him and said, "I will never die."[52] What had been an impression became a declaration, but it is doubtful that Wovoka truly believed himself to be immortal. The differences in the accounts, on the surface quite trivial, nevertheless account for some of the misperceptions about Wovoka.

The last years of Wovoka's life were relatively uneventful, but he lived for nine years after his visit with McCoy. Wovoka, the great Ghost Dance Prophet, died on September 20, 1932, and was buried in the heart of the Paiute Country. Joseph McDonald of the *Reno Evening Gazette* wrote an obituary about Wovoka, explaining that after the prophet's death in Yerington, his body was taken to the Paiute cemetery at Schurz. As family and friends shoveled dirt into his grave, a Christian missionary, the Reverend E. H. Emig, recited prayers. "Whether a special marker will be placed over the grave," McDonald wondered, "has not been decided. It is in the family plot in the Indian burying ground, but Indians at Schurz and vicinity have indicated that it will represent no special shrine of worship for them . . . though Wovoka once was the powerful Paiute of the tribe. Of late years he has acted as a medicine man, but failing health caused him to become very inactive recently."[53] Ironically, the same newspaper reported the following month that "Indians were staging a ghost dance at Pine Grove under the direction of Jack Wilson, the Indian Messiah."[54]

James Mooney, a professional anthropologist employed by the Smithsonian Institution's Bureau of American Ethnography, provided the most comprehensive study of Wovoka.[55] Between 1890 and 1894, Mooney studied the prophet and his religion, documenting a good deal of his information directly from Wovoka. Mooney left an extensive work on Wovoka, a classic memoir entitled "The Ghost Dance Religion and the Sioux Outbreak of 1890." Aside from this study, Wovoka's life and religion evoked little interest until 1957, when Bailey published the first and only biography of the prophet. Like Mooney's study, Bailey's book is sympathetic to Wovoka but intimates that the prophet trifled with fate and reaped the whirlwind. According to Bailey, Wovoka's religion "came at a time when the Indian was a beaten, frustrated, starved creature, without hope." And, according to Bailey, Wovoka, "whether divinely inspired prophet, or opportunist and faker, provided hope for numerous Indians." The inference drawn by Bailey is that chance, in all its perversity and irony, intervened and swept along the prophet and his vision of a restored Indian world toward an unimagined destiny.[56]

Although Wovoka was one of the foremost Indian prophets of his time, no one has erected a monument in his honor at his gravesite at Schurz, Nevada. However, in 1975, at a cost of $900.00, the Yerington Paiute tribe placed a marker as its bicentennial project in the town where Wovoka spent the last twenty years of his life.[57] In the windswept cemetery at Schurz, the wood grave marker first placed there in 1932 still stands and records the birth and death not of Wovoka, the Ghost Dance Prophet, but of Jack Wilson. The mound of sand, well-tended, bears the weathered gifts and offerings—mostly sprigs of sage, flags made of ribbon, and now dessicated flowers in dry mason jars—left there periodically by those who still honor his memory. Anthropologists, historians, and buffs have written thousands of words about Wovoka, trying unsuccessfully to unravel the mysteries that conceal the character of the man. In all the speculation, use of imagination, and other methods of their art, no person has written a more fitting epitaph than that of Edward A. Dyer Jr., son of Wovoka's trusted friend. "Despite the narrow opinion of some of Jack's white contemporaries in Mason Valley," Dyer wrote, "I submit that he was a very great man who without help, tools, or understanding tried to better the lot of his people who were hit by a cataclysm with which they were unable to cope."[58]

Like Joel, Paul, and countless other prophets and religious leaders, Wovoka had dreamed a dream and had seen a vision. That his vision was unshared by the majority of his countrymen should not diminish his contributions to the rich religious heritage of the American people. Rather than dismiss Wovoka as an opportunist whose doctrine unwittingly inflamed a large number of American Indians who longed for a deliverer, one might envision a sincere prophet who misdiagnosed the end of the world. In this regard, he was far from unique. He was probably as surprised and disappointed as his coreligionists when his dream failed and the glory of the Indian millennium failed to unfold.

The Ghost Dance religion, identified as a "revitalization movement" more than a half century after its dissolution, was only one of many such Indian movements. Like the others, it sought to return the world to a happier time. However, none of the Indian movements, up until 1890, were as widespread or as popular as the Ghost Dance. Wovoka, the Ghost Dance Prophet, offered American Indians surcease through the intervention of the supernatural to the tragic confrontation with the dominant society. As Joel had promised the Israelites, if they rededicated themselves to the religion of their fathers, God would pour out his blessings. Wovoka told his followers to lay aside their differences, celebrate their heritage, and await the blessings of the Creator. By any standard, Wovoka, the Ghost Dance Prophet, was one of the most significant holy men ever to emerge among the Indians of North America.

NOTES

1. Joel 2:28 (King James Version).
2. Whether or not the Ghost Dances of 1870 and 1890 originated in deprivation has long been an item of contention among ethnohistorians. Michael Hittman presents a cogent summary of argumentation and argues persuasively that the earlier Ghost Dance, contrary to the speculations of Leslie Spier and Cora DuBois, had its origin in deprivation

created by Euro-American expansionism rather than from diffusion of Basin Plateau ceremonialism. See Michael Hittman, "Ghost Dances, Disillusionment and Opiate Addiction: An Ethnohistory of Smith and Mason Valley Paiutes" (PhD diss., University of New Mexico, 1973); Hittman, "The 1870 Ghost Dance at Walker River Reservation: A Reconstrction," *Ethnohistory* 20 (1973): 247–78.

3. *Annual Report of the Commissioner of Indian Affairs, 1889* (Washington, D.C.: Government Printing Office, 1889).

4. For general sources, see Francis P. Prucha, *American Indian Policy in Crisis: Christian Reformers and the Indian, 1865–1900* (Norman: University of Oklahoma Press, 1976); Henry E. Fritz, *The Movement for Indian Civilization, 1868–1890* (Philadelphia: University of Pennsylvania Press, 1966); Robert W. Mardock, *The Reformers and the American Indian* (Columbia: University of Missouri Press, 1971). The quote from Commissioner of Indian Affairs Thomas Jefferson Morgan is found in *Annual Report of the Commissioner of Indian Affairs, 1890* (Washington, D.C.: Government Printing Office, 1890), 178.

5. The quotes are from James Mooney, "The Ghost Dance Religion and the Sioux Outbreak of 1890," in *Fourteenth Annual Report of the Bureau of Ethnology* (Washington, D.C.: Government Printing Office, 1896), 928. For information on other revitalization movements, see Anthony F. C. Wallace, "Revitalization Movements," *American Anthropologist* 58 (April 1956): 264–81; Robert M. Utley, *Last Days of the Sioux Nation* (New Haven: Yale University Press, 1963); Henry F. Dobyns and Robert C. Euler, *The Ghost Dance of 1889 Among the Paiute Indians of Northwestern Arizona* (Prescott, Ariz.: Prescott College Press, 1967); Hazel W. Hertzberg, *The Search for an American Indian Identity: Modern Pan-Indian Movements* (Syracuse, N.Y.: Syracuse University Press, 1971); Weston La Barre, *The Ghost Dance: Origin of Religion* (Garden City, N.Y.: Doubleday, 1970).

6. Mooney suggested that Wovoka was born in 1854, but an article that appeared in the *Mason Valley News* December 26, 1975, Wovoka's year of birth is given as 1856, giving Wovoka's birthplace as Smith rather than Mason Valley. However, the prophet's grave marker at Schurz, Nevada, records that he was seventy-four when he died, thus placing his birth in 1858. Mooney provisionally rendered Wovoka "Cutter" from a verb signifying "to cut." Other names for the prophet were Wopokahte, Kwohitsaug, Cowejo, Koittsow, Kvit-Tsow, Quoitze Ow, Jack Wilson, Jack Winson, and John Johnson. Lieutenant Nat P. Phister listed the names Kvit-Tsow and Wo-po-kah-tee. Judge Eli S. Ricker, in his research among the Sioux Ghost Dancers, found the names Jocko Wilson and Jakey Wilson. See Mooney, "Ghost Dance Religion," 764–65; Nat P. Phister, "The Indian Messiah," *American Anthropologist* 4 (April 1891): 105–8; Eli S. Ricker, "Short Bull's Story," in Eli S. Ricker Notebook 17, p. 94, Eli S. Ricker Collection, Nebraska State Historical Society, Lincoln, Nebraska; Cora DuBois, *The 1870 Ghost Dance*, Anthropological Records 3 (Berkeley: University of California Press, 1939): 3–7; and see the Arthur Chapman account in the *Annual Report of the Secretary of War, 1892*, House Executive Document,

52nd Congress, 1st Session, 192–93; DuBois identified the 1870 prophet as Wodziwob, and Mooney identified the prophet as Waughzeewaughber but assumed that it was another name for Tavivo. Hittman, who conducted extensive field work among the Paiutes of Mason and Smith Valleys, writes that Wodziwob, contrary to DuBois's assertion, did not die around 1872 but became a Native doctor at Walker River. "Fishlake Joe," who appears frequently in the records of Walker River Reservation after 1872, and Wodziwob were the same person. Wodziwob had come from the southern part of Nevada in the 1860s to Walker River. See Edward C. Johnson, *Walker River Paiutes: A Tribal History* (Salt Lake City: University of Utah Printing Service, 1975), 42.

7. Mooney, "Ghost Dance Religion," 764.

8. Paul Bailey, *Wovoka the Indian Messiah* (Los Angeles, Calif.: Westernlore Press, 1957), 35.

9. E. A. Dyer Sr. to George Friedhoff, May 16, 1965, Dyer Collection, Manuscripts Division, Nevada Historical Society, Reno.

10. Leslie Spier first suggested that the Paiute Ghost Dance had its origins in the Prophet Dance of the Northwest plateau and that the Paiute Ghost Dance was simply part of a recurring phenomenon. Willard Park wrote that, among the Paiutes, "ceremonial performances are meager and mostly confined to shamanistic curing" and that "the curing rite . . . constitutes almost the entire ceremonial life of the Paviotso." He also wrote that not only was the Round Dance the most popular dance of the Paiutes but, with the exception of shamanistic curing rites, that the "significant religious beliefs and activities [of the Paiutes] are associated only with the Round Dance." Using these and other references from Park, Hittman concludes that the Ghost Dance fits into traditional forms of Paiute ceremonialism and were, therefore, not inspired by extratribal ceremonialism such as the Prophet Dance. See Leslie Spier, "The Ghost Dance of 1870 Among the Klamath or Oregon," *University of Washington Publications in Anthropology* 2 (1927): 39–56; Leslie Spier, Wayne Suttles, and Melville J. Herskovits, "Comment of Aberle's Thesis of Deprivation," *Southwestern Journal of Anthropology* 15 (1959): 84–89; Willard Z. Park, *Shamanism in Western North America: A Study in Cultural Relationships*, Northwestern University Studies in the Social Sciences 2 (Evanston, Ill.: Northwestern University Press, 1938), 12, 71; Willard Z. Park, "Cultural Succession in the Great Basin" in *Language, Culture and Personality*, ed. Leslie Spier, A. Irving Hallowell, and Stanley Newman (Menasha, Wisc.: Sapir Memorial Publication, 1941), 183–84; Hittman, "1870 Ghost Dance," 263–71.

11. Bailey, *Wovoka*, 50.

12. Wovoka's afterlife experiences and his rise to the status of Prophet is consistent with that of other Indian religious leaders, including those found in this publication.

13. Bailey, *Wovoka*, 67.

14. E. A. Dyer Sr., "Wizardry," Manuscripts Division, Nevada Historical Society, Reno.

15. While it is possible that Wovoka learned about Smohalla and the Washani religion, it is very unlikely that Smohalla and Wovoka ever met. See Clifford E. Trafzer and Richard D.

Scheuerman, "Smohalla, Washani, and Seven Drums: Religious Traditions on the North-west Plateau," chapter 6 in this volume.

16. Mooney, "Ghost Dance Religion," 763; Chapman, *Annual Report of the Secretary of War*, 192–93.

17. Mooney, "Ghost Dance Religion," 770–71.

18. Round Dances were usually held for five consecutive all-night sessions and were presided over by a singer who stood inside of the dance circle, and also by a dance leader who prayed for rain, fish, game, pine nuts, and good health.

19. Orner C. Stewart, "The Ghost Dance," in *Anthropology on the Great Plains*, ed. W. Raymond Wood and Margot Liberty (Lincoln: University of Nebraska Press, 1980), 181; Hittman, "1870 Ghost Dance," 263.

20. James O. Gregory to S. S. Sears, February 18, 1890, Records of the Walker River Indian Agency, Box 314, Copy Book 1, 80–81, Records of the Commissioner of Indian Affairs, RG 75, LR, Federal Archives and Records Center (FARC), San Bruno, California (SB).

21. L. G. Moses, "Jack Wilson and the Indian Service: The Response of the BIA to the Ghost Dance Prophet," *American Indian Quarterly* 5 (1979): 295–313; Brad Logan, "The Ghost Dance Among the Paiute: An Ethnohistorical View of Documentary Evidence, 1889–1893," *Ethnohistory* 27 (1980): 267–82.

22. Charles F. Ashley to Commissioner of Indian Affairs (CIA), *Annual Report of the Commissioner of Indian Affairs, 1891* (Washington, D.C.: Government Printing Office, 1891), 178.

23. *Walker Lake Bulletin*, March 20, 1889.

24. Ray Wilson, Ohiyesa: Charles Eastman, Santee Sioux (Urbana and Chicago: University of Illinois Press, 1983), 51.

25. Kay Graber, ed., *Sister to the Sioux: Memoirs of Elaine Goodale Eastman* (Lincoln: University of Nebraska, 1978), 74; Elaine Goodale Eastman, "Ghost Dance War and Wounded Knee Massacre of 1890–91," *Nebraska History* 26 (1945): 28; Utley, *Last Days*, 48, 49, 60, 72; James C. Olson, *Red Cloud and the Sioux Problem* (Lincoln: University of Nebraska Press, 1965), 306–19. The Sioux bill passed Congress in 1889, dividing the Great Sioux Reservation—established by the Sioux Treaty of 1868 and modified by the revised agreement with the Sioux of 1876—into six reservations: Standing Rock, Cheyenne River, Lower Brule, Crow Creek, Rosebud, and Pine Ridge. It was not until February 1890 that President Benjamin Harrison announced the acceptance of the Sioux bill by a "majority" of Teton Lakota males and thereby created the separate reservations.

26. Mooney, "Ghost Dance Religion," 77.

27. John S. Mayhugh to CIA, November 24, 1890, Special Case 188, "The Ghost Dance, 1890–98," RG 75, Reel I, Frames 25, 32, 653, National Archives (NA), Washington, D.C.; hereafter cited as Special Case 188.

28. Ibid., Reel I, Frame 274.

29. Mooney, "Ghost Dance Religion," 780–81; Mooney to CIA, February 20, 1892, Records of the CIA, LR, RG 75, NA.

30. Mooney, "Ghost Dance Religion," 843–94.

31. Moses, "Jack Wilson and the Indian Service," 295–313; Logan, "Ghost Dance Among the Paiute," 267–88.

32. John C. Ewers, "The Emergence of the Plains Indian as Symbol of the North American Indian," in *Smithsonian Institution Annual Report, 1964* (Washington, D.C.: Government Printing Office, 1964), 531–44.

33. Oliver Knight, *Following the Indian Wars* (Norman: University of Oklahoma Press, 1960), 311; Elmo S. Watson, "The Last Indian War, 1890–91: A Study in Newspaper Jingoism," *Journalism Quarterly* 20 (1943): 205–319.

34. Logan, "Ghost Dance Among the Paiute," 274–75. C. C. Warner, agent at Pyramid Lake, informed the commissioner on November 18, 1890, that he planned within the next few days to visit Wovoka. The meeting, however, never took place.

35. John G. Neihardt, *Black Elk Speaks* (Lincoln: University of Nebraska Press, 1932), 276; Mooney, "Ghost Dance Religion," 657.

36. Utley, *Last Days*, vii.

37. L. G. Moses and Margaret Connell Szasz, "Indian Revitalization Movements of the Late Nineteenth Century," *Journal of the West* 23 (1984): 13.

38. Elaine Goodale Eastman, *Pratt the Red Man's Moses* (Norman: University of Oklahoma Press, 1935), 173–80; Hertzberg, *Search for an American Indian Identity*, 16.

39. Raymond J. DeMallie would take exception to these and to some of Utley's interpretations. About the Ghost Dance among the Sioux, DeMallie argues that standard historical interpretation "takes *too* narrow a perspective. It treats the ghost dance as an isolated phenomenon, as though it were divorced from the rest of Lakota culture. It also refuses to accept the basic religious nature of the movement. . . . To dismiss the ghost dance as only a reaction to land loss and hunger does not do it justice; to dismiss it as merely a desperate attempt to revitalize a dead or dying culture is equally unsatisfactory." DeMallie also suggests "that the ghost dance could be a valid religion was incomprehensible to the whites." In fairness, however, a number of contemporary white observers did see the Ghost Dance as a valid religion and used relativistic language to suggest its validity to the commissioner and others in the Indian service. Prominent among these were Lieutenant H. L. Scott, John S. Mayhugh, Frank Campbell, and Captain Jesse M. Lee. See Special Case 188 and Raymond J. DeMallie, "The Lakota Ghost Dance: An Ethnohistorical Account," in *Religion and American Culture*, ed. David G. Hackett (New York: Routledge, 2003), 329.

40. Dyer, "Wizardry," 3.

41. Grace Dangberg, "Wovoka," *Nevada Historical Society Quarterly* 11 (1968): 5–51. The author states that "the acceptance of money for objects 'blessed' is not . . . peculiar to the

Indians. . . . No blessing is conferred by the objects or by the treatment of disease unless it is paid for. The fact that the feathers and ochre [paint] were paid for in negotiable currency is an accident of the times and a measure of the extent of influence of Wovoka which was promoted by the white man's civilization" (16).

42. *Elko Daily Independent*, August 22, 1894.

43. Dyer, "Wizardry," 16; Nelson Hammond to Warner, October 28, 1891, Records of the Walker River Agency, Box 314, Copy Book 1, 228, RG 75, FARC, SB. A portion of the letter is recorded here. In October 1891, Josephus, captain of Indian police at Walker River and respectful of Wovoka's spiritual powers, reported to the farmer-in-charge that there were "several Indians coming over from Wadsworth [Pyramid Lake] to kill Jack Wilson the messiah. The names of the Indians are Natches, Lee Winnemucca, one Indian from [Walker?] river, . . . one from the Sink of the Carson named Johnson, also one from Humbolt named Humbolt Natches. Josephus is anxious for you [C. C. Warner] to retain these Indians and not allow them to come here."

44. Dangberg, "Wovoka," 34; *Mason Valley News*, December 26, 1975.

45. Dyer, "Wizardry," 15–16; Grace Dangberg, ed., "Letters to Jack Wilson, the Paiute Prophet, Written Between 1908 and 1911," *Bureau of Ethnology Bulletin* 164 (1957): 284–85; Logan, "Ghost Dance Among the Paiute," 280.

46. Dangberg, "Letters to Jack Wilson," 285.

47. Tim McCoy, *Tim McCoy Remembers the West*, with Ronald McCoy (Garden City, N.Y.: Doubleday, 1977), 222.

48. Dyer, "Wizardry," 5–7.

49. Bailey, *Wovoka*, 207.

50. Dyer, "Wizardry," 7.

51. Bailey, *Wovoka*, 207.

52. McCoy, *Tim McCoy*, 222.

53. *Reno Evening Gazette*, September 20 and October 4, 1932.

54. Ibid., November 8, 1932.

55. Mooney, "Ghost Dance Religion."

56. Bailey, *Wovoka*, 207.

57. *Mason Valley News*, December 26, 1975.

58. Edward A. Dyer Jr. to Friedhoff, May 16, 1965.

9

CALIFORNIA INDIAN WOMEN, WISDOM, AND PRESERVATION

अर्

MICHELLE LORIMER AND CLIFFORD E. TRAFZER

S O MUCH OF AMERICAN INDIAN HISTORY focuses on Native American men. In part, this is because non-Indian men wrote most of the historical documents about Indian history and did not know a great deal about the internal affairs of Indian people. However, women within all tribes, communities, and families played important roles among their people, a fact recognized by Native Americans throughout Indian Country. Women have always contributed significantly into many areas of Indian life, and their importance grew over time during the late nineteenth and early twentieth centuries when settlers, government agents, and the military destroyed Native American economies, forcing men to seek wage labor in towns and ranches surrounding Indian lands. During the transitional era of American Indian history, from roughly 1870 to 1950, gender roles shifted as new economic needs and pressures forced Native men to venture away from American Indian communities to work as migrant laborers in rural and urban areas.[1] The First and Second World Wars also pulled Native men away from their homes as the U.S. government called on Indian men to fight for a country that had relegated Native Americans to social peripheries.

Under the stress from decades of violence tantamount to genocide, waves of epidemics, forced assimilation, kidnapping of indigenous children to off-reservation boarding schools, and increased urbanization that lured people away from Native communities, many components of Indian cultures and traditional practices declined, such as the role of men within Indian communities. During the late nineteenth and early twentieth centuries, select powerful women emerged as spiritual and communal leaders in a number of Native communities, including those in California. Native American women often carried on the medicine ways of the people, if not as shaman, then as keepers of traditions. With the decline of male leadership within some tribes, women took on that mantle, sometimes becoming tribal spokespeople. They also directed or encouraged revitalization movements as tribal historians and spiritual leaders. Women embraced new roles as keepers of tribal traditions, ceremonies, songs, stories, and religions. Remarkably, during the twentieth century, several California Indian women assumed spheres of power and leadership formerly held primarily or solely by men. Influenced by the changing world around them, strong female leaders such as Annie Jarvis, Essie Parrish, Mable McKay, Flora Jones, Jane Dumas, Katherine Siva Saubel, Carmen Lucas, and Pauline Murillo worked to strengthen their Native Californian communities and educate the broader public by collaborating with scholars to revive, protect, and preserve customs and traditions for future generations. They are just a few examples of the women who rose to positions of power within Native American communities and are known throughout Indian Country as people of wisdom, knowledge, and action. They left their marks on Native American history and have earned a place in the written chronicles of the Native Universe.

The changing economic and political landscape of California significantly influenced the lives of many Native people during the late nineteenth century. In the early nineteenth century, Kashaya Pomo people found work at the Russian colony of Fort Ross, where they settled and worked seasonally among the newcomers. Under this arrangement, the Kashaya faced relatively less pressure to adopt Euro-American ways of life than other California Indians, who were compelled to navigate Spanish colonial institutions, especially the mission system. This allowed the Kashaya to maintain their language and traditions to a much greater extent than other California Indians living along the Pacific Coast.[2] In the early 1840s, Russian settlers abandoned Fort Ross. About the same time, American, Mexican, and other foreign squatters, ranchers, and laborers moved into the region, restricting access of Kashaya Pomo and Native Americans to traditional Indian lands, resources, and food. With increased foreign occupation, Native American men began to work as migrant wage laborers. They contributed to ranch economies and various urban labor positions to support their families and communities.

Kashaya Pomo continued to adapt to changes, as many Pomo settled at Haupt Ranch and Stewart Point but continued to find seasonal work on ranches, farms, and lumber camps.[3] In 1919, a majority of Kashaya people relocated as the Bureau of Indian Affairs created the Kashaya Reservation. Not long after creating a confined reservation, officials began allotting the reservations. Federal agents assigned Pomo people forty acres, a meager piece of land on a hilltop previously purchased by the state of California in 1914. In the midst of these changes that threatened Pomo cultural ways of life, Kashaya Pomo people developed a religious and social movement that turned inward to maintain and enhance their culture and language. Because of their passionate religious and cultural beliefs, the Kashaya Pomo developed a strong religious resurgence movement, not a military movement, in the form of the Bole Maru (Dream Dance) religion.[4] Dreamers had emerged after the 1850s with Smohalla and others, but the Dreamer religion became latent among Pomo people waiting for a rebirth. Some Pomo met, sang, and dreamed during the late nineteenth and early twentieth centuries, but the major rebirth of Dreamers came in the 1930s as the Bole Maru. During the Great Depression, Pomo people experienced a reawakening led by deep thinking women of action. Annie Jarvis and Essie Parrish emerged as Dreamer leaders of the Kashaya Pomo, and they became the most powerful and vocal Dreamers, or leaders of the Bole Maru.[5] These extremely influential women shaped and reshaped Kashaya Pomo society by preserving and protecting the history, religion, beliefs, and language of Kashaya people. Like many shamanistic movements, leaders of the Bole Maru drew on ancient beliefs of the people, reframing old beliefs and encouraging people to use their new medicine ways to restore harmony, balance, and order to end the chaos brought on by the white invasion and genocidal acts of war, confinement, economic destruction, forced removal, and ever-changing Indian policies.

Bole Maru is a fusion of traditional Pomo beliefs and practical adaptations to the postcolonial world. As a result of contact with non-Indians and the policies of the state and federal governments during the nineteenth century, many Pomo died from diseases (including smallpox, measles, influenza, tuberculosis, and others) and from wars of extermination that white settlers, state-sponsored militias, and the United States Army perpetrated against them. As non-Indians stole Indian land and claimed it as their own, Pomo populations and those of their neighbors felt the effects of starvation and anomie. Newcomers prevented Pomo and others from taking their Native foods, and the desperate situation led some Pomo to seek the help of their Creator. Since war was not an option, Kashaya Pomo prayed and sang to dream of new directions to cope with newcomers and help the people survive the invasion. As a result, innovative religious movements arose during the early 1870s, including the Bole Maru, which called on the Almighty to aid Pomo people. Over the years, many Pomo men had led the so-called Dreamers during ceremony, but in the early twentieth century, women, too, became leaders of the religious movement.[6] Within the Bole Maru religion, Dreamer women such as Essie Parrish conducted ceremonies and imparted wisdom from both their dreams and cultural narratives, often influenced by their traditional oral stories that emerged among the people at the time of creation.

Ceremonies of the Bole Maru took place in arenas constructed specifically for the dance, with the fire or a central pole as an important fixture that symbolized "the world's center, a path that connected humans with the ultimate source of power."[7] Bole Maru regalia incorporated symbols such as the cross and heart to convey their beliefs. Pomo people retained traditional beliefs and stories, but some participants wore modern manufactured textiles rather than deerskin or clothing made from traditional Native plant materials. Pomo Dreamers added new songs and rituals to ancient musical and narrative motifs. The religion proved to be dynamic in its approach to song, dance, and worship so that the Bole Maru could survive in the modern world of indigenous people. Within this religion, Dreamers such as Essie Parrish took on shamanic roles, serving as healers and philosophers for a people adapting to changing conditions.[8] Anthropologists Lowell Bean and Dorothea Theodoratus noted that the increasing number of men forced to find work as migrant laborers may have contributed to the transfer of leadership roles to women.[9] No doubt the economic change among Native Americans altered internal leadership roles within many Indian tribes, including the Pomo. Settlers took over gathering and hunting/fishing areas and refused to allow Indians access to these lands that had been gifts from Creators to Indian people. California State and federal game and fish departments regulated Indian hunting and fishing, incarcerating Indians for hunting, fishing, and gathering where they had always practiced their economic pursuits. The Bureau of Indian Affairs regulated Native American economies and movements. These and other actions destroyed the traditional economy of Pomo people and all indigenous people of North America. As Indian economies waned, men sought wage labor jobs in white communities and Pomo women rose within Indian communities to become spokespeople, ceremonial leaders, doctors, historians, and keepers of tribal traditions. Throughout California and beyond, women became the important leaders who kept traditions and languages alive, often by creating revitalizations based on a foundation of traditional beliefs, songs, stories, and laws. So it was among the Kashaya Pomo and other tribes in California.[10]

Between the 1920s and 1940s, a time of extreme change and upheaval in greater American society, Pomo people faced intense hardships caused by the Great Depression. Indian economies failed and jobs became scarce. The influx of Anglo-American laborers from the Midwest into Northern California seeking farm work reduced employment opportunities for Native American people. Many Indians turned inward to traditional subsistence patterns for relief, in spite of federal and state regulators. The return to Native economic ways, tending Indian land, and increased sharing between groups led to cultural revitalizations among Pomo people and neighboring Native American communities. This economic change also influenced a shift in traditional Pomo gender roles. Before the 1930s, Pomo men had led most ceremonies and held the positions of Dreamers and healers, but after 1930, with the changing times of modern America, Pomo women such as Annie Jarvis and Essie Parrish ascended to such community positions.[11]

FIGURE 9.1. Mabel McKay was known in California, Oregon, and Nevada as a powerful shaman. She healed by calling on her power and directing it to heal patients. She was also an accomplished basket maker. Collectors and museum curators cherish baskets make by McKay. Courtesy of the State Indian Museum, California State Parks.

Between 1912 and 1943, Annie Jarvis served the Pomo people as a community leader, and she became the first female Kashaya Pomo Bole Maru Dreamer priest. Ghost Dance ideas, doctrines, and methods informed Jarvis's teachings. Revivalist principles of the Ghost Dance included the preservation of Native beliefs and isolationism. For instance, Jarvis prohibited marriages to non-Indians, forbade gambling and alcohol consumption, banned community members from sending children to Indian boarding schools, and discouraged unnecessary contact with white Americans. More specifically, Jarvis promoted and encouraged marriages between Kashaya Pomo so they could preserve their traditions, culture, language, religion, and kinship ties. Jarvis consented to allowing Kashaya Pomo to marry within other Pomo groups. She told her followers that Kashaya Pomo children could find suitable matches among the Central Pomo of Stewarts Point and other Pomo, but she felt strongly that Pomo parents should not allow children to marry outsiders or attend Indian schools created by the Bureau of Indian Affairs. These schools functioned to destroy Native American cultures, religions, and languages through cultural genocide, and Jarvis opposed any attempt to damage traditional cultures of her people.[12]

Jarvis had seen the ill effects of American Indian boarding schools and witnessed cultural destruction. To end this destructive trend, Jarvis encouraged Pomo parents not to allow their sons and daughters to attend Sherman Institute, Stewart Indian Boarding School, Chemawa, Phoenix, Albuquerque, Santa Fe, or any of the other off-reservation American Indian boarding schools operated by the Bureau of Indian Affairs. These schools, she knew, sought to assimilate Indian children and supplant Indian languages and cultures with the English language, market economy, American government, Christianity, and mainstream culture of the United States. Jarvis encouraged Pomo people to limit their interaction with non-Indians, especially Christian missionaries who also wanted to replace Native American religions with Christianity.[13]

Increased contact with Euro-American populations after Jarvis's death in 1943 ushered in a new era for the remaining Kashaya Pomo population.[14] Under the spiritual leadership of Essie Parrish, beginning in 1943, Kashaya people adopted a more open policy. Parrish accepted more interaction with non-Indians, believing that building relationships, contacts, and educational opportunities for the Kashaya people would help promote and defend their tribal interests.[15] She even allowed outsiders to create documentary films about the Bole Maru, including filming her during healing ceremonies when she sang sacred songs and danced in the way of the Bole Maru. Parish decided to share details about the religion and healings to inform non-Indians about the nonviolent religion and the important power of the healing spirit within the Bole Maru. Unlike Jarvis, Parrish advocated formal, Western-style education for Pomo children and accepted the outside organized religion of the Church of Jesus Christ of Latter Day Saints, while still maintaining traditional Kashaya beliefs and practices.[16]

In her belief system, followers could seek many paths to the Creator. The Bole Maru did not die with Jarvis or Parrish, as many of the Pomo continue to follow the teachings and tenets of Essie Parrish today and pass on to their children the Dreamer ways.

Essie Parrish, the last Kashaya Pomo Dreamer, was born in 1902 in Sonoma County, California, on the Haupt Ranch.[17] Parrish learned tribal history from her maternal grandmother, Rosie Jarvis, a "hand curer" and tribal historian. Jarvis had the gift of healing and could summon her power and heal others with it as it emanated through her hand. She taught Parrish the history of the land and people, and both women kept the oral history of the Kashaya Pomo alive.[18] As a child, Parrish listened to other tribal elders who talked about the old ways, the ancient and historical past. Parrish expressed more interest in learning about culture, traditions, and spiritual matters than other children her age.[19] Kashaya elders recognized early on that Parrish would be a prophet and healer as well as a spiritual leader for the people. Rosie Jarvis and Annie Jarvis served as teachers, consultants, and confidants for Parrish, who had her first dream as a child of nine years old. As a youth, she treated and cured her first patient. And at this young age, Kashaya Pomo people recognized Parrish as a shaman and seer, one who would lead the people by way of the spirit that worked through her.[20]

Following Annie Jarvis's death in 1943, Parrish inherited the role of Dreamer or official religious leader of the Bole Maru.[21] In this important tribal role, Parrish treated the sick, oversaw religious events, and communicated messages from her dreams, spiritually directing Kashaya Pomo people. She taught participants necessary traditions, dances, songs, rituals, and rules within these sacred activities and directed ceremonial protocols and the construction of ceremonial regalia, with particular attention to construction materials and objects used in ceremony. She also created new dances and ceremonies that enriched the religion and accommodated modern situations, including the threat of losing Pomo boys and men during the Second World War. Significantly, shortly after the Japanese attacked Pearl Harbor and the government instituted conscription of men to fill the ranks of the military, Parrish created and directed the Star Hoop Dance (Ka'mamot pilili ko'o). Mothers conducted the dance to safeguard their sons serving in the armed forces during World War II, and the Star Hoop Dance proved very effective in protecting young Pomo men.[22] Not one Kashaya Pomo person died fighting in World War II. Contemporary Pomo continue to believe that the Star Hoop Dance and ceremony saved the lives of Pomo men during the war. Rosie and Annie Jarvis passed on a great deal of the Kashaya Pomo tribal knowledge to Parrish, but she also added a good deal to the revitalization of the Pomo people, helping them maintain many traditional activities.

Parrish continued the tradition of tribal historian passed on by Rosie Jarvis. In the early and mid-twentieth centuries, when American culture influenced many Pomo communities, Parrish protected Kashaya traditions and history from outside interruptions by keeping oral narratives, songs, and stories alive. To help preserve her culture, including the Bole Maru, Parrish cooperated with and informed anthropologists and other scholars interested in documenting aspects of Kashaya Pomo culture. She used newcomers knowingly and willingly in an action designed to have non-Indians document her work for future generations, thus preserving traditions through new mediums that her people could access long after she passed. Parrish cooperated with scholars so that her people could retrieve the taped and filmed archives of song, dance, and methodologies used to bring the medicine forward. Parrish worked with linguists such as Robert Oswalt to document Kashaya Pomo history, stories, and language in *Kashaya Texts*.[23] Parrish's daughter, Violet Chappell observed, "Mom just told the stories like that for the language. He [Oswalt] wanted to collect stories to study the language and put in a book. We kids heard the stories different."[24] Undoubtedly, Parrish mediated these stories and descriptions for Oswalt and other scholars. Most importantly, she preserved her knowledge for her people, who are still able to retrieve this knowledge through the use of modern technologies.

Similarly, through the American Indian Film Series in Ethnology, anthropologists at the University of California, Berkeley, including Alfred L. Kroeber and Samuel A. Barrett, documented Parrish as she led dances for both men and women. Parrish arranged the documentary, invited Native American participants, and narrated documentary films that described the history and meaning of dances, songs, rituals, clothing, and healings.[25] Specifically, these ethnographic accounts and documentary films detailed aspects of the Bole Maru that Parrish chose to share with scholars. For instance, one film documents Parrish performing a sucking ceremony, wherein she demonstrates how to extract sickness via objects from a person as dictated by her dreams. Other films show Parrish collecting, processing, and cooking acorns, while another series focused on basketry. Through these films, Parrish facilitated the creation of visual records that preserved aspects of Kashaya Pomo life for all people, including future Native American generations and her Pomo people.[26]

Despite these efforts to preserve and protect Kashaya traditions, not all Kashaya people accepted Parrish's teachings, her participation in scholarly inquiries, or her initial tolerance of the Mormon religion. Beginning in the 1950s, some Kashaya Pomo divided along religious lines. However, Parrish's continued teachings and spiritual practices demonstrated that Kashaya culture superseded all other belief systems, as it was "heterogeneous and pluralistic and always present in a dynamic manner."[27] Along with being a spiritual and political leader, Parrish also expertly wove prized Pomo basketry. Again, she consulted with scholars at the University of California, Berkeley, and the Lowie Museum (today, Phoebe Hearst Museum) regarding Pomo use of Native Californian plants and basketry. Parrish also wove sacred baskets that she made to help cure people, such as one she made for Senator Robert F. Kennedy, who visited the Kashaya Reservation in the late 1960s, shortly before his assassination in June 1968.[28]

Parrish devoted much of her time to healing and leading her people spiritually. However, she was also a mother of fifteen children—teaching them "to be proud, how great it was to be Indian and [to] know who [they] are."[29] In accordance with Bole Maru doctrine, following Parrish's death, the prayers, songs, and dances created by her stopped unless otherwise "given" to another person. New Dreamers and related ceremonies could only emerge through tribal consensus.[30] Thus, the death of Essie Parrish marked the passing of Kashaya Dreamers, although some people have knowledge of the Dreamers and personally adhere to those old beliefs. Before her death, Parrish passed much of her knowledge on to her daughter, Violet Chappell, who was tribal historian in the 1990s, and Mabel McKay (Cache Creek Pomo). Following Parrish's death in 1979, McKay became a Bole Maru Dreamer, but not the official Dreamer of the Kashaya Pomo. Although she was not Kashaya Pomo, many of Parrish's followers respected and followed McKay as a spiritual leader and consultant.[31]

Like Parrish, McKay excelled in basket weaving. Raised under the influence of strong women and skilled basket makers, McKay learned the art known internationally as some of the finest basketry in the world. But she is also known as one of the great leaders of the Bole Maru. Richard Taylor, McKay's brother, was the first Bole Maru Dreamer. In the winter of 1871–1872, Taylor had predicted that a great flood would sweep white people from the world.[32] More than one thousand people gathered in semisubterranean earth lodges to be protected from the flood. Although the flood never developed, the revivalist message of the Bole Maru spread to tribes throughout central California.[33] In addition to Taylor, four other Kashaya Pomo Dreamers emerged. The first two were men, Jack Humboldt and Big José, while the last two were women, Jarvis and Parrish. Both women were exceptionally strong.[34] McKay did not directly follow in this line because she was Cache Creek Pomo, not Kashaya. However, McKay, born in 1907, was the last Bole Maru Dreamer and reportedly the last Pomo sucking doctor. McKay could locate disease within a human body and find the cause of a person's ailment. Once located, McKay sucked out the source of the illness, which manifested in objects that she withdrew from the patient's body and destroyed. She sucked up negative strengths in the tradition of many sucking doctors found throughout Northern and Southern California.[35]

Similar to the Bole Maru and other revivalist prophecies, Flora Jones, a Wintu shaman born in 1909, dreamed that the end of the world was imminent due to the excesses of white people.[36] Prophecies of apocalyptic destruction, such as earthquakes or the great flood predicted by Richard Taylor, were not new to Wintu people. Influenced by the arrival of the Ghost Dance movement to Wintu territory in 1871, Wintu prophet Paitla had communicated to the people about the Earth Lodge religion that stressed the end of the world and return of the dead.[37] He instructed the people to build dance houses to protect Indian people, but the spiritual movement of 1872 proved short-lived because the dead did not return to Fall River as Paitla had prophesized. Nevertheless, the Earth Lodge religion and ceremonial components of the Bole Maru influenced the creation of the Dream Dance (Yetcewestconos) religious movement among Wintu people. Lus, a female dreamer and primary developer of Dream Dances among the Wintu, significantly influenced the spread of the spiritual movement from 1875 to 1895. Throughout most of Wintu territory, she taught her people Dream songs and dances that she performed in different villages. Cora DuBois, an anthropologist who wrote in the 1930s, noted that dreaming of songs continued until about 1920. DuBois observed that Indian people continued to perform "the barest skeleton of a Dream dance formation" into the 1930s.[38]

Wintu spiritual beliefs responded to the negative impacts of Euro-American invasion, including the violence and disease that decimated Wintu populations.[39] Like the Ghost Dance and other American Indian revitalization movements, the Dream Dance emerged for a time and then became latent, alive but quiet among the people in preparation of a reemergence at a later time.[40] Cultural responses by Wintu spiritual leaders included the adherence to traditional beliefs combined with new practices influenced by modern situations and personal revelations. Flora Jones's life experiences encompassed these dual processes, and she drew on traditions and revelations to guide her people spiritually during the twentieth century.

As a young woman, Jones idolized Hollywood actresses and was baptized a Methodist. She even received a formal education in government schools. At the same time, her Wintu-speaking mother raised Jones, and the family sought health care from Wintu shamans. Jones was exposed to traditional spiritual medicine as a girl and learned from the tribal elders about healing. At an early age, Jones encountered animal spirits in dreams and visions that helped inform and guide her.[41] Jones had her first trance and encounter with her "helping spirit" at age seventeen.[42] As a result of her power, which gained intensity by spiritual means, she became a shaman. When she became a healer, Jones lived at a time when many Wintu and other Indians of the region had stopped attending traditional ceremonies or seeking the help of medicine men and women. During the twentieth century, many Indian people had stopped participating in the Doctor's Dance or the communal spirit quest. While these traditions were not in use to any great extent, elder shamans assisted Jones in her initiation in culturally customary ways. Elder teachers, shamans, and community leaders cared for Jones, provided medicine, and took her to sacred places to pray. Through trances, Jones' helping spirit taught her doctoring songs and the art of shamanic or spiritual healing. By embracing this new identity, Jones found peace with the inner contradictions of an adolescent.[43] Significantly, Jones eventually traveled to Panther Meadows on the slopes of Mount

FIGURE 9.2. Wintu Flora Jones earned a positive reputation within many Indian communities of Northern California as an effective healer. Native Americans considered her a powerful shaman. She is known for taking patients to Panther Meadows on the slopes of Mount Shasta in Northern California. Courtesy of the State Indian Museum, California State Parks.

Shasta, a sacred and powerful place of healing energy, where she conducted ceremonies and practiced some of her medicine, thereby helping patients.

Jones demonstrated abilities in several shamanistic specialties but described herself primarily as a healing doctor. She diagnosed illnesses using her hands during "ecstatic healing séances."[44] However, she also occasionally used sucking to heal. Due to amnesia induced by her trances, Jones used tape recorders or an assistant/interpreter during ceremonies to help her uncover the "supernatural dialogue." Jones explained that spirit helpers used her as a tool to communicate future events and appropriate treatment. Jones acquired the help of additional spirits as she became a more experienced doctor, obtaining the assistance of numerous spirits such as the trickster suckerfish spirit, the hostile black wolf spirit, and star, moon, and mountain spirits. During a séance or healing ceremony, Jones entered into a trance and allowed spirit-healers to work through her, sensing through her hands any pains or irregularities in a patient's body. The spirits, not Jones, detected sickness and prescribed treatment that Jones implemented once awakened from her trance and was informed of the spiritual diagnosis.[45] Jones's use of spirit helpers corresponds with methodologies of many Native American healers who called on their familiars to bring knowledge, power, and healing to patients. Through song and prayer, Jones brought familiars nearby so she could use them to heal others. Like many healers, she gave credit to spirits for the healing because the spirits brought the power necessary for curing people.[46]

While Jones primarily healed Native people, she also treated non-Indians, saying, "We have to live almost half in the white man's way and half in my own way I will never forget my own way but I have to steer myself with the white ways."[47] Still, she observed that the presence of white people and the use of technology, such as video recorders, often disturbed her trances and sometimes offended her spirit-healers. Adapting to changing conditions, Jones and spirit-healers acknowledged the presence and influence of Euro-Americans. Jones once said that the spirits understood that they occupied a world with white intruders. "I was told by the spirits one time when I was doctoring," she explained, "that I must help my white brothers as well, if I am to be a thoroughly spiritual doctor."[48] Other Indian doctors explain that the spirit world knows no differences of race among human beings, and some doctors believe they are obligated to help anyone asking for assistance. The continued presence of settlers also expanded the possible causes of disease, and Jones recognized that many and new forms of disease existed among Native Americans because of the spread of viruses and bacteria brought by newcomers.

In the past, shamans such as Jones examined patients for disease caused by self-inflicted stress and/or spirit possession resulting from the violation of traditional tribal laws or the loss of souls to evil spirits. Pain or disease objects (*yapaitu dokos*) inflicted by an offended spirit or a sorcerer caused traditional forms of disease.[49] Non-

Indian Americans brought "white man's diseases" or "traveling diseases" such as small-pox, whooping cough, and cholera. The invasion of newcomers also contributed to increased and harmful conditions such as stress, starvation, drugs, and alcohol. Jones considered cirrhosis of the liver, ulcers, and certain cancers white man's diseases that were beyond the healing power of shamans if not treated early. Jones's treatments were primarily preventative measures against white man's diseases. She criticized pro-cessed foods and did not drink tap water. Instead, Jones traveled several miles to gather water from a sacred spring and restricted herself to an indigenous diet established by her spirit-healers that strengthened her power as a shaman. These dietary measures reflected Jones's prophetic beliefs that white people corrupted the planet and would eventually cause the world to end.[50]

Jones was a Wintu shaman and pushed for spiritual revival of all Native Ameri-cans but especially Wintu. Informed by Wintu laws, religion, and customs, Jones wit-nessed the pain caused by the destructive behavior of Euro-Americans against the earth.[51] During her lifetime, Jones saw lumber companies strip mountains of their timber, miners dig deep into the earth, and government agencies and private indi-viduals take over and exploit former Indian lands. Jones had a direct relationship with the spirit world, and she often learned from her spirit-healers. She claimed that the spirits had informed her that she must call on the Wintu people and other Native Americans from diverse tribes to join together to "wake up" their sacred places. In an effort to do this, in 1973, Jones contacted the United States Forest Service, asking per-mission to use traditional Wintu lands then controlled by the Forest Service so that she could conduct doctoring ceremonies in appropriate traditional power sites. The Forest Service controlled thousands of acres of land in Northern California, includ-ing the slopes of Mount Shasta, the site of Panther Meadows. The volcano is a sacred mountain to the Wintu and numerous other tribes of the region, who do not use the upper slopes of Mount Shasta due to its sacred nature. Some Indians believe the mountain contains a great basket filled with goodness that spreads across the world, and it is therefore against their belief system to travel too far up the mountain. But Jones was an exception because of her abilities as a medicine woman and healer.

Jones used Panther Meadows and other areas on the mountain for her medicine, taking patients to the site for healing. Officials of the Forest Service attempted to prevent Jones from using the mountain slopes, saying they were protecting her from bear attacks. But Jones could not be dissuaded from using the mountain for her heal-ing and eventually convinced officials of the Forest Service. They accommodated her request to occupy areas of the mountains for her medicine ways, and they allowed her to utilize one acre of land for what they deemed "Indian doctor practices."[52] For thou-sands of years, the Wintu and other Indian people held dominion over their sacred lands, but after the United States claimed this part of Indian Country, the newcomers assumed control of the slopes of Mount Shasta and millions of other acres, often preventing Indian people from making traditional use of the land and its resources. In the case of Flora Jones, despite the contention of the Forest Service that bear encounters could prove hazardous, officials approved of this particular Native use of Panther Meadows. This was a major victory for American Indian people, as the Forest Service previously had excluded Native use of much of the mountain and required permits for Indians to gather native plants. Jones encouraged Native Americans to stand up for their rights, a lesson learned and practiced by many Wintu and their neighbors in Northern California.

Flora Jones advocated for Native American people to keep their songs, stories, dances, medicine, beliefs, ceremonies, traditions, and languages alive.[53] In 1981, Jones gathered Indian people together in the state capital of Sacramento, California, for a California Indian Day Celebration. American Indians and non-Indians from around the United States committed to preservation of American Indian culture joined Jones to encourage Native Americans of California and beyond to continue to use and perpetuate Native traditions. The Committee for Traditional Indian Health developed out of this gathering, and soon after, a program of the California Rural Indian Health Board emerged supporting the continuation of Native American traditions in California. Flora Jones was small in stature but large in her commitment to Indian rights, which she fought for until her death. Influential Native leaders such as Kumeyaay plant expert Jane Dumas continued a California Indian tradition championed by Jones. Dumas expanded the work of cultural revitalization by offering traditional knowledge of her people to Indians and non-Indians alike through workshops, demonstrations, field trips, and lectures. She is an expert in traditional Indian medicine, healing, and plant use.[54]

Jane Dumas was born in 1924, a member of the Kumeyaay people of Southern California and northern Mexico. She was a member of the Jamul band of Kumeyaay Indians in East San Diego County, California, and she was born into a leadership family. Chief José Manuel Polton Hataam was her great-grandfather, and he was a village and regional chief of Kumeyaay people.[55] He was also known as a man of great power, a medicine person who wielded influence in many different ways. Dumas's family lived a traditional life long into the twentieth century. Dumas grew up speaking her language, continuing spiritual ways of Kumeyaay, and passing along her knowledge to Kumeyaay and others, Indians and non-Indians alike. Dumas made a special effort to learn about Kumeyaay culture, songs, medicine, and language so that she could keep traditions and the wisdom of her ancestors alive through teaching other Kumeyaay people and by giving cultural presentations to the public.[56] Dumas's mother, Isabel Thing, taught Dumas much about traditional remedies, herbs, and plants. Her father, Ambrosia Thing, was a famous healer with great power, which was a tradition in her family and one used by Dumas throughout her life. During her childhood, Dumas learned many uses of native plants of the San Diego area, from the Pacific Ocean to the deserts of Imperial Valley. According to Dumas, Isabel Thing was a midwife or birthing doctor and medicine woman, known as a *cha'ak kuseyaay* (healer). Dumas and many of her relatives followed in the leadership legacy of Isabel Thing, who learned directly from the women of her family.[57]

Dumas stressed the importance and value of knowing about Native culture and history, especially for American Indians living in increasingly modern and urban societies.[58] She spoke Kumeyaay as her first language and is one of the last fluent speakers. In 1981, Dumas helped establish the San Diego American Indian Health Center, where she worked as a community nurse for many years, offering her expertise that included the use of customary medicine of the Kumeyaay. She worked among urban and reservation Indians. She has the remarkable ability of relating to indigenous people from many diverse backgrounds and from many parts of North America, including Mexico, Guatemala, and South America. Most of all, she cared for her Kumeyaay people. Dumas served as a community health nurse and herbal doctor for more than thirty years, often offering courses on herbal medicine on and off reservations.[59] She touched the lives of thousands of American Indians, and she began teaching ethnobotany classes at the San Diego Museum of Man and at Kumeyaay Community College on the Sycuan Indian Reservation.[60] Over the years, she gave hundreds of lectures on plant use and Indian medicine at San Diego State University; the University of California, Riverside; Grossmont College; and other institutions. She held a regular position at the San Diego Museum of Man and offered classes to students and adults alike throughout California and beyond.

In April 2002, officials in San Diego County inducted Jane Dumas into the San Diego County Women's Hall of Fame. County officials recognized her for her work among the Kumeyaay and the larger population of San Diego County, saying that Dumas was a highly esteemed elder, teacher, and community leader. The same year, the California Wellness Foundation at the University of California, Berkeley, School of Public Health, honored Dumas as a senior leader for her community building and commitment to healthy aging.[61] What's more, in 2005, she won the annual Dragonfly Award from the Dorothy Ramon Center of Banning, California, for her "high-soaring achievements in saving and sharing Southern California Indian cultures."[62] In essence, these awards recognized Dumas as a "cultural activist" who helped revive Native American culture and traditions for younger generations.[63] The Dorothy Ramon Center in Banning, California, near the Morongo Indian Reservation recognized her for preserving knowledge and language related to plant medicine, foods, tools, and other material culture. The focus of her work had been plant knowledge among the Kumeyaay, but she encourages all people to learn about Native uses of plants.

Because of Dumas's teachings, young Kumeyaay people increasingly participate in cultural activities. For example, more people have taken up the art of basket weaving and learn the appropriate use of traditional medicines and natural remedies. In addition, Dumas has encouraged hundreds of young Kumeyaay boys and men to learn Bird Songs, a song complex unique to many different Indians of Southern California and western Arizona. The Kumeyaay are Yuman-speaking people, closely related to the Quechan of the Fort Yuma Indian Reservation near Yuma, Arizona.[64] Like the Quechan, Dumas understood that Kumeyaay people had experienced the devastating impact of forced assimilation during the nineteenth and twentieth centuries, as well as urbanization and economic destruction. In the late twentieth and early twenty-first centuries, the Kumeyaay suffered from their integration into mainstream American society. Dumas and many Kumeyaay felt their language and culture compromised by the imposed school systems of the United States. Dumas lived through the changing times of the twentieth century. She survived to see the revitalization of her language and culture, which has benefited from an infusion of funds from casinos located on several Kumeyaay Indian reservations.

During the late twentieth century, economic development on the reservation brought about by high-stakes casino revenue allowed many Kumeyaay communities to fund cultural education and language programs to a greater extent than in the past.[65] Jane Dumas was in the forefront of preservation since the 1960s, but her work accelerated after the 1980s. Native cultures remain alive through the continuation of traditional practices. Like many women of her era, she learned basket weaving from female role models. She inherited the traditional art forms from her mother, grandmothers, aunts, and female elders who were the premiere basket makers among Kumeyaay people. In addition to learning how to make baskets, these women had deep knowledge about plants and the ecological landscapes. They became vessels of tribal knowledge about the ethnobotany of their people. Dumas learned to be a skilled basket weaver, and she once noted that "basketry is a part of our life, it's our history. After we're gone, it's going to be here for our future generations."[66]

In 2009, the Alliance for California Traditional Arts Apprenticeship Program recognized Dumas as a master artist of Kumeyaay basketry, and she used her knowledge to teach others. A natural teacher, Dumas informed thousands of students of all ages about basketry and the plants important to the production of the art. But Dumas had far more knowledge about plants. She spent her life teaching about plants her people used for food, medicine, and the production of homes, tools, and numerous other material items. Dumas taught many different people about plants of Southern California, including her apprentice, an amazingly talented Luiseño scholar named Richard Bugbee. For many years, they worked together to gather, identify, and help native plants propagate. Bugbee has been a student of Jane Dumas for more than thirty years, and he often presented with Dumas at the San Diego Museum of Man, reservations, and throughout the United States.

Bugbee is heir to the knowledge Dumas accumulated throughout her life. Both Dumas and Bugbee had earned a reputation as authorities of native plants of Southern California, and tribal members and academics often consulted them to learn the many uses of these plants. Before Dumas's death on May 3, 2014, she and Bugbee completed a comprehensive compilation of native plants, using their scientific, common, and Kumeyaay names. The document is a superior source of information on edible and medicinal plants as well as those used in housing and tools.[67] Native female leaders who work to keep their cultures alive, like Jane Dumas, use modern education campaigns, notable institutions, and Native languages as key components of their work. A contemporary of Dumas who shared a passion for cultural preservation is Kwaaymii elder Carmen Lucas, one of the few Kwaaymii remaining in the world. Lucas grew up in San Diego and Imperial Counties in Southern California with her famous father, Tom Lucas, who fought the Bureau of Indian Affairs to keep the former Laguna Indian Reservation as his own property without the interference of that office. Lucas left the region for years to pursue a career in the Marine Corps, but when she returned to Southern California, she determined to preserve American Indian remains, cultural resources, trails, and histories that remained in her beloved homeland of the forests of Mount Laguna and the deserts and valleys below that lead to the winter village sites of the Kwaaymii. During the early twenty-first century, Lucas has made her mark protecting Native American sites and remains in the face of extensive and destructive development of wind and solar energy plants pushed by President Barrack Obama and Governor Jerry Brown.

Katherine Siva Saubel shared the commitment of Carmen Lucas and Jane Dumas to identify, collect, and preserve cultural resources of significance to Native Americans. While Dumas and Lucas lived in Southern California among the Kumeyaay and Kwaaymii (both Yuman-speaking Indians) near the Mexican border, Saubel was Cahuilla, raised in the Uto-Aztecans language, and born on the northern edge of San Diego County, California. Saubel was born in 1920 among the Mountain Cahuilla Indians at *Pachawal pa* on the Los Coyotes Reservation. Now deceased, she was a famous scholar and respected elder-leader who has shared and preserved Cahuilla language, ethnobotany, and culture. During her life, Saubel collaborated with many scholars from many different countries, including Japan and Germany. She worked with linguists, anthropologists, and historians similarly interested in documenting and preserving Cahuilla history, language, culture, and literature. Saubel's parents,

Melan Seivatily and Juan C. Siva, raised her speaking their Native dialect of Mountain Cahuilla.[68] Saubel's mother taught her Cahuilla traditions, botany, and history. As a child and young woman, Saubel closely watched her mother collect and prepare plants to treat different ailments. Both Saubel and her mother were herbal doctors, treating patients using plant medicines, which they infused with power and spirit through prayers and proper treatment—ritual treatment—of the plant medicines. Saubel meticulously kept a notebook of the Cahuilla names and uses of plants. With this information, she and her friend and colleague, anthropologist Lowell Bean, worked several years on an expanded version of Saubel's notebook to create *Temalpakh: Cahuilla Indian Knowledge and Usage of Plants*. After forty years, the book is still in print and used widely by Indians and non-Indians alike who are interested in the plant life of Cahuilla Indians and their neighbors.[69]

Saubel learned her appreciation for the earth from her Cahuilla customs. Her mother was an herbal healer, and both Saubel and her mother used this knowledge to help others. In 2000, for example, Saubel cured a researcher with herbal medicine. The researcher had injured vocal chords by continuing to lecture with a sore throat. The researcher had consulted medical doctors and had been on medication for months when Saubel proclaimed, "When we return to the Morongo Reservation, I will cure your throat."[70] Once back on the reservation, Saubel instructed the researcher to drive southeast toward Palm Springs, get off Interstate 10, and approach a creosote bush living far from the highways. Saubel told the researcher that once he got there he should tell the creosote bush of his ailment and ask for help. Then he was to pick the green ends of the plant, place them in a paper bag, and take home the stems to make a hot tea. The researcher followed the instructions and took the tea twice a day. Within three days, his throat had healed sufficiently that he could speak in a normal voice. Saubel had closely observed her mother's doctoring and had healed the researcher with plant medicine.[71]

Saubel did not receive a formal education until she was eight years old. She attended a segregated elementary school in Palm Springs, California, where she learned English.[72] At the age of thirteen, Saubel recognized that the encroaching American society and its English-speaking population surrounded Cahuilla people and threatened the survival of their culture and language. At this young age, Saubel resolved to work for the preservation and continuation of Cahuilla language and culture.[73] Refusing to go to an off-reservation boarding school, Saubel maintained her fluency in Cahuilla language and close connections to tribal traditions, noting later in life, "I really understand my own heritage, who I am, what lineage I belong to and what clan I am a member of. I know myself."[74] Following her primary education, Saubel attended a high school situated in the heart of Cahuilla Country.[75]

Saubel expressed her fear that Cahuilla culture and language might disappear, forecasting that Cahuilla will be gone in one to two generations. She urged Cahuilla people to intermarry and have children who could speak the Cahuilla language and "adhere to the laws of the old people so that things could be right again."[76] Saubel noted that this was just a dream and often expressed pessimism about the future. She observed that "everything has taken a turn for the worse. It is not going to get any better in the future. He [the white man] is just going to kill us off in the future."[77] Saubel's commentary mirrored the pessimism of Flora Jones and other women of power among the tribes of California. They feared the destructiveness of white ways, the English language, and a culture divorced from tribally based communities.[78] Like other leaders among California Indians, Saubel, Jones, Parrish, Dumas, and others decried the destruction of the environment for development. Economic development, housing, roads, and exploitation of minerals, water, timber, and other natural resources threatened plant and animal habitats throughout the state.

Saubel observed that historically, white people took possession of the land, destroyed trade between Indian communities, uprooted mesquite and acorn trees to build houses, and dumped toxic waste on Indian land.[79] Regardless of these fears and troubling thoughts of the future, Saubel spent her life fighting to conserve and preserve. She became an ardent supporter of careful and planned growth, working with the Native American Heritage Commission, Bureau of Land Management, California State Parks, and United States Forest Service to protect the environment, including plants Indian people used for food, medicine, basketry, and other material culture. In addition, she continually worked to preserve and pass along to future generations Cahuilla culture, song, story, and language. Her work was not in vain, as many Cahuilla, Luiseño, and Kumeyaay of Southern California followed her instruction and have started language programs, encouraging children and adults to speak the language in order to preserve it. These programs use culture as the context within the language and teach language and culture simultaneously. These programs have taken root, and the number of speakers of Native American languages in Southern California has increased in large part because of the advocacy and actions of Katherine Saubel.

In the early 1960s, Saubel worked with William Bright, a linguist at the University of California, Los Angeles, to document the Cahuilla language and compare it with other proto–Uto-Aztecan languages.[80] For many years in the early twenty-first century, she also collaborated with linguist Eric Elliott to produce her personal narratives, *'Isill Héqwas Wáxish—A Dried Coyote's Tail*, two extensive volumes of Cahuilla history, language, and culture. This classic work, written in Cahuilla and translated into English, documents many aspects of Saubel's life as a Cahuilla Indian living in Southern California, and explores Native customs conducted before the Euro-American invasion, including the making of acorn mush, herbal medicine, shamanism, education, plant use, and personal experiences that illustrate prejudice and racism against American Indians.[81] Her work to document and teach Cahuilla language and culture has earned Saubel international respect, an honorary doctoral degree, other degrees, and countless awards. While focusing much of her time on the Cahuilla, Saubel also traveled the world to see other indigenous people and learn about their cultural revival and educational programs.[82]

In 1964, Saubel; her husband, Mariano; and Jane K. Penn founded the Malki Museum on the Morongo Indian Reservation in Banning, California, to demonstrate that "we are still here."[83] Based on cultural knowledge and an initial collection of material items donated by Penn, the Malki Museum became the first American Indian museum created and operated by Native people on an Indian reservation within California. This physical manifestation of Saubel's life work still stands. The museum established a successful publishing company, Malki Museum-Ballena Press, that still publishes works focusing on California Indian cultures. The museum also publishes the *Journal of California and Great Basin Anthropology*. In 2000, the Malki Museum Press published a remarkable work on Dorothy Ramon, who had worked for ten years to preserve her Serrano language with linguist Eric Elliott. Together, they published *Wayta' Yawa' (Always Believe)*, a book supported by Malki Museum Press president Katherine Saubel.

Saubel contributed significantly to Native American communities throughout California by serving for more than twenty years on the California Native American Heritage Commission. This state agency protects American Indian remains and attempts to secure sacred sites within the state. Each year, developers originate new construction projects and the California Transportation Agency builds new roads, bridges, exits, and off-ramps that endanger human remains and other cultural resources. As a commissioner, Saubel served with an elite group of Indian people dedicated to protecting remains and sites as well as navigating politics between different American Indian groups, particularly about issues involving American Indian "most likely descendants." For many years, Saubel was the leading tribal elder on the Native American Heritage Commission, and she often spoke her mind about the proper handling of human remains. At a meeting in Santa Barbara, she told a young Native woman that if people accepted money to rebury American Indian human remains, those people were no longer Native because they had lost sight of their ancient and sacred spiritual obligation to rebury the dead and sing over them.

At another meeting of the California Native American Heritage Commission, Saubel and her fellow commissioners challenged the United States Forest Service for allowing a developer to build a ski lodge on the slopes of Panther Meadows on Mount

FIGURE 9.3. Vivienne Jake was a Southern Paiute leader who encouraged her people to speak and sing to the earth. She often told others the earth loves to hear songs. She was a Salt Song singer and one of the leaders of the Salt Song Project. She helped establish the project to encourage people to learn and sing the sacred body of songs. Her efforts have led to a continuance of the special song complex of Nuwuvi people. Courtesy of Philip Klasky.

Shasta, a known sacred place to Flora Jones and many other Indian people living in the surrounding area of Northern California.[84] Saubel and her fellow commissioners helped sway national policies of the Forest Service, and the federal agency withdrew its approval to lease sacred lands to a foreign company interested in building the ski lodge. This is but one example of Saubel's influence within the state and nation. Coincidently, living a few miles from Saubel on the San Manuel Indian Reservation, a Serrano-Cahuilla Indian woman grew up to become one of the most significant women in Native America. Pauline Manuel Ormego Murillo—known by her friends and family as Dimples—spent her life openly and eagerly teaching people of all ages and all races about the history, language, culture, medicine, and religion of her people.

Murillo was born on the San Manuel Indian Reservation on February 3, 1934, and she spent her childhood on the reservation located north of San Bernardino next to the town of Highland, California. Murillo remembered her childhood like a dream, spending a "wonderful life of adventure and make believe as many children do."[85] Murillo felt a special relationship with the hills on the reservation at the southern base of the San Bernardino Mountains, where she ran "through the hills and up the canyons on the reservation with my cousins, having much fun."[86] Murillo's "magical memories" surround the reservation, the center of her world, and the women who influenced the course of her life.[87] Murillo was born into a leadership family that began with Chief Santos Manuel, known commonly to his people as Pakuuma. Murillo's mother, Martha Teresa Manuel Chacon, was the great-granddaughter of Santos Manuel, the Serrano hero who had saved his people from a campaign of extermination launched by militia in 1866, determined to kill Indian men, women, and children and drive them out of the San Bernardino Mountains. Murillo knew this story well and was proud that her ancestor had brought the people out of the mountains safely to settle closer to non-Indians, demonstrating their peaceful intentions toward newcomers. Women of the Manuel family, as well as men, helped keep the families together at San Manuel village through difficult times during the late nineteenth and early twentieth centuries. Murillo's mother, grandmother, and great-grandmothers greatly influenced her life, because these women had led the people in the cultural preservation of Serrano and Cahuilla Indian history, language, religion, art, and ceremony.[88] Dolores Crispeen Manuel, Murillo's great-grandmother, had warned the people that change would come to Indian people, but she asked the Manuel family to stay close to one another and to keep their traditions alive. She asked her family to maintain and protect their unique identities as Serrano and Cahuilla people.

One evening during the late nineteenth century, Dolores sat with members of her family, peering off toward the south and west.[89] From the slopes of the foothills, she could see far off in every direction. She asked her people to look, listen, and remember, saying, "Look now you see that I am telling you this so you can pass it on to your

FIGURE 9.4. This photograph depicts an intelligent and confident Martha Manuel Chacon. Born and raised on the San Manuel Indian Reservation, Martha was a member of the prominent Manuel family. Many members of her family were shaman, including the tribal Keeka Pakuuma, or Chief Santos Manuel. For many years, Chacon kept the Big House on the San Manuel Reservation alive and active. Courtesy of the Murillo family.

children. Hear me well, see that faint little speck of light way down there from the homes of whites. Someday there will be more and more. I won't see it, but you will and you'll see the changes all around you. But never forget who you are or where you come from. Always remember we were here and they came. Try and live as we always have and maybe things will work out. We don't know."[90] Like Dolores Crispeen Manuel, Martha Manuel Chacon and her daughter, Pauline Murillo, spent their lives preserving the traditions of Serrano and Cahuilla people by teaching the language, conducting ceremonies, following ancient funeral rituals, archiving tribal documents, and teaching elements of Serrano culture and history in public schools. In addition, they consulted with scholars so that academics could have accurate and detailed information directly from indigenous scholars.

The Manuel family took seriously the charge given to them by Dolores, and they have never forgotten their obligation to keep the traditions, language, ceremonies, and history alive. In the twenty-first century, members of the extended Manuel family led the tribe and championed programs of cultural preservation, especially the women. Murillo epitomized this obligation, spending her life learning and sharing. She often said that she shared with others "so you will get it right."[91] For Murillo, no room existed for assumptions about Serrano and Cahuilla culture and history. She believed tribal elders should tell others about the history and culture of the people so that outsiders would represent Indians correctly. Murillo learned a great deal about her tribe's history from her grandmother, Jesusa Manuel, a Cahuilla woman originally from the Los Coyotes Indian Reservation; her mother; and her aunt, Louisa Manuel, or Wee-Sha. All of them spoke Serrano, Cahuilla, and English. In addition, they knew some Spanish because their friends and neighbors spoke Spanish. Murillo learned Serrano and Cahuilla as a young girl, and she grew up speaking these languages at home. However, Murillo and her siblings spoke English while attending elementary, junior high, and high school. In addition, she participated in ceremonies at the tribal ceremonial house, generally referred to as the Big House, a sacred religious and community dwelling that served the people deep into the twentieth century. Murillo also participated in the last female puberty ceremony conducted on the San Manuel Indian Reservation.[92]

One morning Murillo woke up feeling ill with a severe stomachache and talked to her grandmother, Jesusa, about her condition. Her grandmother recognized that Murillo was about to begin her first menses, so Jesusa "went to our old stone garage and started digging in the earth under our garage." Jesusa prepared a shallow pit so she could "bake" Murillo as part of the female puberty ceremony. "She burned wood and got it hot and then covered the coals with a thin layer of dirt and then a blanket so I would be real warm and had me lie down in there from morning until evening."[93]

FIGURE 9.5. Serrano elder Dorothy Ramon provided the most comprehensive account of her tribe's medicine ways in her classic book with Eric Elliott, *Wayta' Yawa' (Always Believe)*. Her nephew, Ernest Siva, has carried on her work in language and cultural preservation, sharing knowledge of indigenous spiritual medicine. Courtesy of the Dorothy Ramon Learning Center. Photo by Alice Kotzen.

Jesusa had Murillo sit in the pit and covered her first with a blanket and then the dirt taken out to create the pit. Her grandmother placed "beautiful baskets"—art objects made and used by women—all around her. Throughout the day, Jesusa sang traditional songs. "My grandmother sang and just sat there," Murillo explained in her autobiography, "then when it was almost evening, she called my Aunt Louisa to help her get me out and take me to the old rock house."[94] The women washed her hair with the leaves of the eucalyptus trees so that it would always be black, and then they dried it. They fed her *atole*, or corn mush, and flour tortillas with no salt or lard. She ate this bland diet for seven days, and she was told always to drink her broth or soup with two hands so that one of her breasts would not be larger than the other.[95] Murillo wrote about her puberty ceremony and often told the story in detail when she presented to the public, including children in elementary and high schools who were fascinated with such a personal and tribal story.

Not long after Pauline Murillo underwent the puberty ceremony, tribal elders at San Manuel met to discuss her future. Pauline was twelve at the time, and George Murillo, her childhood friend, was thirteen. All the children had been playing when the elders summoned Pauline and George to the Big House to participate in the community meeting. At the time, Pauline's mother was working in Los Angles and not on the reservation. Still, Pauline and George went to the Big House, where they learned the tribal elders had made a decision about them. "They said that since George and Dimples have been seeing each other for a while now," Pauline recorded in one of her books, "it was time that they got married or lived together."[96] When the children heard this decision, they ran in different directions. And when Martha returned from Los Angeles, she scolded the tribal elders for following the old tradition of arranged marriages, in part because her own arranged marriage to Pablo Ormego from the Torres Martinez Reservation had not worked out.[97] Like Martha, Pauline was pragmatic about tribal traditions, but both women adhered to the basic elements of the culture and worked hard to preserve them through education, which they both championed.

Murillo attended public schools, where most students treated her and other Indian students from San Manuel in positive ways. Some teachers took a special interest in Murillo's education, which encouraged her to continue to learn after completing her formal education. Her mother had attended Saint Boniface Indian School, an off-reservation boarding school in Banning, California, operated by the Catholic Church. In one nasty experience, a nun slapped Martha, Martha responded by slapping the nun, and a priest whipped Martha. When she returned home for a visit, Martha informed her parents that she would not return to the Catholic school. After that, she attended public school and encouraged her children to get as much education as possible. "My mom believed that education was very important," Murillo once wrote, "and she passed this belief down to me, as I have to my children."[98] Murillo "learned a lot from [her] mother and continued learning from her all [her] life."[99] Murillo and Martha got together often to speak Serrano and Cahuilla, sharing words, phrases, songs, and stories. They also traveled to public and private schools, as well as colleges and universities, to share their knowledge, and they met with individuals to teach them their languages. After the turn of the twenty-first century, Murillo encouraged her tribe to establish a language program, which has functioned for years teaching young children the Serrano language.

Murillo's interest in language preservation extended to keeping songs and stories alive. She sang many Bird Songs, a song complex among the Cahuilla, Serrano, and other Indians of Southern California and western Arizona that began at the time of Native creation, when the people scattered like birds traveling to many diverse areas to meet different plants and animals. Generally men sang Bird Songs, and both men and women danced to the ancient songs, accompanied only by gourd rattles.[100] But Murillo heard the songs all her life, and she could sing the Bird Songs just like her mother and grandmother before her. Murillo was a talented bird dancer as well, one of the first people to dance whenever men began singing in public. She was part of the revival of Cahuilla Indian Bird Songs during the 1950s and 1960s, and she encouraged young men on her reservation to keep singing the songs. Since the 1980s, numerous young men and boys on the San Manuel Indian Reservation have sung Bird Songs, and women of all ages join the singers to dance the Bird Songs. Murillo influenced the revitalization of Bird Songs and bird dancing. She has shared her traditional stories widely, often telling researchers about the rich oral literature of her people. She has also written about the rebirth of Bird Songs and dances and about traditional stories of Serrano people.[101]

Like many California Indian women, Murillo had a masterful knowledge of plant use by Serrano and Cahuilla Indians. Her grandmother, mother, and aunts taught Murillo many uses of plants—basketry, houses, tools, bows, arrows, homes, and a host of other things. She often spoke publically about the use of eucalyptus leaves that Indians used in a large tub of extremely hot water. They placed "a chair or stool in the middle of it" before having a person sit on the chair while others covered the entire affair with a blanket so the patient would take in the steam of the leaves. Although eucalyptus was not a native plant, ingenious people learned of its use and added it to their medicine ways. Murillo also learned to use native tobacco as a medicine. She used smoke from tobacco to blow into the ears of people suffering from earaches. She also used tobacco to ease the pain of sores or burns on the skin. "We used to take the leaf and put it on top of the stove to toast it. Then we would peel off the first layer to reveal the shiny bottom layer. It is the shiny part that you put down over a sore, wound, or burn and wrap it up." Murillo gave credit for her knowledge about plants to her elders, saying, "My grandmother, my mother, and aunts were all wonderful women who were very knowledgeable about the old ways."[102] Murillo passed along her knowledge to her children, grandchildren, and every researcher eager to learn about traditional ways of her people. She was forthcoming about numerous topics, generously giving her time to teach others without compensation; she only wanted people to learn and represent her people correctly.

Murillo helped keep traditions alive through her knowledge and teachings, and this included the sensitive matter of Serrano and Cahuilla spiritual and medicine ways. Murillo grew up in a family with deep knowledge of herbal and spiritual medicine.

Her father, Pablo Ormego, and members of her family were medicine men and women. The women knew herbal medicine and practiced it widely, but the men understood spiritual medicine. When working with patients, Indian shamans among the Cahuilla and Serrano called on their power, sang their songs, and used their rituals to access healing power and direct it into patients. As a child, Murillo assisted her father in his healings, handling sacred items and watching procedures used by her father and other medicine men. Murillo remembered, "The medicine men and women were very important among our people. There were several medicine men and a few women." The medicine people "healed people in many ways" and they "have the power to heal and they can give you peace of mind." Murillo compared Indian medicine men and women to Western doctors "in that they can provide a sense of security."[103] The medicine men also healed many people, including Murillo's mother.

When Martha Manuel was a girl, she used to play with her cousin, Vincent Morongo. One day they played in a wash near the reservation, but a medicine man named Ignacio Ormego, commonly called Chappo by the people, was in the area and told the children to leave the area. The children did not know that Ormego had "a vendetta against someone" and had placed some bad medicine in the wash to harm the other person. The children did not listen to Ormego, and once he left the wash, they entered the area he had told them to avoid. Martha became very ill, and her family put her in the hospital in San Bernardino until they realized her sickness derived from Indian disease or staying medicine.[104] They took her to *Sehi*, or Palm Springs, to see Pedro Chino, a *puul amnewet*, or highest level medicine man, who healed Martha by sucking out the disease inside her leg—the bad medicine placed in the wash by Ormego. Murillo often told the story of her mother's healing so others might understand the nature and methods of Indian medicine, some of which Murillo practiced in her life, but always to help others, not to harm them.[105]

Murillo lived her life for others, keeping the traditions alive and sharing with others in order to perpetuate the culture of her people. She made a huge impact on the revitalization of the Native culture among her people and other Indian tribes of the region. Throughout her life, Southern Paiute leaders believed that indigenous people needed to speak and sing to the landscapes of California, Arizona, Utah, and Nevada. She spent years guiding the Salt Song Project with Chemehuevi people of California. In 2004, she joined a group of Salt Song singers and sang to the Oasis of Mara, the first time songs had been sung there since 1911, when the villagers left the area. In 2004, she also joined Salt Song singers that sang at the school cemetery of Sherman Institute, an off-reservation American Indian boarding school in Riverside, California.

Each of the women addressed in this work represent different Indian communities. They used varied methods to practice, preserve, and share their Native cultures. All of them knew songs in their Native languages, and all of them sang to the earth.

FIGURE 9.6. Pauline Manuel Ormego Murillo spent her life preserving the language, history, culture, arts, songs, and stories of the Serrano and Cahuilla people of Southern California. Murillo had deep knowledge of plant medicine and spiritual medicine because her father was a *puul*. She published two books and was a well-known bird dancer. Courtesy of the Murillo family.

Each of them were prayer leaders, sharing prayers in public that called for the preservation of the good earth. Every one of these women had learned about language, religion, and culture from older women who served as their role models and educators. In turn, each of these women passed on their indigenous knowledge to younger women who would act as keepers of the traditions. From many sources, these California

Indian women learned their lessons and determined to preserve their languages, creation narratives, traditional laws, songs, stories, and religions. They used knowledge passed on to them through oral traditions, primarily by other women, as well as songs and stories with particular "attention to the sacredness of language, concern with landscape, affirmation of cultural values and tribal solidarity."[106]

Like tribal elders before them, they passed along knowledge first through the oral traditions of their people, but then also in written and spoken English. Some of these women—especially Vivienne Jake, Carmen Lucas, Jane Dumas, Pauline Murillo, Katherine Saubel, and many others too numerous to list—preserved culture by speaking publically and writing narratives in their Native languages and English. All of the women discussed in this chapter represent the many unnamed women within all the tribes, communities, and families who struggled for the well-being of their people by reviving Native interest in preserving their culture, language, and spiritual ways. These female leaders, like their male counterparts, acted on behalf of their tribes in the face of increasing modernization and urbanization in California. All of them have been pushed and pulled toward tradition and adaptation into a changed and modern world. All of these women were born of rich tribal traditions and societies that had to "come to terms with the impact of white culture on their people and their own lives."[107]

Native American societies and cultures in California have changed dramatically since the Spanish period, but in every tribal community, American Indian women have played significant roles in the preservation of rich Native arts, cultures, religions, laws, and languages. The role of women within Indian communities has not diminished over time. In fact, during the twentieth century, the roles of women grew in importance because of changing circumstances, declining economies, and new gender roles. During the twentieth century, women ascended in power and importance among some California Indian tribes. Gender roles proved dynamic, and women from leadership families and others grew in stature within their own communities and among non-Indians. Native women brought intelligence, experience, and knowledge to many elements of modern Indian life throughout the United States and in California, where several became leaders of their people. Their contributions, too long ignored, were great indeed.

NOTES

1. William Bauer has written an extensive study of labor among Indians living on the Round Valley Indian Reservation that focuses on the importance of work with, for, and among non-Indians during the nineteenth and twentieth centuries. His thesis can be

applied to many American Indian people during the transitional era of American Indian history, including the communities presented in this chapter. See William Bauer, *We Were All Like Migrant Workers Here: Work, Community, and Memory on California's Round Valley Reservation, 1850–1941* (Chapel Hill: University of North Carolina Press, 2009).

2. Greg Sarris, *Keeping Slug Woman Alive: A Holistic Approach to American Indian Texts* (Berkeley: University of California Press, 1993), 8–9; Robert Oswalt, *Kashaya Texts* (Berkeley: University of California Press, 1964), 4–6.

3. Oswalt, *Kashaya Texts*, 4–5.

4. Ibid.

5. Sarris, *Keeping Slug Woman Alive*, 10.

6. Ibid., 10–11.

7. Lowell J. Bean and Sylvia Brakke Vane, "Cults and Their Transformations," in *Handbook of North American Indians*, vol. 8, *California*, ed. Robert F. Heizer (Washington, D.C.: Smithsonian Institution Press, 1978), 671.

8. Ibid.

9. Lowell J. Bean and Dorothea Theodoratus, "Western Pomo and Northeastern Pomo," in Heizer, *Handbook of North American Indians*, 8:300–302.

10. Victoria D. Patterson, "Evolving Gender Roles in Pomo Society," in *Women and Power in Native North America*, ed. Laura F. Klein and Lillian A. Akerman (Norman: University of Oklahoma Press, 1995), 142–44.

11. Ibid.

12. Patterson, "Evolving Gender Roles in Pomo Society," 142–144; Greg Sarris, "Keeping Slug Woman Alive: The Challenge of Reading in a Reservation Classroom," in *The Ethnography of Reading*, ed. Jonathan Boyarin (Berkeley: University of California Press, 1993), 238–69.

13. Sarris, "Challenge of Reading in a Reservation Classroom," 257–58.

14. Oswalt, *Kashaya Texts*, 4–5.

15. Sarris, "Challenge of Reading in a Reservation Classroom," 245.

16. Sarris, *Keeping Slug Woman Alive*, 10–11.

17. Greg Sarris, "Parrish, Essie," in *Native American Women: A Biographical Dictionary*, ed. Gretchen M. Bataille (New York: Garland Publishing, 1993), 197–98.

18. Sarris, "Jarvis, Rosie," in Bataille, *Native American Women*, 123.

19. Oswalt, *Kashaya Texts*, 9.

20. Ibid., 5; Sarris, "Parrish, Essie," in Bataille, *Native American Women*, 97–198.

21. Sarris, "Parrish, Essie," in Bataille, *Native American Women*, 197.

22. Alfred L. Kroeber and Samuel A. Barrett, *Dream Dances of the Kashia Pomo: The Bole-Maru Religion Women's Dances*, American Indian Film Series in Ethnology, (Berkeley: University of California, Department of Anthropology, 1963), videocassette, 30 min.

23. Oswalt, *Kashaya Texts*, 9.

24. Sarris, *Keeping Slug Woman Alive*, 185.

25. Alfred L. Kroeber and Samuel A. Barrett, *Kashia Men's Dances: Southwestern Pomo Indians*, American Indian Film Series in Ethnology, (Berkeley: University of California, Department of Anthropology, 1963), videocassette, 45 min.

26. Sarris, *Keeping Slug Woman Alive*, 65.

27. Ibid., 79.

28. Sarris, "Parrish, Essie," in Bataille, *Native American Women*. Sarris noted that Kennedy visited the Kashaya Reservation in 1967; however, a news report announced Kennedy's visit on January 4, 1968. See KPIX Eyewitness News, "Robert Kennedy Visits School on Kashia Reservation," January 4, 1968, San Francisco Bay Area Television Archive, 16 mm, b&w comagnetic silent/sound film, 2:43, accessed June 13, 2011, https://diva.sfsu.edu /collections/sfbatv/bundles/190088.

29. Sarris, "Parrish, Essie," in Bataille, *Native American Women*, 197–98.

30. Sarris, *Keeping Slug Woman Alive*, 177.

31. Ibid., 11. Mabel McKay passed away in 1993.

32. Thomas Buckley noted that the Bole Maru most likely originated among the Hill Patwin with Lame Bill, a prophet who supported the Earth Lodge religion. Thomas Buckley, introduction to *The 1870 Ghost Dance*, by Cora DuBois (Lincoln: University of Nebraska Press, 2007), 1–4.

33. Sarris, *Keeping Slug Woman Alive*, 65–67.

34. Ibid., 126, 176.

35. For a brief description of sucking doctoring, see Sarris, *Keeping Slug Woman Alive*, 65.

36. Willard Johnson, "Native American Prophecy in Historical Perspective," *Journal of the American Academy of Religion* 64 (Autumn 1996), 575–612; 595.

37. Wintu territory encompassed parts of present-day Shasta, Trinity, Siskiyou, and Tehama Counties in Northern California. Frank A. Lapena, "Wintu," in Heizer, *Handbook of North American Indians*, 8:324–40.

38. DuBois, *1870 Ghost Dance*, 128–29.

39. Peter M. Knudtson, *Wintun Indians of California and Their Neighbors* (Happy Camp, Calif.: Naturegraph Publishers, 1977), 15–17.

40. Gregory E. Smoak, *Ghost Dances and Identities: Prophetic Religions and American Indian Ethnogenesis in the Nineteenth Century* (Berkeley: University of California Press, 2006), 165–175.

41. Knudtson, *Wintun Indians of California*, 15–17, 59–60; William S. Lyon, *Encyclopedia of Native American Healing* (New York: W.W. Norton, 1996), 122–24.

42. Knudtson, *Wintun Indians of California*, 61–62.

43. Ibid.

44. The other specialties Jones recognized included dreamers and singers, who possessed clairvoyant abilities, while tracers specialized in locating things and/or souls. Healers

and sucking doctors focused on healing people, with sucking doctors traditionally seen as the most powerful, locating and curing pain by "sucking" while in a trance state. Knudtson, *Wintun Indians of California*, 63.

45. Ibid., 62–64.

46. Kenneth Coosewoon, a Comanche healer, also emphasized that the Healing Spirit worked through him to bring about healing. Chemehuevi shaman Dutch Eddy could only heal once his bat familiar brought him spiritual healing power. The source of healing originates from the spirit world, not the shaman. The shaman serves as the vessel through which power is transferred from the spiritual world to patients, at times through an intermediary like a bat, scorpion, wolf, cloud, wind, etc.

47. Knudtson, *Wintun Indians of California*, 65.

48. Ibid.

49. Ibid., 66–67.

50. Ibid., 66.

51. David Suzuki and Peter Knudtson, *Wisdom of the Elders: Honoring Sacred Native Visions of Nature* (New York: Bantam Books, 1992), 200–202.

52. Knudtson, *Wintun Indians of California*, 67.

53. John Dart, "Religious Freedom and Native Americans," *Theology Today* 38 (July 1981), 174–81.

54. Linda D. Navarro, "The Committee for Traditional Indian Health: A Program of the California Rural Indian Health Board, Inc.," *News from Native California* 14, (Winter, 2000/2001).

55. Richard Carrico, *Strangers in a Stolen Land* (San Diego: Sunbelt Publications, 2008), 124–27.

56. In 2010, Jane Dumas and her brother, Adolph Thing, participated in a documentary DVD of songs of Southern California Indian people; Clifford E. Trafzer, William Madrigal, and Jonathan Ritter, *Keeping the Songs Alive: Southern California Indians*, (Riverside: University of California, California Center for Native Nations, 2010).

57. Jane Dumas was a member of an important leadership family among the Kumeyaay. According to scholar Richard Carrico, Dumas was a descendent of a prominent shaman named José Manuel Polton Hatam. The Thing-Dumas family developed from several components of the Kumeyaay leader's family. José Manuel was his baptized Spanish name, the name Polton came from his Indian godfather, and Hatam was the name of his powerful clan. Along with his Native language, Hatam spoke Spanish and English, allowing him to communicate effectively with local Euro-American officials. For more on Chief Hatam, see Carrico, *Strangers in a Stolen Land*, 124–27.

58. "Meet Jane Dumas: Respected Native American Elder," Plant Conservation Alliance—Medicinal Plant Working Group, *Green Medicine*, accessed June 15, 2011, http://www.nps.gov/plants/medicinal/spotlight/members/jane.dumas.htm.

59. Barbara A. Gray-Kanatnosh, *Kumeyaay* (Edina, Minn.: ABDO Publishing, 2005), 26–27.

60. "Jane Dumas: Kumeyaay Traditional Plant Use," Alliance for California Traditional Arts, accessed June 20, 2011, http://actaonline.org/content/jane-dumas.

61. Roy Cook, "San Diegan Jane Dumas, Kumeyaay Selected as Senior Leader," American Indian Source, accessed June 20, 2011, http://americanindiansource.com/dumasaward .html.

62. "Jane Dumas," Dorothy Ramon Learning Centers, Inc., accessed June 15, 2011, http:// www.dorothyramon.org/JaneDumas.html.

63. L. Frank and Kim Hogeland, *First Families: A Photographic History of California Indians* (Berkeley: Heyday Books, 2007), 132.

64. Clifford E. Trafzer, *Yuma: Frontier Crossing of the Far Southwest* (Wichita, Kans.: Western Heritage Press, 1980), 3–7, 31–68.

65. Ibid., 132.

66. Jeanine M. Pfeiffer and Elizabeth Huerta Ortiz, "Invasive Plants Impact California Native Plants Used in Traditional Basketry," *Fremontia: Journal of California Native Plant Society* 35 (Winter 2007), 7–13.

67. "Jane Dumas: Kumeyaay Traditional Plant Use."

68. Clifford E. Trafzer, "Saubel, Katherine Siva," in Bataille, *Native American Women*, 229; Katherine Siva Saubel and Eric Elliott, *'Isill Héqwas Wáxish - A Dried Coyote's Tail*, vol. 1, (Banning, Calif.: Malki Museum Press, 2004), xxxiii–xxxiv.

69. Lowell John Bean and Katherine Siva Saubel, *Temalpakh: Cahuilla Indian Knowledge and Usage of Plants* (Banning, Calif.: Malki Museum Press, 1972).

70. Katherine Saubel, oral interview by Clifford E. Trafzer, March 2000.

71. Saubel and Elliott, *'Isill Héqwas Wáxish*, 1:64; Saubel, interview.

72. Saubel and Elliott, *'Isill Héqwas Wáxish*, 1:13–14.

73. Ibid., 1:xxxiii; 1:831–32.

74. Darryl Wilson, "Five Hundred Years from Now: An Interview with Katherine Saubel," *News from Native California* 5 (February-April 1991), 11–13.

75. *We Are Still Here: Katherine Siva Saubel and the Cahuilla Indians of Southern California*, directed by Leigh Podgorski (Van Nuys, Calif.: Under the Hill Productions, 2007), DVD, 57 min.

76. Saubel and Elliott, *'Isill Héqwas Wáxish*, 1:68.

77. Ibid., 1:96–97.

78. Ibid.

79. Ibid., 1:105–12.

80. William Bright, "The History of the Cahuilla Sound System," *International Journal of American Linguistics* 31 (July 1965), 241–44.

81. Saubel and Elliott, *'Isill Héqwas Wáxish*, 1:64. Katherine noted that among the Cahuilla, women were never shamans. Rather, some women, such as Saubel's mother, had intensive knowledge of plants and acted as herbal healers.

82. *We Are Still Here.*

83. Ibid. Penn, Saubel, and others formed the Malki Museum on the Morongo Indian Reservation near Banning, California, and the museum still offers a robust program of preservation.

84. Minutes of the Native American Heritage Commission, Capitol Mall, Sacramento, California. Clifford Trafzer served as a commissioner with Saubel (1989–2012) and attended the meetings mentioned in this chapter.

85. Pauline Murillo, *Living in Two Worlds: The Life of Pauline Ormego Murillo* (Highland, Calif.: Dimples Press, 2001), 23.

86. Ibid., 228–29.

87. Ibid., 401.

88. Ibid., 30, 42, 100, 223.

89. Murillo shared this story often, including in an oral interview by Clifford E. Trafzer, September 7, 2000.

90. Pauline Ormego Murillo, *Never Forget Who You Are or Where You Came From* (Highland, Calif.: Dimples Press, 2001), 21.

91. Murillo, interview.

92. Murillo, *Living in Two Worlds*, 100, 115, 223, 401, 409, 411.

93. Ibid., 151, 163.

94. Ibid., 163, 167.

95. Ibid., 167–68.

96. Ibid., 125, 137.

97. Murillo, interview.

98. Murillo, *Never Forget Who You Are*, 12.

99. Murillo, *Living in Two Worlds*, 223.

100. Trafzer, Madrigal, and Ritter, *Keeping the Songs Alive.*

101. Ibid., 181, 213, 395, 399, 409, 411.

102. Ibid., 168.

103. Ibid., 350.

104. For an understanding of staying medicine, see Donald Bahr, "Pima and Papago Medicine and Philosophy," in *Handbook of North American Indians*, vol. 10, *Southwest*, ed. Alfonso Ortiz (Washington, D. C.: Smithsonian Institution Press, 1983), 195–99.

105. Ibid., 386, 387; Murillo, interview.

106. Gretchen M. Bataille and Kathleen Mullen Sands, *American Indian Women: Telling Their Lives* (Lincoln: University of Nebraska Press, 1984), 3–4.

107. Ibid., 20, 24.

10

COOSEWOON

ᚨ

Visions, Medicine, and Sweat Lodge

CLIFFORD E. TRAFZER

IN SOUTHWESTERN OKLAHOMA, Mount Scott rises up majestically, breaking the monotony of the southern plains. Mountains, plateaus, and valleys radiate out from this sacred mountain, trailing off where trees, bushes, flowers, and prairie grasses provide a home for many animals. Water flows through streams and creeks, making the area highly desirable for many indigenous people, including Comanche, Kiowa, Kiowa-Apache, and Chiricahua Apache. For many American Indians and newcomers, Mount Scott and its lush environment is a sacred place. The shadow of the mountain is home to many people and families among the Kiowa and Comanche tribes. Mattie Kaulie, a beautiful Kiowa woman, lived on the family's ranch under the shadow of Mount Scott. When she married a handsome Comanche man named Abner Coosewoon, the couple lived in her family's home at Meers, near Medicine Park, Oklahoma. On September 29, 1929, Mattie gave birth to Kenneth Coosewoon.[1]

Today, Kenneth Coosewoon is known in many parts of Indian Country, especially in Oklahoma, for his remarkable healing abilities. He has won many awards and has been recognized by the state and many diverse groups. But most importantly, he is an example of a contemporary healer, a man that has devoted his life to using the sweat lodge ceremony to heal others. Coosewoon is an example of a modern-day Native American healer, a man that gives of himself without expecting anything in return. Coosewoon was not born into sweat lodge healing, although as an adult he learned that his grandparents had been medicine people and had used the sweat lodge on property not far from his home at Meers, Oklahoma. Coosewoon grew up and has lived his life in the shadow of Mount Scott and the gateway into the Wichita

FIGURE 10.1. Comanche healers Kenneth and Rita Coosewoon open many ceremonies with songs and prayers. They are contemporary healers that generally use the sweat lodge to heal patients from physical, mental, and spiritual sicknesses. Even without entering the sweat lodge, Coosewoon uses spiritual power to heal people. Editor's photograph.

Mountains. Lake Lawtonka is situated at the base of Mount Scott and not far from Coosewoon's home, which is located a mile or so from the Kiowa Methodist Church where his mother and father took him to pray as a Christian.

Coosewoon's mother's conversion to Christianity led her to raise her son away from the "Good Red Road." She opposed him practicing the old religion of Comanche and Kiowa people. Instead, he grew up in the Methodist Church and did not learn about the medicine ways or culture of his people. Significantly, Coosewoon was raised at a time when some indigenous parents, like his own, attempted to shield their children from the "primitive" religions, languages, and medicine ways of past generations. Mattie Coosewoon did not want her children to learn the Kiowa or Comanche languages. She did not want them practicing "heathenistic" ceremonies, dances, and songs of the people. Mattie Coosewoon believed that knowledge of traditional medicine ways would hold her son back in a world controlled by white Americans. She wanted Coosewoon raised as "mainstream" as possible to provide him far more educational and economic opportunities than those known to Coosewoon's mother, father, and other kin.

Born on the Kiowa-Comanche-Apache Reservation in southwestern Oklahoma, Coosewoon became a well-known healer among American Indians and non-Indians. Through his own indigenous education and spiritual revelations as an adult, Kenneth Coosewoon came to believe that all people were the same—all children of Grandfather, the great healer. Coosewoon never discriminated against non-Indians, helping them just as he did American Indian people, but asking one and all to believe in the power of Grandfather. Coosewoon continues to live near Mount Scott and Lake Lawtonka on the same land and in the same house as his parents and maternal grandparents. For his sweat lodge ceremonies, he gathers willow shoots near the shore of Lake Lawtonka, rocks from the hillsides near his home, and red berry cedar for smudging on Longhorn Mountain in the Wichita Range. He gathers ancient rocks to bring the fire of the earth into the sweat lodge, where water transforms the hot rocks and water into steam. Coosewoon explained that the steam penetrates the skin, hearts, minds, and souls of patients.

Through the sweat lodge ceremony, Coosewoon has healed many people with numerous kinds of sicknesses over the course of several years. He is a spiritual doctor that calls on the Grandfather, or Healing Spirit, for power, which he directs into patients to cure them. He is a modern wisdom spirit, a man of power and foresight. In the past, he received revelations that led him into indigenous medicine and curing. He explained that he continues to receive visions from the spiritual world and uses gifts given to him by Grandfather to help all people—Indians and non-Indians alike. However, Coosewoon has not always been a holy man and healer. For many years he fought alcoholism, egotism, insecurity, and other demons before Grandfather forever changed his life. Over time, Coosewoon found his American Indian identity and his agency, using his knowledge of Native American culture to uplift and cure hundreds of people. Through song and prayer, Coosewoon continues his work today through acts of healing.

Kenneth Coosewoon grew up in a loving family and carefree environment. In his youth, he rode horses everywhere across the plains and onto the slopes of Mount Scott. He excelled as an athlete in every sport, and while a student at Elgin High School, made the all-star basketball team in Comanche County four years in a row.[2] Two colleges offered him basketball scholarships, and he chose to attend Cameron College in Lawton, Oklahoma, located not far from his home at Medicine Park. At college, Coosewoon fell in love with Juanita Doraline Taylor, but the two left college in 1951 to marry and begin a life together.[3] After a short stint in the United States Army, Coosewoon returned to the rural area around Medicine Park, Oklahoma, with his wife, where he worked at various jobs and ran a successful dry-cleaning business. For years he battled alcoholism, until Doraline committed him to the Indian hospital in Lawton for treatment. While in the hospital, Coosewoon experienced his first visions.[4]

FIGURE 10.2. In the home of Cahuilla elder Bill Madrigal, Coosewoon used red berry cedar from Longhorn Mountain in Oklahoma, sage, and his eagle fan to heal Gloria Delgado, kneeling, and Florence Majo Lawfton, sitting to Coosewoon's right. Editor's photograph.

While strapped to a gurney and in recovery at the hospital, Coosewoon reported seeing "little people," or tiny spirits that looked like miniature human beings. Little people poked fun at Coosewoon and berated him for being such a fool to harm himself and others. Coosewoon recovered for a spell but later fell into his old patterns again. Doraline committed him to the hospital again, and while he was recovering, Coosewoon said he saw a clouded mass that came under the door and floated across the room. At the foot of the bed, the shadowy mass took human form and spoke to Coosewoon, saying, "If you stop drinking, you will live to wear out many blue jeans," but the spirit warned that if Coosewoon took another drink, it would be the end of his life. The spirit asked Coosewoon if he was ready to enter the spirit world, and when he declined, the spirit left the hospital.[5] "At the time, I didn't know what or who it was," Kenneth explained. "But I know now. He was the Grandfather, the Great Spirit, God, the Healing Spirit or whatever you want to call it."[6] Coosewoon explained that the spirit had come to lead him on a new journey—into the world of traditional healing.

When Coosewoon returned from the hospital, his life changed forever. He decided never to drink again. In 1964, his brother-in-law took him to Alcoholics Anonymous (AA), and the organization helped him refrain from drinking. He stopped drinking for ten years, but lapsed badly into alcoholism and nearly died four times. But Doraline, psychologist Richard Downey, and his family helped Coosewoon with his health recovery. He returned to AA, where American Indian participants helped him reconnect with his Indian roots and culture, which began him down the path of the Good Red Road.[7] Coosewoon remembered this as a turning point, when he turned inward, reassessing his life and actions. He remembers deciding to change his life in many ways. Rather than look for fistfights, he decided to become generous, caring, and calm as a human being. He began being retrospective, deciding to end his prejudices. He gradually rekindled his Native American identity, learning from other Indians and reading more about his own people and healers such as Black Elk and Lame Deer. He began to live a hero's place within Native American culture by serving others and not gratifying his ego. For many years, Coosewoon directed drug and alcohol centers, helping American Indian men and women end their drinking and find a new life. Coosewoon excelled at this work, drawing on lessons he had learned as an alcoholic to help other Indian people suffering from the scourge.

While he "was running an alcohol treatment center" at the old Fort Sill Indian School near Cache Creek in Lawton, Oklahoma, called Men for Men, some of his clients asked if they could establish a sweat lodge near the counseling center.[8] At the time, Coosewoon knew nothing about the sweat lodge as a healing space. Although he had heard of sweat lodges before, he thought people used them to lose weight. He soon learned the sweat lodge united humans with the spiritual world, especially Grandfather or the Moving Spirit. Coosewoon explained that he learned that the sweat lodge was the "little church" for Indian people, offering many forms of healing.[9] He also later learned that his mother's family had been deep into the sweat lodge for years before his birth, but because of his mother's conversion to Christianity, she had not taught him about the tradition.[10]

Approximately thirty-five clients sought treatment at Men for Men, including a young Cheyenne-Arapaho man and a Kiowa fellow. Both of these men had previously used a sweat lodge for healing, and one day while walking "down at the bridge" across the creek close to the Fort Sill Indian School, they found an appropriate site for a sweat lodge. They approached Coosewoon, and said, "Kenneth, we found a good place to build a sweat lodge." They planted the seed for the treatment center to supplement other forms of healing with the sweat lodge. These two men and others became enthusiastic about building a sweat lodge. Coosewoon helped them build the structure, which faced east, using local willows and covering it with a tarp. The men brought ancient rocks from Mount Scott, and they led Coosewoon's first sweat lodge ceremony. During that first session, Coosewoon decided he liked the experience, and he reported seeing the spirits of his relatives that had run sweat lodge ceremonies in the past. The ceremony on Cache Creek was Coosewoon's first experience in the sweat lodge and led him forward on his path of becoming a healer.[11] He experienced many things during this first ceremony, and he wanted to learn more. But before his next sweat lodge ceremony along Cache Creek, he would experience a remarkable revelation far from his home in southwestern Oklahoma.

As director of Men for Men, Coosewoon often joined other directors in workshops and retreats. In 1978, he attended such a gathering of American Indian directors held at Dwight Mission in Cherokee Country. Dwight Mission sits on the edge of thick deciduous woods in the Cookson Hills east of Tulsa, Oklahoma, where Sallisaw Creek runs behind the mission at the edge of the woods. It is an ideal location, quiet and pastoral. The creek snakes its way through meadows and woods on the lower end of a cemetery for the children and parishioners that attend the Baptist school and church. Along Sallisaw Creek not far from the cemetery and mission, two Lakota shamans, Wallace and Gracie Black Elk, had erected a sweat lodge for participants in the director's workshop and had been asked to conduct a sweat lodge ceremony. Coosewoon did not know the Black Elks, but they soon became Coosewoon's mentors and guides. According to Coosewoon, the Black Elks knew that Grandfather has selected him to heal others, and the Black Elks went out of their way to encourage Coosewoon in helping others. Before Coosewoon was to leave Dwight Mission, Gracie Black Elk gave him tape recordings of power songs so that he could listen and learn them for use in his own sweat lodge ceremony. At the time, Coosewoon had no intension of using the tapes or learning the songs. He was not a healer and had no plans to run a sweat lodge. All he knew was that he liked to participate in the sweat lodge ceremony because of the positive, uplifting feeling it gave him.

During the workshop for directors, Kenneth and the other men joined in the sweat lodge with the Black Elks. Coosewoon reported that during his second sweat lodge, he "experienced everything . . . I didn't know existed," including "moving spirits" and "sparks that jumped around in the sweat." The sparks flickered in front of him in the dark sweat lodge as if someone was striking a cigarette lighter, creating sparks in the total darkness. But the sparks started "dancing all around me," and "a rattle appeared in front of me but no one was shaking the rattle." It appeared spiritually, and Coosewoon reported seeing it for some time. He heard the sound of that spirit rattle and reported it "was the most beautiful thing I think I ever heard."[12]

Coosewoon reported he experienced other inexplicable phenomena during this same ceremony. Something in the center of the red glowing rocks in the middle of the lodge caught his eyes. "I looked down at the rocks," he later said, and "could see a little spark down in them rocks." He kept looking at the spark, and soon a light "just like a flashlight pen" beamed out of the rocks and cast a small light on Coosewoon's heart. At the time, he felt the light penetrated his heart, and soon he saw "blood spurting out of his chest." Although blood squirted out of his heart each time his heart beat, he felt no pain and the blood simply disappeared. He believed the spirit world was "flushing out my meanness." At first, only he saw the stream of light beaming out of the rocks and onto his heart. Then he asked the man sitting next to him if he saw the light. At first the man said he did not see it, but after Coosewoon asked him to move closer and look carefully, the man remarked, "Yeah, it's shining right on your heart."[13]

Coosewoon was moved by all these events, which he believed were spiritual in nature and were intended to help him become a better person. The moving sparks and shaking rattle had caught his attention and made him feel positive about the entire experience. The tiny beam of light shining on his heart created the flushing action, which cleaned his blood of all the hate and anger he had harbored for years. He fully believed Grandfather did these things to purify his blood and clean his mind to think in positive ways about his own life and his relationship with all his "relatives" on earth. Then another momentous event occurred in the sweat lodge. Coosewoon reported that the spirit of a large bald eagle entered the lodge. The great bird walked up to Coosewoon, spread its wings, and began fanning his face, shoulders, and body with its great wings. He felt the wind generated by the wings and felt the eagle was spiritually cleansing him. He remembered "floating" and having a good feeling while the eagle fanned him. He was also somewhat confused. "Spiritually, I felt good, great, clean," Coosewoon said, adding that with time, he received a profound message to change his ways and begin life anew. He felt that as a man, he had to walk the Good Red Road and follow a more positive path during his life. His days of drinking, fighting, and acting foolishly to feed his ego were behind him. He wanted to be a better person.[14]

At dusk during the course of the sweat lodge ceremony, Coosewoon volunteered to take care of the fire heating the rocks outside the lodge. The other men left the sweat lodge and walked up a small hill to Dwight Mission to have supper. After they had left, the camp was quiet and serene. Coosewoon stood over the fire, leaning on a shovel and taking care to keep the fire under control. Then all of a sudden, several sparks burning blue flew from the rocks into the air and onto the ground surrounding the fire keeper. Coosewoon watched the sparks and noticed one of the blue glowing embers pulsating a blue light. "I kept looking at it and it kept getting brighter and brighter." Something spoke to him, telling him to pick it up. "When I first picked it up," he explained, "it felt like it was hot and I started to throw it back down."[15] However, the blue ember turned cool to his touch. He heard someone clearly speak to him, but when he looked about, he saw no one. In his hand, the blue ember continued to glow a bright blue. Then Coosewoon heard someone tell him to walk down to Sallisaw Creek. He looked around and saw no one, but the words came from "a big bird by the creek" that spoke to him, telling him to walk down to the stream's edge. "So I had that in my hand and as I was walking down toward where he was calling me, that thing started getting brighter and brighter." Although confused by these events, Coosewoon explained he was not scared: "I knew it was something spiritual."[16] He began to pray to himself when "a big gust of wind" blew through the edge of the woods where he stood holding the blue ember, and soon the wind "went right through me and by me and I looked up into the sky and there was lightning."[17]

The vision continued when he heard the roar of thunder but found no clouds. Lightning and thunder popped around him, and the entire scene was just "like in the movies." By this time, Coosewoon began "getting scared" but mostly because he did not understand the meaning of these dramatic events. All of a sudden, a large oak tree in front of him "started dancing and shaking." In fact, Coosewoon felt an earthquake all around him as "the whole earth just shook and I jumped about ten feet in the air." Then, across the creek, deep in the dark woods, Coosewoon saw two lights moving together through the forest, looking "like two eyes, and it kind of blinked." On the far bank of Sallisaw Creek, the two lights turned into a single ball of blue light, glowing in the darkness, and then diffused into a blue glowing fog that crossed the stream and surrounded him. "It circled me, that blue glow, and I tried to reach and get some of it." When Coosewoon reached down to touch the blue light, a voice came from the light, saying, "No, don't touch me." So he raised his hand, all the while holding the blue ember in his other hand.[18]

From the blue light surrounding him, Coosewoon heard a spiritual male voice address him, saying that the Healing Spirit—or Grandfather—would always be with him. "You run the sweats," the spirit said, "and "I'll show you how to run them. I will always be with you. I'll never leave you." The spirit voice promised to teach him all that he needed to know and provide him with all his needs in order to lead the sweat lodge ceremony and heal people. "Grandfather," Coosewoon said, "promised always to help me with the sweat lodge," provided "I was willing to help others." The spirit continued, saying, "You'll see many miracles and many things will happen." But Coosewoon's first thoughts were, "I don't have nothing to run the sweats, and he said, get a water bucket and a dipper." He understood that the spirit was referring to the leader of the sweat lodge using a bucket and dipper to pour out water onto the glowing hot rocks to create steam inside the sweat lodge. "Start with that," the spirit demanded, and "that's what I done." Soon after, Coosewoon answered the calling from the spirit world, and many things came his way. People gave him songs, eagle feathers, a drum, an eagle bone whistle, a pipe, cedar, sage, and other sacred items. But "when I first started," he explained, "I had a dipper and water bucket." Other things came to him over time, and in this way, he learned patience. "We want something right now, but he doesn't do it that way. When he's ready for you to have the next step, he will provide it."[19]

After these experiences, Wallace and Gracie Black Elk and the other directors returned to the sweat lodge to continue the ceremony. They found Coosewoon as they had left him, tending the fire with his shovel. He said nothing to any of them about

FIGURE 10.3. Kenneth Coosewoon builds his sweat lodges from young willow shoots, which he gathers near Lake Lawtonka. He uses large, round tan stones gathered in or near the Wichita Mountains of southwestern Oklahoma. For many years, he has lived in his mother's home in Meers, Oklahoma. Editor's photograph.

what he had experienced, assuming they would not believe him and think him to be "crazy." So he said nothing but was much changed spiritually by the experience, determined to be a better person and help others. He still was not convinced he would ever lead a sweat lodge ceremony or heal other people. He had never been a healer or ceremonial leader, and he made no plans to begin such work. He quietly participated in the workshops with the others and accepted the tapes Gracie Black Elk gave him. He returned home to work at the Fort Sill Indian School with his clients, not sharing with his family or clients anything that had transpired at Dwight Mission. Coosewoon remained skeptical of the Healing Spirit (a manifestation of Grandfather) and the messages he received, but he remembered the voice saying, "Son, don't worry about it! Whenever anything good happens, don't worry about it." Coosewoon learned to "put a smile on your face and keep going."[20]

Many tribes have their own method of conducting the sweat lodge ceremony, but Coosewoon runs his sweat lodge in the larger tradition of the northern and southern Great Plains tribes. "I'm Comanche and Kiowa, but I don't run the sweat in any tribally specific manner, just the way I grew into the ceremony."[21] The Black Elks tutored

Coosewoon and gave him songs and structure. His sweat lodge is influenced by Lakota culture, but Coosewoon also draws on Comanche and Kiowa beliefs. From the beginning, he believed the sweat lodge ceremony was about health and healing, not about the form and format of the ceremony. "We are all different tribes . . . and the ceremony means the same to all Native Americans that practice the sweat lodge." Coosewoon believed that "it's not bad" for tribal healers to follow their tribe's traditions in conducting the sweat lodge. In fact, he believed it was natural for healers to do so, but Coosewoon employed the ways he learned from others and the Healing Spirit, the Grandfather.[22]

When Coosewoon conducts a sweat lodge ceremony, especially a healing sweat, he makes more than one hundred tobacco ties, wrapping small red cloths around tobacco and praying for healing as he creates each tiny red bundle. He makes "ropes, tobacco ropes, for each of the four directions." In addition, during some sweats, Coosewoon introduces water, corn, meat, berries, and fish into the sweat as offerings. "We take them in for the spirits," and often the elements given to the spirits disappear during the course of the ceremony. But the foundation for Coosewoon's method of running the sweat lodge evolved from that of the Black Elk Sweat Lodge, the place where he forgave himself and shed his negative feelings toward himself and others. His Great Vision pointed him on a new path to control his own hatred, anger, suspicion, jealousy, envy, and other base feelings. Instead, the ceremony led him to embrace the Healing Spirit and share the positive benefits of the sweat lodge with anyone that sought his help or advice.[23]

After the Great Vision, Coosewoon found his Indian identity, an element of his personal life that had long evaded him. He ended his personal desire to be popular, recognized, or rewarded for his work. He no longer wanted to be a "big man." Coosewoon is the first to say that he is human and influenced by people and events around him, but he strives to think of others and not his ego. He stopped worrying about the way others perceive him as a man, father, Indian, or healer. The Great Vision taught him to be honest about his life and transformation. He often explains to groups that the spirit world has given him a charge to help, guide, counsel, and heal. He has spent his life calling on spirits and using the wisdom they impart to help others. He never pushes his beliefs or ceremonies on people but shares them with those interested in learning or healing through the Indian way. Kenneth received power as a result of his encounter with the spirit world, and part of the power included practical medicine he uses in his healing way.[24]

After his Great Vision at Dwight Mission, Coosewoon remained silent to everyone about what had happened. With time, however, he began to share his vision and its meaning with people and the various elements of the vision came to have meaning to him, such as the glowing blue embers. The wood of the blue glowing ember became his medicine, which he carries with him and gives to patients who take it orally. "The wood is blue when I find it, blue glow, the gift that was given to me." Coosewoon sees the medicine glow blue, especially in the dark, but most people see it as a dark brown. When he offers healing to a person, he sometimes has them eat a small portion of the blue medicine wood, insisting the person ingests it. At first he was not certain the blue chip in his hand was to be his medicine, but he learned from the spirit world to allow "them to eat a little piece of that wood, and with the prayers and the eagle feather, they get well."[25]

Coosewoon was convinced that "the wood has some spiritual effect to it, some way, but I don't know how." A few years after the Great Vision, Wallace Black Elk told Coosewoon that Grandfather "gave you that medicine, and you are to use it, not question what it is" in terms of chemical makeup. Kenneth learned that when the items the Grandfather put before him proved effective in his healing, then he should use it without questioning the power of the item or procedures shown to him. But like other spiritual gifts, the power has to be infused through prayer into the wood, water, flowers, seeds, sage, cedar, sweet grass, pipe, tobacco, or other material item. Coosewoon developed his ceremony and relationship with Grandfather over time, but almost immediately after his vision, circumstances unfolded that drew him closer into the spiritual world of wisdom drawn from the Healing Spirit.[26]

A short time after the Great Vision at Dwight Mission, Coosewoon was working at home in Medicine Park when the telephone rang and signaled another major step in his journey to becoming a healer. Coosewoon received an emergency call from his daughter, Deanna. She reported that her boyfriend, Jayme, had been shot point-blank with a .38-caliber revolver during a holdup at a convenience store. Jayme was in the hospital and it appeared he would die. Deanna begged Coosewoon to come to the hospital to be with her and Jayme. At the time, Coosewoon did not want to go to the hospital, knowing Jayme's family would be there crying, and he simply did not want to be part of the grief. Deanna persisted, asking her father to come to the hospital just to be with her. Finally he agreed but told her he could do little or nothing. After the call, Coosewoon cleaned up, taking a shower. While he was showering, he reported that once again he heard the same voice he had heard at Dwight Mission, saying, "Kenneth, go and help Jayme." When Coosewoon responded, saying, "I don't know what to do," the Healing Spirit responded, saying, "Kenneth, you do not know the power I have given you. I will always be with you. Now, go and help Jayme!"

Coosewoon drove from Meers into Lawton to the hospital, not knowing what he might do to help Jayme, but he knew he could be a comforting presence to Deanna. When he arrived at the hospital, he found his daughter, who took him to look in on Jayme. At the same time, he learned that the bullet had severely damaged Jayme's liver, blowing it into small pieces. His liver was not working and he was on life support systems to keep him alive. When Coosewoon and Deanna got to Jayme's bed in the emergency room, they watched as a priest gave Jayme his last rites. At the same time, in his head, Coosewoon heard the spiritual voice speak in his ear, saying that Jayme was going to "make it" and that Coosewoon must conduct sweat lodge for him. He received another message from the spiritual world: Jayme would live! When the priest left and the room became quiet, he walked to Jayme, bent over the unconscious man, and whispered in his ear, saying, "Don't believe that. I have been told you are going to be ok, so hang in there. We're going to do sweat lodge and bring you healing."[27] Jayme opened his eyes briefly and blinked at Coosewoon in acknowledgment that he had heard him.[28]

In response to the emergency and in an effort to save Jayme's life, Coosewoon called the Indian men and clients at the rehabilitation center meeting at the Fort Sill Indian School. Accompanied by Ronald Cooper, Coosewoon's grandson, the men met behind the center at the sweat lodge. When Coosewoon arrived at the sweat lodge, "I saw thousands of birds circling the sweat lodge, eagles, hawks, robins, sparrows, all kinds," and "I took this as a good sign." At the time of this gathering to pray for Jayme, Coosewoon had participated in only two sweat lodge ceremonies. He readily admitted he did not know how to lead the ceremony. But when he entered the sweat lodge, he calmed down, remembering the Healing Spirit had said, "I will always be with you. I will always help you in whatever you need." Coosewoon addressed the participants, admitting he did not know what he was doing but that he believed "our collective prayers for Jayme will have more strength than just my prayer." He asked them to pray with him for Jayme's life. They prayed for his miraculous recovery.[29]

Coosewoon led his clients in four rounds of ceremony that night. When they concluded the last round and final prayers, Coosewoon and the participants crawled out of the lodge to a wondrous sight. The door to the sweat lodge opened to the east and was located very near the edge of Cache Creek, which had cut a deep channel into the earth. The west bank of the creek was glowing a deep blue and shimmering color, "much like a neon light." In the dark night, the stars sparkled and the entire scene conveyed the message that the Healing Spirit head heard the prayers. The participants all took the blue glow as a positive sign. Coosewoon and Ron Cooper drove home together and the next day returned to the hospital. Jayme's health had stabilized slightly but remained in critical condition. The doctors told Coosewoon that during surgery they had collected parts of Jayme's liver in a plastic surgical baggy. They had attempted to reconnect blood vessels into the mass of liver, but the mess was most vexing. They told Coosewoon they had reattached blood vessels but needed the blood to begin flowing through the reconstituted organ. Coosewoon responded by meeting once again at the sweat lodge with his clients to ask Grandfather to make the blood flow, and soon Jayme's blood began flowing through his liver. In time, Jayme stabilized sufficiently so hospital personnel could airlift him from Lawton to the University of Oklahoma Medical Center in Oklahoma City. Jayme progressed over time but had to fight off gangrene infection, which he did with the help of another sweat lodge ceremony led by Coosewoon. Jayme's condition improved until he was able to return to Lawton and resume a normal life. As of 2017, Jayme remains alive, a friend of the Coosewoon family.[30]

Jayme's recovery was nothing short of a miracle. Coosewoon explained that the horrible circumstances taught him to trust in the Healing Spirit and to follow a new path of helping and healing others. He always tells people seeking his help that they must believe in Grandfather's power, as the healing does not stem from Coosewoon but from the Healing Spirit. From his experience with Jayme, he learned that "prayers are the most powerful things on earth" but also recognized that humans have a hard time putting their trust in Grandfather. Still, Coosewoon had to learn by his own experience and passes on the belief in Grandfather's power to everyone he encounters. Coosewoon also learned to tell others about his experiences at Dwight Mission and with Jayme, all of which changed his life and provided others with an example of hope. Coosewoon explained that he could not promise a cure to anyone, but he could provide hope and wholeness. He could offer people a measure of balance through ceremony and prayer, asking Grandfather to intervene and help patients suffering from numerous maladies. His experience with Jayme taught Coosewoon he was walking the right path, taking the journey the holy ones wanted him to take. From that time forward, Coosewoon has explained that he prays often, asking for guidance, saying, "He wants me to remember that He will always be with me and will help me." Coosewoon asks those seeking his help to believe that they are not alone and that Grandfather watches over all people, helping them in His own unique way.[31]

After healing Jayme, people began asking Coosewoon to help them, and he developed his own style of sweat lodge ceremony. For nearly forty years, he has helped men, women, and children, sometimes praying and singing for them in the lodge, and other times simply meeting with them and offering spiritual medicine. At other times, Coosewoon receives telephone calls and prays for those in need without organizing a full-scale ceremony. To bring about strong healing, Coosewoon believes that the power "comes in" the best when males and females are involved. He has conducted ceremony only with men, but he feels that having a woman or women involved in ceremony better concentrates healing power.

After healing Jayme, Coosewoon often asked his wife Doraline to help him in sweat lodge ceremonies. Unfortunately, Coosewoon lost his first wife. In time, he married his longtime friend Rita, so he and Rita made a healing partnership. Rita Coosewoon is one of the few speakers of the Comanche language and is a tribal judge. She also is a healer in her own right. Coosewoon and Rita were among the first

Indians to enter men and women's prisons to doctor the people. Coosewoon was the first Native American medicine man to bring the sweat lodge into prisons, and he has conducted hundreds of ceremonies for men in prisons. With the help of Rita, he has also entered women's prisons to lead prayer circles and listen to the needs of prisoners. The Coosewoons became famous throughout the United States for their healing sessions in prisons, using the sweat lodge whenever possible and simply leading prayer sessions when they could not conduct full ceremonies.[32]

When Rita was unable to accompany Coosewoon to conduct sweat lodge, Cherokee healer Beverly Patchell served as the female component of the sweat lodge ceremony or healing sessions in prayers. Over a forty-year period, Coosewoon helped people with physical, mental, and spiritual problems, calling on the Healing Spirit to intercede. In spite of his fame within Native American communities, he never claimed to be a medicine man. "I don't even know what a medicine man is," he once explained. Regardless, Coosewoon has earned the title many times over as he has healed hundreds of people and never charged a person for his help. He explained that his power to help others would leave him if he charged people for prayers in or out of the sweat lodge. He also never discriminates due to race, religion, or belief system. He believes that all people are the same—children of Grandfather—and all people need the help of the Healing Spirit. Whenever asked to help anyone, Coosewoon agrees to help to the extent he is able. For him, "There are no races of people in the spirit world. We are all in one spirit. There are no religions in the spirit world. We are all of the Spirit and we should help everyone." Coosewoon follows the same ritual procedures when conducting the sweat lodge ceremony no matter what the background or heritage of the person.[33]

Since his experience at Dwight Mission, Coosewoon has used blue medicine as part of his healing ways. The wood that created the blue glow is his blue medicine. Most people see the wood as tan or gray, but the wood appears blue to Coosewoon. According to him, when he runs out of the wood, he goes to a private place and prays to the Healing Spirit to provide it for him, "and it comes to me, all around me, and I see it glowing blue." During healing ceremonies or prayer sessions, he has people eat the medicine, which places the Healing Spirit within the wood into the patient's body. To help patients, Coosewoon prepares small leather medicine bags that people wear around their necks. These pouches contain prayers and a small portion of his blue medicine. He prepares for ceremony by tying small red cloth into bundles, placing tobacco into each little red cloth and tying the end with string, which is a tradition of many Plains Indians as well as others. He uses the bundles to pray for ill people before they enter the sweat lodge.

Tying tobacco bundles places Coosewoon's mind and spirit in the direction of healing, asking Grandfather to intervene at this early stage before the ceremony. He generally uses seven little bundles in a single prayer tie, placing them in the roof ribs of the lodge. The blue medicine and prayer bundles are part of the larger ceremony found within the sweat lodge or the "first little church." He builds his sweat lodge on "our holy land." The earth was a gift from Grandfather to indigenous people, and the earth contains wisdom that Coosewoon draws on before, during, and after ceremony. He gives thanks to Grandfather for providing all the elements of the earth—the willow branches, rocks, wood, and ground below him; the sky, moon, and stars above him. For Coosewoon, the entire length of North and South America is holy land, a gift from Grandfather to Native Americans. Coosewoon feels that the sweat lodge ceremony is an extension of Grandfather's many gifts to human beings, and people must be humble and thankful for these gifts. He remembers the elements in his prayers before and during the sweat lodge ceremony. Grandfather, Great Spirit, Moving Spirit, God, the Creator—known in Native American languages by many names—made this land for indigenous peoples. It holds spiritual power in special places, and this power concentrates at the site of every sweat lodge ceremony.[34]

Coosewoon feels strongly that the land of his forefathers and other Native Americans is "holy land here," because "this is where the Grandfather placed us." Many other Native Americans have proclaimed the same message, including Yakama Chief Owhi, who explained, "God looked one way then the other and named our lands for us."[35] Coosewoon believes the sweat lodge was the first way of praying among Native Americans, a place to give thanks to "Grandfather, God." He believes that "at one time, all the Indians had the sweat lodge, but through Christianity and over the years, we lost it." He points out that agents of the Bureau of Indian Affairs and Christian missionaries working in Indian country discouraged, forbade, or outlawed sweat lodge ceremonies, believing it was a pagan, anti-Christian gathering. Some Christians tied sweat lodge ceremonies to Satan and devil worshiping. But in the late twentieth century, Native American spiritual leaders, including Wallace and Gracie Black Elk and Kenneth and Rita Coosewoon, revived the wider use of the sweat lodge ceremony. They ministered to others and encouraged people, especially Native Americans, to use the sweat lodge for spirituality, psychology, prayers, purification, thanksgiving, counseling, and healing.[36]

In large part, the success of the sweat lodge ceremony centers on the rocks that emit heat and steam. Coosewoon gathers the rocks used in his sweat lodge from a wide area surrounding Mount Scott in the heart of Comanche and Kiowa country. He explains that Mount Scott is an ancient mountain and contains rocks that provide excellent heat in the sweat lodge. They rarely break and never pop or explode from the extreme heat of the fire. When he heats the ancient rocks, he feels he brings new life to them, returning the essence of the rocks back to creation, when intense heat within the earth formed them. Coosewoon places the large heated round rocks in the center of the sweat lodge, where he pours water over them, creating a great deal of steam that fills the lodge. The "steam is like the Grandfather, it penetrates and goes through you, cleaning you, healing you, purifying you." The sweat lodge "cleans you" physically, mentally, and spiritually. The ceremony requires participants to keep an open mind and allow the Healing Spirit into their bodies, hearts, and minds. Coosewoon begins the sweat lodge ceremony by enjoining Grandfather, singing "Great Spirit, Great Spirit, have pity on us. We're having a hard time, and we need your help." Wallace and Gracie Black Elk taught Kenneth this calling song, giving it to him and urging him to use it to open each ceremony, a tradition he has maintained for many years and continues today.[37]

When Coosewoon conducts ceremony, he asks everyone to pray either out loud or to themselves, ending with "All My Relations," to indicate the person has completed the prayer. This is a Lakota tradition that the Black Elks taught Coosewoon, but it is also used commonly by many spiritual leaders from numerous tribes. Coosewoon opens his ceremony with song and then prays for everyone in the sweat lodge, asking for healing for each person. If he knows the personal needs of people in the sweat lodge, he asks the Healing Spirit to address issues for specific people and help them cope with whatever ails them. He asks for healing in a deep manner. Kenneth prays, asking participants to turn everything over to Grandfather, especially those things beyond human control. He asks everyone to be humble and believe Grandfather can help heal them, sometimes touching each person with his large eagle feather. Grandfather is the Healing Spirit, and he works many wonders to help people better heal or live with their illness. Coosewoon remembers a man with terminal cancer who entered the sweat lodge, asking only that he be able to live out his days serving his family and preparing for his death. The man asked to be able to continue his work until he died. He did not ask to be healed, but his cancer disappeared.[38] Another woman was so impaired that she remained outside the sweat lodge in her wheelchair, praying with the others. After the ceremony, the woman was able to leave the wheelchair and walk for the first time in years.[39]

One day in the spring of 2008, a woman in California sought the help of a medicine man. Medical doctors had determined that her breast cancer was so severe and progressing so rapidly that she should have both breasts removed. She reported this to a friend who happened to be leaving the next day to visit various Native American healers in Oklahoma, including Kenneth Coosewoon. At a hotel room, the friend consulted with Kenneth and Rita Coosewoon, explaining the situation. During the consultation, Coosewoon prayed, asking for help from the Healing Spirit. His eyes turned upward and he seemed to place himself into another realm. He prayed and then announced he would be able to destroy the cancer.[40]

Coosewoon told the woman's friend, "You tell her to believe the healing is working now and it's coming now. It's already happening, and it going to come to her and she's gonna get well." Kenneth instructed the friend to return home, meet with the

FIGURE 10.4. In the opening stages of a sweat lodge ceremony, Kenneth Coosewoon prays outside the lodge, asking Grandfather and spirits to join the people in ceremony. He asks for guidance.

women, use an eagle feather to smudge her, pray with her, and make her eat the blue medicine. When her friend returned to California, the two met and followed Coosewoon's instructions. For three weeks they met, and on the third week, they went through the ritual of smudging, praying with the feather, and eating the blue medicine. After completing the ritual, the woman explained she had gone through her preoperation screening where technicians had scanned her body to track the progress of the cancer. The images showed no cancer, at which point her doctors biopsied her body but found no cancer cells. To the day of this writing, the woman has remained cancer free.[41]

Coosewoon laughed on the telephone when he learned this good news, but he never claimed that his healing power destroyed the cancer. Instead, he insisted the Healing Spirit defeated the cancer. The woman views her cure as a miracle, but Coosewoon explained later that the Healing Spirit works in mysterious ways. And so it is with each patient Coosewoon helps. His doctoring has not saved everyone, but his use of spiritual power to heal have helped everyone, even nonbelievers, cope with their problems. In May 2012, Coosewoon doctored a Lakota woman, a recovering

alcoholic who needed a liver transplant. At the same time, he used spiritual medicine on a non-Indian woman recovering from cancer. He sang and prayed for them
both, using sweet grass and his feather to smudge them. He asked Grandfather for
healing, and after the smudging, he gave them each blue medicine to eat. When his
prayer ended, Kenneth could hardly walk. He allowed everyone to leave the area as
he leaned against a brick wall. Once alone, he announced to his host, "Something
powerful just happened. Something good went on in there. Someone or both of them
received healing."[42]

His session with these two women cured the woman with the liver ruined by alcoholism, and the cancer patient remains cancer free, earning a doctorate in psychology.
He doctored both of these women just as he has helped thousands of prison inmates,
returning combat veterans, and mentally impaired children at San Marcos Treatment
Center in San Marcos, Texas. For many years, Cassie Schmitt, director at San Marcos
Treatment Center, hired Coosewoon to work with the children in their treatment
plan, introducing them to sweat lodge. For more than ten years, Coosewoon spent
every Christmas and New Year's in San Marcos with the children, taking care of their

FIGURE 10.5. Healers use spiritual power and plant medicine to cure people. Comanche
healer Kenneth Coosewoon uses, from top to bottom, hawk feathers, sage, an eagle feather,
stone, bone whistle, red berry cedar, and sweetgrass in healing ceremonies. Coosewoon gathered the cedar on Longhorn Mountain and gathered the sage in the Wichita Mountains. Editor's photograph.

spiritual needs when they are not able to return home. In this and many other ways, he follows the tradition of past Native American healers, prophets, and holy people. He uses spiritual power to help and heal others, drawing on song, prayer, ritual, and ceremony to call the Healing Spirit and ask for assistance. His grandson, Ronald Ray Cooper, continues the work and has learned directly from his grandfather how to conduct ceremony and heal. Coosewoon is one of many recent examples of leaders drawn to the sacred, calling on the spirit world for power and wisdom that will continue to influence traditional Native Americans and believers in unseen powers. He lives in contemporary society, but he draws on ancient traditions of healing to help people today. He is only one example of a modern healer influenced by a vision and direction provided by spiritual powers not generally understood or used by people today.[43]

In recent years, Coosewoon has lived in a veteran's center in Lawton, Oklahoma, where he has thrived. As in the past, Coosewoon has visited patients at the center and helped anyone interested in learning from the Comanche healer. In December 2016, Coosewoon explained that in January 2017, he planned to build a sweat lodge on the grounds and conduct sweat lodge ceremonies for his fellow mates at the center. He anticipated helping others and continuing to follow recent messages from the spiritual world asking him to do this work for others and to remember that the Healing Spirit would be with him forever, guiding him to conduct ceremony and prayers for the benefit of others. At the time of this writing, Kenneth Coosewoon is planning to gather willow shoots at Lake Lawtonka, tan rocks from the slopes of Mount Scott, and dry firewood in the woods near Cache Creek. He is presently wrapping red prayer bundles in preparation for the sweat, and with each bundle, offering healing prayers for the patients living at the veteran's center on the south side of Lawton, Oklahoma.[44]

NOTES

1. Kenneth and Rita Coosewoon, oral interview by Clifford E. Trafzer, November 17, 2011; Kenneth Coosewoon, video interview, Coosewoon Collection, Medicine Park, Oklahoma.

2. Coosewoon, interview, November 17, 2011; Kenneth and Rita Coosewoon, oral interview by Clifford E. Trafzer, April 14, 2008.

3. Coosewoon, interview, November 17, 2011.

4. Coosewoon, interview, April 14, 2008.

5. Kenneth and Rita Coosewoon, oral interview by Clifford E. Trafzer, May 17, 2011.

6. Ibid.

7. Coosewoon, interview, November 17, 2011.

8. Beverly Patchell, oral interview by Trafzer, May 13, 2012.

9. Ibid.

10. Coosewoon, interview, April 14, 15, 2008.

11. Coosewoon, interview, November 17, 2011.

12. Coosewoon, interview, April 14, 2008.

13. Ibid.; Coosewoon, video interview.

14. Ibid.; Coosewoon, interview, November 17, 2011.

15. Coosewoon, interviews, April 14, 2008, and November 17, 2011.

16. Ibid.

17. Ibid.

18. Ibid.; Coosewoon, video interview.

19. Coosewoon, interview, April 14, 2008.

20. Ibid.

21. Beverly Patchell, Sweat Lodge Video, Coosewoon Collection, Medicine Park, Oklahoma.

22. Ibid.

23. Ibid.; Patchell, interview, May 13, 2012.

24. Beverly Patchell, oral interview by Trafzer, December 12, 2012.

25. Coosewoon, interview, April 14, 2008. On a trip to Oklahoma in April 2008, the author visited Dwight Mission, the cemetery, and the site of Coosewoon's Great Vision. Little or no development has occurred on the landscape for the past forty years.

26. Coosewoon, interview, April 15, 2008.

27. Kenneth and Rita Coosewoon, oral interview by Trafzer, May 4, 2008. During Coosewoon's visits to the hospital to see Jayme, he fought off death, which he said came in the form of a great horned owl. Coosewoon said the owl planned to take Jayme's soul, but he spoke to the owl, telling it that good medicine would prevail and Jayme would live. He commanded the owl to leave, which it did, flying off during the daytime.

28. Kenneth Coosewoon, oral interview by Trafzer, April 12, 2015, Longhorn Mountain gathering of red berry cedar, Wichita Mountains, Oklahoma.

29. Coosewoon, interview, April 14, 15, 2008.

30. Ibid.

31. Coosewoon, interview, April 12, 2015.

32. Coosewoon, interview, May 4, 2008.

33. Ibid.; Coosewoon, interview, November 17, 2011; Patchell, interview, May 13, 2012.

34. Coosewoon, interview, April 15, 2008; Patchell, Sweat Lodge Video.

35. Clifford E. Trafzer and Richard D. Scheuerman, *Renegade Tribe: The Palouse Indians and the Invasion of the Inland Pacific Northwest* (Pullman: Washington State University Press, 1986), 54.

36. Coosewoon, interviews, April 14, 2008, and November 17, 2011; Patchell, interview, May 13, 2012.

37. Coosewoon, interview, May 17, 2011.

38. Ibid.; Coosewoon, interview, April 14, 2008; Patchell, interview, May 13, 2012.

39. Coosewoon, interview, April 12, 2015.

40. Coosewoon, interview, April 14, 2008.

41. Ibid; Coosewoon, interview, April 15, 2008; Kenneth Coosewoon, telephone interview by Trafzer, May 30, 2008.

42. The event took place in May 2012 at the annual Medicine Ways Conference, University of California, Riverside, where Coosewoon spoke and doctored two people in a quiet, secluded entryway to a conference room. In addition to this healing, the author received a phone call on March 23, 2013, from a Native American participant of the 2012 conference that reported that Coosewoon had prayed for her daughter who had cancer and given her a medicine bundle. Her daughter's cancer disappeared, and she has no new cancer cells.

43. Coosewoon (lecture, Medicine Ways Conference, University of California, Riverside, May 2012). Cassie Schmitt and Richard Downey have contributed to this essay through information they provided the author.

44. Kenneth Coosewoon, telephone interview by Trafzer, December 25, 2016.

CONCLUSION

🍂

N UWUVI, OR SOUTHERN PAIUTE PEOPLE, share a common belief in their origins. They say at the beginning of time, Hutsipamamau, or Ocean Woman, fell from the Upper World to the Middle World, or earth. Tribal scholars say she fell to earth in the form of a worm but soon took the form of a woman with supernatural power that had come with her to earth. She walked on the surface of a primordial sea that enveloped the earth. At the time, no land existed, but Hutsipamamau had a vision of solid earth, and like the Iroquoian creator, Ataentsic, she used the power she had brought with her to begin the creation process that resulted in the first "people," which included plants, animals, landforms, and the cosmos.[1] All these and many other animate and inanimate things interacted with each other in the first historical drama. At the same time that Hutsipamamau fell to earth, a web of spiritual power or energy also came to earth.[2] Power encircled the earth in the form of a web or spiral that pulsated and moved. According to Nuwuvi scholars, the web of power enjoyed intelligence and will.[3]

Southern Paiute people call this original power *puha* and say that it concentrates in specific places within the landscape, especially on Mount Charleston in the Spring Mountains of Nevada. *Puha* also concentrates in the minds and bodies of special people chosen by spirits to have access to and use of power. Southern Paiute called these people *puha'gaants*, people who Nuwuvi reported have unusual power to heal. *Puha'gaants* had "special friends" known as *tutuxub*, commonly called familiars. They lived in their own spiritual environments until the shaman called them through a special song. Contemporary tribal elder, singer, and historian Larry Eddy, from the Colorado River Indian Reservation, reported that his grandfather, Dutch Eddy, was

FIGURE C.1. In order to keep the songs alive, a group of Salt Song singers sang to the Old Woman Mountains located in the heart of the eastern Mojave Desert. The group of Southern Paiute, Chemehuevi, and Cahuilla singers sang in praise of power located at that holy indigenous place. The Cultural Conservancy sponsored the sing. Singers include Robert Chavez, Matthew Leivas, Larry Eddy, Eunice Ohte, Vivenne Jake, and Lalovi Miller. Courtesy of Philip Klasky.

a *puha'gaant*. Like other healers, the elder Eddy called on his power through song.[4] "He'd sing and sing until the red hawk or eagle got there, or whatever" familiar he had obtained through visions or dreams. A person's familiar appeared to him and imparted power to the *puha'gaant* so he could heal patients. For Eddy's grandfather, a bat served as his *tutuxub*, a powerful familiar.[5]

To attract a concentration of *puha* to conduct healing, shamans used song, which brought the familiar. According to Larry Eddy, spirit helpers loved songs, especially those songs of the Indian doctor specifically about the familiar.[6] *Puha'gaants* "called and they called, and that helper wherever he was, he heard that song. He could hear it for miles, and he heads in the direction to that doctor. When he gets there, then the doctor knows, well, I'm going to save this guy."[7] When medicine people call their familiars, "nobody sees that animal but him. He calls that animal through his songs." For a shaman, "it was all done in his songs," which were his way of "beckoning to his familiar," and it came "out from the mountain or from the valley or wherever he was at." The familiar "would come down to this doctor," where the spirit helper played "around the sick person," which "may have been [part of] the healing process." Now and then the familiar would "jump towards or come towards the doctor, and the doctor would sit there and watch him like he's nothing, like he's not paying attention." Once the familiar got close to the *puha'gaant*, in a flash of a moment, the shaman reached out and grabbed his familiar in his hand, capturing it.[8] "This is when that healing power would be transferred to him, to the doctor, to the patient. That's how they healed." In this manner, shamans "healed their sick person or ailing person."[9]

Speaking of his grandfather, Larry Eddy remembered that "as a kid, I must have been about eight or nine or ten years old, I used to go here, go there with my grandfather, and he was a healer." Since his grandfather was well-known, "A lot of people came to him for different cures, and he would perform cures." As his grandfather visited people in need, they sat outside. Dutch Eddy conducted healings out of doors, many times at night around a fire. Other times, he sat outside by himself where "he sang his songs" and called his power. Through this ritual or ceremonial act of singing, he also called *puha* to come to him, carried by his familiar. Then "when that time came for him to heal . . . something would happen there in the middle of the night to attract everybody, and that was the time that his healing progressed or whatever he did happened." That was the moment he used the power given to him by his spirit helper to transfer *puha* and its healing power from the shaman into the patient to cure the individual.[10]

Many American Indian tribes still believe that webs of power concentrate in certain areas within the environment, and medicine people travel to these places to gain energy that they use for the benefit of others.[11] Each tribe and community has knowledge of such places, including Southern Paiute. Within a thousand miles of Salt Song Trail, many sites of power or *puha* exist. In July 2016, contemporary Salt Song singer Matthew Hanks Leivas traveled to a place of power in the Old Woman Mountains, situated in the eastern Mojave Desert, to "recharge his energy."[12] He traveled with a friend, Jeff Johnson, the manager of the Old Woman Mountain Preserve. At the Painted Rocks in the preserve of the Native American Land Conservancy, Leivas prayed in his Native language to the landscape and animals. As Leivas sang the quail song in his Native language, "About fifteen to twenty baby quail came from the bushes and headed toward Painted Rocks and Matthew."[13] All the while, Johnson walked away from Leivas to allow him privacy, but he watched from afar, quietly taking in a panoramic view of the whole area, including the granite monolith at the base of which Leivas sang to the birds. All of a sudden, Johnson's gaze stopped on the granite monument called Painted Rocks. "There on top of a small boulder not more than thirty feet away from Matthew was a bighorn sheep standing over him." The bighorn watched on as the quail hovered near Leivas and two crows circled overhead, calling

FIGURE C.2. Luke Madrigal is a well-known Cahuilla Bird Song singer. He grew up hearing the songs, and as a young college student he started learning Bird Songs from master teacher Robert Levi (sitting right) of the Torres Martinez Indian Reservation. James Ramos sits to the left holding a gourd rattle. Editor's photograph.

out in their language. Then Leivas began singing a Salt Song in Nuwu, not knowing the bighorn stood above him. The scene created a "powerful and inspiring" energy. For fifteen minutes, Leivas sang while the bighorn looked on. The bighorn "surprisingly walked down from the petroglyph panel above the ceremonial site. He looked at us, then he was gone." Later Leivas explained, "The bighorn clan are my ancestors."[14]

From the time of indigenous creations to the present, American Indians have continued to believe in the power of the spirit, which manifests in many different forms. Spiritual power lies at the heart of Native American cultures, past and present, and indigenous belief in power is prologue to the future of indigenous communities. In the past, non-Indians defamed Native American religions, ceremonies, beliefs, and leaders, often labeling medicine people fakes, frauds, and charlatans. Pilgrims and Puritans characterized Native Americans as savages, heathens, and devils. Their negative views persevered throughout most of American history and remain extant in some quarters of American life. Ministers and leaders portrayed indigenous spiritual leaders as counterimages to Christians and "civilized" Europeans. Settlers targeted medicine men and women for destruction and denigrated holy people, calling them children of Satan, certainly not God's children. Native Americans were outside the Christian covenant and remained so during most of American history. Settlers justified the killing of spiritual leaders and their followers, committing genocide through acts of war, fire, and starvation in the name of God.[15] Furthermore, Native American spiritual leaders generally did not fit the image held by non-Indians of great Indian leaders. Settlers admired the abilities of male war leaders, including Pontiac, Little Turtle, Brant, Tecumseh, Looking Glass, Crazy Horse, and Cochise.[16]

Settlers did not generally respect spiritual leaders and medicine people with their "new-fangled religious delusions."[17] Christians believed in the written stories found in the Bible, including miraculous healings, deaths, and resurrections by Old Testament prophets and Jesus. In 1 Corinthians, 12:1–11, the apostle Paul spoke of humans receiving spiritual gifts to do miracles, prophesize, and heal. These gifts, he argued, all came from the same source, the Spirit. According to Paul, "To one given through the Spirit the utterance of wisdom, and to another the utterance of knowledge according to the same Spirit, to another faith by the same Spirit, to another gifts of healing by the one Sprit, to another the working of miracles, to another prophecy."[18] Many healers would agree with Paul, arguing the source of power to heal and help others came from the Spirit, not mankind. Longhouse leader and *towat* Andrew George, a major spiritual leader and healer on the Columbia Plateau, explained that the source of positive power on earth derives from the same spirit. In the longhouses of the Northwest, "The Seven Drums beating and the words of the song speak the same truths as are in the Bible. Listen, you can hear them. Truth is the same everywhere."[19] But Christian settlers and leaders denied the efficacy of indigenous miracles, prophecies, and healings. They denied the veracity of oral stories of miracles, power, and healing that Native Americans claimed derived from the Spirit, even when they witnessed such events and described them.[20]

Negative portrayals of indigenous people and their religions led to justifying settler violence, encroachment, and assimilation. During the nineteenth and twentieth centuries, the United States Army, the Office of Indian Affairs, school superintendents,

FIGURE C.3. Roland Maldonado and Matthew Leivas sing Salt Songs to the Oasis of Mara. Ten years before, Paul and Jane Smith sponsored a gathering of Salt Song singers at the 29 Palms Inn in the Mojave Desert. In November 2016, the Smiths and Patricia Flanagan hosted a Gathering of Tribes at the Oasis of Mara. More than one hundred Salt Song singers and dancers prayed for the ancient oasis. Editor's photograph.

and Christian missionaries targeted Native American religions and spiritual leaders in an attempt to diminish, discredit, and destroy indigenous spiritual beliefs, religious ceremonies, and healings, thereby committing physical and cultural genocide as defined by the United Nations Convention on the Prevention and Punishment of the Crime of Genocide, 1948.[21] Non-Indians outlawed American Indian sacred customs, stole sacred sites, exploited environments, destroyed food sources from flora and fauna, and dictated laws prohibiting ancient medicine ways. Newcomers quickly changed the names of millions of places in Indian Country, renaming sites on maps in an attempt to erase the American Indian past and presence on the landscape. Settlers and government agents separated children from their parents, people, and places in an attempt to reprogram indigenous students at boarding schools. Government agents and missionaries used wars, removals, reservations, treaties, and other means to annihilate Native American people and cultures, especially their religious beliefs and medicine ways. In spite of the government's great effort and the expenditure of millions of dollars, the United States could not completely destroy indigenous people and communities or their connection with the spiritual world.

Native Americans have survived modernity, and so have many spiritual beliefs of the Native Universe. Each year, Pueblo people gather to open their kivas and renew their ceremonial cycle. Lakota, Dakota, Crow, Blackfeet, and others prepare for their annual Sun Dances. Each winter, Navajo *yeis* comb communities seeking donations in support of the next Yeibichai Dance designed to heal patients in ceremony. In the early summer each year, the Haudenosaunee gather in longhouses for strawberry festivals, where they listen to orations about the Gawaiio, the Good Word of Handsome Lake. At the same time, Northwestern Coastal and Plateau people gather in First Food Ceremonies, blessing the fish, deer, roots, and berries. They eat their sacred foods in communion with the spiritual world that provided them life through indigenous foods. In the spring, Cocopa people of southern Arizona gather with their people in Baja California to conduct a Blessing of the Water Ceremony. In 2016 and 2017, water protectors from Standing Rock, many other Native nations, and non-Indians that support the tribes and their efforts to protect the environment exercised their sovereign freedom and ancient commitment to preserve the precious gift of water. They claim that water is a spiritual gift that sustains all life on earth. They continue to protest, sing, and pray for guidance and assistance from the spiritual world that has watched over them for generations, not simply for themselves but for all life that needs water to survive. Indigenous water protectors ask the nation and world to consider what is best for living beings: water and health for many or wealth for a few. Water protectors stand in harmony with ancient Native beliefs in relationship with plants, animals, and human beings centered on life and spirit.[22]

Today, American Indians everywhere conduct ceremony and connect with the spiritual world. Nuwuvi people in Arizona, California, Nevada, and Utah continue to hold ceremony every month, calling on Salt Song singers to conduct ceremonies for their loved ones that have passed. Nuwuvi people have used Salt Songs in healing ceremonies for generations. They say that during the time of creation, two women entered Ting-i-aay, a holy cave in western Arizona, where they received a message from the spirit world to take a hero's journey.[23] According to oral tradition, the women received a message from spirits located in the cave to take a Salt Song Trail from Arizona to Utah and into Nevada as far north as the Spring Mountains. From there, the women parted. One sister left the other, her soul or spirit going north and ascending into the sky. She left this life on earth for another life, traveling in spirit into the Milky Way. The sister remaining on earth traveled south into California past the Old Woman Mountains, Oasis of Mara, Palm Springs, and east to the Colorado River. When the woman reached the Colorado River south of present-day Blythe, California, she walked north past the giant intaglios, following a well-worn trail on the west bank of the Colorado River to the Riverside Mountains. At this point, adjacent present-day Poston, Arizona, she swam the Colorado River into Arizona. From the Parker Valley, this holy woman traveled north to the Bill Williams River just above

FIGURE C.4. Fort Sill Apache-Cahuilla elder Lorene Sisquoc and Paiute-Shoshone elder Galen Townsend have used Indian medicine all their lives. This photograph depicts them sharing their tribal knowledge at a Medicine Ways gathering in the Rupert Costo Library, University of California, Riverside. Editor's photograph.

present-day Parker Dam and traveled east to the holy cave Ting-i-aay. She concluded a one-thousand-mile journey on foot through deserts, mountains, and valleys highly significant to all Nuwuvi people. She ended her great trek where she had started. Southern Paiute reenact this journey in song every time a person dies. During funeral and memorial ceremonies, Salt Song singers re-create the heroic journey of the Salt Song Trail. They sing and hold ceremony to heal the living and help the deceased leave their homeland and travel north to the Spring Mountains and the entryway into the Milky Way.[24]

Like other tribes, Southern Paiute believe that *puha* is sentient, alive with meaning, potential, and possibilities. It sits within things animate and inanimate, seen and unseen. Traditionally, Nuwuvi people believed *puha* had intelligence and will, with the ability to give or withhold power. Since they conceived the earth and universe in a state of constant equilibrium, humans purposely and carefully interacted with *puha* and other forces of the spiritual world. Southern Paiute people connected with *puha* through songs, prayers, rituals, and ceremonies. Like other tribal people, they followed rules or laws governing their interactions with *puha*, which could create positive, constructive results or negative, destructive outcomes.[25] Nuwuvi people continue to interact with *puha* and encounter its concentration during ceremony, including wakes and memorials. Many Southern Paiute people continue to interact with puha, including those that have visited the Oasis of Mara.

To talk about the future of the Salt Songs, in November 2016, more than one hundred Southern Paiute people and their Native and non-Native friends met at the Oasis of Mara, present-day Twentynine Palms, California, to share a portion of their sacred song complex and honor a holy site on the Salt Song Trail.[26] Matthew Leivas, Bonita Eddy, Iris Burns, Robert Chavez, Hope Hinman, Mary Drum, Roland Maldanado, Bridget Eddy, and many other Salt Song singers joined their voices in unison in the heart of the Mojave Desert while young boys and girls danced in a circle near the oasis pond on the current property of the 29 Palms Inn. Singers and participants interacted positively with *puha*, honoring the oasis and the Chemehuevi and Serrano people that had lived and died at this place they once called home. The Gathering of Tribes at the Oasis of Mara encouraged indigenous circles on the Colorado River Indian

FIGURE C.5. The Plateau Indian Center at Washington State University hosted a conference honoring Palouse Indians. These men from the Colville and Nez Perce Reservations provided presentations. From left to right: Albert Andrews Red Star is the leader of the Seven Drums Longhouse on the Colville Reservation. Michael Finney is a historian and author from the Colville Reservation. Gordon Fisher was a tribal scholar with rare information on significant tribal elders. Courtesy of Richard D. Scheuerman.

and Shivwits Indian Reservations to host future gatherings of Salt Song singers.[27] At all these gatherings, tribal elders pass along their ancient ceremonies and encourage young people to learn the songs. Throughout Indian Country today, a cultural confluence has developed between elders and young people who are committed to the continuum of American Indian medicine ways. For many, spiritual power of the past remains alive and active today. Contemporary ceremonies have contributed to increased use of spiritual power, which has enhanced tribal and spiritual sovereignty and encouraged future generations to remember the songs, power, and medicine ways.

NOTES

1. Clifford E. Trafzer, *A Chemehuevi Song: Resiliency of a Southern Paiute Tribe* (Seattle: University of Washington Press, 2015), 21–25.

2. Ibid.; Kathleen Van Vlack, Richard Stoffle, Evelyn Pickering, Katherine Brooks, Jennie Delfs, *Unav-Nuquaint: Little Springs Lava Flow Ethnographic Investigations*, Bureau of Applied Research in Anthropology (BARA), Tucson, University of Arizona (2013), 23–25; Richard Stoffle, Richard Arnold, Kathleen Van Vlack, Larry Eddy, Betty Cornelius, "Nuvagantu, 'Where Snow Sits': Origin Mountains of Southern Paiute," in *Landscapes of Origin in the Americas: Creation Narratives Linking Ancient Places and Present Communities*, ed. Jessica Christie, (Tuscaloosa: University of Alabama Press, 2009), 32–44.

3. Clifford E. Trafzer, "Where Puha Sits: Salt Songs, Power, and the Oasis of Mara" (paper presented at the Indigenous Environments Conference, University of East Anglia, UK, July 8, 2016).

4. Larry Eddy, interview by Clifford E. Trafzer, October 18, 2007, Colorado River Indian Reservation, Parker, Ariz.

5. Ibid. Ocean Woman is the most powerful familiar, or *tutuxub*, for Southern Paiutes. She manifests herself in many forms and characters in creation narratives and songs.

6. Eddy, interview. Donald Bahr addresses the importance of using song to engage spirit helpers. See Donald Bahr, Juan Gregorio, David I. Lopez, and Albert Alvarez, *Piman Shamanism and Staying Sickness* (Tucson: University of Arizona Press, 1974), 230, 234–35.

7. Eddy, interview.

8. Ibid. During the interview, Eddy explained that a person would think that a familiar of a shaman would come directly to the Indian doctor, but in his grandfather's case, it was not so. When Eddy was a boy, he saw his grandfather's familiar during a healing ceremony, and the bat was not cooperative but was attracted by his grandfather's singing, slowly moving closer to the *puhagaant*. During the interview, Eddy bent over in his seat and started grabbing at the ground, as if chasing an excited puppy that jumped from side to

side, close to and far away from the shaman. Then Eddy pretended to have captured the familiar and announced, "Then he could do the healing."

9. Eddy, interview.

10. Ibid.

11. Lowell John Bean, *Mukat's People: The Cahuilla Indians of Southern California* (Berkeley: University of California Press, 1974), 161–62, 180–82.

12. Kurt Russo, e-mail communication to Clifford E. Trafzer, July 10, 2016. This e-mail provided the report Jeff Johnson made to Russo regarding his journey to the Old Woman Mountain Preserve with Matthew Leivas.

13. Ibid.

14. Ibid.

15. Francis Jennings, *The Invasion of America: Indians, Colonialism, and the Cant of Conquest* (New York: W. W. Norton, 1975), 3–31; Roger M. Carpenter, *"Times Are Altered with Us": American Indians from First Contact to the New Republic* (Chichester, UK: John Wiley & Sons, 2015), 110–24; Clifford E. Trafzer, Jean A. Keller, and Lorene Sisquoc, eds., *Boarding School Blues: Revisiting American Indian Educational Experiences* (Lincoln: University of Nebraska Press, 2006), 11–22, 24–29.

16. For a discussion of great warriors as heroic figures, see R. David Edmunds, *Tecumseh and the Quest for Indian Leadership* (Boston: Little, Brown, and Company, 1884), 122–25.

17. This phrase derives from General Oliver O. Howard's remarks about worshipers of the Washani faith on the Columbia Plateau. The "Christian General" did not disguise his contempt of the so-called Dreamers of the Northwest. "Report of Civil and Military Commission to the Nez Perce Indians, Washington Territory and the Northwest," in *Annual Report of the Secretary of Interior, 1877* (Washington, D.C.: Government Printing Office, 1877), 607–9; Oliver O. Howard, *Nez Perce Joseph* (Boston: Lee and Shepherd, 1881), 30, 37, 43, 54; Clifford E. Trafzer and Richard D. Scheuerman, *The Snake River-Palouse and the Invasion of the Inland Northwest* (Pullman: Washington State University Press, 2016), 129–33.

18. 1 Cor. 12:8–10b (English Standard Version).

19. These are the words of Andrew George (Tipiyeléhne Xáyxayx, or White Eagle), a *towat*, or medicine man, of the Palouse and Nez Perce. See Richard D. Scheuerman and Clifford E. Trafzer, *River Song: Naxiyamtáma (Snake River-Palouse) Oral Traditions from Mary Jim, Andrew George, Gordon Fisher, and Emily Peone* (Pullman: Washington State University Press, 2015), 75.

20. Several examples of miracle healings by shamans appear in Vine Deloria's last book. A few are cited here. See Vine Deloria Jr., *The World We Used to Live In: Remembering the Powers of the Medicine Men* (Golden, Colo.: Fulcrum Publishing, 2006), 47–49, 52, 55–60.

21. Jack Norton, *When Our Worlds Cried: Genocide in Northwestern California* (San Francisco: Indian Historian Press, 1979), 153–63; Brendan C. Lindsay, *Murder State: California's*

Native American Genocide, 1846–1873 (Lincoln: University of Nebraska Press, 2012), 11–23; Benjamin Madley, *An American Genocide: The United States and the Indian Catastrophe* (New Haven: Yale University Press, 2016), 4–8, 11, 14, 172–83, 350–59, 551–54.

22. As of spring 2017, several internet sites provide information on the struggles of the people of Standing Rock to prevent the Dakota Access Pipeline from crossing and possibly polluting the Missouri River. The struggle to protect water, sacred sites, holy places, trails, and other cultural features, former homelands, and human remains will continue throughout the twenty-first century.

23. Salt Songs always mention Ting-i-ayy, a sacred cave. Elders are careful not to share the exact location of this cave, which provided direction to the two women that entered the cave in ancient time to begin their journey and led to ceremonies used often in contemporary society to send souls to heaven.

24. Trafzer, *Chemehuevi Song*, 3–8; Eddy, interview, October 18, 2007, and March 5, 2016.

25. Lowell John Bean, ed., *California Indian Shamanism* (Menlo Park, Calif.: Ballena Press, 1992), 21–32.

26. *A Gathering of the Tribes on the Oasis of Mara*, (Twentynine Palms, Calif.: November 11–13, 2016), program brochure.

27. The editor attended the Salt Song Gathering of the Tribes at the Oasis of Mara, and information here derives from field notes taken after the ceremony concluded.

CONTRIBUTORS

The editor of this volume, CLIFFORD E. TRAFZER, is Distinguished Professor of History and Rupert Costo Chair in American Indian Affairs at the University of California, Riverside. He served many years as the director of the California Center for Native Nations. Most recently, he authored *A Chemehuevi Song: The Resilience of a Southern Paiute Tribe* (University of Washington, 2015) and co-edited *The Indian School on Magnolia Avenue: Voices and Images from the Sherman Institute* (Oregon State University Press, 2015). He co-edited the inaugural book for the Smithsonian's National Museum of the American Indians, *Native Universe: Voices of Indian America*, co-authored *The Snake River-Palouse and the Invasion of the Inland Northwest* (1986, revised edition, 2016), which won the Governor's Writer's Day Award for nonfiction. His book *Death Stalks the Yakama: Epidemiological Transitions and Mortality on the Yakama Indian Reservation, 1888–1964* won best nonfiction from the Wordcraft Circle of Native American Writers.

Historian RICHARD D. SCHEUERMAN is associate professor of education at Seattle Pacific University and vice president of the Washington State Historical Society. He is co-author with Clifford Trafzer of *The Snake River-Palouse and the Invasion of the Inland Northwest*, original published as *River Song: Naxiyamtáma (Snake-River Palouse) Oral Traditions*, and with Michael O. Finley of *Finding Chief Kamiakin: The Life and Legacy of a Northwest Patriot*. He is presently conducting research on agrarian traditions and heritage grains of the Spanish missions along the El Camino Real.

TROY R. JOHNSON (deceased) was professor of history and director of Native American Studies at California State University, Long Beach. He is best known for his book on the American Indian occupation of Alcatraz, 1969–1970.

R. DAVID EDMUNDS is the Watson Professor of American History-Emeritus, at the University of Texas at Dallas and is the author or editor of ten books and more than one hundred essays or articles. The past president of both the Western History Association and the American Society for Ethnohistory, he has held fellowships from the Guggenheim and Ford Foundations, and from the National Endowment for the Humanities. Edmunds currently serves as a consultant to several tribal governments in litigation defending reservations and tribal homelands.

JOSEPH B. HERRING is retired. He is the foremost scholar of Kenekuk and best known for his book on the Kickapoo Prophet. The essay in this collection is a new and updated analysis of Kenekuk based on archival sources.

AL LOGAN SLAGLE, now deceased, was a member of the Keetoowah band of Cherokee and taught many years at the University of California, Berkeley. He was a scholar, professor, and member of the Indian Shaker Church.

For many years, L. G. MOSES has taught at Oklahoma State University. His early work focused on James Mooney, the Ghost Dance religion, and Wovoka—the topic of his essay on the Ghost Dance Prophet.

BENJAMIN JENKINS is archivist and assistant professor of history at the University of La Verne, where he also directs the new Public History Program. He received his PhD in history at the University of California, Riverside, in 2016. His current research focuses on the interactions between citrus agriculture and railroad transportation in Southern California. His recent publications include "Steel, Steam, and Citrus: The Economic Transformation of Southern California" in the *Journal of the West* and *The Digital Frontier: Archival Digitization and Modern Usage of the Human Record*.

MICHELLE LORIMER is a tribal scholar for the Pechanga band of Luiseño Indians and an instructor at California State University, San Bernardino. In 2016, Great Oaks Press of the Pechanga tribe published her book, *Resurrecting the Past: The California Mission Myth*.

INDEX

Carnard River, 79
Canyon de Chelly, 56, 60
Carleton, General James, 21
Carson, Kit, 21
Castle Dome Mountain, 14, 51, 53
Catholicism, 29, 88–90, 96–98, 145, 146, 148, 169, 246
Cayuga, 109, 110, 115–17
Cayuse, 23, 31, 146, 151, 152, 163, 164, 166, 168, 170; and Indian War, 148, 151; nonreservation, 23; nontreaty, 168; prisoners of war, 23
ceremonies (Native American), 3, 5–8, 14, 20, 24–35, 46–48, 53–65, 72, 74, 89, 93, 95–97, 107, 125, 127–32, 135, 142, 145, 147, 148, 152–54, 155–61, 165, 167, 170, 172, 173, 186, 194, 196, 203, 204, 206, 222–24, 227, 228, 230, 232–34, 256–58, 260–74, 279–86; Coyote Way Ceremony, 22, 56; False Face ceremony, 30, 112, 115–21; Feather Ceremonies, 159; First Food Ceremonies, 156, 158, 159, 283; gun ceremony, 134; peyote ceremony, 28, 139, 140; puberty ceremony, 47, 63, 244, 246; salmon ceremonies, 10, 124, 155–57; sweat lodge ceremony, x, 24, 35, 53, 256, 258, 260–65, 267–72, 274. See also Navajo ceremonies; Iroquois Ceremonial of Midwinter; World Renewal ceremonies; and under Cahuilla
Chacon, Martha Manuel, 25, 242–44
Chappell, Violet, 228, 229
Charleston Peak, Nevada, 11
Charley, Deleliah, 198
Charley, John, 183
Chasing Crane, 208
Cheeters, Watt, 26
Chemehuevi, 3, 4, 8, 10–12, 33, 34, 35, 248, 278, 285
Cherokee, 17, 24, 32; Country, 261; language, 26; people, 19, 26; Stomp Dance, 189
Cheyenne, 30, 125; River Reservation, 137
Chickasaw, 19
Chino, Pedro, 9, 248
Chippewa, 72, 79
Chiricahua Apache, 133, 256
Choctaw, 19, 20, 72
Christians/Christianity, 12, 14, 15, 20, 26, 27, 29, 46, 88, 89, 93, 95–98, 99, 141, 145, 146, 148,

150, 157, 159, 160, 162, 164, 166, 167, 169, 179, 180, 182, 187, 189, 194–96, 204, 214, 226, 257, 260, 270, 281, 282; Christianity as universalizing, 15, 94, 170
Christmas, 78, 273
Church of Jesus Christ of Latter Day Saints, 205, 226, 228
Civil War (American), 21, 99, 108
Claiborne, General Ferdinand, 20
Clark, William, 148
Cochise, 281
Cochrane, Admiral Alexander, 20
Cocopa, 49, 283
Colorado, 55, 56; River, 8, 11–14, 26, 27, 47, 49, 51, 53–55, 132, 283; River Indian Reservation, 12, 25, 277, 285
Columbia Plateau, 24, 31, 145–51, 153, 156, 161–63, 169, 171, 173, 281
Columbia River, 10, 146, 148, 150, 151, 153, 154, 156, 169–72
Colville Indian Reservation, 196, 285
Comanche, 8, 24, 31, 35, 125, 127, 139, 140, 209, 256–58, 264, 265, 268, 270, 273, 274
Comanche County, 258
Commissioner, Special Indian, 94
Commissioner of Indian Affairs, 162, 202, 203, 205, 208
Committee for Traditional Indian Health, 234
confederacy, 15, 18–21, 29, 79, 81, 83; Confederate Army, 21; Penacook, 15; Tecumseh's, 18–21, 79, 81, 83
Cooley, Kathleen, 189
Cooper, Ronald Ray, 267, 274
Cookson Hills, 261
Coosewoon, Abner, 256
Coosewoon, Deanna, 266, 267
Coosewoon, Juanita Doraline Taylor, 258, 259, 268
Coosewoon, Kenneth, 24, 35, 127, 257–74; and alcoholism, 258–60; first healing experience, 266–68; Great Vision, 262–66; work in prisons, 268, 269. See also ceremonies (Native American): sweat lodge ceremony
Coosewoon, Mattie Kaulie, 256, 257
Coosewoon, Rita, 35, 257, 268–71
Corn Beetle, 56
Corn Mother, 111
Cornplanter, Chief, 16, 17, 116, 119